Full Speed Ahead

FULL SPEED AHEAD
Stories and Activities
for Children on Transportation

Jan Irving
and
Robin Currie

Illustrated by
Karen Wolf

1988
TEACHER IDEAS PRESS
A Division of
Libraries Unlimited, Inc.
Englewood, Colorado

TEACHER IDEAS PRESS
A Division of Libraries Unlimited, Inc.
P.O. Box 3988
Englewood, Colorado 80155-3988

Library of Congress Cataloging-in-Publication Data

Irving, Jan, 1942-
    Full speed ahead : stories and activities for children on
transportation / Jan Irving and Robin Currie ; illustrated by Karen
Wolf.
    xiv, 244 p. 22x28 cm.
    Includes index.
    ISBN 0-87287-653-5
    1. Storytelling.   2. Libraries, Children's--Activity programs.
3. Children--Books and reading.   4. Transportation in literature.
5. Transportation--Study and teaching (Elementary)   6. Children's
literature--Study and teaching (Elementary)   I. Currie, Robin,
1948-   . II. Title.
Z718.3.I77 1988
372.6--dc19   88-29540
                                                            CIP

This book is bound with Type II nonwoven material that meets and exceeds National Association of State Textbook Administrators' Type II nonwoven material specifications Class A through E.

We would like to dedicate this book to the cars that started for us on cold mornings, the airplanes that helped us get together to write this book, and to all the vehicles that will take us to our future destinations.

Contents

Introduction

Full Speed Ahead is a source book for program planning. It is similar in purpose and structure to *Mudluscious: Stories and Activities Featuring Food for Preschool Children* (Libraries Unlimited, 1986) and *Glad Rags: Stories and Activities Featuring Clothes for Children* (Libraries Unlimited, 1987). These books introduce children to quality picturebook literature and provide enrichment activities in which children can actively participate. The stories and activities are appropriate for children preschool age through third grade.

Full Speed Ahead uses transportation as the "vehicle" to appreciation of language just as *Mudluscious* used the theme of food and *Glad Rags* used the theme of clothes. Children will learn such expressions as "out of steam," "reinvent the wheel," and "all hands on deck" through stories and activities. New story interpretations for such experiences as a "traffic jam" and being "stuck in a rut" will encourage children and teachers to explore figurative and literal meanings of language. Traditional folk literature does not feature transportation as much as it includes the food and clothing themes of our previous books, but we have re-examined the Cinderella story with a focus on the pumpkin coach and retold the Hare and the Tortoise fable with a contemporary approach. The 150 picture books we have annotated in the eight chapters of *Full Speed Ahead* provide a wide range of stories from simple board books for the youngest child to the rhythmic texts of modern classics such as *Mike Mulligan and His Steam Shovel*.

Schools, childcare centers, and libraries are developing literature-based programs that extend interests beyond basal readers and workbook exercises. The stories and activities in *Full Speed Ahead* will encourage reading readiness and promote the enjoyment of story so that young readers will stay interested in books beyond decoding skills and classroom assignments.

The theme of transportation holds fascination for children even though they may not have had direct experience with all the vehicles mentioned in this book. Children are full of movement themselves and naturally curious about the world around them—from animals that move in the natural world to locomotives and jets that speed ahead in our fast-paced world of technology. Through the theme of transportation children will learn self-awareness and explore a broader world through role playing. We have made an effort to dispel rigid sex role stereotypes so both girls and boys will be encouraged to drive buses, fly airplanes, and reinvent the wheel.

The scope of the chapters ranges from child-manipulated vehicles to those that children ride in as passengers or those they see in operation. The first chapter, "Feet and Flippers," begins with the simplest form of transportation—moving on your own two feet. Chapter 2 progresses to skates, swings and other vehicles children operate on their own. Chapter 3, "Take Me Along," includes vehicles we ride in as families or in small groups, and larger group transportation—buses, trains, and ships—are included in chapter 4, "We All Go Together." Work-related vehicles are the focus of chapter 5, "Tractors and Tow Trucks," air-related vehicles, the focus of chapter 6, "Up in the Air," and more fantastic flights of fancy are included in chapter 7, "Magic Carpets and Merry-Go-Rounds." The final chapter, "Trolley Cars and Rickshaws," provides an overview of transportation around the world and through the ages. The range of experience of the book is broad—some vehicles may be unique to a culture (e.g., dog sleds) or to an occupational group (e.g., farm tractors), but others may be as common to most children as family automobiles and school buses.

Each chapter is structured in parallel form. The chapter introduction presents the overall theme and purpose of the subject. The literature section of each chapter annotates picture books on a subtheme, and then includes related literature activities from fingerplays and action rhymes to a wide variety of storytelling methods such as flannel-board and participatory stories told with masks. Games follow the quieter literature activities to provide a change of pace and crafts are included as well. The final section of each chapter includes take-home activities. This replaces the cooking and tasting section in *Mudluscious* and the visual display section in *Glad Rags.* The logic for this change is twofold. First, it is more appropriate to the theme of transportation, and second, it reinforces the idea that people on the go need activities to share together. Take-home activities will encourage parent-child interaction in the learning activities introduced at school or in childcare centers.

The two-part skills index will guide you in selecting activities that teach cognitive and social inter-action skills. The fifteen skill areas include self-awareness, gross motor, color recognition, size and shape recognition, rhythm and rhyming, following directions, group cooperation, musical, artistic, role and dialogue invention, sequencing, classification, word recognition, directional orientation, and health and safety. The index is organized into a "Breakdown of Activities by Skills Area" and an "Alphabetical Index of Activities Showing Associated Skills." A "Literature Index" that includes authors and titles of all annotated picture books is also provided.

We would like to thank the many people who have enthusiastically responded to both *Mudluscious* and *Glad Rags* and asked for more. We would also like to thank the following people: David Loertscher, Shirley Lambert, Karen Wolf, Carol Elbert, Paula Brandt, Ginny Cameron, Lorna Caulkins, Bruce Currie, Pat Franzen, and Phyllis Hilston.

Setting Up the Program

We suggest books and activities so that you might create your own program. Your final selection of the type and length of activities and stories should be based on your own situation. But here are two sample programs the way we might set them up. The programs are derived from chapters 1 and 6.

FEET AND FLIPPERS

Sample Program*

Initiating Activities:	Begin with "Off to a Silly Start" (p. 1) as children arrive. Repeat this several times until all children can introduce themselves. When all children come, begin with song "Baby Walk" (pp. 5-6).
First Story:	Begin with *The Hare and Tortoise* (p. 14). The picture book version of this familiar story will make everyone want to take off running.
Related Activities:	Follow up this story with "Hare and the Tortoise Retold" (pp. 13-14) so children can enjoy another experience. This new version uses your own two hands and repeated refrains. Then continue with the song "Fast and Slow" to reinforce the idea of different walking speeds.
Second Story:	Now you are ready for another picture book about racing. Read *Get Set! Go!* by Watanabe (p. 3).
Related Activities:	After you've read this picture book about racing, share the draw-and-tell story, "The Great Race" (p. 23). Then allow for some movement with the game "Fast and Slow" (p. 29).
Third Story:	Now use a more participatory story telling method by reading the picture book *I'm Going on a Bear Hunt* (p. 3).
Related Activities:	Continue in this vein with another participatory story, "Dog Hunt" (pp. 3-5).
Final Activities:	Conclude the program with the song "Seasonal Walks" (p. 5) and give children the take-home activity "Walk with Your Eyes Diary" (p. 31).

---

*Based on chapter 1.

UP IN THE AIR

Sample Program*

Initiating Activities: Begin with "Welcome Aboard" (p. 135) so children can introduce themselves and get into the spirit of flight preparations.

First Story: Young children will enjoy *Jamie Goes on an Airplane* (p. 136) to prepare for flight take off. You may wish to substitute *First Flight* (p. 136) for children that are a little older.

Related Activities: Sing "Going Flying" (p. 137) to recreate the steps in getting ready to take an airplane trip. Continue with the flannel-board story "Carry On" (pp. 138-39) to recall the experience of boarding aircraft with ridiculous consequences.

Second Story: Read *Little Helicopter* (p. 144).

Related Activities: Before you tell the next story, sing the "Helicopter Song" (p. 146). Then get the children involved with "Whirlybird to the Rescue" (p. 145).

Third Story: Read *They Came from Aargh!* (p. 148).

Related Activities: Follow this story with a similar story told with flannel-board, "Willy's Spaceship" (pp. 150-52). Then conclude with an "Out of This World Vacation" (pp. 153-54) told with active participation.

Final Activities: Play the game "Great Galaxies" (p. 158). Then show the children how to make their own spaceships by constructing as a group a "Refrigerator Carton Rocket" (p. 159). Give them each a "Flight Bag Take-Home Activity" (p. 164) so they can reenact the day's fun again and again.

---

*Based on chapter 6.

1

Feet and Flippers
Ways to Go on Your Own

INTRODUCTION

The first chapter in this book on transportation barely leaves the ground because it focuses on the first form of getting around—using your own two feet. Other chapters will explore inventions as simple as the ox cart and as technologically advanced as supersonic jets, but most of the world still depends upon the use of feet to move.

The first subtheme, "Run and Walk," focuses on ways people move. We have included books with animals walking and running in this section if they are anthropomorphic (having human attributes) or take on human characteristics. Running, walking, and dancing books may focus on feet activities. In *My Two Feet* by Schertle, walks in different seasons—winter in *The Snowman Who Went for a Walk* or spring in *A Walk in the Rain* or dancing and jogging fun in *Max* and *Bear and Duck on the Run*—suggests that walking may serve a utilitarian or "pedestrian" function or it may also be just for fun. Follow up these stories with a new version of the traditional "Bear Hunt" story with the participatory story "Dog Hunt," recall a child's first steps by singing "Baby Walk," and encourage families to record sights they see on walks together with our take-home activity.

The second subtheme, "Waddle and Paddle," explores ways animals move in distinctly animal-like ways. The popularity of the picture books *Jump, Frog, Jump* and *Rosie's Walk* is evidence of children's enthusiasm for imitating animal actions. Follow-up activities will help you tell other stories on your own with methods from draw and tell to masks and shadow figures so children can more readily visualize these fun ways to get around.

INITIATING ACTIVITY

Off to a Silly Start

Begin story time with a funny rhyme the children will learn right away. Each child can have a turn to say his or her name; have everyone repeat it and clap the syllables.

> A-B-C, 1-2-3
> I've got feet below my knees!
> They can jump, and they can run.
> Say your name, and we'll have fun!
> (*Carol*)
> Let's all say it.
> (*Carol*)
> Let's all clap it.
> (*Clap-clap*)

LITERATURE-SHARING EXPERIENCES

Books for Run and Walk

Aesop. **The Miller, His Son and Their Donkey**. Illustrated by Roger Duvoisin. Whittlesey House, 1962.
> This traditional tale of who rides on whom and too much good advice is humorously illustrated.

Curious George Goes Hiking. Edited by Margret Rey and Alan Shalleck. Houghton Mifflin, 1985.
> Based on an animated film, in this book George the monkey gets into trouble losing the picnic food for the hike, but becomes a hero as he helps everyone find the way back home.

Delton, Judy. **Bear and Duck on the Run**. Illustrated by Lynn Munsinger. Albert Whitman, 1984.
> Duck is into jogging and tries to convince Bear to join him. Bear has more relaxed ways to spend his time and the two friends finally compromise.

Hest, Amy. **Crack-of-Dawn Walkers**. Illustrated by Amy Schwartz. Macmillan, 1984.
> Sadie and her grandfather enjoy the sights and sounds of their early morning walks.

Hill, Eric. **Spot's First Walk**. Putnam, 1981.
> Spot, the familiar puppy, finds lots of surprises concealed under the flaps of this picture book about his first walk outside.

Hillert, Margaret. **Take a Walk, Johnny**. Illustrated by Yoshi Miyake. Follett, 1981.
> Once bored with his daily walks, Johnny finds walking and observing more exciting than he thought.

Hughes, Shirley. **Alfie's Feet**. Lothrop, Lee and Shepard, 1982.
> Alfie's feet fit his new boots—most of the time. Children will understand his right-left dilemma.

Isadora, Rachel. **Max**. Macmillan, 1976.
> After Max walks his sister to ballet class, he finds dancing more interesting than baseball.

Kessler, Leonard. **On Your Mark, Get Set, Go**. Harper & Row, 1972.
> Animal Olympics are exciting for everyone except the worm, but they all have fun training anyway.

Lobe, Mira. **The Snowman Who Went for a Walk**. Illustrated by Winifried Opgenoorth. Morrow, 1984.
> In a quest for longer life before melting, Snowman sets off to find the perfect climate.

Miller, Elizabeth. **Cat and Dog Have a Parade**. Illustrated by Victoria Chess. Franklin Watts, 1981.
> Left and right are a problem for Dog and threaten to spoil the parade until Cat helps by painting L and R on the correct feet.

Scheffler, Ursel. **A Walk in the Rain**. Illustrated by Ulises Wensell. Putnam, 1986.
> New rainware is a cause for celebration and a walk in the rain for Jamie and Grandma.

Schertle, Alice. **My Two Feet**. Illustrated by Meredith Dunham. Lothrop, Lee and Shepard, 1985.
> A little girl demonstrates activities using her feet throughout the year.

Shannon, George. **Dance Away**. Illustrated by Jose Aruego and Ariane Dewey. Greenwillow, 1982.
> Rabbit's dancing is a bother to his friends until it saves them from the fox.

Sivulich, Sandra. **I'm Going on a Bear Hunt**. Illustrated by Glen Rounds. Dutton, 1973.

Caves, streams, and trees impeded the progress of these bear hunters. The story is written to be participatory fun.

Taylor, Mark. **Henry the Explorer**. Atheneum, 1966.

Henry and his dog don the garb of great explorers but rarely leave the familiar territory.

Watanabe, Shigeo. **I Can Take a Walk**. Illustrated by Yasuo Ohtomo. Philomel Books, 1984.

The preschool bear enjoys his solo walk away from home, but is glad to have Father Bear along for the return trip.

Watanabe, Shigeo. **Get Set! Go!** Illustrated by Yasuo Ohtomo. Philomel Books, 1981.

Bear may not win the race, but he makes an effort children will understand and admire.

Wildsmith, Brian. **Goat's Trail**. Knopf, 1986.

When a wild goat leads a sheep into town, and unties a cow, a pig, and a donkey hitched to a cart, confusion and a traffic jam result.

Related Activities for Run and Walk

Dog Hunt

Set the pace for this imitation of the "Bear Hunt" by tapping on knees and making other sound effects as indicated.

I'm going on a dog hunt
for my dog named Rags.
Here, Rags, here!
Not there!
Let's go down the street.
walk
walk
walk
walk
Here Rags!
Not here.
Oops. Here is a puddle.
Can't step over it.
Don't want to go around it.
Have to go through it!
splash
splash
splash
splash
Shake off the water.
walk
walk
walk
walk
Here, Rags
Not there.
Oops! Here is a mud hole.

Can't go over it.
Don't want to go around it.
Have to go through it.
glup
glup
glup
glup
Wipe off feet.
walk
walk
walk
walk
Here, Rags, here.
Not there.
Oops! Here is a sandbox.
Can't go over it.
Don't want to go around it.
Have to go through it.
swoosh
swoosh
swoosh
swoosh
Dust off.
walk
walk
walk
walk
Oops! Here is a pile of leaves.
Let's jump in.
run
run
run
run
jump
crunch
Arf
Arf?
RAGS!
Let's go home.
walk
walk
walk
walk
Back through sand.
swoosh
swoosh
swoosh
swoosh
Back through the mud.
glup
glup
glup
glup

Back through the puddle.
splash
splash
splash
splash
We're home, Rags!
And just in time for dinner!

Seasonal Walks
(To the tune of "Mulberry Bush")

Spring time walks sound
splish, splash, splish,
splish, splash, splish,
splish, splash, splish.
Spring time walks sound
splish, splash, splish.
Spring time walks are fun.

Summer walks feel sizzle hot,
sizzle hot,
sizzle hot.
Summer walks feel sizzle hot.
Summer walks are fun.

Autumn walks sound
crunch, crunch, crunch.
crinkle, crunch,
crinkle, crunch,
Autumn walks sound
crunch, crunch, crunch.
Autumn walks are fun.

Winter walks feel freezy cold,
freezy cold,
freezy cold,
Winter walks feel freezy cold,
Winter walks are fun
COME!

Baby Walk
(To the tune of "Mary Had a Little Lamb")

Imitate the actions of the baby learning to walk and remind the children of the "good old days" when they were young!

Baby learns to creep and crawl,
Creep and crawl, creep and crawl.
Baby learns to creep and crawl,
You're going on your way.

Baby learns to pull and stand,
Pull and stand, pull and stand.
Baby learns to pull and stand,
You're going on your way.

Baby tries to take a step,
take a step, take a step.
Baby tries to take a step,
You're going on your way.

Baby tumbles—catch him fast!
Catch him fast! Catch him fast!
Baby tumbles—catch him fast!
You're going on your way.

Baby takes another step,
Another step, another step.
Baby takes another step—
Now you're on your way.
Hooray!

Long Walk Home

(A Flannel-board Story)

Make flannel-board figures of a kitten, fire truck, pine cone, cookies, and ducks. These objects are placed on the board in the second half of the story. For the first half, place two pieces of yarn on the board to outline a sidewalk.

"Hurry, Jonathan, hurry!" said mother. "I have to get these brownies to the bake sale by 3 o'clock."

Jonathan stepped out onto the sidewalk. He put the heel of his right foot to the toe of his left foot. Then he put the heel of his left foot to the toe of his right foot. Right, left, right, left.

"Hurry, Jonathan, hurry!" said mother.

Jonathan skipped three skips forward and two skips backward. Then he skipped four skips forward and three skips back. Skip forward, skip back.

"Hurry, Jonathan, hurry," said mother.

Jonathan took one giant step and stopped. He took another giant step and stopped. Start and stop, start and stop.

"Hurry, Jonathan, hurry!" said mother. And she took hold of his hand and marched him firmly along with no more fooling around. They arrived at the bake sale at two minutes to 3. Mother dropped off the brownies and bought some chocolate chip cookies, and they started home.

On the way home, Jonathan said, "Can we go my way home?"

"Of course," said mother. "I am in no hurry now."

They walked past the pet store and looked at the kitten in the window.

They walked to the fire station and looked at all the fire trucks.

They walked to the park, and they picked up some pine cones along the path.

(Text continues on page 9.)

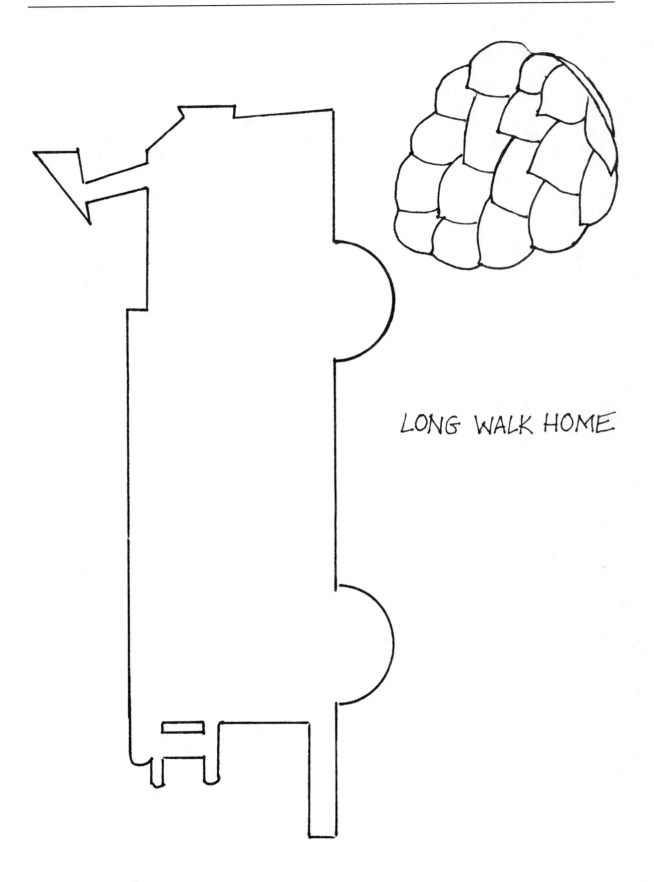

LONG WALK HOME

LONG WALK HOME

When they came to the garden in the park, Jonathan and mother sat down and ate the cookies.

Then Jonathan led mother by the duck pond. They fed the crumbs from the cookies to the ducks.

Jonathan was getting tired from so much walking. "Hurry, Mommy, hurry," said Jonathan. "I am tired."

"No wonder," said mother. "We did take the long way home. But look at how much we got to see along the way."

Tumbling Tricks
(A Chant with Actions)

After the children have learned the words and actions for this chant, repeat it faster and faster.

Somersault,   *(Roll hands)*
Cartwheel,   *(Palms flat, circle hands)*
Handstand,   *(Slap knees)*
Flip.   *(Swing arms up overhead)*
Which stunt is
Your favorite trick?

Hopscotch Song
(To the tune of "Ten Little Indians")

One little,
Two little,
Three squares of hopscotch,
Four little,
Five little,
Six squares of hopscotch,
Seven little,
Eight little,
Nine squares of hopscotch,
Ten squares on the street.
Ten little,
Nine little,
Eight squares of hopscotch,
Seven little,
Six little,
Five squares of hopscotch,
Four little,
Three little,
Two squares of hopscotch,
One square for my feet!

The Gingerbread Kid
(A Cut and Tell Story)

Fold an 8½ x 11 inch paper three times so that the piece is 1 1/8 x 8½. As you tell the story, cut and open as indicated in the directions (see illustration).

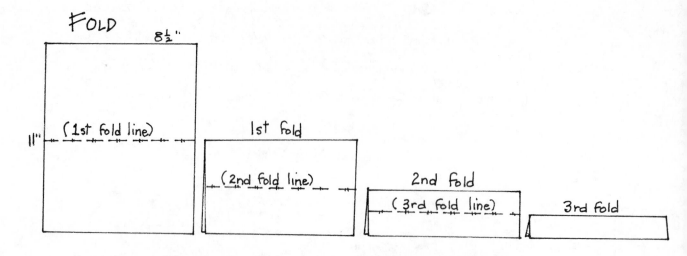

One day an old woman decided to make gingerbread. She got out a big bowl and a big spoon and a big pan. She stirred and mixed and rolled and cut. There on the pan was a wonderful gingerbread kid. She baked it ever so carefully for just the right amount of time, and took it out to decorate. She added raisin eyes and three red candy buttons. As she placed the very last button on it, she said, "My, you look good enough to eat. You should stay close to home."

But as soon as she said that, the gingerbread kid jumped off the pan and ran toward the door. He said,

"You can't make me stay
I will run
And run away!"

He ran out the door and up the hill. (*Make first cut.*)

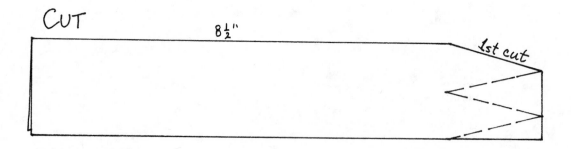

At the top of the hill he met the rooster. The rooster crowed, "My, you look good enough to eat. You should stay close to home!"

But the gingerbread kid just ran on and called to the rooster,

"You can't make me stay
I will run
And run away!"

He ran down the hill. (*Make second cut.*)

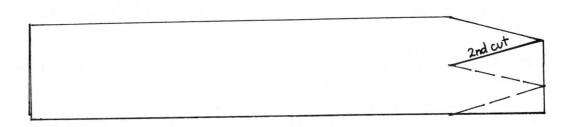

At the bottom of the hill, he met a woodchuck. The woodchuck chucked, "My, you look good enough to eat. You should stay close to home!"
But the gingerbread kid just ran on and called to the woodchuck,

> "You can't make me stay
> I will run
> And run away!"

He ran up the next hill. (*Make third cut.*)

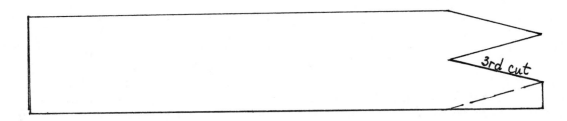

At the top of the hill, he met a sheep. The sheep bleated, "My, you look good enough to eat. You should stay close to home!"
But the gingerbread kid just ran on and called to the sheep,

> "You can't make me stay
> I will run
> And run away!"

He ran down the next hill. (*Make fourth cut.*)

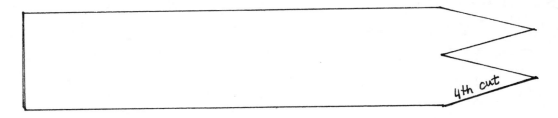

At the bottom of the hill, he met a horse. The horse nagged at him, "My, you look good enough to eat. You should stay close to home!"
But the gingerbread kid just ran on and called to the horse,

"You can't make me stay
I will run
And run away!"

He ran straight into a dark cave.
He couldn't see at first, but he felt something big and fuzzy. Then he saw a long line of sharp teeth! (*Open paper and hold up so jagged edge is at the bottom.*) CHOMP!

OPEN and TURN

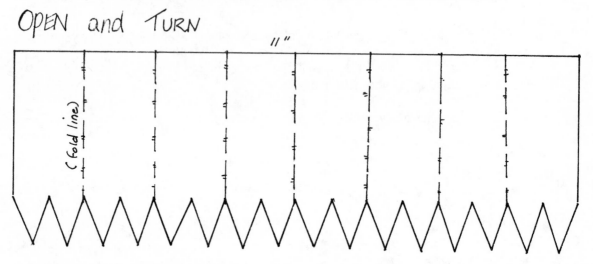

Something thought he looked good enough to eat. The gingerbread kid ran and ran and ran all the way home and did not stop until he was safe inside his own picket fence. (*Open paper and hold up so jagged edge is at top.*)

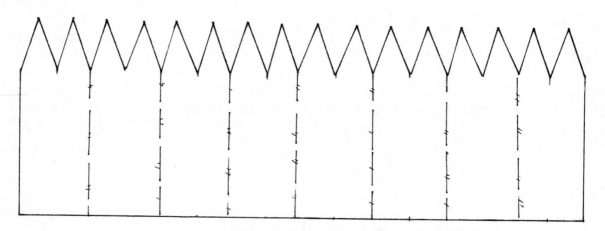

And after that he stayed close to home where he lived happily ever after.

Dancer
(To the tune of "I'm a Little Teapot")

I'm a little dancer on my toe—
Round and round I like to go.
I can arabesque and pirouette,
And do the very best curtsey yet.

Hare and Tortoise Retold
(A Finger Story)

Use the fingers of one hand to form ears for the hare. Hold the fingers of the other hand down so they make the feet of the tortoise. Move the animals as they run the race in the story.

Once upon a time there was a hare—which is another name for a rabbit—who liked to think he was the fastest animal in the forest. Not only did he like to think that, but he liked to tell everyone that he was the fastest animal in the forest.

I can run at a powerful pace
I challenge anyone to a race!

But no one wanted to race with the Hare, partly because he was very fast and partly because he bragged so much.

Now in this forest there also lived a tortoise—which is another name for a turtle. He had been closed up in his own little world inside his shell for so long that he had not heard Hare's bragging or had seen how fast Hare could run. So when he heard Hare say,

I can run at a powerful pace
I challenge anyone to a race!

Tortoise liked to have fun and a race sounded like fun. So he called back to Hare,

Keep on moving'—steady, slow—
Takes me where I want to go.

So it was agreed that Tortoise and Hare would race the next day. All the animals in the forest came out to see it. They lined up at the starting line and Owl called, "On your mark, get set, GO!" And the race began.

Hare jumped off the starting line and was way ahead in no time. He called back over his shoulder:

I can run at a powerful pace
I certainly will win this race!

Tortoise did not exactly take off with a jump. He almost needed a jump start. But at last he looked out of his shell and ambled down the road. He hummed a little hum to himself and said:

Keep on movin'—steady, slow—
Takes me where I want to go.

Hare was far ahead when he came to a field of lovely daisies. He decided to take a little time off to smell the daisies and weave a daisy chain. Then he hopped on the road and called back over his shoulder:

I can run at a powerful pace
I certainly will win this race!

Tortoise was moving slow enough that he did not need to stop to smell the daisies. He could smell them as he went by. He did not waste any time making daisy chains. He hummed a little hum to himself and said:

> Keep on movin'—steady, slow—
> Takes me where I want to go.

Hare did not see Tortoise at all when he came past the Dance Hall. But when he looked inside he saw that everyone was doing the Bunny Hop. He could not resist just a dance or two. Or three. He hopped and hopped and hopped. And finally hopped back on to the road and confidently called:

> I can run at a powerful pace
> I certainly will win this race!

Tortoise heard the music from the dance hall, but he did not stop even to do the Minute Waltz. He hummed a little hum to himself and said:

> Keep on movin'—steady, slow—
> Takes me where I want to go.

Hare was getting a little sleepy after all those daisies and dances. When he saw the pokeberry bush he decided to take a doze. Soon he was deep asleep.

Tortoise kept right on moving—slow but steady. He moved past the pokeberry bush, and down the last hill to the finish line. He was just six turtle steps short of the finish line when Hare woke up. He jumped back on the road and said,

> I can run at a powerful pace...

But just then Tortoise crossed the finish line and said:

> But this time I have won the race!

And after that Hare and Tortoise became good friends. In fact, if you get up very early in the morning you can see them out together—jogging!

Books for Waddle and Paddle

Aesop. **The Hare and the Tortoise.** Illustrated by Paul Galdone. McGraw-Hill, 1962.

> The traditional tale of "slow and steady wins the race" is enhanced by Galdone's lively pictures. The tortoise wins again to the delight of children everywhere.

Florian, Douglas. **A Bird Can Fly.** Greenwillow, 1980.

> Birds, beavers, ants, and others are observed in their locomotion and activities.

Freschet, Bernice. **Little Black Bear Goes for a Walk.** Illustrated by Glen Rounds. Scribner, 1977.

> Little Black Bear has a series of adventures from falling in ponds to finding out about bees on his first walk away from mama bear.

Hutchins, Pat. **Rosie's Walk.** Macmillan, 1967.

> Rosie the hen unknowingly misses one close encounter after another with the fox, who always gets the bad end and at last runs off and leaves Rosie to her walk.

Kalan, Robert. **Jump, Frog, Jump.** Illustrated by Byron Barton. Greenwillow, 1981.

> The only way for the frog to get away from the children is to jump, but can he catch the fly for dinner, too?

Kent, Jack. **Joey Runs Away.** Prentice Hall, 1985.

> Mother Kangaroo rents out her pouch after Joey leaves home, but they both find he is the best occupant.

Lionni, Leo. **Swimmy**. Pantheon, 1963.

Swimmy is just a little fish in a big school until he thinks up a plan to save them all from being eaten by a big fish.

Maris, Ron. **Better Move on, Frog!** Franklin Watts, 1982.

All the holes frog tries are already taken until at last he finds one that is just right.

Miles, Miska. **Swim Little Duck**. Illustrated by Jim Arnosky. Little, Brown, 1976.

After trying the big wide world, Little Duck comes back happily to the pond.

Rockwell, Anne. **Willy Runs Away**. Dutton, 1976.

Willy the Dog finds when he runs away there is no place like home.

Related Activities for Waddle and Paddle

How Do They Do It?

Show pictures of the various animals as you say this rhyme the first time. Then enjoy acting out all these kinds of animal movements with the children.

> The animals never
> Make a big fuss
> If they don't take a subway
> Or ride on the bus.
>
> The elephant lumbers.
> The turkeys can strut.
> The pigs love to wallow.
> The goats ram and butt.
>
> The ducks waggle tails.
> The cat tiptoes by.
> The horses can gallop.
> The eagles can fly.
>
> The fish all go swimming.
> The kangaroo jumps.
> The snake likes to slither.
> The camel ga-lumps.
>
> With all of these ways
> To go near and far,
> How dull it will seem now
> To ride in the car!

What Do I Do?
(A Circle Story)

Cut two circles of poster board and attach at the center with a brad fastener. On the top one, place a picture of a duckling. Cut a wedge from the side opposite the duckling. On the bottom circle place pictures of a kitten, pony, rabbit, worm, and duck. Turn the wheel to show the character Duckling is talking to. At the end, lead all the children around the room going "waddle-waddle, quack-quack."

(Text continues on page 18.)

WHAT DO I DO?

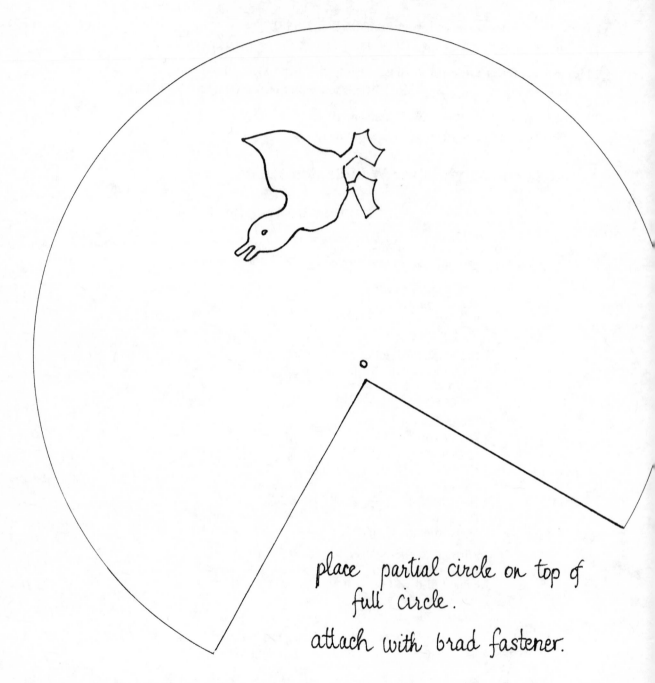

place partial circle on top of
full circle.
attach with brad fastener.

WHAT DO I DO?

Duckling had only been hatched from his egg for fifteen minutes or so when he decided to go for a walk. Mother Duck had said, "I am just going for some breakfast for us. Wait here until I get back." But Duckling was not as patient as he should have been for being only fifteen minutes old, and he did not want to wait. So he decided for himself to go for a walk.

The only problem was he did not know quite how ducklings were supposed to walk. He looked around for someone to ask, and sure enough walking by his nest was Kitten.

"Kitten," said Duckling in a nice way, because even though he was only fifteen minutes old, he had learned to be polite, "Could you show me how ducklings are supposed to walk?"

"Of course," said Kitten who was glad to help, but was not exactly sure how ducklings were supposed to walk. "I'm sure that they walk the same as little kittens do: tippy-toe, tippy-toe, tippy-toe."

"Thank you," said Duckling. He tried to walk tippy-toe, tippy-toe, tippy-toe, but his little webbed feet went flippy-toe, flippy-toe, flippy-toe and he fell on his duckling bill. As he was lying there thinking how to walk, along came Pony.

"Pony," said Duckling. "Could you show me how ducklings are supposed to walk?"

"Of course," said Pony who was glad to help, but was not exactly sure how ducklings were supposed to walk. "I'm sure that they walk the same as little ponies do: gallop-a-trot, gallop-a-trot, gallop-a-trot."

"Thank you," said Duckling. He tried to walk gallop-a-trot, gallop-a-trot, gallop-a-trot, but his little webbed feet went gallop-a-flop, gallop-a-flop, gallop-a-flop and he fell on his duckling bill. As he was lying there thinking how to walk, along came Rabbit.

"Rabbit," said Duckling. "Could you show me how ducklings are supposed to walk?"

"Of course," said Rabbit who was glad to help, but was not exactly sure how ducklings were supposed to walk. "I'm sure that they walk the same as little rabbits do: Hop-hopity-hop, hop-hopity-hop, hop-hopity-hop."

"Thank you," said Duckling. He tried to walk hop-hopity-hop, hop-hopity-hop, hop-hopity-hop, but his little webbed feet went flop-flopity-flop, flop-flopity-flop, flop-flopity-flop and he fell on his duckling bill. As he was lying there thinking how to walk, along came Worm.

"Worm," said Duckling. "Could you show me how ducklings are supposed to walk?"

"Of course," said Worm who was glad to help, but was not exactly sure how ducklings were supposed to walk. "I'm sure that they walk the same as little worms do: Creepy-creepy-crawl, creepy-creepy-crawl, creepy-creepy-crawl."

"Thank you," said Duckling. He tried to walk creepy-creepy-crawl, creepy-creepy-crawl, creepy-creepy-crawl, but his little webbed feet went fleepy-fleepy-fall, fleepy-fleepy-fall, fleepy-fleepy-fall, and he fell on his duckling bill.

Duckling was just about to give up ever going for a walk at all when along came Mother Duck.

"Mother Duck," said Duckling. "Could you show me how ducklings are supposed to walk?"

"Of course," said Mother Duck who was glad to help, and knew exactly how ducklings were supposed to walk. "They walk the same as Mother Ducks do: Waddle-waddle-quack-quack, waddle-waddle-quack-quack."

"Thank you," said Duckling. And when he tried to walk waddle-waddle-quack-quack, waddle-waddle-quack-quack, his little webbed feet went exactly the right way. So he and Mother Duck went waddle-waddle-quack-quack, waddle-waddle-quack-quack all the way back to the nest for breakfast.

Movin' and Groovin' at the Zoo
(To the tune of "Mulberry Bush")

I went on a trip down to the zoo,
to the zoo, to the zoo
To see what the animals could do,
And this is what they did.

The elephants all lumbered by,
lumbered by, lumbered by
The elephants all lumbered by,
That is what they did.

The kangaroos took great big jumps,
Great big jumps, great big jumps.
The kangaroos took great big jumps,
That is what they did.

The snakes all slithered on their scales,
on their scales, on their scales.
The snakes all slithered on their scales,
That is what they did.

The monkeys all were swinging high,
Swinging high, swinging high.
The monkeys all were swinging high,
That is what they did.

The fish were swimming here and there,
Here and there, here and there.
The fish were swimming here and there,
That is what they did.

The bats were hanging upside down.
Upside down, upside down.
The bats were hanging upside down,
That is what they did.

Sandy Claws
(A Shadow Figure Story)

This original pourquoi story would make a wonderful shadow figure story. Cut figures of the bottle, crab, and genie. To make the genie more effective, attach bits of cotton balls and pull them out thin so the shadow appears to have mist around it. Mount the pieces on dowel rods. Shine a bright light from the back onto a sheet or lay the pieces on an overhead projector.

(Text continues on page 22.)

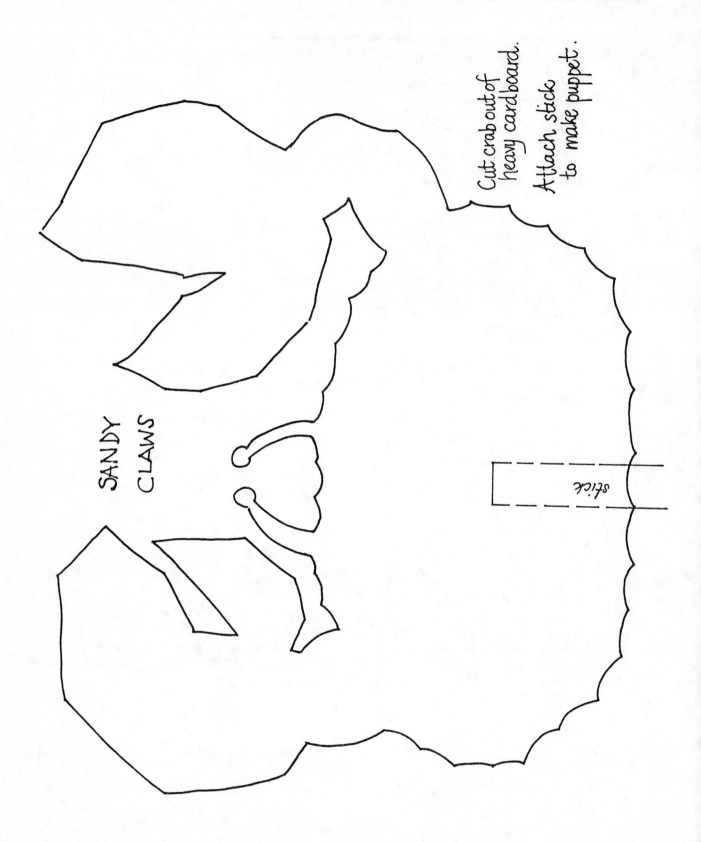

SANDY CLAWS

Cut crab out of heavy cardboard. Attach stick to make puppet.

stick

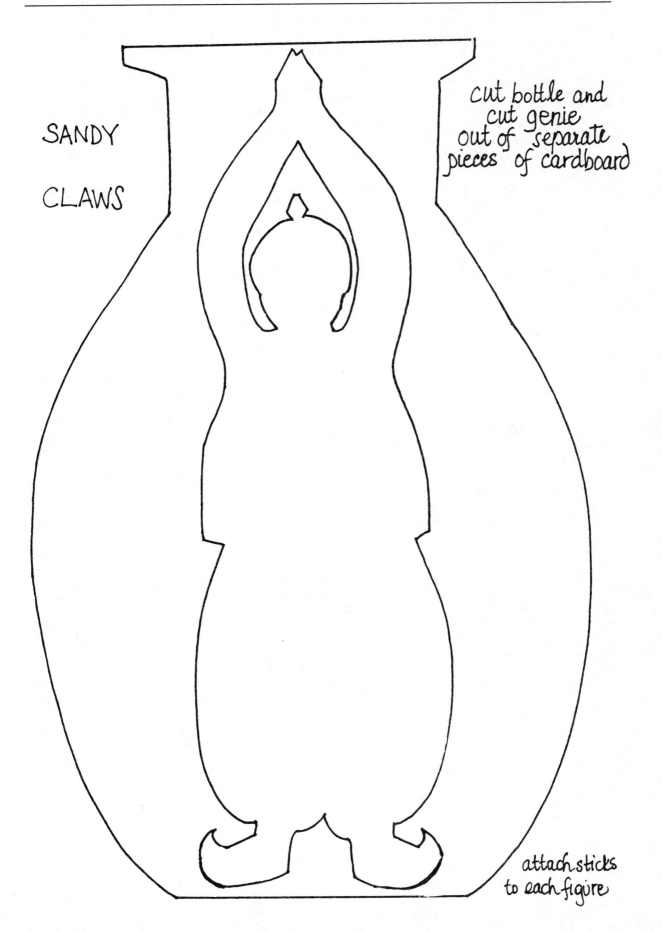

SANDY

CLAWS

cut bottle and
cut genie
out of separate
pieces of cardboard

attach sticks
to each figure

Now crabs have a hard shell with prickly spikes. They have sharp pincher claws that are always full of sand. And when they walk, they do not go to the front or to the back, but rather to the side. It was not always so. There was a time when crabs could walk as straight as anything, but those days are gone. And this is how it came to be.

Long ago a crab rested thinking in the sun. Crab knew that with her prickly shell and claws full of sand, she was not beautiful, but with the sun on her back and the ocean nearby she didn't mind. Still and all, when a strange bottle washed up on the shore and looked as if it could contain a magic genie of some sort, Crab walked straight up to give it a try. It is not easy to rub a bottle when your claws are full of sand, but finally a whiff of smoke and a poof of light brought the genie out of the bottle.

Now this bottle had been floating a long time in the water and the genie inside had grown fat and lazy from lack of magic exercise so he did not want to try anything too tricky. Instead of offering the crab anything she wanted, he said, "My powers are limited. I can only grant wishes about the way you move. You can wish to move any way you want, but that is all I can do."

Well, Crab thought it was a shame she could not wish herself to be a beautiful mermaid or at least get the sand out of her claws, but there was still the sun on her back and the ocean nearby to make her happy. She decided it might be a very good thing to move some other way, so she said, "I would like to stand on two feet and waddle like a sea gull."

"Whatever," said the genie and in a whiff and a poof, Crab was up on two feet waddling like a sea gull.

After Crab had waddled around for a while, she began to wonder if there were other ways to move so she rubbed the bottle again with her sandy claw and the genie appeared.

"Now remember," he said. "My powers are limited. I can only grant wishes about the way you move. You can wish to move any way you want, but that is all I can do."

"That's all right," said crab. "I think now I would like to gallop like a horse."

"Whatever," said the genie and in a whiff and a poof, Crab was galloping like a horse.

After Crab had galloped around for a while, she began to wonder if there were other ways to move. She rubbed the bottle again with her sandy claw and the genie appeared.

"Now remember," he said. "My powers are limited. I can only grant wishes about the way you move. You can wish to move any way you want, but that is all I can do."

"Well, here's a challenge for you," said crab. "I think now I would like to dance like a ballet dancer."

"Whatever," said the genie and in a whiff and a poof, Crab was dancing like a ballet dancer.

After Crab had danced around for a while, she began to wonder if there were other ways to move. She rubbed the bottle again with her sandy claw and the genie appeared.

"Now remember," he said. "My powers are limited. I can only grant wishes about the way you move. You can wish to move any way you want, but that is all I can do. And this is the last time I can come out."

"I'll make it good, then," said Crab. "What I really want is to be able to whiff and poof and vanish like a genie."

Now the genie was getting pretty tired of Crab always changing her mind. Besides his magic had gotten lazy and he did not know how many more spells he could do. When Crab asked to whiff and poof and vanish like a genie, he did not say a word. He rolled up his sleeves and shot a great bolt of lightning. "There," he said, "that will teach you to be greedy. I just changed you back to walk like a crab." And he disappeared for good.

Unfortunately his magic was more rusty than he thought and the spell to change Crab back to walk like a crab missed its mark by a little. So when Crab tried to walk instead of going straight to where she was going, she moved first to one side and then the other until she finally got there. At first she was upset, but after a time she realized that with the sun on her back and the ocean nearby she was not really in a hurry to get anywhere anyway.

Which is a good thing, because that is how a crab moves to this very day.

Particular Penguins

As you say the word "waddle" place arms at sides with hands flat and palms down at hip level. Move flat footed with heels together.

My penguin loves the South Pole
He likes the cold and snow.
He skates upon the icy lake,
And this is how he goes:
Waddle, waddle, waddle, waddle,
Waddle, waddle, waddle.

I took him to Hawaii
To see the sandy turf.
He wore his yellow swim trunks
And this is how he surfed:
Waddle, waddle, waddle, waddle,
Waddle, waddle, waddle.

No matter where I take him,
No matter how we go,
He'll always be a penguin
From his head down to his toes!
Waddle, waddle, waddle, waddle,
Waddle, waddle, waddle.

The Great Race
(A Draw and Tell Story)

Draw the simple lines shown to help the children figure out who finally beat Crow in a race—but only after dark!

Sometimes Crow drove everyone crazy. He constantly bragged about how fast and far he could fly. All day long he sat on the fence and told the sparrows and the ducks and the chickens how fast and far he could fly. They all had to admit that, even though he drove them crazy, he could fly faster and farther than any of them. So they listened to his bragging and tried to think of a way to make him stop.

Finally Duck came up with an idea. "Let's find someone who can beat Crow in a race." The others thought it was a wonderful idea, but who could beat Crow? Duck didn't know, but she set out to find someone.

She left at eight o'clock in the morning and traveled up the hill to where Goose lived. (*Draw first line.*)

"Goose," she called. "Please come beat Crow in a race."
Goose called back,
"Once I flew against the Crow
I lost to him, I'll have you know

I do not wish to hear him brag or
Watch him strut and see him swagger."
And Goose would not come race Crow.

At ten o'clock in the morning Duck traveled down the hill to Owl's house. (*Draw second line.*)

"Owl," she called. "Please come beat Crow in a race." Owl called back,
"Once I flew against the Crow
I lost to him, I'll have you know
I do not wish to hear him brag or
Watch him strut and see him swagger."
And Owl would not come race Crow.

At twelve o'clock Duck traveled around the bend to Dove's house. (*Draw third line.*)

"Dove," she called. "Please come beat Crow in a race." Dove called back,
"Once I flew against the Crow
I lost to him, I'll have you know
I do not wish to hear him brag or
Watch him strut and see him swagger."
And Dove would not come race Crow.

At two o'clock in the afternoon Duck traveled up another hill to Lark's house. (*Draw fourth line.*)

"Lark," she called. "Please come beat Crow in a race." Lark called back,
"Once I flew against the Crow
I lost to him, I'll have you know
I do not wish to hear him brag or
Watch him strut and see him swagger."
And Lark would not come race Crow.

At four o'clock in the afternoon Duck traveled down the other hill to Pigeon's house. (*Draw fifth line.*)

"Pigeon," she called. "Please come beat Crow in a race." Pigeon called back,
"Once I flew against the Crow
I lost to him, I'll have you know
I do not wish to hear him brag or
Watch him strut and see him swagger."
And Pigeon would not come race Crow.

Duck felt so bad she sat down at the bottom of the hill and almost cried. Where could they find someone to beat Crow? Pigeon heard her sniffing and said, "Maybe there is someone who can help. Follow the path through the woods for five turns and there you will find someone."

Duck jumped up and ran down the path. The path had lots of curves and could hardly be said to be as straight as the crow flies. Even though she went as fast as possible by the time she got there it was eight o'clock in the evening and already dark. But Pigeon was right. There was someone who could beat Crow. When this someone went back with Duck, the race was held right then and Crow was beaten soundly. Never again could Crow brag.

Do you know who Duck found? After Duck traveled around those five curves, she found—BAT! (*Draw scalloped line across the bottom.*)

And that was that!

Slow and Fast
(To the tune of "The Farmer in the Dell")

Have all the children imitate the actions of the animals in the song. Older children can name other fast and slow animals for more verses and actions.

The turtle walks so slow.
The turtle walks so slow.
I can walk like turtle walks.
The turtle walks so slow.

The frog goes hopping fast.
The frog goes hopping fast.
I can hop just like a frog.
The frog goes hopping fast.

The snail comes crawling slow.
The snail comes crawling slow.
I can crawl just like a snail.
The snail comes crawling slow.

The horse can gallop fast.
The horse can gallop fast.
I can gallop like a horse.
The horse can gallop fast.

Who's Moving Outside?
(A Story with Puppets)

Make paper plate puppets with mouths that open. Staple two paper plates together around the edges. Fold them both in half and cut a slit in the outside plate to insert fingers. Add eyes on the top, teeth and tongue inside the fold. Make a bear, moose, owl, rabbit, and mouse. Give puppets to children to hold as indicated in the story and when the time for the yawning comes in the story, have them open the mouths of the puppets.

(*Give Bear puppet to first child.*) Bear was tired. It was half past October, and he was all ready for a long winter's sleep. Bear walked toward his cave: lumber, lumber, lumber. He turned around three times and lay down to sleep. (*Have child turn around three times and sit down.*) Good night, Bear.

But Bear could not get to sleep. Someone was moving outside. Bear got up to see who it was. (*Have first child get up.*) It was Moose. (*Give Moose puppet to second child.*) Crunch-crunch, crunch-crunch. Moose was walking on dried leaves. Moose walked to his cave. Crunch-crunch, crunch-crunch. He turned around three times and lay down to sleep. Good night, Moose. (*Have child turn around three times and sit down.*) Bear walked back to his cave: lumber, lumber, lumber. He turned around three times and lay down to sleep. (*Have child turn around three times and sit down.*) Good night, Bear.

But Bear and Moose could not get to sleep. Someone was moving outside. Bear and Moose got up to see who it was. (*Have children get up.*) It was Owl. (*Give Owl puppet to child.*) Flap-flap, flap-flap. Owl was flying around the tree tops. Owl flew to his hole in the big tree. Flap-flap, flap-flap. He turned around three times and lay down to sleep. (*Have child turn around three times and sit down.*) Good night Owl. Moose walked back to his cave. Crunch-crunch, crunch-crunch. He turned around three times and lay down to sleep. (*Have child turn around three times and sit down.*) Good night, Moose. Bear walked back to his cave: lumber, lumber, lumber. He turned around three times and lay down to sleep. (*Have child turn around three times and sit down.*) Good night, Bear.

But Bear and Moose and Owl could not get to sleep. Someone was moving outside. Bear and Mouse and Owl got up to see who it was. (*Have children get up.*) It was Rabbit. (*Give Rabbit puppet to child.*) Hop-hop-hop. Rabbit was hopping over the dry ground. Rabbit hopped into his hole in the ground. Hop-hop-hop. He turned around three times and lay down to sleep. (*Have child turn around three times and sit down..*) Good night, Rabbit. Owl flew back to his hole in the big tree. Flap-flap, flap-flap. He turned around three times and lay down to sleep. (*Have child turn around three times and sit down.*) Good night, Owl. Moose walked back to his cave. Crunch-crunch, crunch-crunch. He turned around three times and lay down to sleep. (*Have child turn around three times and sit down.*) Good night, Moose. Bears walked back to his cave. Lumber, lumber, lumber. He turned around three times and lay down to sleep. (*Have child turn around three times and sit down.*) Good night, Bear.

WHO'S MOVING OUTSIDE?

One whole paper plate stapled to two halves

Opening for hand

Attach eyes, ears, etc. to this half

Attach tongue to lower half of whole plate

But Bear and Moose and Owl and Rabbit could not get to sleep. Someone was moving outside. Bear and Moose and Owl and Rabbit got up to see who it was. (*Have children get up.*) It was Mouse. (*Give Mouse puppet to last child.*) Scurry-scurry-scurry. Mouse was hurring over the bare earth. Scurry-scurry-scurry. Mouse scurried into his hole in the ground. And while all the others watched, Mouse did an amazing thing.

Mouse yawned (*open mouth on Mouse*), then he turned around three times and fell right to sleep. (*Have child turn around three times and sit down.*) Good night, Mouse.

When Rabbit saw Mouse yawn, he got so sleepy he hopped into his hole in the ground. Hop-hop-hop. He yawned (*open mouth on Rabbit*), turned around three times and fell right to sleep. (*Have child turn around three times and sit down.*) Good night, Rabbit.

When Owl saw Rabbit yawn, he got so sleepy he flew to his hole in the big tree. Flap-flap, flap-flap. He yawned (*open mouth on Owl*), turned around three times and fell right to sleep. (*Have child turn around three times and sit down.*) Good night, Owl.

When Moose saw Owl yawn, he got so sleepy he walked back to his cave. Crunch-crunch, crunch-crunch. He yawned (*open mouth on Moose*), turned around three times and fell right to sleep. (*Have child turn around three times and sit down.*) Good night, Moose.

When Bear saw Moose yawn, he got so sleepy he walked back to his cave. Lumber, lumber, lumber. He yawned (*open mouth on Bear*), then he yawned again (*open mouth on Bear*). He turned around three times and fell right to sleep. (*Have child turn around three times and sit down.*) Good night, Bear.

And the only sound in the forest then was z-z-z-z-z-z. Good night.

Animal Parade

Have fun imitating the animals in this chant. Do it first in a group and then make a parade around the room. Older children may want to take the parts of the different animals or add some of their own.

> The pig leads the way.
> The pig leads the way.
> Wallow-wallow, oink-oink,
> Animal parade.
>
> Next comes the cat.
> Next comes the cat.
> Tip-toe, meow.
> Wallow-wallow, oink-oink,
> Animal parade.
>
> Look, it's a mule.
> Look, it's a mule.
> Clip-clop, hee-haw,
> Tip-toe, meow.
> Wallow-wallow, oink-oink,
> Animal parade.
>
> I see the sharks.
> I see the sharks.
> Swish-swish, chomp-chomp,
> Clip-clop, hee-haw,
> Tip-toe, meow,
> Wallow-wallow, oink-oink,
> Animal parade.

Here come the snakes.
Here come the snakes.
Slither-slither, hiss-hiss,
Swish-swish, chomp-chomp,
Clip-clop, hee-haw,
Tip-toe, meow,
Wallow-wallow, oink-oink,
Animal parade.

GAMES FOR FEET AND FLIPPERS

1-2-3-4-Moose

Play this version of "Duck Duck Goose" to encourage children to imitate the movements of a number of different animals. One child chosen to be "it" walks around the circle tapping heads and counting aloud. When he taps one and names an animal, both children race around the circle in the manner of that animal: hopping for kangaroos, crawling for worms, etc. The first one back to the opening sits down and the other becomes "it."

Flippity-Flop

Relay race wearing swim flippers for a frog, put a cardboard box on each foot for horseshoes, jumping in a sack for a kangaroo. Prizes are animal crackers, of course!

Fast and Slow

Sit in a circle. Name various animals and have the children call out "fast" for animals that move quickly or "slow" for lazier animals. After the children understand the game, let individuals raise hands to identify "fast" and "slow" and then be the leader to call out the next animal. Even greater challenge to name them in alphabetical order!

Strut Your Stuff

Give children pictures of animals who move in distinctive ways, then invite them to imitate the strut, waddle, or walk for other children to guess who they are. Making noises is NOT allowed. Just strut your stuff.

CRAFTS FOR FEET AND FLIPPERS

Fans of the Foot

This activity was included in *Readers on the Move*, I READ program for Illinois, 1986. Edited by Robin Currie.

Trace around each child's foot. Decorate to make faces by adding wiggle eyes, yarn hair, fake fur moustaches and beards. Attach to wide craft sticks and wave away.

Tracks and Trails

Give each child a piece of paper and glue. Lay out an assortment of dried beans, macaroni, rice. Children spread a line of glue on the paper and lay items on it to make a set of tracks. When the project is dry, tell about the imaginary creature who made the tracks, where he is going, and what noise he makes.

What Big Feet You Have!

Quick-change anyone's feet into animal feet with poster board cutouts and yarn. Decide what kind of feet to make and how they will move. Cut the animal foot shape out of poster board and punch two holes in the center about six inches apart. Stand on the animal foot, and string ends of yarn through holes. Tie on top and waddle or lumber away. Be careful walking on stairs.

TAKE-HOME ACTIVITY FOR FEET AND FLIPPERS

Walk with Your Eyes Diary

Provide children with their own booklets to record things they see on walks with their families. You might "jog" their memories with one-line suggestions at the tops of several pages such as:

"Five living things I saw on my walk to school were:"
"In spring one day I saw these three changes outside:"
"On our block I saw these two things today that I never saw before:"

This activity will not only open up children's eyes, but it should open up communications with parents and children.

2

Skates and Swings
More Ways to Go on Your Own

INTRODUCTION

Soon after children learn to walk, they quickly run and jump aboard tricycles, sleds and skateboards. These vehicles give children their first real experiences in independence. They can go around the block or beyond the neighborhood on skates and bicycles. The vehicles in this chapter are the ones children operate themselves. They may also be vehicles adults enjoy, but this is as carefree as sailing up in a swing or as anxious as learning to ride a two-wheel bike without training wheels. Children will already have the experience to plunge right into these stories and activities.

The first subtheme of the chapter, "Round and Round: Going on Wheels," includes bicycles and skateboards. Picture books range from a child learning to master the skill of skating in *Wait, Skates!*, or learning about winning and losing a big-wheel race in *Wheels* to animals performing tricks in *Bears on Wheels* and *Curious George Rides a Bike*. Children will practice counting skills, empathize with Sandy's uncertainties in the story "Too Many Training Wheels" and sing a chorus of "Roller Rink Round" as follow-up activities after you read the picture books.

The second subtheme, "Up and Down: Other Ways to Go," includes ice skates, skis, swings, stilts and pogo sticks. Stationary pieces of playground equipment have not been included. Few picture books have been written about these kinds of transportation so we have created sled songs and a cut-and-tell story as well as other varieties of fun and skills development for your children.

INITIATING ACTIVITY

Moving Around

To get the children thinking about various kinds of transportation they may ride, teach them the following chant. Do it at first as a group, then divide into parts as indicated. Last of all try it as a round.

   I. Roller, roller, roller skates
       Roller, roller, roller skates.   *(Roll hands over each other.)*

  II. Sleds and skis,
       Sleds and skis.   *(Arms out shoulder level, sway.)*

 III. Swing high,   *(Pause and swing arms up.)*
       Swing low   *(Pause and swing arms back.)*

 IV. Bicycles, tricycles, big wheels,   *(Circles in front, flat palms.)*

       GO!   *(Clap.)*

LITERATURE-SHARING EXPERIENCES

Books for Round and Round: Going on Wheels

Berenstain, Stan, and Jan Berenstain. **Bears on Wheels**. Random House, 1969.
Unicycle fun for one wheel and lots of bears as they perform tricks in the air.

Breinburg, Petronella. **Shawn's Red Bike**. Illustrated by Errol Lloyd. Crowell, 1975.
Shawn works hard and saves his money to buy a red bike. When he finally gets the bike, he has to learn to ride it on his own.

Chlad, Dorothy. **Bicycles Are Fun to Ride**. Illustrated by Lydia Halverson. Children's Press, 1984.
Safety rules are taught as a boy rides his new bike. Fun and instructive for older children.

Johnson, Mildred. **Wait, Skates!** Illustrated by Tom Dunnington. Children's Press, 1983.
Beginning reader with controlled vocabulary but plenty of action as skates provide a child humorous excitement the first time out.

Keats, Ezra Jack. **Skates**. Four Winds, 1981.
In this near wordless book, two dogs almost give up trying to learn to roller skate, but they catch a stranded cat in their hat and wheel safely away.

Monroe, Lynn Lee. **The Old-time Bicycle Book**. Carolrhoda, 1979.
This easy-to-read non-fiction book describes the invention of the bicycle from the first model, the French hobby horse of 1791 to the tricycles and various two wheelers of the 1800s.

Petrie, Catherine. **Hot Rod Harry**. Illustrated by Paul Sharp. Children's Press, 1982.
Hot Rod Harry's bike can really fly like the wind. This is a beginning reader with controlled vocabulary.

Rey, Hans. **Curious George Rides a Bike**. Houghton Mifflin, 1952.
This familiar monkey is up to all kinds of tricks and trouble with his new bike.

Rockwell, Anne. **Bikes**. Dutton, 1987.
Bikes with one, two, three wheels as well as some that just stay in one spot are clearly described and colorfully illustrated.

Schertle, Alice. **Bim Dooley Makes His Move**. Illustrated by Victoria Chess. Lothrop, Lee and Shepard, 1984.
Bim takes part in a rescue of a moving van with all his family's goods inside. Bim's daring feat is performed from his bicycle.

Silver, Rosalie. **David's First Bicycle**. Illustrated by Mordicai Gerstein. Western Publishing, 1983.
David progresses from training wheels to riding his two wheeler to school on his own.

Thomas, Jane. **Wheels**. Illustrated by Emily Arnold McCully. Clarion, 1986.
Elliott learns about winning and losing on big-wheel bikes when he races his new one with his friends.

Watanabe, Shigeo. **I Can Ride It**. Illustrated by Yasuo Ohtomo. Philomel Books, 1982.
The familiar preschool bear tries out all kinds of transportation fun from skateboards to sports cars.

Related Activities for Round and Round: Going on Wheels

Skateboards—Be Careful!
(To the tune of "Sing a Song of Sixpence")

Sing a song of skateboards
Sailing down the street.
Watch me! I can "hang ten"!
And wave to folks I meet.
If I am not careful
A crack I do not see,
I'll sing a song of band aids for
My poor old skinned up knees!

Skateboard Song
(To the tune of "Mary Had a Little Lamb")

See me glide on my skateboard,
My skateboard, my skateboard,
See me glide on my skateboard,
My skateboard's lots of fun!

See me turn from side to side,
Side to side, side to side.
See me turn from side to side,
My skateboard's lots of fun!

See me zig zag in and out,
In and out, in and out,
See me zig zag in and out,
My skateboard's lots of fun!

See me hang ten, I'm a sport.
I'm a sport, I'm a sport.
See me hang ten, I'm a sport.
Skateboarding is fun—COME!

Race for Three Wheels
(A Participatory Story)

All the children may make the sounds indicated or they may divide into groups and take parts as the yellow trike versus the big wheel.

Rhonda and Ricky had a lot in common. They lived right next door to each other. They both thought chocolate ice cream was the best food in the world. And they both had exactly the same birthday.

Rhonda and Ricky opened their presents on the day of their birthdays. Rhonda got a trike. It was her older sister's, but Daddy had painted it a beautiful yellow just for her. The wheels still went squeek-squeek-squeek, but there was a brand new horn on the handlebars that went beep-beep. Rhonda was very excited and could hardly wait to show Ricky her new trike.

But when she took it outside, there was Ricky with his birthday present. He had a brand new wonderful big-wheel bike that went rumble-rumble-rumble as it went on the sidewalk. On the handlebars it had a siren that said whoooeee. Ricky was very happy with his new big-wheel and he could hardly wait to race Rhonda on her new trike.

Rhonda knew she could not go very fast on her trike, but she agreed to race Ricky around the block. Her sister came out to start the race.

"On your mark. Get set. Go!" she said.

Ricky took off in a flash. Rumble-rumble-rumble. He turned the first corner and sounded his siren: whoooeee. He was out of sight.

Rhonda pushed one pedal on the yellow trike and then the other. Squeek-squeek-squeek. She did not go fast, but she kept moving along. When she got to the first corner she sounded her horn: beep-beep. She did not see Ricky, but she was having a good time riding her new trike.

Ricky looked back but he did not see Rhonda. He got off his big-wheel and ate a box of raisins. Then he jumped back on and raced away: Rumble-rumble-rumble. As he turned the second corner, he sounded his siren: whoooeee. He was out of sight.

Rhonda kept on pushing one pedal and then the other on the yellow trike. Squeek-squeek-squeek. She did not go fast, but she didn't stop for anything. When she got to the second corner she sounded her horn: beep-beep. She did not see Ricky, but she was having a good time riding her new trike.

Ricky looked back but he did not see Rhonda. He got off his big-wheel and watched an ant carry a crumb of cake all the way across the sidewalk and onto the anthill. Then he jumped back on and raced away: Rumble-rumble-rumble. As he turned the third corner, he sounded his siren: whoooeee. He was out of sight.

Rhonda kept on pushing one pedal and then the other on the yellow trike. Squeek-squeek-squeek. She saw the ant on the anthill, but she didn't stop for anything. When she got to the third corner she sounded her horn: beep-beep. She did not see Ricky, but she was having a good time riding her new trike.

Ricky looked back but he did not see Rhonda. He got off his big-wheel and said hello to his friend Sam. He even let Sam sit for a minute on his new big-wheel. Then he jumped back on and raced away: Rumble-rumble-rumble. As he turned the last corner, he sounded his siren: whoooeee. He was out of sight.

Rhonda kept on pushing one pedal and then the other on the yellow trike. Squeek-squeek-squeek. She waved hello to Sam, but she didn't stop for anything. When she got to the last corner she sounded her horn: beep-beep.

After Ricky turned the corner, he was in front of his own house. He decided to go in and get a drink of juice. Rhonda saw his big-wheel in front of his house as she came around the last corner. She came closer and closer and finally passed the big-wheel. She crossed the finish line just as Ricky came back outside. What a surprise to see that Rhonda had won!

Rhonda's sister gave them both dishes of chocolate ice cream because they were good racers. Then Ricky let Rhonda ride his big-wheel bike: Rumble-rumble-rumble. He even let her sound the siren: whoooeee. He was busy riding the yellow trike: Squeek-squeek-squeek. He pushed the pedals and sounded the horn: beep-beep. But he never did figure out how Rhonda won that race!

Too Many Training Wheels
(A Flannel-board Story)

Use a figure of a bike and eight small circles for the training wheels. Place them on the board as Sandy's mother adds and subtracts them in the story. Have the children count the wheels with you.

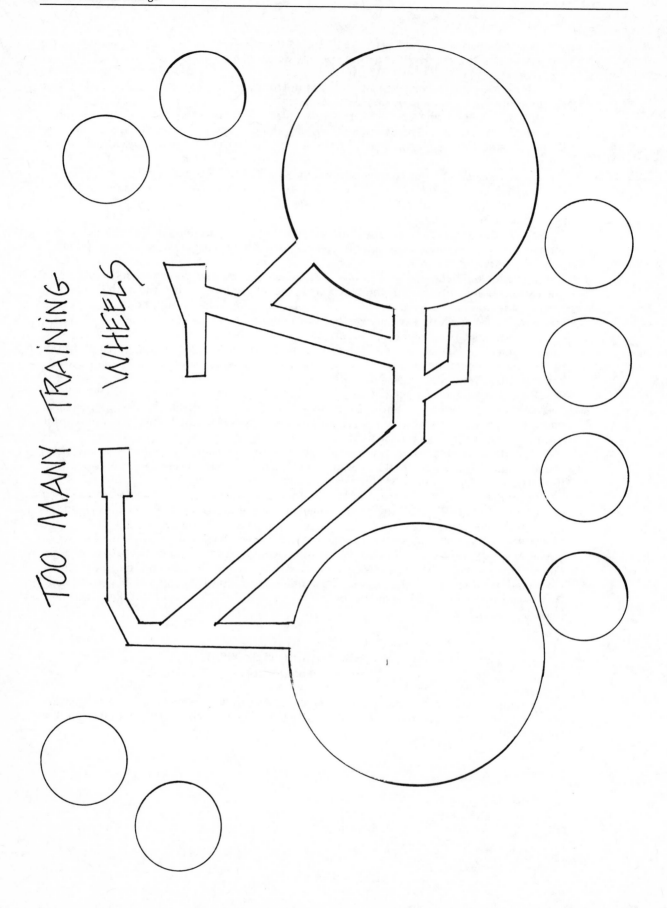

TOO MANY TRAINING WHEELS

Sandy had a brand new bike. It had a red seat and green handle bar grips and blue and white streamers that blew in the wind. But Sandy was afraid to ride his new bike. He was afraid he would fall.

Sandy's mother understood the problem so she bought Sandy two training wheels and put them on the back wheel of his bike.

"1-2 training wheels," she said. "Now you won't fall, Sandy."

But Sandy was still not sure. "Could I have two more training wheels?" he asked. "Just to be sure I won't fall."

Sandy's mother said, "I never heard of that many wheels." But she got two more training wheels and put them on the front wheel of Sandy's bike.

"1-2-3-4 training wheels," she said. "Now I'm sure you won't fall, Sandy."

But Sandy was still not sure. "Could I have two more training wheels?" he asked. "Just to be very sure I won't fall."

Sandy's mother said, "I never heard of that many wheels." But she got two more training wheels and added them to the back wheel of Sandy's bike.

"1-2-3-4-5-6 training wheels," she said. "Now I'm very sure you won't fall, Sandy."

But Sandy was still not sure. "Could I have two more training wheels?" he asked. "Just to be very, very sure I won't fall."

Sandy's mother said, "I never heard of that many wheels." But she got two more training wheels and put them on the front wheel of Sandy's bike.

"1-2-3-4-5-6-7-8 training wheels," she said. "Now I am very, very sure you won't fall, Sandy."

So Sandy tried to ride his new bike. On Monday he rode it with eight training wheels, and he did not fall. But he did not go very fast either. So Monday night his mother took off two training wheels. That left 1-2-3-4-5-6.

On Tuesday he rode it with six training wheels, and he did not fall. He went a little faster, but not really fast. So Tuesday night his mother took off two training wheels. That left 1-2-3-4.

On Wednesday he rode it with four training wheels, and he did not fall. He went kind of fast, but not really very fast. So Wednesday night his mother took off two training wheels. That left 1-2.

On Thursday he rode it with two training wheels, and he did not fall. He went pretty fast, but not as fast as he wanted. So Thursday night his mother took off two training wheels. That left none.

On Friday Sandy rode his bike all day. The blue and white streamers sailed out behind him in the wind as he went fast and faster. Sometimes he did fall, but he did not get hurt. And he was not afraid.

So on Saturday he gave all the training wheels to the little boy next door who was just learning how to ride a bicycle.

The Very Best Bike
(To the tune of "Mary Had a Little Lamb")

I want the best bike in the world,
in the world, in the world,
On the best bike in the world
Is lots of fancy stuff.

It has to have a silver bell,
Silver bell, silver bell.
It has to have a silver bell
And other fancy stuff.

It has to have furry seat
Furry seat, furry seat
It has to have furry seat
And other fancy stuff.

It must have streamers on the bars
On the bars, on the bars
It must have streamers on the bars
And other fancy stuff.

It has to have a raccoon tail
Raccoon tail, raccoon tail
It has to have a raccoon tail
And other fancy stuff.

Now it's the best bike in the world
In the world, in the world
But I can see no room for me
I think that is enough
STUFF!

Bicycle Built for Five
(A Participatory or Flannel-board Story)

To use as a participatory story, cut two circles of red poster board, and one each of blue, green, purple, and orange. Punch a hole in the center of each one and push onto the end of a dowel rod so the child holding the rod can turn the wheel as he or she moves around the room. Move the children as indicated in the story. Use the names of the children participating for the children in the story. Have all the children say "ding-ding" when the bell is mentioned. This may also be a flannel-board story. See illustration for flannel-board shapes.

BICYCLE BUILT FOR FIVE

Cut 1 bicycle

Cut 4 unicycles

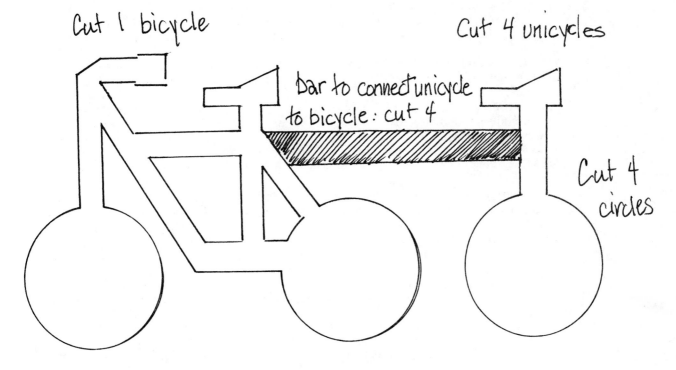

Bar to connect unicycle to bicycle: cut 4

Cut 4 circles

Flannelboard story

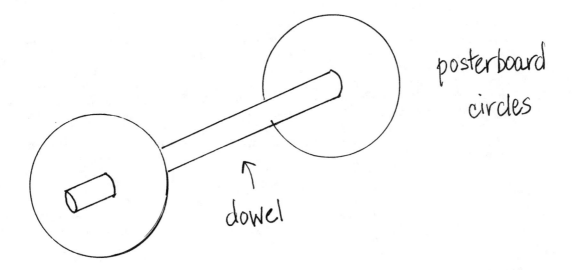

posterboard circles

dowel

participatory story

Roger had a brand new bike. (*Give first child two red circles.*) It had a red seat and two red wheels and a silver bell. (*Ding-ding.*) Roger rode his new bike up Maple Street, turned onto Elm, turned again onto Oak and then back down Chestnut to home. (*Walk child around room, turning sharply at the corners as you name the streets.*) What fun!

As he rode down Maple Street again, Bruce saw him. "Can I ride, too?" he called.

"This bike is not safe for two," said Roger. "But let's see if my dad can fix it so we can both ride."

They went back to Roger's house and sure enough, his dad added one blue wheel and one blue seat. (*Give second child blue circle and have him place one hand on shoulder of first child.*) So Bruce rode on the blue and Roger rode on the red with the silver bell. (*Ding-ding.*) They rode up Maple Street, turned onto Elm, turned again onto Oak and then back down Chestnut to home. (*Walk children around room, turning sharply at the corners as you name the streets.*) What fun!

As they rode up Elm Street, Gary saw them. "Can I ride, too?" he called.

"This bike is not safe for three," said Roger. "But let's see if my dad can fix it so we can all ride."

They went back to Roger's house and sure enough, his dad added one green wheel and one green seat. (*Give third child green circle and have him place one hand on shoulder of second child.*) So Gary rode on the green, Bruce rode on the blue and Roger rode on the red with the silver bell. (*Ding-ding.*) They rode up Maple Street, turned onto Elm, turned again onto Oak and then back down Chestnut to home. (*Walk children around room, turning sharply at the corners as you name the streets.*) What fun!

As they rode along Oak Street, Paul saw them. "Can I ride, too?" he called.

"This bike is not safe for four," said Roger. "But let's see if my dad can fix it so we can all ride."

They went back to Roger's house and sure enough, his dad added one purple wheel and one purple seat. (*Give fourth child purple circle and have him place one hand on shoulder of third child.*) Paul rode on the purple, and Gary rode on the green. Bruce rode on the blue, and Roger rode on the red with the silver bell. (*Ding-ding.*) They rode up Maple Street, turned onto Elm, turned again onto Oak and then back down Chestnut to home. (*Walk children around room, turning sharply at the corners as you name the streets.*) What fun!

As they rode back down Chestnut, Oliver saw them. "Can I ride, too?" he called.

"This bike is not safe for five," said Roger. "But let's see if my dad can fix it so we can all ride."

They went back to Roger's house and sure enough, his dad added one orange wheel and one orange seat. (*Give fifth child orange circle and have him place one hand on shoulder of fourth child.*) Then Oliver rode on the orange, Paul rode on the purple, and Gary rode on the green. Bruce rode on the blue, and Roger rode on the red with the silver bell. (*Ding-ding.*)

They rode up Maple Street but as they turned onto Elm the bike was too long and it tipped over. (*Walk to first corner. Have children sit down and then get up.*) They put it up again, but as they turned onto Oak the bike was too long and it tipped over again. (*Walk to second corner. Have children sit down and stand up.*) They put it up, but as they came around the corner onto Chestnut the bike tipped again. (*Walk to third corner. Have children sit down and stand up.*) This was no fun at all!

(*Walk children back to front.*) Back they went to Roger's house. "Dad," said Roger, "We all want to ride but we want to have fun, too. Can you fix the bike once more?"

Roger's dad looked at the bicycle built for five and had an idea. He took off the orange wheel and gave it to Oliver. (*Have fifth child drop hand off shoulder of fourth and step aside.*) He took off the purple wheel and gave it to Paul. (*Have fourth child drop hand off shoulder of third and step aside.*) He took off the green wheel and gave it to Gary. (*Have third child drop hand off shoulder of second and step aside.*) He took off the blue wheel and gave it to Bruce. (*Have second child drop hand off shoulder of first and step aside.*) Now each one had a unicycle and Roger had a red bike with a silver bell. (*Ding-ding.*) They rode up Maple Street, turned onto Elm, turned again onto Oak and then back down Chestnut to home. (*Lead children around room in line but not holding on, turning sharply at the corners as you name the streets.*) What fun! They all rode together, but they didn't tip over. And Roger rang the silver bell. (*Ding-ding.*)

Not for the Birds!
(A Participatory Story with Masks)

In preparation for this story, make grocery bag masks for the following animals: Rabbit, Duck, Goose, Turkey, and Ostrich. Select five children to wear these masks before you tell the story. As each animal climbs on Rabbit's racing bike, position the children in a line behind one another.

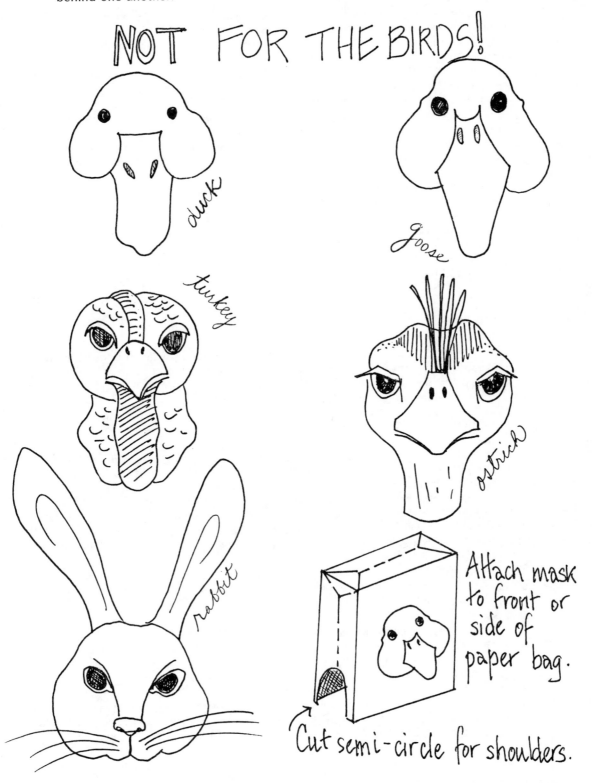

NOT FOR THE BIRDS!

duck

goose

turkey

ostrich

rabbit

Attach mask to front or side of paper bag.

Cut semi-circle for shoulders.

Rabbit had a new racing bike. It had a fancy black leather seat, shiny silver wheels, and ten speeds to make it go zooo-m! Rabbit loved to go zooo-m on her new racing bike.

"Zoomedy zoom," said Rabbit. "I like my bike!"

But when Duck saw Rabbit, Duck saw Rabbit's new bike.

"Oooo, I like that bike!" said Duck. "Please, Rabbit, make room. I want to go zooo-m!"

So Rabbit let Duck hop on the back of her bike. The bike did not go quite so fast with two, but it still went zooo-m!

Now when Goose saw Rabbit and Duck on Rabbit's new bike, Goose said, "Oooo, I like that bike! Please, Rabbit, make room. I want to go zooo-m!"

So Rabbit let Goose get on the back of her bike behind duck. The bike did not go nearly so fast with three, but it still went zooo-m!

Now when Turkey saw Rabbit and Duck and Goose on Rabbit's new bike, Turkey said, "Oooo, I like that bike! Please, Rabbit, make room. I want to go zooo-m!"

The bike was starting to be crowded, but Rabbit let Turkey get on the back of her bike behind Duck and Goose. The bike did not go fast with four, but it still managed to go zooo-m.

Now the next animal to see Rabbit was Ostrich. Ostrich was a very large bird. Ostrich had never tried to get on a racing bike before, but Ostrich loved to go fast. So, Ostrich called out to Rabbit, "Yahoo, Rabbit! Oooo, I like your bike. Please, Rabbit, make room. I want to go zooo-m!"

Well, Rabbit took one look at Ostrich. Then Rabbit looked at her bike with all her friends on the back. There were Duck and Goose and Turkey. Now Ostrich wanted to go, too.

"No," said Rabbit. "This is too much. This bike is not for the birds. This bike is for me—Rabbit. Everybody get off."

So off hopped Turkey and Goose and Duck. (*Ostrich never got on in the first place.*) And, then, Rabbit really took off—zooo-m!

Cheap Skates

Andy had a pair of skates that he got from his mother's cousins friends' son. They were not wonderful, but they had the right number of wheels and, as his mother pointed out, the price was right. They were cheap skates. Andy used them, but what he really wanted most was to have a pair of nice new skates of his very own.

So he was very excited one day to see a sign in the window of the sporting goods store: "Big Skating Contest Tomorrow. Grand Prize: New Redball Skates! Meet at the park at 3 o'clock."

At 3 o'clock the next day Andy was at the park ready to go. So were about fifty other boys and girls all hoping to win the Redball Skates! The first contest was a race to see who could go the fastest on a straight path. At the end of the race, Andy was in first place, but he had lost the back wheels on his right skate. They were cheap skates.

Luckily the next contest was rolling down a hill. Andy could do that on his left skate and the toe of his right skate so the missing wheels did not matter. At the end of the hill roll, Andy was in first place. But he also lost the front wheels off his right skate. They were cheap skates.

Luckily the next contest was who could go the farthest on one foot. Andy could do that on his left foot so the missing wheels did not matter. At the end of the one footed glide, Andy was in first place. But he also lost the back wheels off his left skate. They were cheap skates.

Luckily the next contest was a fancy dance contest. Andy did the whole dance on one toe of his left skate. At the end of the fancy dance contest, Andy was in first place. But he also lost the front wheels off his left skate. They were cheap skates.

Then Andy's luck ran out. The next contest was for speed skating all around the park. Andy could not skate anywhere because the last wheels had fallen off his skates. All he had left was a pair of laced-up skate shoes with metal bottoms where the wheels used to be. Andy slowly started to walk home with his cheap skates going scrape-clunk, scrape-clunk on the sidewalk. He did not look up until a man ran up to him.

"Stop, stop, that noise is wonderful!" cried the man. "I am trying to make a monster picture called *Return of the Clumsy Monsters* and all I hear is the rumbler-rumble of skates. Your inventive shoes have exactly the sound I want my monster to make as he walks in the park. May I buy those fabulous shoes? Name your price!"

Andy was so surprised it took him a minute to realize that the movie director was buying his old skates. He said, "These are just cheap skates. You can have them. I just need something to wear home."

The movie director looked in the van and found a pair of Redball Skates. "Would these do?" he asked. "They are left over from the movie *Roller Monsters Take Over Latvia*."

So that is how Andy got a pair of brand new skates and never wore cheap skates again.

Roller Rink Round
(To the tune of "Pop Goes the Weasel")

Sing this little song as a group or in several groups as a round.

> Round and round the roller rink
> The roller skaters travel —
> Forward, backward, hand in hand.
> Oops! Down they tumble!

Books for Up and Down: Other Ways to Go

Curious George Goes Sledding. Edited by Margret Rey and Alan Shalleck. Houghton Mifflin, 1984.
Adapted from a Curious George film, the mischievous monkey uses his sled to save a child.

Long, Ruthanna. **Tiny Bear and His New Sled**. Illustrated by Joan Allen. Golden Press, 1969.
Tiny Bear and all his friends enjoy winter fun on his sled. Easy reader format, but clear pictures for story time.

Peters, Sharon. **Santa's New Sled**. Illustrated by Kathy McCarthy. Troll Associates, 1981.
In this beginning reader, Santa's old sled breaks down, so he buys a snowmobile to make his journey.

Radin, Ruth Yaffe. **A Winter Place**. Illustrated by Mattie Lou O'Kelley. Little, Brown, 1982.
Up a winding hill past houses and trees, a family ice skates on a lake in the clearing. The folk art paintings and evocative text recall sights and sounds of ice skating on a winter afternoon.

Seuss, Dr. **The King's Stilts**. Random House, 1939, 1976.
King Burtram enjoys playing on his stilts at the end of a hard day until the evil Lord Droon steals them. In the end, Eric, the page, recovers them and restores happiness in the kingdom.

Shortall, Leonard. **Ben on the Ski Trail**. Morrow, 1965.
Ben takes ski lessons to learn to ski and does so well he gets the ski patrol to come when an injured skier needs help.

Yolen, Jane. **Mice on Ice**. Illustrated by Lawrence Di Fiori. Dutton, 1980.
Gomer the Rat King kidnaps Miss Rosa, star of the Mice Capades, but Horace, the famous inventor of the ice-making formula and the mice ice skaters rescue her.

Related Activities for Up and Down: Other Ways to Go

Just Enough Ice for the Mice

The first of December came on a Monday at Slipandslide Lake. Meeny, Miny, and Moe, the mouse triplets, begged Mama Mouse to let them go ice skating on the lake.

"Please, Mama," said Meeny.

"Wouldn't it be nice," asked Miny.

"To go out on the ice?" finished Moe.

Mama Mouse tiptoed carefully outside to see if the ice was thick enough for her three little mice to go skating. Mama measured one inch of ice.

"No, my little mousekins. One inch is not enough ice for mice."

On Tuesday the second of December, Meeny, Miny, and Moe asked Mama again.

"Please, Mama," said Meeny.

"Wouldn't it be nice," asked Miny.

"To go out on the ice?" finished Moe.

Mama Mouse tiptoed carefully outside to see if the ice was thick enough for her three little mice to go skating. Mama measured one, two inches of ice.

"No, my little mousekins. Two inches are not enough ice for mice."

On Wednesday the third of December, Meeny, Miny, and Moe asked Mama again.

"Please, Mama," said Meeny.

"Wouldn't it be nice," asked Miny.

"To go out on the ice?" finished Moe.

Mama Mouse tiptoed carefully outside to see if the ice was thick enough for her three little mice to go skating. Mama measured one, two, three inches of ice.

"No, my little mousekins. Three inches are not enough ice for mice.'

On Thursday the fourth of December, Meeny, Miny, and Moe asked Mama again.

"Please, Mama," said Meeny.

"Wouldn't it be nice," asked Miny.

"To go out on the ice?" finished Moe.

Mama Mouse tiptoed carefully outside to see if the ice was thick enough for her three little mice to go skating. Mama measured one, two, three, four inches ofice.

"Well, my nice little mice. Four inches are mighty nice, but they are not quite enough for three nice little mice."

On Friday the fifth of December, Meeny, Miny, and Moe were afraid to ask Mama again. They just looked up at her and said, "Please!"

Mama Mouse tiptoed outside carefully—oh, so carefully because there had been a deep freeze. And this time Mama counted one, two, three, four, five inches of ice.

"Yes," said Mama. "This is just right. Five inches of ice is nice. It is just enough ice for MY LITTLE MICE!"

So Meeny, Miny, and Moe put on their little ice skates and they skated round and round Slipandslide Lake. But they never ever fell down or fell into the lake because the ice was just right for the three little mice.

Fred's Sled
(A Cut-and-Tell Story)

Make the cuts as shown to help tell this story. Make the cuts along the lengthwise side of a piece of typewriter paper so the resulting worm will be long enough.

Fred Fox got a sled for Christmas. It was a bright red sled. Fred was so excited to ride his red sled that he jumped right on and slid down the hill. (*Make first cut like this:*)

"Whee! What a spree!" he shouted. "Riding a red sled is fun!"

Riding downhill was fun. But when Fred tried to ride his sled uphill, it wouldn't go.

"This sled won't go in the snow!" said Fred. And Fred was right. He needed a little help to make the sled go uphill.

Fortunately, Bill Beaver lived at the bottom of the hill in Beaver Hollow.

"Bill, if you help me pull my new sled up this hill, you can slide down the next hill with me," said Fred.

"It's a deal! That will be real fun," said Bill. So Bill and Fred pulled Fred's sled up the second hill. (*Make second cut like this*:)

Then they jumped on the sled and slid down the hill. (*Make third cut like this*:)

But when Fred and Bill tried to get on the sled to ride it up the next hill, the sled wouldn't go.

"This sled won't go in the snow!" said Bill.

"We need a little help," said Fred.

Fortunately Olivia Otter lived at the bottom of Otterhill.

"Olivia, if you help us pull my sled up Otterhill, we'll let you slide down the otter side," said Fred.

"It's a deal. That will be real fun," said Olivia.

So Fred Fox, Bill Beaver, and Olivia Otter pulled Fred's sled up Otterhill. (*Make fourth cut like this*:)

Then they slid down the otter side. (*Make fifth cut like this*:)

By the time the three friends got to the bottom of the otter side of Otterhill, the sun was going down. Fred Fox knew that his mother would be cross if he got home late for dinner.

"My sled won't go in the snow," said Fred. "And I'll be late for dinner."

"We just need a little help," said Olivia and Bill.

Well, just then the sled started to go up and then it went down. And then it went up, and then it went down. And once more it went up and down and up. (*Make last long cut like this*:)

"Whee! That was some spree!" said Fred.

"This sled can really go in the snow!" said Bill.

"I think we got a little help," said Olivia.

And she was right. They all looked under the sled, and there was a big fat earthworm. All the commotion had awakened him from his long winter's nap. The earthworm gave them all a ride all the way home and just in time for dinner. (*Hold up worm shape.*)

Sled Song

(To the tune of "Jingle Bells")

Slip and slide, slip and slide
On a wooden sled.
Use a plastic circle
Or a cardboard box instead.
Belly flop, on your back,
Come and take a ride!
There will be hot chocolate when
We finally go inside.

Skis, Please

Walrus ran the Ski Lodge at Tumbledown Mountain. Every winter he waited for it to snow the first big snow so the people would come skiing.

So he was very excited when one night it snowed sixteen inches at one time. Sure enough the next day the schools were closed, but the Ski Lodge was open and ready for business.

The first one to show up at the Ski Lodge was Hippo. "Skis, please," she called.

Walrus said, "Please be careful. The new snow might be a little soft. Maybe you should wait until some smaller animals have packed it down."

But Hippo said, "I am an expert skier. I don't need to wait for anyone." And she put on her skis and was off down the hill.

The next one in line was Moose. "Skis, please," he called.

Walrus said, "Please be careful. The new snow might be a little soft. And watch out for Hippo."

But Moose said, "I am an expert skier. I don't need to watch for anyone." And he put on his skis and was off down the hill.

The next one in line was Dog. "Skis, please," he called.

Walrus said, "Please be careful. The new snow might be a little soft. And watch out for Hippo and Moose."

But Dog said, "I am an expert skier. I don't need to watch for anyone." And he put on his skis and was off down the hill.

The next one in line was Cat. "Skis, please," she called.

Walrus said, "Please be careful. The new snow might be a little soft. And watch out for Hippo and Moose and Dog."

But Cat said, "I am an expert skier. I don't need to watch for anyone." And she put on her skis and was off down the hill.

The next one in line was Rabbit. She was a real snow bunny and did not take any chances. "Do you think the snow is too soft?" she asked.

"Not if you are careful," said Walrus. "Watch out for Hippo and Moose and Dog and Cat."

"Oh, I will," said Rabbit. She strapped on her skis and carefully went slowly down the slope. At the first tree she saw Cat, stuck in the soft snow. Rabbit helped pull her out and they skied on together.

At the second tree they saw Dog, stuck in the soft snow. Rabbit and Cat pulled him out and they skied on together.

At the third tree they saw Moose, stuck in the soft snow. Rabbit and Cat and Dog pulled him out and they skied on together.

At the fourth tree they saw Hippo, stuck in the soft snow. Rabbit and Cat and Dog and Moose pulled and pulled and pulled, but they could not get Hippo out. They pulled and they pulled and they pulled some more, but Hippo was stuck in the soft snow. Just when Hippo was about to cry because she would be stuck until spring, Rabbit had an idea.

"Jump!" she said.

"Jump?" the others asked.

"Yes, jump," said Rabbit. And she began to hop around on her skis. She looked very funny, so funny that Hippo laughed instead of crying. Soon the others started jumping up and down, too. All that jumping packed the soft snow down around Hippo until it was hard enough she could climb out all on her own.

The friends skied down the hill together. Then they went into the Ski Lodge to tell Walrus about their great adventure and have a cup of cocoa.

See Saw Chant
(An Action Rhyme)

See saw
Up down
High low
Touch the ground

I go up.
You go down.
But don't jump off —
I'll bust my crown!

Stilt Walk
(To the tune of "Paw Paw Patch")

I can walk up high on stilts.
I can walk up high on stilts.
I can walk up high on stilts,
If I walk so carefully.

I can turn around in circles.
I can turn around in circles.
I can turn around in circles,
If I turn so carefully.

Now my legs begin to wobble.
Now my legs begin to wobble.
Now my legs begin to wobble.
Let's jump down so carefully —
TIMBERRRRRR!

Slightly Stilted
(A Poem)

I cannot reach the cookies
Because of my short height.
I need my legs made longer:
Some stilts would be just right.

It might take a little practice,
So I don't tip and swing,
But then I would be tall enough
To reach most anything.

So watch out, silly cookies,
Hiding safely on the shelf.
I'm going to learn to use my stilts,
And I'll get to you, myself!

Bouncity-Bounce
(An Action Rhyme)

There will be no wiggles left in anyone after this jumping rhyme!

Bouncity-bounce, bouncity-bounce!
I can jump like a kangaroo.
Bouncity-bounce, bouncity-bounce!
I can hop like a bullfrog, too.
Bouncity-bounce, bouncity-bounce!
I can leap like a rabbit—quick.
Bouncity-bounce, bouncity-bounce!
I'm having fun on my pogo stick.

Kangaroo Countdown
(An Action Rhyme)

Jump like kangaroos or clap this rhyme as you recite the bouncy words.

One Kangaroo
On a pogo stick
Jumpin' along
And doin' a trick!
Two Kangaroos
On a pogo stick,
Along came another
Hopped on quick!
Three Kangaroos
On a pogo stick,
Clickety clickety
Clickety click!
Four Kangaroos
On a pogo stick
Here comes another
Just watch him kick!
Five Kangaroos
On a pogo stick,
Just one more
Makes number six!
Six Kangaroos
On a pogo stick
Let's get off—
This is making me sick!
6-5-4-3-2-1
We're all done!

Higher, Daddy

Dolly liked to go high, higher, highest in her swing. But she could not pump herself that much. She needed someone to push her. And the best swinger in the world was her daddy.

"Daddy, push me high," Dolly would call. "I want to touch the treetops." And Daddy would push her high enough to touch the treetops.

"Daddy, push me higher," Dolly would call. "I want to touch the white clouds." And Daddy would push her higher so she could reach the white clouds.

"Daddy, push me highest," Dolly would call. "I want to touch the little silver stars." But Daddy would never push her high enough to touch the little silver stars.

"If I did that," he said, "you might slide off into the sky, and I could never give you another hug."

One day Daddy was weeding the garden and he could not push Dolly in the swing. So she decided to pump herself. She leaned forward and back, forward and back. Pretty soon she was high.

"Look, Daddy," she called. "I can touch the treetops."

Dolly leaned forward and back, forward and back. Pretty soon she was higher.

"Look, Daddy," she called. "I can touch the white clouds."

Dolly leaned forward and back, forward and back. Before long she was highest.

"Look, Daddy," she called. "I can touch the little silver stars."

Dolly let go of the swing to grab one of the little silver stars, but the stars would not hold her up. She started to fall and fall and fall. Daddy saw her fall and ran as fast as he could. He caught her just before she landed in a sticker bush.

"Thank you," said Dolly in a little voice. And she gave him a big hug.

Now Dolly swings high to touch the treetops. She swings higher to touch the white clouds. But she has decided she would rather have a hug from Daddy than any of the little silver stars.

Swing Song

(To the tune of "Mary Had a Little Lamb")

Swing up high, and swing down low,
See the trees, far below.
Swing down low, and swing up high,
Toes can touch the sky.

Swing at dawn or in the dark.
Fly and sing, like a lark.
Swing at dusk or in the light,
And always hang on tight.

GAMES FOR SKATES AND SWINGS

Bicycle Built for Everybody

Scatter the children throughout the room. Pick one to "ride" the front of the bicycle and lead that child around the room as everyone sings the following words to the tune of the "Farmer in the Dell."

Oh, come and ride my bike
Come and ride my bike
Jump aboard and we'll have fun
This bike is built for two.

When the song stops the nearest child stands behind the first and places hands on waist of one in front. The song is repeated as the children go around the room.

Oh, come and ride my bike
Come and ride my bike
Jump aboard and we'll have fun
This bike is built for three.

Continue adding children to the line until the bike is full and the room is empty. Then lead the whole line to the next activity.

Swing Things

Play this variation of "I Packed My Grandmother's Trunk" by naming things you see when you are up in a swing. Begin with the words, "Way up in the swing, I see...." Youngest children can just name things they would see outside. They will also enjoy incorporating as many sound effects as possible, but don't expect them to remember the whole lists as individuals. Older children will enjoy the sound effects, too, and be challenged by naming the items in alphabetical order and reciting them from memory.

Winter Wonderland

For some children skis and skates are commonplace every year—other parts of the country never see the snow! Get the thrill of the chill with this variation of charades.

Divide into two teams—Skiers and Skaters. Each team must think up five winter activities and write them on pieces of paper. They swap papers, then as individuals or in groups of two act out the winter activity for the rest of their team to guess. The team to get the most right out of five gets to be first in line for hot chocolate.

Balancing Act

Bikes, skateboards, or ice skates all require a certain amount of balance. Help the children in your group improve their balance with this game. Tape masking tape strips or pieces of yarn in various areas of the room in straight lines or at angles. Children "walk the line" placing one foot carefully in front of the other and not stepping off. When the basic skill is mastered, add some imagination and simple props. Place an article of clothing at the beginning of each balancing tape for the children to wear while walking it. Wrap on a scarf to go skiing or put on some wild shorts for surfboard fun.

Mini Olympics

Many of the activities in this chapter are fun for the children, but also pursued by adults and even Olympic athletes. Bicycle racing, skiing, speed and figure skating are not "just for kids" anymore. Set up areas in the room with books for the children to look at and imitate the various sports pictured. They may move freely or as small groups, but at the end of the allotted time, they all come together to pantomime the activity they would most like to pursue. Younger children will enjoy copying the pantomimed activity, older ones will want to guess the sport shown. If a sporting goods store will allow a display or demonstration of some of the adult equipment, you may introduce a potential Olympic contender to his or her sport, or at least offer lifelong alternatives to TV viewing to the children you contact.

CRAFTS FOR SKATES AND SWINGS

Everybody Rides

Make a mural to decorate the room and encourage group cooperation. Draw a long horizontal line in the center of the mural paper. Cut a construction paper wheel for each child to decorate. The wheels will be pasted below the line. Each child will draw a self-portrait above the line right over his or her wheel. Provide fabric scraps and yarn for clothing and hair. At the top, write "Cooperation is the Only Way to Ride!"

cooperation is the only way to ride

EVERYBODY RIDES

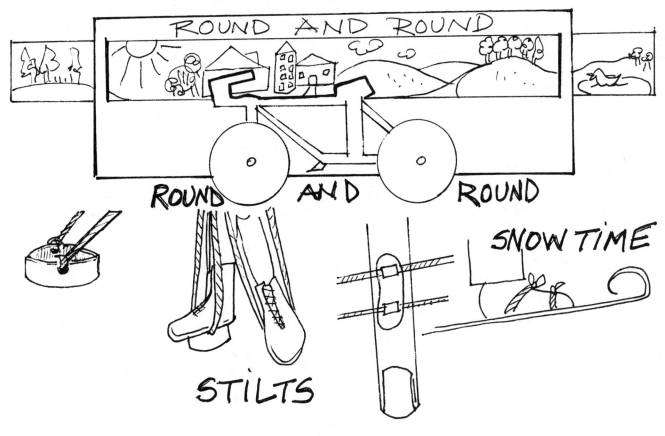

ROUND AND ROUND

ROUND AND ROUND

STILTS

SNOW TIME

ICE FOR MICE

REAL SWINGERS

Round and Round

Adding wheels that move make a bike picture come alive. Make these special with moving backgrounds! First draw a simple bike on 8½ x 11-inch white paper. Cut a 4½-inch slit in each end of the paper and cut out the top half of the bike as shown. Add paper wheels with brads so they can turn.

Cut another sheet of paper in half lengthwise and tape the ends together to make a 4¼ x 22-inch strip. Draw on a variety of trees, houses, animals. Slip the strip through the slits and behind the bike. When you move the strip the bike appears to move.

Stilts

This idea was part of *Readers on the Move*, I READ Program Manual for Illinois, 1986, edited by Robin Currie.

Use two similar-sized clean tin cans for each child. Punch two holes in the opposite sides of each can near the upper edge. Provide children with self adhesive paper to cover and decorate the cans, yarn to string through the holes and plenty of space to try the stilts out. To use, stand one foot on each can and hold the yarn. (Tie the ends of the yarn together so the child can hold them while standing straight.) Walk carefully on a flat surface.

Snow Time

Use strips of poster board for indoor skis. Cut to allow about 12 inches in front of the child's foot and 6 inches behind. The child may curl the tip by rolling around a paper towel tube. Draw around the child's foot on each ski and tape two pieces of yarn to the ski at the ball and heel of the drawn foot. Children place feet on the drawn ones and tie front yarn over toes and back yarn around ankle. The poster board skis will glide on either carpeted or tiled surface, but remove before going downstairs!

Ice for Mice

After telling the story "Just Enough Ice for the Mice," make these little pictures of the mice as they finally go skating. Give each child a sheet of white paper for snow. Cut free-form shapes from tin foil for the frozen Slipandslide Lake. Children can form mice of two paper cones, one for the body and one for the head as shown. Add paper eyes and ears. Attach pipe cleaner legs by taping inside the body cone, bending the feet and attaching scraps of foil for skates. Tape the mice to stand up on the lake or encourage the children to move them about as if skating.

Real Swingers

Give a pipe cleaner person a ride on a swing. Use five drinking straws to form the swing set as shown. Tape pieces of yarn to the bottom of a rectangle cut from construction paper and tie to the top straw. Shape a person of two pipe cleaners to sit on the swing. Wrap hands around the yarn and push the swing.

TAKE-HOME ACTIVITY FOR SKATES AND SWINGS

Your Kind of Town

Kids love maps of all kinds and as they become more mobile, encountering the world on skates and bikes, knowledge of the community becomes more important. Draw a simple map of your community. Identify some landmarks and leave others blank for the family to note as they travel around town. Encourage the families to not only fill in the blanks, but to complete the map by adding special restaurants or people's homes that are meaningful to them.

3
Take Me Along

INTRODUCTION

Young children always in motion rarely have to be persuaded to go along in the car. Since they are already "on the go," they will quite naturally beg "take me along." This chapter capitalizes on this enthusiasm in its focus on vehicles we ride in as families or in small groups. Larger vehicles for group transportation are included in chapter 4, "We All Go Together."

The first theme of this chapter covers automobiles and car trips. The range of picture books includes Daniel Pinkwater's wild and wacky *Tooth-Gnasher Superflash* as well as Peter Spier's restored antique *Tin Lizzie*. A car trip from a young child's perspective includes motion sickness and frequent bathroom stops in Helen Oxenbury's *The Car Trip*, but it also recalls a family cozily piled into a station wagon in Cynthia Rylant's *The Relatives Came*. These picture books and our activities give children opportunities to reenact everyday practices of buckling seat belts as well as to explore an unlikely explanation of a traffic jam.

The second theme of "Take Me Along" transportation includes vans, campers, wagons, baby carriages, and even shells of turtles and snails—nature's own built-in mobile home. Begin with *Max's Ride* and follow it up with several rounds of "Baby Buggy Chant." "Come for a Ride" becomes an add-on chant to enjoy after you read *Sam's Wagon*.

Through games, crafts, and stories, young children will learn such expressions as "stuck in a rut," and "road hog." They will role play through songs about going to the gas station, and they will be reminded to click on their seat belts in another song. We have combined fun activities with health and safety features so young children will happily relate these experiences to their own world.

INITIATING ACTIVITY

Park Your Car

To get storytime started, invite children to pretend to drive cars into a place you designate. Then they can tell their names and everyone claps.

> Here's a place to park your car
> Drive in. Tell us who you are!
> (Points to child who gives name. For example, Tommy.)
> Let's all say it: Tommy.
> Let's all clap it: Tommy. (*Clap two times.*)

Proceed until all children have had a chance to "park" and tell their names.

LITERATURE-SHARING EXPERIENCES

Books about Cars

Berenstain, Stan, and Jan Berenstain. **The Berenstain Bears and the Big Road Race**. Random House, 1987.

Little Red car races against the bigger racing cars—orange, yellow, green, and blue. Despite their boasts and nasty tricks, Little Red wins. Concepts and colors are taught along with the story.

Burningham, John. **Mr. Gumpy's Motor Car**. Crowell, 1973.

Cumulative tale about Mr. Gumpy's human and animal friends that join him for a cheerful ride in the car—until the weather changes from sun to rain.

Caines, Jeannette. **Just Us Women**. Illustrated by Pat Cummings. Harper & Row, 1982.

A little girl and her aunt plan a car trip complete with maps, box lunch, and plenty of time to enjoy the trip along the way for wandering down back roads and stopping for breakfast at night.

Cameron, Polly. **The Green Machine**. Illustrated by Consuelo Joerns. Coward, McCann, 1969.

A nonsense verse about the trek of a green classic sports car through the garden that makes the garden "tremble in its roots." When the car picks up speed and loses control, the plants and garden tools mutter such comments as " 'He'll turn over,' said the clover" and " 'Hit the brake,' said the rake." When the car sinks into the brook, the violet pushes him out, the garden bids him adieu with " 'Don't forget us,' said the lettuce."

Davis, Maggie. **The Best Way to Ripton**. Illustrated by Stephen Gammell. Holiday House, 1982.

An automobile driver asks a farmer pig the best way to Ripton, but after hearing the dangers he is likely to encounter on each route, the driver decides to change his travel plans.

Fowler, Richard. **Mr. Little's Noisy Car**. Grosset & Dunlap, 1985.

This "Lift-the-Flap" book is a funny story of lots of animals that make the strange noises in Mr. Little's car. The animals are seen when you lift the flap (the hiss in the tire comes from a snake, for example). The book also teaches lots of names for car parts.

Gackenbach, Dick. **Binky Gets a Car**. Clarion, 1983.

Binky McNab gets a shiny red pedal car for his birthday, but drives it so carelessly that he's confined to his own yard until he learns to be more careful.

Gay, Michel. **Little Auto**. Macmillan, 1986.

When Little Auto goes on a beach vacation, he gets off to a poor start with Sand Crab. In the end they become friends as Crab's claws come in handy to repair Little Auto's faulty parts.

Gibbons, Gail. **Fill It Up! All about Service Stations**. Crowell, 1985.

Large, bright illustrations clearly show the activity of a service station and garage, a subject fascinating to most small children.

Grahame, Kenneth. **The Open Road**. Illustrated by Beverly Gooding. Scribners, 1979.

The second chapter of the classic *Wind in the Willows* told in a picture book version introduces Rat and Mole's leisurely river boat travel, but the main focus is Toad's fixation on the alluring motor car.

Hurd, Thacher. **Axel, the Freeway Cat**. Harper & Row, 1981.

Axel, the Freeway Cat, lives in an abandoned car and works for the department of highways as a litter collector. His life is lonely until he helps out a stalled motorist during a traffic jam.

Lindgren, Barbro. **Sam's Car**. Illustrated by Eva Eriksson. Morrow, 1982.

In a small and very simple picture book, Sam and Lisa argue over a toy car until mother resolves the situation with a second car.

McPhail, David. **Emma's Vacation**. Dutton, 1987.

Cooped up in the family car for a long drive to get to the mountains, Emma becomes restless. Once there the family continues to go—on a boat, a bus, a train, and an amusement park rocket ship. Finally Emma insists on quieter times—wading in the brook, climbing trees and hiking.

Newton, Laura P. **William the Vehicle King**. Illustrated by Jacqueline Rogers. Bradbury, 1987.

William chooses a bright blue car, a light brown sedan like Mama's, and a shiny orange car plus vans, racing cars, tow trucks and a red fire engine—all to help him become "William the Vehicle King."

Oxenbury, Helen. **The Car Trip**. Dial, 1983.

A young child describes his "best car trip ever," but his parents see the experience from another perspective. The noise, frequent bathroom stops, motion sickness, and car trouble combine to make the trip difficult from their point of view.

Peet, Bill. **Jennifer and Josephine**. Houghton Mifflin, 1967.

A stray cat named Josephine who lives in Jennifer, an old touring car, looks out for the car's welfare when a reckless driver tries to abandon her.

Pinkwater, Daniel. **Tooth-Gnasher Superflash**. Four Winds, 1981.

When Mr. and Mrs. Popsnorkle and the five little Popsnorkles test drive the Tooth-Gnasher Superflash, they discover it can turn into a dinosaur, a galloping elephant, a turtle and a flying chicken so they decide to trade in their own green Thunderclap-Eight.

Rockwell, Anne. **Cars**. Dutton, 1984.

Big, clear pictures make cars fun for individual study or storytime learning.

Rylant, Cynthia. **The Relatives Came**. Illustrated by Stephen Gammell. Bradbury, 1985.

All the relatives come to visit from Virginia in their old station wagon that "smelled like a real car" and is stuffed with snacks, luggage, and people. This warm family story begins and ends with the trip in the family car, their home away from home.

Spier, Peter. **Tin Lizzie**. Doubleday, 1975.

The proud possessors of a vintage Model-T Ford are described from 1909 to the present owners.

Related Activities about Cars

Packing the Car

This chant will be fun if you can show each item as it is mentioned. Use a stuffed dog and cat. Show a toy car for the last verse.

> Time to pack the car
> For vacation near or far
> Everyone can help out
> When we pack the car!
>
> Father brings the suitcase
> Father brings the suitcase
> Everyone can help out
> When we pack the car!
>
> Mother brings the road maps
> Mother brings the road maps
> Everyone can help out
> When we pack the car!

Brother brings the tape deck
Brother brings the tape deck
Everyone can help out
When we pack the car!

Sister brings the cooler
Sister brings the cooler
Everyone can help out
When we pack the car!

Baby brings the diaper bag
Baby brings the diaper bag
Everyone can help out
When we pack the car!

Grandma brings the pillows
Grandma brings the pillows
Everyone can help out
When we pack the car!

Grandpa brings the dog and cat
Grandpa brings the dog and cat
Everyone can help out
When we pack the car!

Oops! The car is full now!
Oops! The car is full now!
Everyone can go ride
In the other car!

Stuck in a Rut
(A Mask Story)

See the illustration for making masks for a cow, goat, sheep, pig, and goose. You may make a wasp mask or use a finger puppet or cut out wasp. Give children the masks and have them sit and pull as indicated in the story.

paper plate puppets

draw wasp onto paper plate or cardboard

attach dowels, sticks, etc. for handle

STUCK IN A RUT

Cow had a new red car. He wanted all his friends to see his new car and take them for a ride. So he stopped at Goat's house.

"Hey, goat. Look at my new car. Come on in and have a spin!" So Goat got in the new car and they went to Sheep's house.

"Hey, Sheep. Look at my new car. Come on in and have a spin!" So Sheep got in the new car and they went to Pig's house.

"Hey, Pig. Look at my new car. Come on in and have a spin!" So Pig got in the new car and they went to Goose's house.

"Hey, Goose. Look at my new car. Come on in and have a spin!" So Goose got in the new car and they went for a long ride. They rode over high hills and low valleys. They crossed bridges and went in and out of woods. And it was in the big woods that Cow's new car got stuck in a rut.

"Oh, bother," said Cow. "Look at my new car. It's stuck in a rut. You will have to push it out."

Now Goat and Sheep and Pig and Goose liked to ride, but they did not like to push. So Goat pushed a little, then he sat in the road to rest. But Cow's new car was still stuck in a rut.

And Sheep pushed a little, then he sat in the road to rest. But Cow's new car was still stuck in a rut.

Then Pig pushed a little, then he sat in the road to rest. But Cow's new car was still stuck in a rut.

Finally Goose pushed a little, then he sat in the road to rest. But Cow's new car was still stuck in a rut.

But when Goose sat down, he sat on a wasp. "Yipe!" said Goose. He jumped up and began to push Cow's new car as hard as he could. The car moved a little.

When Pig saw Goose working so hard, he jumped up and began to push Cow's new car as hard as he could. The car moved a little more.

When Sheep saw Pig and Goose working so hard, he jumped up and began to push Cow's new car as hard as he could. The car moved a little more.

When Goat saw the others working so hard, he jumped up and began to push Cow's new car as hard as he could. The car moved a little more and a little more until POP! It was out of the rut!

"Hurrah!" said all the animals and they started to get back into the car. But Cow had seen the whole thing, and he knew who really got the car out of the rut.

And Cow let Wasp ride all the way home in the front seat.

Seat Belt Song

(To the tune of "Pop! Goes the Weasel")

When you climb into your car,
Before you start the engine,
First thing you should always do:
Click (*click tongue*) on your seat belt!

Don't forget you silly head!
Don't give me excuses!
Stretch the belt across your tum:
Click (*click tongue*) on your seat belt!

Mr. Bumpenrumble's New Car

(A Flannel-board Story)

Tell this flannel-board story using cut out parts of cars. You will need a back end, front end with grill and headlights, wheels, top, and an antenna with a raccoon tail tied on. Place the pieces on at random during the story and then assemble them in the end.

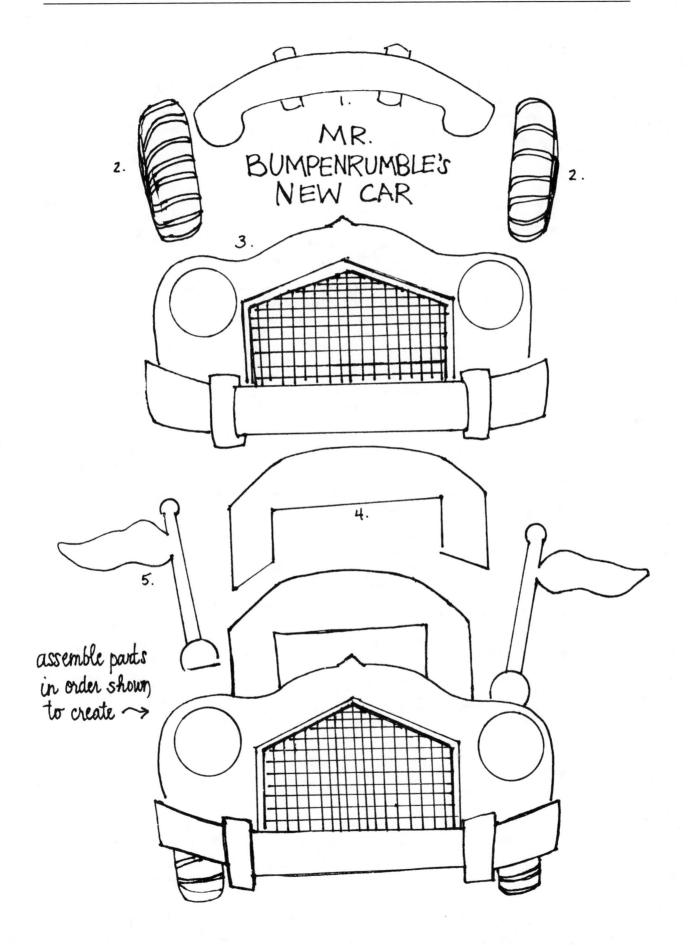

MR. BUMPENRUMBLE'S NEW CAR

1.

2.   2.

3.

4.

5.

assemble parts in order shown to create ⟶

Mr. Bumpenrumble owned a junkyard. When people sold him their old cars, Mr. Bumpenrumble put each car in the car crusher and as fast as you could say smoosh-and-smash, the car was all flat and ready to be recycled. Mr. Bumpenrumble liked taking old worn-out cars and getting them ready to recycle. But it made him sad when he had to crush a whole car while part of it was still like new.

On Monday a woman brought in her old car. It was all worn out except for the back end. The back end was still like new. Mr. Bumpenrumble put the back end to one side and faster than you can say smoosh-and-smash the rest of that car was crushed and ready to recycle. But Mr. Bumpenrumble had saved the back end. (*Place back end of car on flannel board.*)

On Tuesday a man brought in his old car. It was all worn out except for the front end. The front end was still like new. Mr. Bumpenrumble put the front end to one side and faster than you can say smoosh-and-smash the rest of that car was crushed and ready to recycle. But Mr. Bumpenrumble had saved the front end. (*Place front end of car on flannel board.*)

On Wednesday a woman brought in her old car. It was all worn out except for the wheels. The wheels were still like new. Mr. Bumpenrumble put the wheels to one side and faster than you can smoosh-and-smash the rest of that car was crushed and ready to recycle. But Mr. Bumpenrumble had saved the wheels. (*Place wheels on flannel board.*)

On Thursday a man brought in his old car. It was all worn out except for the top. The top was still like new. Mr. Bumpenrumble put the top to one side and faster than you can say smoosh-and-smash the rest of that car was crushed and ready to recycle. But Mr. Bumpenrumble had saved the top. (*Place top of car on flannel board.*)

On Friday a woman brought in her old car. It was all worn out except for the antenna with the raccoon tail. The antenna with the raccoon tail was still like new. Mr. Bumpenrumble put the antenna with the raccoon tail to one side and faster than you can say smoosh-and-smash the rest of that car was crushed and ready to recycle. But Mr. Bumpenrumble had saved the antenna with the raccoon tail. (*Place antenna with the raccoon tail on flannel board.*)

On Saturday, Mr. Bumpenrumble did not crush any cars. He went to his junkyard and looked at all the pieces he had set aside during the week. (*Point to the pieces as you mention them.*) There was a front end, a back end, some wheels, a top, and an antenna with a raccoon tail. What do you think Mr. Bumpenrumble did? He made those spare pieces into a brand new car. (*Assemble car or have children come add pieces one at a time.*)

Then on Sunday, Mr. Bumpenrumble went for a long drive in his brand new car!

Gas Station Song
(To the tune of "Mary Had a Little Lamb")

Gas stations are fun for me
Fun for me, fun for me.
Gas stations are fun for me
Bring your family!

Mommy pumps the gas like this (*Mime pumping action.*)
Gas like this, gas like this,
Mommy pumps the gas like this
Fill'er, fill'er up!

Daddy squirts some air in tires (*psssst*)
Air in tires, air in tires
Daddy squirts some air in tires
So they won't go flat!

Pop the hood up, check inside (*clap*)
Check inside, check inside
Pop the hood up, check inside
Is everything all right? Right!

Now drive through our free car wash (*Wiggle fingers overhead.*)
Free car wash, free car wash
Now drive through our free car wash
But roll the windows up. Yup!

Traffic Jam
(An Auditory Participatory Story)

Use this story to teach two meanings of the word "jam." To involve the children, divide them into three groups. Each one represents one of the trucks and makes the appropriate noise. Gooseberry truck goes chunkety-chunk. Strawberry truck goes pinkety-pink. Watermelon truck goes rumbley-rum. You may wish to follow this activity by making jam sandwiches.

Chunkety-chunk, chunkety-chunk. The delivery truck from Grandma's Gooseberry Farm was headed toward the city. Inside was a big load of gooseberries to make gooseberry pie for Grandma's world famous restaurant.

Pinkety-pink, pinkety-pink. The tiny truck from Sam's Sunnyside Strawberry Patch was headed toward the city, too. Inside were just enough strawberries to make strawberry tarts for afternoon tea.

Rumbley-rum, rumbley-rum. The big watermelon truck from Wayne's Watermelon Warehouse rumbled to the far side of the city. Inside were forty-five of the biggest, juiciest, drippiest watermelons Wayne had for the city market.

Chunkety-chunk. Chunkety-chunk. Along Main Street and down Elm.

Pinkety-pink. Pinkety-pink. Up Cedar and following Grandma's Gooseberry Farm truck down Elm.

Rumbley-rum. Rumbley-rum. Across River Drive and following the Sam's Sunnyside Strawberry Patch truck down Elm.

And right there on the corner of Elm, there was Mother Goose and six little goslings walking across the street.

Chunkety-screech! Pinkety-screech! Rumbley-screech! All three trucks came to a screeching halt and stopped.

Out onto the ground rolled boxes of gooseberries. Out onto the ground rolled quarts of strawberries. And out onto the ground rolled forty-five of the biggest, juiciest, drippiest watermelons Wayne had.

Wayne's Watermelon Warehouse truck backed up. SPLAT! Right over forty-five watermelons.

Sam's Sunnyside Strawberry Patch truck backed up. SPLAT! Right over seventeen quarts of strawberries.

Grandma's Gooseberry Farm truck backed up. SPLAT! Right over twenty-eight boxes of gooseberries.

Grandma's Gooseberry Farm truck rolled forward. Sam's Sunnyside Strawberry Patch truck rolled back. Wayne's Watermelon Warehouse truck lunged forward.

Chunkety-chunk. Pinkety-pink. Rumbley-rum. All three trucks ended up in a terrible jam!

Well, Grandma jumped out of the gooseberry truck and looked at the mess. Then she noticed Mother Goose and the goslings slurping the gooseberry-strawberry-watermelon mess. Grandma dipped her finger in the goo and tasted too. Good. The goo was good!

Grandma called to Sam and Wayne to try some of the new creation. Wayne took one bite and went to call his friend, Bill the Baker. Faster than you can say gooseberry-strawberry-watermelon goo, there was Bill with fresh hot bread. Sam called the street department who brought the street sweepers to scoop the gooseberry-strawberry-watermelon goo onto big slabs of Bill's fresh hot bread.

In the meantime, on Elm Street all the cars got stuck in the traffic jam, but nobody got mad, nobody lost tempers, nobody honked horns. Everyone got out of the cars and made the best of the sticky situation by trying a slab of bread spread with gooseberry-strawberry-watermelon goo.

By the end of the day Grandma, Sam, and Wayne were making a new taste sensation of the gooseberry-strawberry-watermelon goo, but because that name was too long for the labels on the jars, they renamed it World's Finest Traffic Jam.

Traffic Lights
(An Action Rhyme)

Stop, wait, go.
Stop, wait, go.
Traffic lights can tell us when to
Stop, wait, go.

Red on top.
Red on top.
Traffic lights can tell us when to
Stop, stop, stop.

Yellow next.
Yellow next.
Traffic lights can tell us when to
Wait, wait, wait.

Green is last.
Green is last.
Traffic lights can tell us when to
Go, go, go.

Can't Miss
(A Flannel-board Story)

The garage is made up of felt pieces—five rectangular pieces and a triangle. Lay the rectangles side by side on the board and place the triangle above them all. Remove a rectangle each time Aunt Maude gets out her saw and cuts a bigger hole until nothing is left but the triangular roof. The triangle is removed at the very end, too. Use this story when you read *Tin Lizzie* by Peter Spier.

Uncle Clem and Aunt Maude lived in a big old house with a big old garage built way out back the way they used to build garages. In their garage they had a big old car named Tin Lizzie. Tin Lizzie wasn't much to look at because Uncle Clem was such a lousy driver. Oh, he did all right when he got Tin Lizzie out on the open road. But he had a very difficult time getting the car in and out of the garage without bumping or scraping or scratching the fenders.

One Monday evening when Uncle Clem drove Lizzie up the driveway, he missed the door and knocked a hole in the front wall of the garage. So on Tuesday Aunt Maude got out her saw and made the hole a little bigger. "Maybe," she said to herself, "Uncle Clem won't miss the door tonight."

But when Uncle Clem drove Lizzie up the driveway that night, he missed. He missed the door and knocked an even bigger hole in the front wall of the garage. So on Wednesday Aunt Maude got out her saw and made the hole a little bigger. "Maybe," she said to herself, "Uncle Clem won't miss the door tonight."

But when Uncle Clem drove Lizzie up the driveway that night, he missed again. He missed the door and knocked an even bigger hole in the front wall of the garage. So on Thursday Aunt Maude got out her saw and made the hole a little bigger. "Maybe," she said to herself, "Uncle Clem won't miss the door tonight."

Well, you probably won't believe this, but when Uncle Clem drove Lizzie up the driveway that night, he missed again. He missed the door and knocked an even bigger hole in the front wall of the garage. So on Friday Aunt Maude got out her saw and made the hole a little bigger. "Maybe," she said to herself, "Uncle Clem won't miss the door tonight."

On Saturday when Uncle Clem drove Tin Lizzie into the garage he hit the back wall with such a big thud that the whole garage started to shake, swing and sway. Uncle Clem backed Tin Lizzie out of the garage just seconds before the whole thing tumbled to the ground (*remove the triangle*).

Aunt Maude raced from the house and saw the sorry sight. She put her hands on her hips and said, "Clem, maybe we just better turn this garage into a parking lot. Tin Lizzie may get a little wet, but she'll likely hang onto her fenders. And that way you just can't miss!"

And after that he never did!

Parking Meter Rhyme
(A Little Hand Clap Chant)

One coin,
Two coins,
Three coins,
Four—
Tell me
Does it
Need some more?

Turn the handle.
Let it click.
How many minutes
Do you get?
1-2-3-4-5-6?
That's slick!

Books about Vans, Wagons, and Helps along the Way

Alexander, Martha. **I'll Be the Horse If You Play with Me**. Dial, 1975.
   Oliver plays with his younger sister Bonnie as long as she pulls him in a wagon and plays on his terms. Bonnie learns a lesson because she then lets her younger brother play with her when he will pull her in a wagon.

Byars, Betsy. **Lace Snail**. Viking, 1975.
   The generous snail gives her lacy gifts to everyone.

Lindgren, Barbro. **Sam's Wagon**. Illustrated by Eva Eriksson. Morrow, 1986.
   Sam puts all of his favorite things in his wagon—his teddy bear, his doggie, his ball, his car, his cookie. As each falls out, doggie retrieves them—including the cookie.

Lionni, Leo. **The Biggest House in the World**. Pantheon, 1968.
   Snail's dream to have the biggest, most ornate shell proves to be too much of a good thing when it comes true. He is glad in the end to have his plain old shell back.

Mack, Stan. **The Runaway Road**. Parents, 1980.
   The Puddle family always takes Route 100 straight to the mountains when they drive their car on their vacation, but one year the road takes some unexpected twists and turns and runs away to the beach for its own vacation.

Maestro, Betsy, and Giulio Maestro. **Traffic: A Book of Opposites**. Crown, 1981.

Simple concept book traces the journey of a little car over and under the bridge, through a tunnel, up hills and down valleys and through traffic until it arrives home.

McPhail, David. **Captain Toad and the Motorbike**. Atheneum, 1978.

Toad takes to his new motorbike and surprises everyone by coming out of retirement to win his first race.

McPhail, David. **Pig Pig Rides**. Dutton, 1982.

Pig Pig takes off on a variety of vehicles in his imagination only to be reminded by his mother to come back home.

Robbins, Ken. **City/Country**. Viking, 1985.

This is a child's eye view of a car trip showing clear photos for a variety of city and country sights.

Shaw, Nancy. **Sheep in a Jeep**. Illustrated by Margot Apple. Houghton Mifflin, 1986.

This story in rhyme relates the misadventures of a flock of sheep who go riding in a jeep. It won't go over a hill, gets stuck in the mud, wrecks, and in the end, is sold—cheap! The author composed this nonsense verse to entertain her own children on a boring car trip.

Wells, Rosemary. **Max's Ride**. Dial, 1979.

Max the bunny goes over, under, up, and down in this hardboard concept book about his carriage ride.

Related Activities about Vans, Wagons, and Helps along the Way

Let's Take a Taxi
(To the tune of "London Bridge")

When your motor car breaks down,
Car breaks down, car breaks down.
When your motor car breaks down
Take a taxi!

When you're walking and it rains,
And it rains, and it rains.
When you're walking and it rains
Take a taxi!

Walk so far your feet get sore,
Feet get sore, feet get sore?
Walk so far your feet get sore?
Take a taxi!

Caught in traffic? Just get out,
Just get out, just get out.
Caught in traffic? Just get out
And take a taxi.

Wave your hand and whistle loud
Whistle loud, whistle loud.
Wave your hand and whistle loud
Take a taxi!

TAXI! (*Spoken.*)

Camper Caper
(A Participation Story)

Here's another version of the popular "Lion Hunt" participatory story. You might adapt this by letting children suggest their own items to take along in the camper.

We're going in a camper
On a weekend trip
Let's get packed!
Put in the suitcases
Sleeping bags
Tent and flashlight
Take the dog
Don't forget the snackies
Chips and such

Off we go
Over the hills
Under the bridge
Around the curve
Hang on tight!
Out to the woods
Set up camp

Take out the snackies—
Oh, no!
The dog ate them!

Take out the dog.
Get out the flashlight
And set up the tent
The sleeping bags
And the suitcases
All unpacked

Now we're camping
Sun goes down
Moon comes out
All is quiet

Wait! What was that?
Whooooo!

Maybe its a monster.
Maybe its a ghost.
Maybe we should go home!

Pack up the suitcases
Sleeping bags
Tent and flashlight
Grab the dog

Out of the woods
Around the curve
Hang on tight
Under the bridge
Over the hills

And home!

Home in the Van
(To the tune of "Home on the Range")

In our fast-paced society people seem to be constantly on the go. They even take their homes along on vacation! Since many people own or rent vans for family getaways, this song should be a popular modern alternative to the traditional tune "Home on the Range."

Home, home in the van!
It's my home away from my home.
It's better than camp,
'Cause I never get damp—
When it rains
I just stay nice and dry.
Vans! Vans are the best—
It's got all the comforts of home.
With a bed for my head
We will "full speed ahead!"
In a van you're at home when you roam.

Road Hog
(A Participatory Story with Masks and Motion)

For this story give children paper plate masks of the following characters: Hubert the Hog, Henrietta the Hen, Larry the Lamb, Gary the Goat, and Police Chief Bill the Bulldog. Move the children around each other as the story indicates.

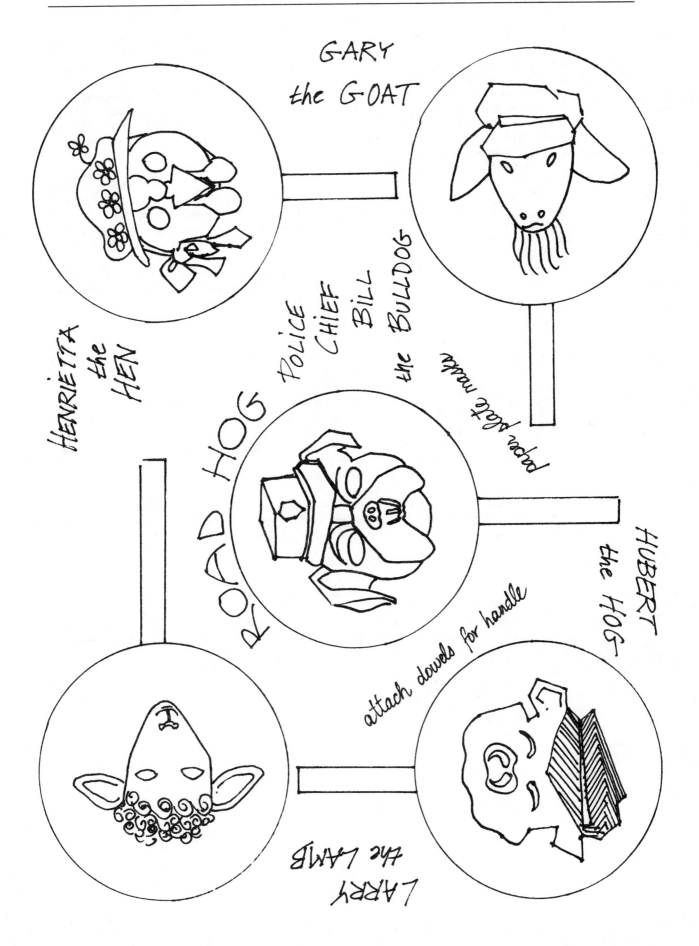

GARY
the GOAT

Henrietta
the
HEN

ROAD HOG
POLICE
CHIEF
BILL
the BULLDOG

paper plate masks

HUBERT
the HOG

attach dowels for handle

LARRY
the LAMB

Hubert was a hog. He always took second and third helpings at every meal—especially if there was corn on the cob for dinner. He always talked louder than anyone else and hogged the conversation. But the worst thing Hubert did was to take up more of the road when he drove his van. Hubert, you see, was a road hog.

One day Hubert drove down the highway in his van. He drove up next to Henrietta the Hen in her little red pick up truck. (*Place Hubert next to Henrietta.*) Hubert snorted. He shook his fists. And he shouted, "Vroom! Vroom! I'm warning you! Get offa my road and give me some room!" And Hubert shoved Henrietta's little red pick up truck to the side of the road. (*Move Henrietta to the side.*)

The next day, Larry the Lamb and Gary the Goat took their motorcycles out on the highway for a spin. (*Give two more children these masks.*) Hubert went around Larry on the left. And Hubert went around Gary on the right. (*Weave Hubert around these two children.*) Hubert snorted. He shook his fists. And he shouted, "Vroom! Vroom! I'm warning you! Get offa my road and give me some room!" And Hubert made Larry and Gary spin around and around until they ended up on the other side of the road. (*Spin Larry and Gary around in circles and lead them to the other side.*)

And the next day when Henrietta and Larry and Gary tried to park their vehicles in the parking lot of the shopping mall, Hubert had parked his van cattycorner. He had taken up the last three parking spaces all by himself. Nobody had any room. (*Have Hubert stretch his arms out to block the way.*)

Well, the next day, when Hubert tried to get his van out of his driveway, he had no room. Henrietta the Hen, Larry the Lamb, and Gary the Goat were making a road block across the road. (*Line up these three children in front of Hubert with their arms outstretched.*)

Hubert snorted. He shook his fists. And he shouted, "Vroom! Vroom! I'm warning you! Get offa my road and give me some room!"

But this time, Police Chief Bill the Bulldog said, "No Hubert. We're warning *you* this time. This is a ticket for being such a rude road hog. If you don't learn some manners about sharing, we'll never let you out on the road again."

So right then and there Hubert decided to reform. He didn't snort. He didn't shake his fists. And he didn't shout. Very, very politely he asked Henrietta and Larry and Gary and Police Chief Bill if they would like to share some of the room in his van to all go for a ride together.

(*Place children one behind the other with hands touching waist of the child in front of them.*) So they all climbed inside Hubert's van. And then everyone shouted happily together, "Vroom! Vroom! There's plenty of room! Come on in. Let's go for a spin."

Come for a Ride
(A Chant)

After the children have done this chant enough to understand the pattern, they may suggest things to put in the wagon. Older children will enjoy the challenge of listing things in alphabetical order or making an action to represent each one.

Come for a ride in my wagon
Come for a ride with me.

I'll put a frog in my wagon.
Come for a ride in my wagon.
Come for a ride with me.

I'll put a rock in my wagon.
I'll put a frog in my wagon.
Come for a ride in my wagon
Come for a ride with me.

I'll put a snail in my wagon.
I'll put a rock in my wagon.
I'll put a frog in my wagon.
Come for a ride in my wagon
Come for a ride with me.

I'll put a worm in my wagon.
I'll put a snail in my wagon.
I'll put a rock in my wagon.
I'll put a frog in my wagon.
Come for a ride in my wagon
Come for a ride with me.

I'll put a cake in my wagon.
I'll put a worm in my wagon.
I'll put a snail in my wagon.
I'll put a rock in my wagon.
I'll put a frog in my wagon.
Come for a ride in my wagon
Come for a ride with me.

I'll put a pup in my wagon.
I'll put a cake in my wagon.
I'll put a worm in my wagon.
I'll put a snail in my wagon.
I'll put a rock in my wagon.
I'll put a frog in my wagon.
Come for a ride in my wagon
Come for a ride with me.

Now there's no room in my wagon.
Cause there's a pup in my wagon.
And there's a cake in my wagon.
And there's a worm in my wagon.
And there's a snail in my wagon.
And there's a rock in my wagon.
And there's a frog in my wagon.
But you can come pull my wagon,
You can help pull with me!

Wagon Song

(To the tune of "Paw Paw Patch")

I like to ride in my little red wagon
I like to ride in my little red wagon
I like to ride in my little red wagon
Bumpity-bump on the holes and cracks.

Wheels go round on my little red wagon
Wheels go round on my little red wagon
Wheels go round on my little red wagon
Bumpity-bump on the holes and cracks.

Hang on tight in my little red wagon
Hang on tight in my little red wagon
Hang on tight in my little red wagon
Bumpity-bump on the holes and cracks.

Come with me in my little red wagon
Come with me in my little red wagon
Come with me in my little red wagon
Bumpity-bump on the holes and cracks.

Baby Buggy Chant

(A Little Lap Clap)

The long-popular tongue twister "rubber baby buggy bumpers" inspired this little chant. Have fun beating out the rhythm of this verse by clapping hands and slapping hands to lap. The words will get mixed up as you go along just as the baby in the verse bumps in the baby buggy. No matter! There's no right or wrong way to proceed. Use this chant to introduce or follow up the book *Max's Ride* by Rosemary Wells.

Snuggy, snuggy baby
In the bumpy baby buggy.
Bumpy, bumpy baby
In the snuggy baby buggy.
Buggy buggy baby
In the bumpy baby snuggy!

There's No Place Like Home

Snail and Turtle were best friends. They lived near the pond by the side of the path. Most of the time they were very happy there, but one day Snail became restless. He looked up and down the path, wondering where it went and what grand adventures he could have on it.

"Oh, Turtle," he sighed. "I do so want to go on a grand adventure. You are my best friend. Won't you come with me?"

Turtle shook his head. "Snail, you are my best friend, too," he said, "but I could never go on a grand adventure. I could never leave my home."

So they continued to live near the pond by the side of the path. And Snail continued to dream of going on a grand adventure.

One day, Porcupine stopped by the pond. "Oh, my friends, I have been on a grand adventure. I saw the lights of the city, and they were beautiful. I am going back now. Won't you come with me?"

Snail looked hopefully at Turtle, but Turtle said, "I could never go on a grand adventure. I could never leave my home."

So they continued to live near the pond by the side of the path. And Snail continued to dream of going on a grand adventure to see the city lights.

One day, Goose stopped by the pond. "Oh, my friends, I have been on a grand adventure. I saw the rolling ocean, and it was beautiful. I am going back now. Won't you come with me?"

Snail looked hopefully at Turtle, but Turtle said, "I could never go on a grand adventure. I could never leave my home."

So they continued to live near the pond by the side of the path. And Snail continued to dream of going on a grand adventure to see the rolling ocean and the city lights.

One day, Moose stopped by the pond. "Oh, my friends, I have been on a grand adventure. I saw the snow-topped mountains, and they were beautiful. I am going back now. Won't you come with me?"

Snail looked hopefully at Turtle, but Turtle said, "I could never go on a grand adventure. I could never leave my home."

So they continued to live near the pond by the side of the path. And Snail continued to dream of going on a grand adventure to see the snow-topped mountains and the rolling ocean and the city lights.

One day, Owl stopped by the pond. "Oh, my friends, I have been on a grand adventure. I saw the tall tree forests, and they were beautiful. I am going back now. Won't you come with me?"

Snail looked hopefully at Turtle, but Turtle said, "I could never go on a grand adventure. I could never leave my home."

But when Owl heard that, he laughed. "Why you silly Turtle," he said. "You and Snail take your houses with you wherever you go. You have built-in mobile homes. You can have the greatest adventures of all without ever leaving home."

"Why you are right, Owl," said Turtle. And from that day on the two friends had all the adventures Snail had ever dreamed of. They saw the lights of the city and the rolling ocean and the snow-topped mountains and the tall tree forests.

And they did it all without ever leaving home!

GAMES FOR TAKE ME ALONG

Assembly Line Game

Guide children in creating a car. Suggest parts for children to imitate such as steering wheel, motor, lights, wipers, wheels. Arrange the children to form the completed car with children pretending to be headlights in front, etc. Then have the car move out of the "factory" and around the room. This activity will teach children to move cooperatively or the car will lose one of its parts.

Put on the Brakes

Teach children to recognize traffic signs, follow directions, and also "get the wiggles out" with this game. First prepare the following traffic signs: a rectangular 35 mile-an-hour SPEED LIMIT sign, a diamond-shaped SLOW sign, a triangular YIELD sign, and an octagonal STOP sign. Children may move in place or around the room for the movement portion on this game. (Gear kind of movement to your own situation.)

Play begins as you hold up the SPEED LIMIT sign to signal that the children may begin moving at a moderate speed. When you hold up the SLOW sign, they must slow down. When you hold up the YIELD sign, they pause (perhaps direct them to pause to the count of five), then move again. And when you hold up the STOP sign, everyone puts on the brakes. Vary the pace of this activity as you like. (See illustration on next page.)

I Helped Pack the Trunk

Play this add on game like the popular "I Unpacked Grandmother's Trunk." The leader tells the children to think of all the things they might pack in the trunk of the family car for a vacation trip, then begin by saying "I helped pack the trunk of our car for a vacation trip, and I put inside an _____ (air mattress, apple, etc.)." The second person repeats the first item and adds an item beginning with the letter B (bicycle, bottle of pop, baseball). Play continues until children name items beginning with every letter of the alphabet.

CRAFTS FOR TAKE ME ALONG

Simple Gas Pump

What young child doesn't like to pretend to be a gas station attendant or want to pump gas like Mom or Dad these days? Let children make their own play gas pumps and use them in "just pretend" games. Provide children with rectangular boxes or oatmeal boxes (or ask children to bring one from home). Punch a hole in the side of the carton for th hose and attach a length of fat yarn. To one end of the yarn, tie a nozzle cut from lightweight cardboard. Provide stick-on numbers for the front of the gas pump, and draw on a gas gauge with felt-tipped markers. (See illustration on page 74.)

A Take Along Bag

For this project, simply let children decorate a lunch bag or grocery bag to take along on a car trip. Fill the bag with craft and game items or include a list of suggestions for parents to complete. The possibilities include pipe cleaner critters, washable felt-tipped markers, small art tablet, finger puppets or fingers cut from old gloves to become instant puppets, three bright-colored pieces of yarn or ribbon tied together that can be braided on the trip.

Paper Snail and Turtle Craft

As a follow-up to the story "There's No Place Like Home," have children make their own snail and turtle craft critters. (See illustration on page 75.) For the snail, cut two paper strips of construction paper approximately 2 inches wide and 10 inches long. On one strip bend back one end of the paper and staple to make a loop for the head. Add two slender paper antennae to the head. Curl the second strip of paper with scissors or by rolling it around a pencil. Tape or staple the curl to the flat strip of paper to make the snail's shell.

For the turtle, cut a 6 inch circle of construction paper. Then cut slashes about 1½ inches long around the other edge of the circle and bend the paper to form the turtle's shell. Overlap the slashed portions and staple or tape so that the shell will form a dome shape. Now make a slash on one end of the turtle's shell and insert a paper strip in this slot. The strip should be approximately 1 inch wide and 7 inches long. Bend back one end of the paper strip and staple to make a loop for the head in the same manner as you did the snail. Cut the other end of the strip in a V to resemble a tail.

Design Your Own Sports Car

Even young children are attracted to sports cars and many would love to design their own. Provide children with a simple rectangular shape with wheels drawn on and the seat portion cut out. Show children how they can draw a few simple lines to design their own sports car model. They can cut along these lines or simply color and decorate the chassis with felt-tipped markers, crayons, or paint. (See illustration on page 76.)

(Text continues on page 77.)

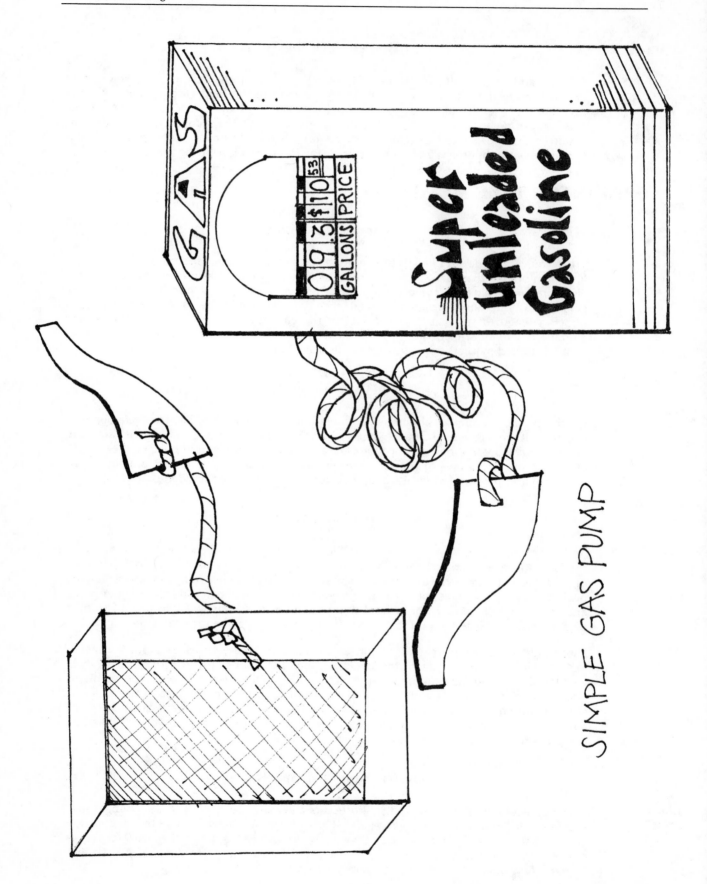

GAS

Super unleaded Gasoline

0 9.3 $10 53
GALLONS PRICE

SIMPLE GAS PUMP

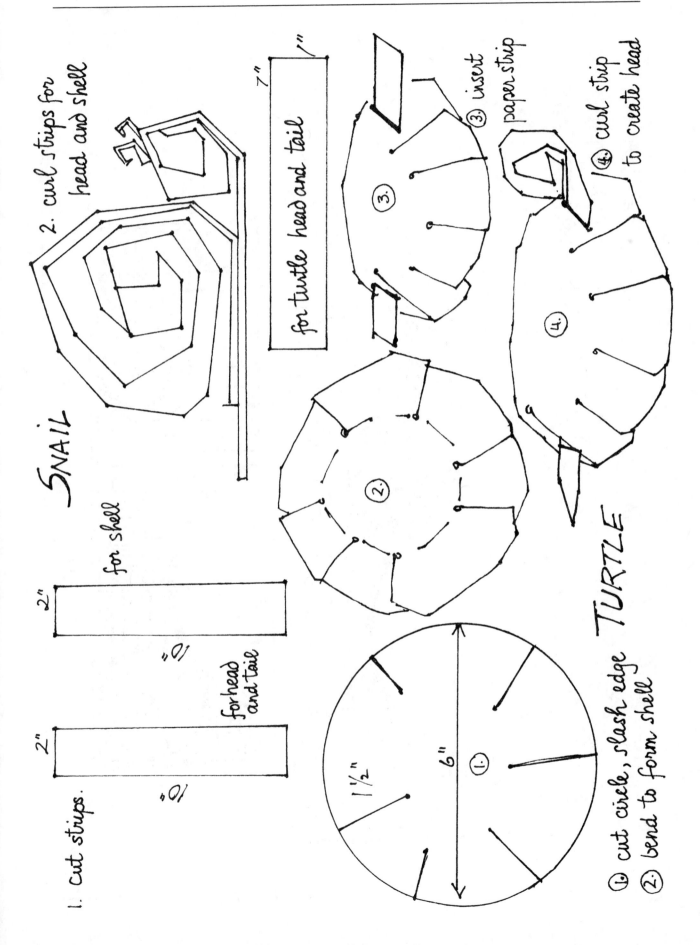

SNAIL

1. cut strips.

2. curl strips for head and shell

2"
for shell
10"

2"
for head and tail
10"

7"
for turtle head and tail
7"

① cut circle, slash edge
② bend to form shell

6"
1 1/2"

① ·
② ·
③ insert paper strip
④ curl strip to create head

TURTLE

TAKE-HOME ACTIVITY FOR TAKE ME ALONG

Family Trip Tricks

Include the words to some of the songs and changes in this chapter such as the "Seat Belt Song" and "Packing the Car" so families can enjoy these together. Here are a few other games to add for families to enjoy in the car on long trips:

A-B-C the Country Game

Keep an alphabetical record of things you see on your trip. The first item should begin with A, the next with a B, and so on. Here are a few ideas to get you going: A—alley, B—barn, C—church, D—dog, E—exit sign. Have an adult or older child record this list and a younger child can illustrate each one. Everyone gets an opportunity to participate.

How Many Miles Before We Get There?

Children impatiently ask "How many miles is it?" so many times on long trips that parents can become irritable. Give them something to do as you count down. Prepare a travel board with one hole for each ten miles you will travel in one day. Punch that number of holes in the top of shoe box. Write down little riddles, tricks to do quietly (count quietly to twenty, think of a rainbow-colored pony and describe to everyone), tongue twisters on slips of paper. Make one slip for each hole in the box. Roll up the slips and place in the holes. After you have traveled ten miles, take out a trick and do it. Then place that slip of paper in the shoe box. After all the tricks and riddles have been completed, your journey has come to a happy end.

Happy journeys!

4

We All Go Together

INTRODUCTION

Over the years trains and boats have been our most important means of transportation. Airplanes and automobiles may be more frequently used for passenger travel in the United States today, but we continue to be fascinated by these more traditional vehicles. Perhaps train whistles and lighthouses suggest the exotic because they are no longer common experiences. Tales of John Henry, Casey Jones, and Piper's *The Little Engine That Could*, then, will be eagerly sought after by today's children.

The first subthemes of this chapter, "We All Go Together on Land," include trains, subways, and buses. Picture books range from the first experience of Crews' *School Bus* and Barton's *Trains* to the fantasy in McPhail's *The Train* and the humorously misrouted subway in Munsch's *Jonathan Cleaned Up, Then He Heard a Sound or Blackberry Subway Jam*. Give children opportunities to create their own train and school bus crafts, participate in the story "No Fuss on the Bus," and chant "Boxcar Count Down" together.

"We All Go Together on Water," the second subtheme, includes boats, ships, and rafts. Picture books will introduce children to the traditional *I Saw a Ship a Sailing* illustrated by Domanska as well as more contemporary experiences in *Ferry Boat* by Maestro. The enrichment activities that follow will encourage active participation from fingerplays and flannel boards to participatory stories.

Since the focus of this chapter is group transportation, many activities naturally will encourage group cooperation, but they also will teach such skills as sequencing, classification and rhyme and rhythm. In addition, children will be introduced to expressions associated with trains and boats so everyone will be eager to "hoist anchor" and climb "all aboard!"

INITIATING ACTIVITY

At the Station

Here's the engine in the front,
Come and join the train.
Do you have your tickets out?
Tell me, what's your name?

LITERATURE-SHARING EXPERIENCES

Books for Going Together on Land

Alexander, Martha. **Move Over, Twerp.** Dial, 1981.

The big kids try to harass Jeffrey by making him give up his seat on the school bus, but he comes up with an effective solution.

Barton, Byron. **Trains**. Crowell, 1986.

Brief text and bold illustrations show different kinds of trains and people associated with trains.

Brown, Margaret Wise. **Two Little Trains**. Illustrated by Jean Charlot. Addison-Wesley, 1949.

Old locomotive and modern train both travel west — at their own speeds and in their own styles.

Burton, Virginia Lee. **Maybelle the Cable Car**. Houghton Mifflin, 1952.

The competition between Maybelle the cable car and Big Bill the new bus takes place in San Francisco. They discover there is a need for both kinds of transportation.

The Busy School Bus. Illustrated by Carolyn Bracken. Grosset & Dunlap, 1986.

As the school bus picks up children along the way, they see other vehicles — a mail truck, a taxicab, motorcycle, and bookmobile — in this "fast rolling" board book on wheels.

Crews, Donald. **Freight Train**. Greenwillow, 1978.

Bold pictures make a trip of a freight train through tunnels and cities a delight.

Crews, Donald. **School Bus**. Greenwillow, 1984.

Crews' bright yellow school buses pick up children, deliver them to school, and take them home again. Bold graphics, simple text the youngest children will relate to.

DiFiori, Larry. **If I Had a Little Train**. Western, 1985.

Simple board book pictures a freight train carrying mail and dogs, traveling above a canyon, across the desert, and to the ocean.

Ehrlich, Amy. **The Everyday Train**. Illustrated by Martha Alexander. Dial, 1977.

Jane waits for the freight train to come by everyday. She waves, plays a game — What-color-is-the-caboose-today — and wonders if there are other people somewhere waiting along the track to watch the train pass by.

Fowler, Richard. **Mr. Little's Noisy Train**. Grosset & Dunlap, 1987.

Mr. Little's freight train is just about ready to leave the railroad yard when he hears various scraping and fluttering noises. The reader then lifts a series of flaps to discover a bat in the smokebox, a dragon in the firebox, a polar bear and penguin in the refrigerator car, a desert rat in the hopper car, an alligator taking a bath in the hatch and an owl on the caboose. Finally Mr. Little runs past them all, hops aboard the engine and rattles out of the yard.

Greene, Graham. **The Little Train**. Illustrated by Edward Ardizzone. Doubleday, 1973.

When a little train tires of his routine, he runs away on a great adventure.

Kesselman, Wendy. **There's a Train Going by My Window**. Illustrated by Tony Chen. Doubleday, 1982.

A host of strange animals ride the train past a girl's window to faraway lands.

Kovalski, Maryann. **The Wheels on the Bus**. Little, Brown, 1987.

Granny takes Joanna and Jenny shopping for new coats, but they have to wait so long for the bus home, they begin singing the song "The Wheels on the Bus." They get so carried away with the song that they miss the bus when it finally comes and end up taking a taxi.

Kroll, Steven. **Toot! Toot!** Illustrated by Anne Rockwell. Holiday House, 1983.

While Lawrence plays with his toy train, he imagines that he goes to visit his grandparents. When his mother interrupts his play, he finds out his grandparents have come to invite him for a visit.

Lewin, Hugh. **Jafta—the Journey**. Illustrated by Lisa Kopper. Carolrhoda, 1983.

In this story of South Africa, Jafta and his mother go by cart to the city where his father works.

Lippman, Peter. **Peter Lippman's Busy Trains**. Random House, 1978.

Passenger trains, freight trains, and all kinds of cars and engines are described including special trains such as mining trains and railroad cranes.

Lyon, George. **A Regular Rolling Noah**. Illustrated by Stephen Gammell. Bradbury, 1986.

When a young boy is hired to guard a boxcar of farm animals, an adventure begins that reaches from Kentucky to Canada.

Mantean, Michael. **The Very Bumpy Ride**. Illustrated by B. Wiseman. Parents, 1981.

Mrs. Fitzwilliam, a gaggle of geese, Mr. Flapsaddle, Granny Smith, a cow, and Billy McNilly and his pet goldfish all climb aboard the bus to go to the fair. The ride becomes noisy, crowded, very bumpy, and full of unexpected good times.

McPhail, David. **The Train**. Little, Brown, 1977.

A little boy climbs out of his bed and onto his toy train that becomes transformed into a life-sized one in his dreams.

Munsch, Robert. **Jonathan Cleaned Up, Then He Heard a Sound or Blackberry Subway Jam**. Illustrated by Michael Martchenko. Annick, 1981.

Jonathan goes to city hall to complain about his house being used as a subway station. The final solution to Jonathan's problem reroutes the subway to an unexpected spot.

Peet, Bill. **The Caboose Who Got Loose**. Houghton Mifflin, 1971.

A little caboose who longs to be free of a train gets her wish one day and ends up in the trees.

Piper, Watty. **The Little Engine That Could**. Illustrated by Ruth Sanderson. Platt, 1976.

This anniversary edition of the 1930 classic features the famous little blue engine who puffs along with courage and spunk.

Rees, Ennis. **Windwagon Smith**. Illustrated by Peter Plasencia. Prentice Hall, 1966.

A fanciful covered wagon with a sail takes Windwagon Smith sailing across the prairie.

Sattler, Helen Roney. **Train Whistles**. Illustrated by Giulio Maestro. Lothrop, Lee and Shepard, 1977, rev. ed. 1985.

Train whistles as signals, a kind of language, are explained and the meaning for the various sounds are given.

Steig, William. **Farmer Palmer's Wagon Ride**. Farrar, Strauss & Giroux, 1974.

A wild ride in Farmer Palmer's wagon leave the pig, donkey and even the farmer in fear of their lives.

Steptoe, John. **Train Ride**. Harper & Row, 1971

The Brooklyn to Times Square train ride is an adventure for Charles when he makes the trip alone for the first time.

Ziefert, Harriet. **Jason's Bus Ride**. Illustrated by Simms Taback. Viking Kestrel, 1987.

When a dog gets in front of the bus, no one can figure out how to move it until Jason takes over.

Related Activities for Going Together on Land

All Aboard
(To the tune of "London Bridge")

Select two children to be the "engines" and form an arch. Sing the song in the traditional manner, having children select which engine to hook on. After everyone has joined one train or the other, lead the two trains around the room singing the song. Then lead them into the "station" to be seated for the next activity.

> Watch the train go 'round the track.
> 'Round the track, 'round the track.
> Watch the train go 'round the track.
> All aboard!

Subway Ride
(To the tune of "Jingle Bells")

Underground subway train
Rumbles round and round.
I hold my ears
When it comes near,
I cannot hear a sound!

Underground subway train—
Lots of people ride.
Hold the straps
Above your head,
And sway from side to side.

No Fuss on the Bus
(A Participatory Story with Puppets)

To prepare for this story, make puppets out of paper plates by folding in half to form a mouth, then add stand up eyes, teeth, tongues to make each character distinctive. Make a hippo, crocodile, frog, cat, and elephant. Make the turtle puppet out of two paper plates for shells. Make a long strip of cardboard with a head on one end and a tail on the other. Insert it between the plates so the children can pull the turtle's head into the shell by pulling on the tail. Use the puppets as indicated in the story.

(Text continues on page 84.)

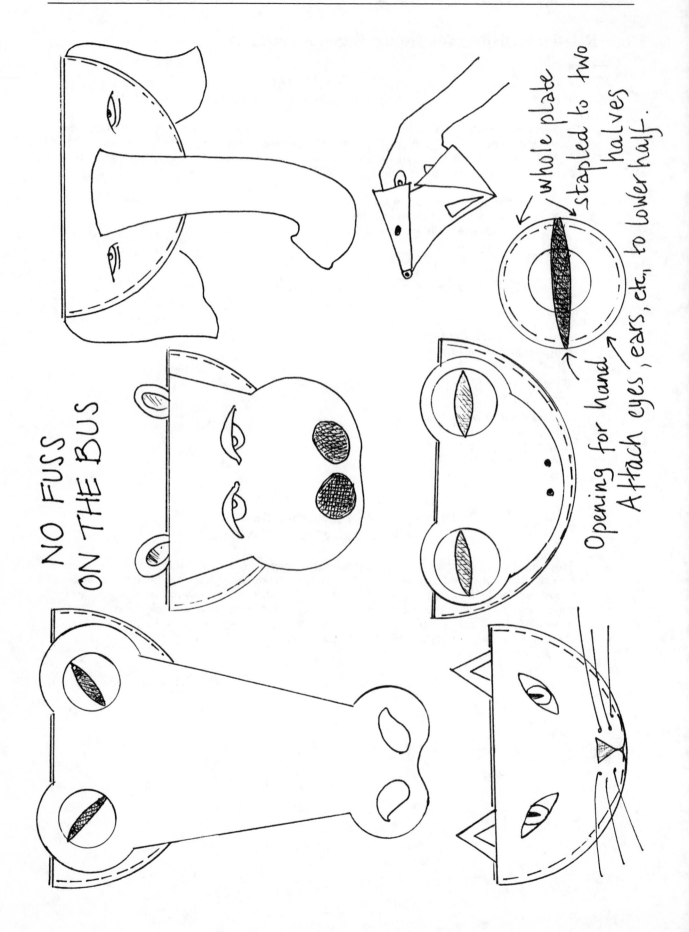

NO FUSS
ON THE BUS

whole plate
stapled to two
halves

Opening for hand
Attach eyes, ears, etc., to lower half.

NO FUSS ON THE BUS

TURTLE PUPPET

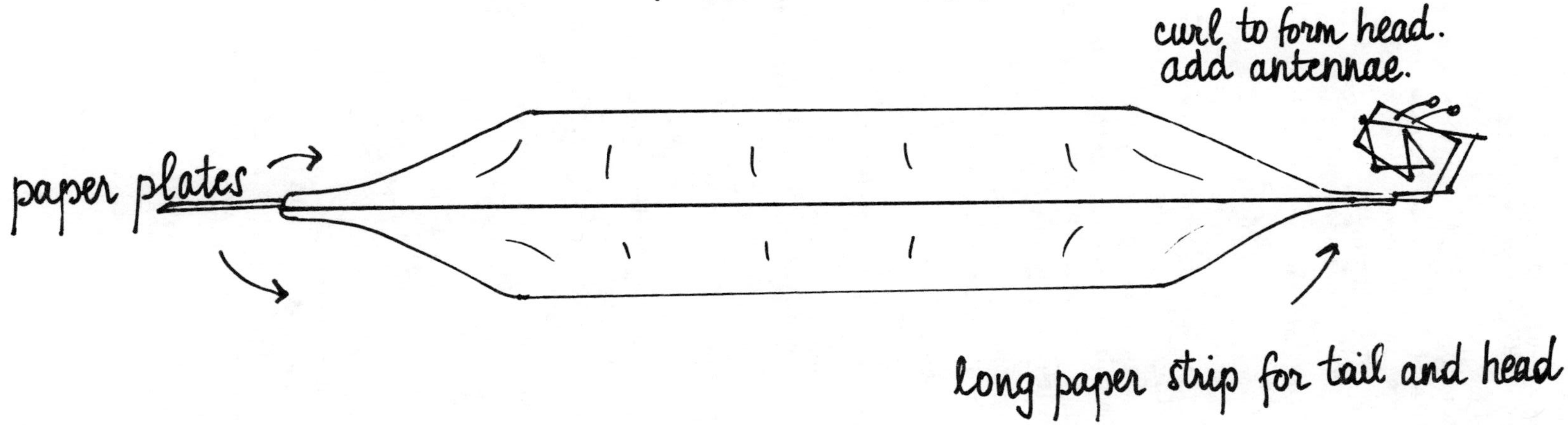

paper plates →

curl to form head.
add antennae.

long paper strip for tail and head

Henrietta the Hippo was a good, solid bus driver. She never got flustered, even in tight situations, even when passengers gave her a hard time.

At seven in the morning Henrietta the Hippo got on her bus. She always sat in the first seat.

At eight in the morning Henrietta the Hippo stopped at Riverside Road and picked up Carl the Crocodile. (*Give crocodile puppet to second child.*) Carl was cross because he woke up on the wrong side of the river bed that morning. When Carl got on the bus he was so snappy he almost bit Henrietta's head off. (*Have child snap crocodile's jaws.*) Henrietta didn't get flustered. She simply said,

> "Please don't raise a fuss.
> Just move on back in the bus."

So Carl took his place in the second seat of the bus.

At nine in the morning Henrietta the Hippo stopped at Dilly Dally Lane and picked up Timothy the Turtle. (*Give turtle puppet to third child.*) Timothy took a long time climbing onto the bus. Carl the Crocodile began to get cross again. He was so snappy he almost bit Timothy's head off. (*Have child snap crocodile's jaws.*) Timothy got so frightened he tucked his head into the shell and refused to budge. (*Timothy puppet can pull in head.*) Henrietta didn't get flustered. She simply said,

> "Please don't raise a fuss.
> Just move on back in the bus."

So Carl took his place in the third seat of the bus and Timothy sat in the second seat.

At ten in the morning Henrietta the Hippo stopped at Polliwog Place and picked up Fredrika Frog. (*Give frog puppet to fourth child.*) Fredrika jumped right on the bus. (*Jump frog puppet.*) But she was so jumpy she made Timothy nervous, and he tucked his head in his shell. (*Timothy puppet can pull in head.*) Carl began to get cross again. He was so snappy he almost bit Fredrika's head off. (*Have child snap crocodile's jaws.*) Henrietta didn't get flustered. She simply said,

> "Please don't raise a fuss.
> Just move on back in the bus."

So Carl took his place in the fourth seat of the bus and Timothy sat in the third seat. Fredrika sat in the second.

At eleven in the morning Henrietta the Hippo stopped at Catnip Corner and picked up Kitty the Cat. (*Give cat puppet to fifth child.*) Kitty pounced onto the bus and began a constant conversation that soon unnerved the entire bus. Fredrika began to get jumpy. (*Jump frog puppet.*) Timothy tucked his head in his shell. (*Timothy puppet can pull in head.*) Carl began to snap. (*Have child snap crocodile's jaws.*) Henrietta didn't get flustered. She simply said,

> "Please don't raise a fuss.
> Just move on back in the bus."

So Carl took his place in the fifth seat of the bus and Timothy sat in the fourth seat. Fredrika sat in the third seat and Kitty took her place in the second seat.

At twelve Henrietta the Hippo made her last stop at Peanut Path. There was Eleanor the elephant waiting. (*Give elephant puppet to sixth child.*) When all the passengers took a look at Eleanor, they knew there was no more room to move back in the bus. So, Carl snapped off the bus, Timothy slowly climbed off the bus, Fredrika jumped off the bus, and Kitty pounced off the bus. Eleanor lumbered onto the bus, but this time Henrietta didn't say anything because there was no more fuss on the bus.

A Boxcar Countdown

Clickety clack clickety clack—
Hear the train come down the track,
Puffing 'cause it's going fast.
Count the cars as they go past.

Clickety-one, clickety-one
Here comes box car number one.

Clickety-two, clickety-two
Here comes box car number two.

Clickety-three, clickety-three
Here comes box car number three.

Clickety-four, clickety-four
Here comes box car number four.

Clickety-five, clickety-five
Here comes box car number five.

Clickety-six, clickety-six
Here comes box car number six.

Clickety-seven, clickety-seven
Here comes box car number seven.

Clickety-eight, clickety-eight
Here comes box car number eight.

Clickety-nine, clickety-nine
Here comes box car number nine.

Clickety-ten, clickety-ten
Here comes box car number ten.

Clickety clack clickety clack—
The train has gone on down the track,
Puffing 'cause it's going fast.
Wave good-bye 'cause it's all past.

Rainbow Express
(A Flannel-board Story)

Make a set of railroad cars that are gray on one side and a bright color on the other (blue engine, green coal car, purple boxcar, yellow passenger car, orange tank car, red caboose). Place pieces on the board with the gray sides showing and turn over as Engineer Ebeneezer washes off the gray dirt and reveals the bright colors underneath. You may wish to bring a whistle to blow at the end.

(Text continues on page 89.)

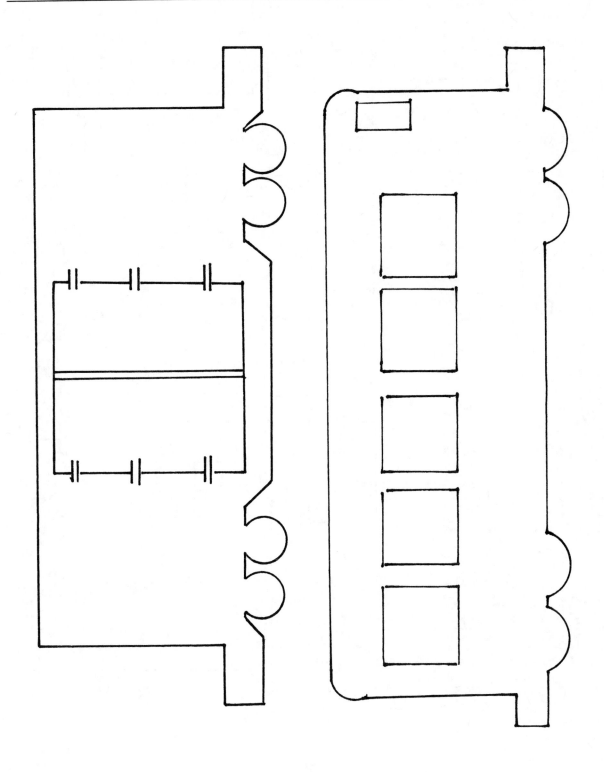

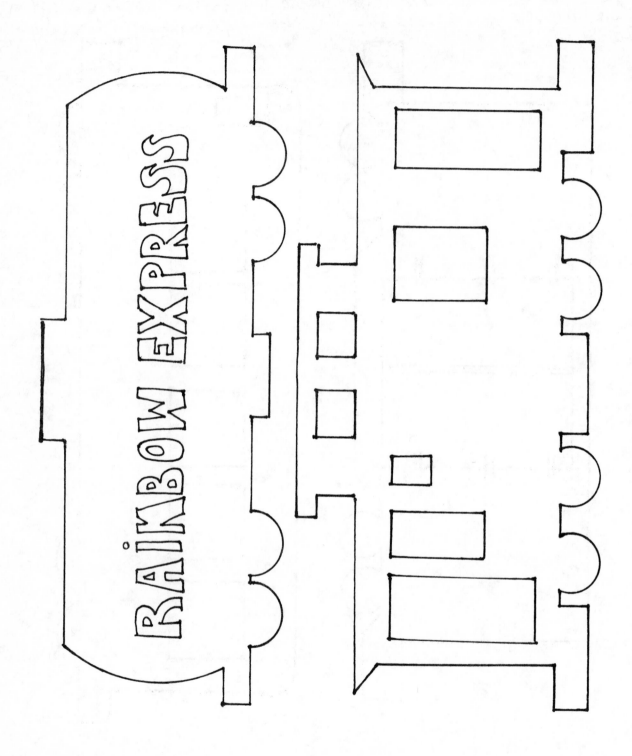

The Old Gray Express was just about at the end of the line. Engineer Ebeneezer had carried passengers for as long as he could remember, but now each year there were fewer and fewer passengers riding the Old Gray Express. The only one who came to the station every day was little Jeremy Joe. He only came to wave to Eb and watch the train go by.

Eb asked the people in town why they did not ride the train anymore.

"Aw, Eb," they said, "the train is no fun. We like to ride in our shiny colorful cars with the loud horns."

"But Old Gray always runs on time," said Eb. "In your wonderful shiny cars with the loud horns, sometimes you are early and sometimes you are late, depending on the traffic. With Old Gray you would always be on time."

But the people still thought Old Gray was no fun and fewer and fewer people rode Old Gray.

Finally the day came when Old Gray had no one to ride, and Eb knew he could only take one more trip.

"Well, Old Gray," he said to the train. "Tomorrow is our last trip. How about if I give you a nice bath tonight. We'll wash all your cars shiny clean."

It had been quite a few years since anyone had washed Old Gray. In fact no one could remember the last time she had a bath. Eb got out the hose and the sponges and the brushes and set to work. Eb scrubbed the engine until all the gray dirt was gone. To his surprise, the engine under all the gray dirt was bright blue.

So Eb scrubbed the coal car until all the gray dirt was gone. To his surprise, the coal car under all the gray dirt was bright green.

So Eb scrubbed the boxcar until all the gray dirt was gone. To his surprise, the boxcar under all the gray dirt was bright purple.

So Eb scrubbed the passenger car until all the gray dirt was gone. To his surprise, the passenger car under all the gray dirt was bright yellow.

So Eb scrubbed the tank car until all the gray dirt was gone. To his surprise, the tank car under all the gray dirt was bright orange.

So Eb scrubbed the caboose until all the gray dirt was gone. To his surprise, the caboose under all the gray dirt was bright red.

"Well, Old Gray," said Eb. "You are full of surprises! Now I have one for you. From now on we will not call you Old Gray. We will call you the Rainbow Express!"

Eb pulled the Rainbow Express into the station right on time the next morning. But almost no one noticed. They were all driving their colorful cars with the loud horns. The only one at the station was Jeremy Joe.

"Wow," said Jeremy Joe. "Old Gray looks great!"

"Call her Rainbow Express now, Jeremy Joe," said Eb. "Come on up for a free ride."

Jeremy Joe climbed into the bright blue engine with Eb, but he could not see out the window.

"Climb up on my shoulders," said Eb. When Jeremy Joe did, he saw an old cord hanging down. A cord that had not been pulled in so long everyone had forgotten it was there.

Jeremy Joe pulled it.

"Tooooot," said the train whistle very softly.

Eb looked up. "Pull it again, Jeremy Joe," he said.

"Tooooooooooot," said the whistle a little louder.

Eb reached up and they pulled together.

"TOOOOOOOOOOOOT-toot-toot!" said the whistle.

And then the people came running! They were so pleased with the Rainbow Express and the whistle, which was louder than any of their car horns, that they rode it everyday. Eb and Jeremy Joe always kept the cars clean and the whistle tuned.

And the Rainbow Express always got the people where they wanted to go on time.

School Bus Song
(To the tune of "Paw Paw Patch")

Where oh where is school bus 7?
    (*Shade eyes and look around.*)
Where oh where is school bus 7?
Where oh where is school bus 7?
Can you see it coming down the street?

Could it be stuck in traffic?
    (*Pretend to steer wheel.*)
Could it be stuck in traffic?
Could it be stuck in traffic?
Can you see it coming down the street?

Did it run out of gas?
    (*Throw hands up in despair.*)
Did it run out of gas?
Did it run out of gas?
Can you see it coming down the street?

Did the tires all go flat?
    (*Clap.*)
Did the tires all go flat?
Did the tires all go flat?
Can you see it coming down the street?

Here it comes—it's right on time.
    (*Wave.*)
Here it comes—it's right on time.
Here it comes—it's right on time.
Hop aboard and we are off to school.

Christmas on the Scooter Limited Express
(A Flannel-board Story)

Cut shapes of four railroad cars to place on the board as the people of the town add cars to the train. Then place a figure of a tree on the top of the cars as the Scooter Limited Express leaves for the Big City.

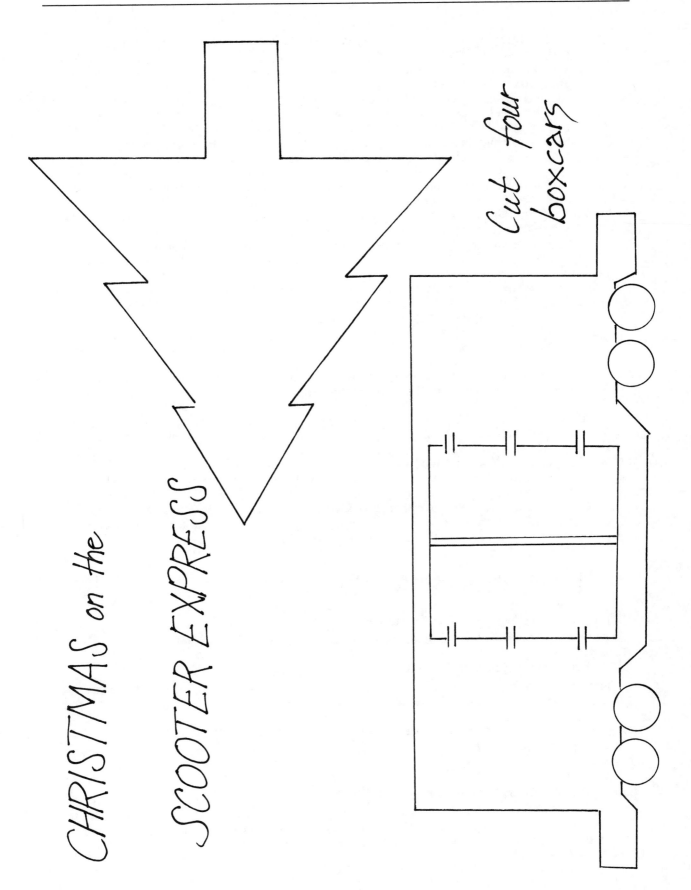

CHRISTMAS on the
SCOOTER EXPRESS

Cut four boxcars

In the town of Ridgeway all the people worked very hard. They spent part of the year planting and weeding and watching things grow. Then they spent the rest of the year chopping and tying and loading. The people in the town of Ridgeway grew Christmas trees and sold them to the people in Big City nearby.

One year the people in Big City had an idea. They wanted a huge, enormous Christmas tree to put in the town square. The people of Ridgeway went out into the forest and found a tree that had been growing since the oldest man in town was a baby. It was so big and so wide and so high that it took all the people in Ridgeway a month to saw through the trunk. It took a week just to fall to the ground. All the horses in Ridgeway were hitched up to the tree and they pulled for two weeks to get it out of the forest and into town. By that time it was the last week in November and the people in Big City were almost ready to decorate the tree. They wanted it to come on the railroad train as soon as possible.

Then the trouble started. Their little train, the Scooter Limited Express, had never had any trouble carrying all the little trees into Big City. But it was not big enough to carry that huge, enormous tree. So they added another boxcar, but it was still not enough. They added another boxcar, but it was still not enough. Finally they added the last boxcar in town and they knew the tree would fit.

But how could they get that huge enormous tree on the train? Some of the people lifted one end, but it was not enough. Some of the people lifted the other end, but it was not enough. Some of the people lifted the middle, but it was not enough.

Then the mayor had an idea. He suggested all the people line up and lift all at once. The people lined up next to the huge enormous tree. They lifted once, but the tree did not move. They lifted again, but the tree did not move.

I think they need help. When I count one-two-three, you all show me how you would lift the tree. One. Two. Three. LIFT! Ummmmmmmm. (*Have all children imitate lifting motion.*) The tree moved a little, but not enough.

Let's try to help again. One. Two. Three. LIFT! Ummmmmmmm. (*Have all children imitate lifting motion.*) The tree moved a little more, but it was still not on the train.

Let's try one more time. One. Two. Three. LIFT! Ummmmmmmm. (*Have all children imitate lifting motion.*) OOF! The tree was finally loaded onto the train. (*Place the tree on top of the train.*) The Scooter Limited Express got the huge, enormous tree to Big City just in time. The people there decorated it and had a wonderful Christmas.

The people in Ridgeway had a wonderful Christmas, too. They loaded themselves onto the train—which was much easier than loading the tree—and had a big celebration. Then they renamed the train the Holiday Extra Special Express.

Books for Going Together on Water

Allen, Pamela. **Who Sank the Boat?** Coward, McCann, 1983.

Too many animals want a ride on the boat! Which one is responsible for sinking it?

Barton, Byron. **Boats.** Crowell, 1986.

Brief text and bold illustrations show boats—including rowboats, sailboats, ferryboats, and tugboats—and some of the activities associated with them.

Benjamin, Alan. **A Change of Plans.** Illustrated by Steven Kellogg. Four Winds, 1982.

A boat ride ends up as a swim when too many friends come along. The picnic afterward, however, is a success in this rhyming text.

Burningham, John. **Mr. Gumpy's Outing.** Holt, Rinehart and Winston, 1970.

A series of animals ask Mr. Gumpy to take them along in his boat on the river, but after awhile they kick, trample, flap and variously muck about until the boat tips over. After the spill they dry out, have tea, and are all promised a ride another day.

Cohen, Carol Lee. **Whiffle Squeek**. Illustrated by Ted Rand. Dodd, Mead, 1987.

The poetic text sings of the adventures of Whiffle Squeek the cat who sails the briny deep by kibitka boat. The cat's "fishy" fashions are eaten one night by a hungry sea monster, but Whiffle Squeek escapes in the end. This story in rhyme is reminiscent of the Scottish ballad "Aiken Drum."

Crampton, Gertrude. **Scuffy the Tug Boat**. Illustrated by Tibor Gergely. Golden Press, 1946.

Scuffy leaves the safety of the bathtub to go down stream and into the open sea. He enjoys the trip, but is glad to be back home.

Crews, Donald. **Harbor**. Greenwillow, 1982.

A busy harbor introduces all kinds of boats and ships.

DiFiori, Larry. **If I Had a Little Boat**. Western, 1985.

The little sailboat sails through a busy harbor, over the ocean to a desert island and back home in this small, simple board book.

Flack, Marjorie, and Kurt Wiese. **A Story about Ping**. Viking Press, 1933.

Boats on the Yangtze River provide an Oriental setting for Ping the duck as he arrives too late to get on his house boat one night.

Gay, Michel. **Little Boat**. Macmillan, 1985.

Translation of a French book, the charming illustrations and text describe a little boat in a big storm.

Gibbons, Gail. **Boat Book**. Holiday House, 1983.

Many kinds of boats from sailboats, kayaks, and canoes to larger boats—aircraft carriers and freighters—are clearly pictured and identified.

Graham, Margaret Bloy. **Benji's Boat Trip**. Harper, 1977.

When Benji the dog's family goes on a trip without him, Benji takes his own surprise boat trip and has some unexpected adventures.

Hutchins, Pat. **One-eyed Jake**. Greenwillow, 1979.

An ill-tempered pirate robs every ship in sight—passenger ships, cargo ships, even fishing ships. He keeps on plundering and filling up his ship until he has to throw his crew overboard. The clever cabin boy throws him the key to the cabin only to see the ship sink with the greedy pirate and his ill gotten gains.

I Saw a Ship a Sailing. Illustrated by Janina Domanska. Macmillan, 1972.

Domanska's geometric lines and bright-colored illustrations accompany this favorite rhyme of a ship "full of pretty things," with sail or silk and masts of gold whose unlikely crew are "four and twenty mice" with a duck as captain. Children will want to set sail, too.

Krasilovsky, Phyllis. **The Cow Who Fell in the Canal**. Illustrated by Peter Spier. Doubleday, 1957.

Children who have not seen a canal will be enchanted with the cow who floats down the narrow waterway like we would drive down the street.

Lasker, Joe. **The Strange Voyage of Neptune's Car**. Viking, 1977.

When Captain Patten falls ill on a voyage around Cape Horn, his young wife Mary Anne becomes the first woman to command a clipper ship there.

Lindgren, Barbro. **The Wild Baby Goes to Sea**. Adapted from the Swedish version by Jack Prelutsky. Illustrated by Eva Erikson. Greenwillow, 1982.

Baby Ben builds a wooden box boat then sails out to sea with his animal crew mates to have many tempest-tossed adventures before returning safe and sound on his mama's floor.

Maestro, Betsy, and Ellen Del Vecchio. **Big City Port**. Illustrated by Giulio Maestro. Four Winds, 1983.

Lifting cargo onto ships and boats pulling in and out of the docks are clearly illustrated in this book about a busy harbor.

Maestro, Betsy, and Giulio Maestro. **Ferry Boat**. Crowell, 1986.

A ferryboat trip by a family will introduce this unusual means of transportation.

Peppe, Rodney. **The Kettleship Pirates**. Lothrop, Lee and Shepard, 1983.

Pip Mouse sets sail on a pirate ship that once was a kettle. He is set to work by the pirates but finds a buried treasure before heading home.

Rockwell, Anne. **Boats**. Dutton, 1982.

A variety of work and pleasure boats are identified by brief text and bright pictures. Those included range from small fishing boats to ocean liners, speed boats pulling water skiers to kayaks. Non-motorized boats (rowboats, sailboats) as well as motor boats from houseboats to tug boats are shown.

Ross, Katherine. **Bear Island**. Illustrated by Lisa McCue. Random House, 1987.

Bear and Rabbit, two good friends, make a boat "from this and that" and go on a terrific voyage until a gale wrecks their craft. Fortunately they land on an island where they stay in peace and happiness for many years.

Williams, Vera B. **Three Days on a River in a Red Canoe**. Greenwillow, 1981.

A girl, her mom, Aunt Rosie and cousin Sam pool their money to buy a red canoe and take a three-day canoe trip on the river. Text and illustrations read like the girl's travel journal with pictures of wildlife, recipes for fruit stew simmered over a bonfire, and a diagram of pitching your own tent.

You Can Pilot a Submarine. Illustrated by Carolyn Bracken. Western, 1983.

This drive-away board book places young readers at the controls of a submarine to see subterranean plants and animals.

Related Activities for Going Together on Water

Who Will Save the Day?
(A Participatory Story)

Teach children the refrain and hand actions before you begin the story so they can all join in with gusto.

REFRAIN:

"We are lost," cried the captain,
　(*Hand to head.*)
As the ship tossed and swayed,
　(*Swing hands right to left.*)
And the crew cried out,
　(*Hands to mouth.*)
"Who will save the day?"
　(*Arms out with palms up.*)
"Not I," said the dog
　(*Shake head for each animal.*)
"Not I," said the cat
"Not I," said the rat
And that was THAT!
　(*Clap three times on last three words.*)

Captain Wayward and his crew had sailed the seven seas on their ship the *Tempest Tossed*. For most of the trip there had been smooth sailing. They had been to Australia, Borneo, Cuba, Denmark, Easter Islands, Fiji, and so on all the way to the Yukon and Zanzibar. Now it was time to go home.

On Monday, they ran into an iceberg off the coast of Iceland. It ripped a hole in the hull.

> "We are lost," cried the captain,
> As the ship tossed and swayed,
> And the crew cried out,
> "Who will save the day?"
> "Not I," said the dog
> "Not I," said the cat
> "Not I," said the rat
> And that was THAT!

So Captain Wayward had to fix the hull all by himself.
On Tuesday they ran into a hurricane near Honolulu. It ripped a hole in the mainsail.

> "We are lost," cried the captain,
> As the ship tossed and swayed,
> And the crew cried out,
> "Who will save the day?"
> "Not I," said the dog
> "Not I," said the cat
> "Not I," said the rat
> And that was THAT!

So Captain Wayward had to fix the mainsail all by himself.
On Wednesday the rudder ran into a sand bar near San Salvador.

> "We are lost," cried the captain,
> As the ship tossed and swayed,
> And the crew cried out,
> "Who will save the day?"
> "Not I," said the dog
> "Not I," said the cat
> "Not I," said the rat
> And that was THAT!

So Captain Wayward had to fix the rudder all by himself.
Finally on Thursday the sun came out. The sea was calm, and it was smooth sailing. They sailed on full speed ahead all day long.

And on Friday, the *Tempest Tossed* docked at home in Boston Harbor in the good old U.S.A.

> "We are home," said the captain,
> With the ship tied fast.
> And the whole crew said,
> "At last, at last!"

A Seaworthy Craftable Craft
(A Story in Rhyme for Participation)

Teach children actions for different animals that will come on board the raft before you begin the story. The lady bug hugs; the frog hops; the newt plays a flute; the chick holds her stomach; the goat holds a thumb out as if hitchhiking; and the cow throws up her hands.

> Jack was a sailor
> Who built a small raft.
> Aye! It was a seaworthy
> Craftable craft.

When the raft was all done,
One bright sunny day,
He picked up some passengers
Along the way.

The lady bug
Gave him a hug,
On the seaworthy craftable craft.

The fat frog
Hopped off her log,
The lady bug
Gave him a hug,
On the seaworthy craftable craft.

The nimble newt
Played her flute,
The fat frog
Hopped off her log,
The lady bug
Gave him a hug,
On the seaworthy craftable craft.

The silly chick
Felt seasick,
The nimble newt
Played her flute,
The fat frog
Hopped off her log,
The lady bug
Gave him a hug,
On the seaworthy craftable craft.

The gypsy goat
Hitched a ride on the boat,
The silly chick
Felt seasick,
The nimble newt
Played her flute,
The fat frog
Hopped off her log,
The lady bug
Gave him a hug,
On the seaworthy craftable craft.

The big moo cow
Cried, "We're sinking now!"
On the seaworthy craftable craft.

This is not however
The end of our tale:
They were saved by a seaworthy
Whale of a whale!

Ship Shape
(A Flannel-board Story)

Cut a crescent of green felt, a thin blue rectangle, small triangle of yellow and large triangle of red. Place on the board as indicated in the story.

On the morning the sea was calm and the sun was shining on all the little waves, four children came to the beach. Each brought sand pails and shovels and inner tubes to play with. And each one had something new.

Chris was the first one to the edge of the water. She had a green crescent. (*Show green crescent.*) Chris told the others, "I like my green crescent. It is new and nice, but I don't know what to make out of it." She put the green crescent in the water where it floated and rocked, but did not go very far. (*Place green crescent on board.*)

Rodney was next to the edge of the water. He had a thin blue rectangle. (*Show thin blue rectangle.*) Rodney told the others, "I like my thin blue rectangle. It is new and nice, but I don't know what to make out of it." He put the thin blue rectangle on the green crescent. The green crescent floated and rocked, and went a little way, but still did not go very far. (*Place thin blue rectangle vertically above green crescent on board.*)

Lil was next on the edge of the water. She had a little yellow triangle. (*Show little yellow triangle.*) Lil told the others, "I like my little yellow triangle. It is new and nice, but I don't know what to make out of it." She put the little yellow triangle next to the thin blue rectangle on the green crescent. The green crescent floated and rocked, and went a little further, but still did not go very far. (*Place little yellow triangle next to thin blue rectangle on board.*)

Boris was last to the edge of the water. He had a big red triangle. (*Show big red triangle.*) Boris told the others, "I like my big red triangle. It is new and nice, but I don't know what tomake out of it." He put the big red triangle across from the little yellow triangle next to the thin blue rectangle on the green crescent. (*Place big red triangle on other side of thin blue rectangle.*) The green crescent floated and rocked, and began to sail away.

"Wait for us," the children cried. They all climbed on board and went for a ride on their nice new sailboat. It was shipshape!

Sailing on the Ocean in Our Boat
(To the tune of "She'll Be Comin' Round the Mountain")

We'll be sailing on the ocean in our boat
We'll be sailing on the ocean in our boat
We'll be sailing on the ocean,
We'll be sailing on the ocean,
We'll be sailing on the ocean in our boat
Anchor's away!

We might run into a sea storm in our boat
We might run into a sea storm in our boat
We might run into a sea storm,
We might run into a sea storm,
We might run into a sea storm in our boat
Pitch and toss.

On the poop deck land lubbers get seasick
On the poop deck land lubbers get seasick
On the poop deck land lubbers,
On the poop deck land lubbers,
On the poop deck land lubbers get seasick
Groan, groan.

At last the sea is clear and smooth as glass
At last the sea is clear and smooth as glass
At last the sea is clear,
At last the sea is clear,
At last the sea is clear and smooth as glass
Ahhhhhh.

We will finally drop the anchor in the port
We will finally drop the anchor in the port
We will finally drop the anchor,
We will finally drop the anchor
We will finally drop the anchor in the port
Land Ho!

Row Your Boat Some More

(To the tune of "Row Your Boat")

Row, row, row your boat
    (*Pretend to row slowly.*)
Gently down the stream
Merrily, merrily, merrily, merrily
Life is but a dream.

Row, row, row your boat
    (*Pretend to row slowly.*)
Slowly down the creek
Lazily, lazily, lazily, lazily
Slowly down the creek.

Row, row, row your boat
    (*Pretend to row quickly.*)
Quickly down the river
Faster, faster, faster, faster,
Quickly down the river.

Row, row, row your boat
    (*Turn in circles while rowing.*)
All around the lake
Circle, circle, circle, circle
All around the lake.

Row, row, row your boat
    (*Sink quietly to seated positions for next activity.*)
Through the sticky swamp
Slugging, slugging, slugging, slugging
Stuck there in the mud.
UGH!

All Hands on Deck

(A Fingerplay)

One fat sailor called the crew
    (*Hold up thumb.*)
Next came sailor number two
    (*Hold up index finger.*)
Number three was tall as the mast
    (*Hold up middle finger.*)
Number four came running fast
    (*Hold up ring finger.*)
Number five was not too tall—
    (*Hold up smallest finger.*)
But he was captain of them all

He called six, seven, and eight
   (*Hold up thumb, index and middle finger of other hand.*)
Nine and ten came a little late.
   (*Hold up all ten fingers.*)
"All hands on deck?" the captain said.
"Hoist the anchor. Full speed ahead!"

GAMES FOR WE ALL GO TOGETHER

School Bus Match

One of the challenges for children when they go to school is to locate the right bus each day. Help them begin to recognize and match numbers with the game.

Make ten circles and ten school bus shapes. Number each set from one to ten. Sit in a ring. Hand the circles to the children to hold in front of them so all can see the numbers. As you hold up a school bus the child with the correct number can come up and match it. This can be done on a flannel board by backing all the pieces with felt or attach the buses to shoe boxes and the numbered circles can be dropped inside the box.

Elevated or Underground

Many children may not be familiar with the "el" or elevated railroad of some larger cities, or even with the idea of riding underground in the subway. This game, based on "London Bridge Is Falling Down" will help them get acquainted with these "city slicker" kinds of transportation.

Sing these words to the tune of "London Bridge Is Falling Down." Raise arms overhead during the first verse, squat and put hands on ground on the second. Sway shoulders in rhythm. Sing the verses alternately until everyone is ready to sit down and listen.

   Ride the elevated train
   Ride the el
   Ride the el
   Ride the el until it goes
   Underground!

   Now it's called the subway train
   Subway train
   Subway train
   Subway train until it comes
   Up again.

Train Tales Game

Use the shoe shoe choo choo train cars craft (p. 102) to play this game. For the game you will need four train cars linked together. Fill the first car with subject/adjective/noun combinations written on index cards. (Examples: The silly snake, the curious cat.) Fill the second car with action verbs written on cards. (Examples: swallowed, caught, sank.) The third car should have object nouns. (Example: a mouse, bubble gum.) The fourth car is filled with prepositional phrases or adverbs. (Examples: in a gulp, with her paws, slowly.)

Children select cards from the boxes, arrange and rearrange them to make sentences and short "train tales." Provide blank cards so children can "write" their own words, phrases, and stories. With teacher assistance, this game can be a great motivator for developing reading and writing skills.

The Captain Says

Play this seaworthy version of the traditional "Simon Says" game by instructing children to listen to a sequence of instructions. They should do what you say if the instructions begin with the words "The Captain Says." They should remain still if you do not tell them "The Captain Says." Include sea terms in the game to add to the fun. For example, "The captain says climb the mast." (All climb.) "The captain says row your boats." (Everyone rows.) "Walk the plank." (Those who are "caught" doing this go to a desert island—one corner of the room—until other children are "caught" during the next adventure. Then children exchange places.)

The Great Train Chain Game

The object of this cooperative game is to create two trains then one great train chain by adding "boxcar children" and by moving around the room without colliding. Two children are selected as engineers to begin play. These children may wear engineer style hats or bright red kerchiefs. The engineers chug around the room and move their arms in circular movement as if they are train engines. The engineers select "cars" by tapping children on the shoulders and by saying "choo." The tapped child responds by saying "choo choo," and grabs the waist of the engineer. Play continues with the cars linking to the growing train chain. After everyone has been linked in one of the two chains, the shorter chain moves to attach to the longer chain so that the result is one great train chain.

CRAFTS FOR WE ALL GO TOGETHER

"All Hands on Deck" Craft

Make a finger puppet sailor from two pieces of stiff interfacing (or heavy paper). Use the pattern below. Glue around the outside edges with a fabric glue. Draw on features, eye patches, etc. with markers. Make small felt priate hats with a cut in each hat so it will fit on a sailor's head. Make the whole merry crew of sailors and attach a cardboard hand that will stand up on a base (see illustration), so you will have "all hands on deck."

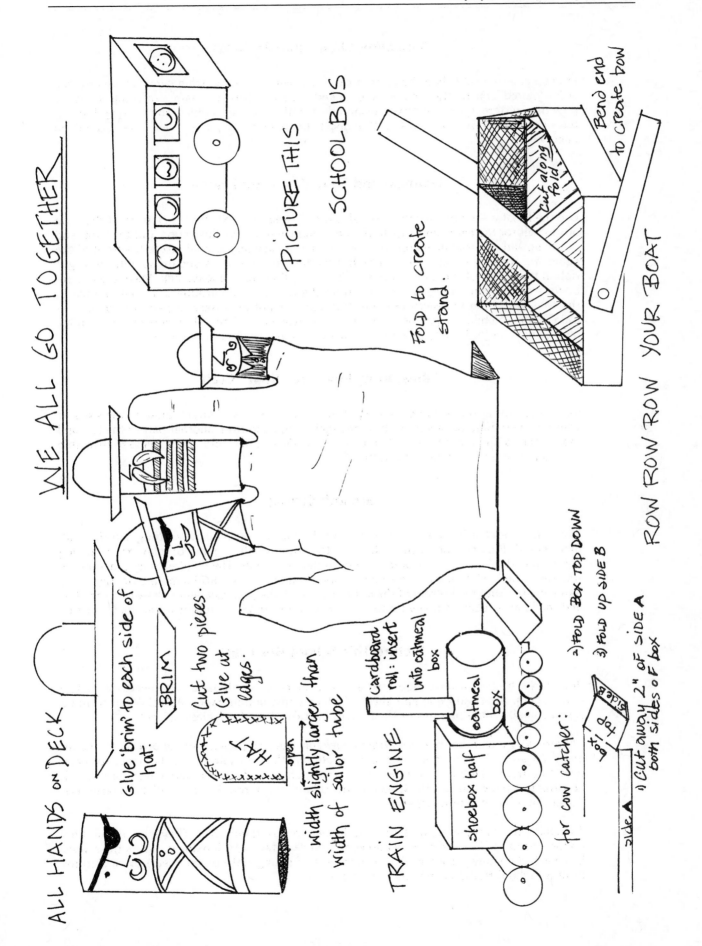

WE ALL GO TOGETHER

ALL HANDS on DECK

Glue 'brim' to each side of hat.

BRIM

Cut two pieces.
Glue at edges.

HAT

open

width slightly larger than width of sailor tube

PICTURE THIS

SCHOOL BUS

Fold to create stand.

Cut along fold

Bend end to create bow

ROW ROW ROW YOUR BOAT

TRAIN ENGINE

Cardboard roll: insert into oatmeal box

oatmeal box

shoebox half

for cow catcher:

SIDE A
SIDE B

1) Cut away 2" of side A both sides of box
2) Fold box top down
3) Fold up side B

Shoe Shoe Choo Choo Train Cars

Provide children with shoes boxes to make their own train cars. Train cars may be covered with colored construction paper and linked together with fat yarn. Vary this craft by providing different sizes of boxes, using lids, small cardboard ladder, and cutting doors in the sides of the boxes. Use this craft in another way by playing the "Train Tales Game" on page 99.

Oatmeal and Shoe Box Train Engine

Use the lid of a shoe box for the base of this train engine. Next, cut the bottom of the shoe box in half for the cabin and glue to the lid as indicated in the illustration. Cut the front end of the box lid and fold down for the cow catcher. Attach an oatmeal box to the front of the cabin with two-sided tape. Then attach a cardboard tube or cardboard spindle from gift ribbon to the top of the oatmeal box. This tube will be your smokestack. Make eight cardboard wheels—four large, four small—from the rest of your cardboard box and attach to the train with brad fasteners. (See illustration.) It is not necessary to paint or cover your train. Younger children may need assistance in attaching wheels. Teachers may use an ice pick to poke holes in the box lid so the brad fasteners will go in more easily.

"Row, Row, Row Your Boat" Craft

Cut the top off a toothpick box. Use the top to make two oars. Attach these to the sides of your boat with brad fasteners. Make a one-inch-wide band from another part of the top and tape it across the boat to resemble the seat. Cut one end and fold in a V shape to resemble the front of a row boat. (See illustration.)

Smooth Sailing

This simple boat will send the children merrily, merrily on their way—they can do it all themselves! Provide for each child a butter tub, small mound of clay or modeling compound, drinking straw or pipe cleaner, square of paper. The children may draw on the squares. Attach with tape to the straw or pipe cleaner for sails. Roll a mound of clay into a ball and press into the bottom of the butter tub. Stick the pipe cleaner or straw into the clay, and the boat is ready. It really floats—you may want to have a tub of water ready for fun.

Picture This School Bus Craft

Provide each child with a shoe box, an extra piece of cardboard, two pieces of yellow construction paper and one half sheet of black construction paper. Ask children to bring several small school pictures of themselves (or take them for a class project).

Children first cover the shoe box with yellow construction paper. Lay the box on the paper and draw around to determine the appropriate length and width to cut the paper for each box. Cut from cardboard four wheels three inches in diameter and cover with black construction paper. Attach the wheels to the school bus of the shoe box with brad fasteners. Cover the lid with yellow paper.

The children may trade pictures, but should keep one of themselves. They glue the pictures on the side of the box and draw windows around each face as if looking out from the school bus. Each child may paste one picture in front (as if sitting in the driver's seat). Extra pictures or other school treasures may be kept in the box.

TAKE-HOME ACTIVITY FOR WE ALL GO TOGETHER

On-the-Go Bingo

Draw a simple BINGO card, 5 x 5-inch squares. In each square show a picture of group transportation: bus, train, subway, boats of all kinds. The center square is FREE. Encourage families to write the date and place each is seen as they vacation or go around town. The card can be brought back to the library for a prize or used as a diary of transportation observations for the family.

5

Tractors and Tow Trucks
Machines That Help Us Work

INTRODUCTION

Early toys and books boys and girls enjoy show the fascination of children with tractors, trucks, and all varieties of work machines. In their role play, children become fire fighters driving bright red fire trucks or mimic the sounds and actions of cement mixers, bull dozers, and steam shovels. This chapter will provide activities to capitalize on these interests and also teach such skills as classification, sequencing, and counting.

The first theme on trucks includes garbage trucks, tow trucks, delivery trucks, and dump trucks. The books range from Donald Crew's nearly wordless *Truck*, to the rhythmic text of Diane Siebert's *Truck Song*. Follow up a reading of these books with "Truck Talk Chant" or sing "Dump Truck Song."

Tractors and other helpers are the focus of the second part of this chapter. Virginia Lee Burton's classic *Mike Mulligan and His Steam Shovel* and Gail Gibbons' more recent *Fire! Fire!* are but a sampling of the excellent picture books to select. Then invite the children to participate in "Three Tractors and Buba" and to sing one of the fire truck songs so they will become even more aware of transportation that helps us carry on our daily lives.

INITIATING ACTIVITY

Things That Help Us Work

Teach the children this rhyme about all different kinds of things that help us do the work we need done. If there is time, children may suggest other sounds and actions for more verses. Very young children may prefer to do only one verse at a time without repeating the whole series of sounds and actions.

> Here are things that help us work.
> Work, work, watch them work.
> Steam shovel: Grrrrr.
> (*Bend low and pretend to scoop dirt.*)
>
> Here are things that help us work.
> Work, work, watch them work.
> Fire Engine: Ding-ding-ding.
> (*Pretend to spray with hoses.*)
> Steam shovel: Grrrrr.

Here are things that help us work.
Work, work, watch them work.
Bull dozer: Scraaaape.
(*Bend elbows; move arms back and forth like big wheels.*)
Fire Engine: Ding-ding-ding.
Steam shovel: Grrrrr.

Here are things that help us work.
Work, work, watch them work.
Dump truck: Duuuuuump.
(*Raise arms slowly; then drop hands to legs.*)
Bull dozer: Scraaaape.
Fire Engine: Ding-ding-ding.
Steam shovel: Grrrrr.

Here are things that help us work.
Work, work, watch them work.
Police car: Eeeeeeee.
(*Run in place.*)
Dump truck: Duuuuuump.
Bull dozer: Scraaaape.
Fire Engine: Ding-ding-ding.
Steam shovel: Grrrrr.

LITERATURE-SHARING EXPERIENCES

Books for Trucks

Alexander, Anne. **ABC of Cars and Trucks**. Illustrated by Ninon. Doubleday, 1956.
  Verse describes trucks the children may not see often anymore from auto trailer to zone truck.

Barrett, N. S. **Trucks**. Illustrated by Tony Bryan. Franklin Watts, 1984.
  An introduction to the many varieties of heavy trucks and the work they are designed to do.

Barton, Byron. **Trucks**. Crowell, 1986.
  Brief text and clear illustrations present a variety of trucks and what they do.

Busy Farm Trucks. Illustrated by R. W. Alley. Grosset & Dunlap, 1986.
  Board book with wheels on the cover shows grain trucks, tank trucks, horse trailers, livestock wagons, feed wagons, and hay wagons.

Crews, Donald. **Truck**. Greenwillow, 1980.
  A bright red trailer truck loads up, travels hundreds of miles through city traffic signs, tunnels, highways and over bridges to its destination in this nearly wordless picture book.

Curious George and the Dump Truck. Edited by Margaret Rey and Alan Shalleck. Houghton Mifflin, 1984.
  This mischievous monkey gets into trouble when he spills a load of sand from a dump truck. He is a hero when the sand blocks the way of the jewelry thieves.

Gay, Michel. **Little Truck**. Macmillan, 1985.
  A little truck describes its journey carrying heavy rocks and sand.

Gibbons, Gail. **Trucks**. Crowell, 1981.

Gibbons' clear drawings with bright colors picture a variety of trucks at work — delivering cargoes, moving loads, pushing earth and snow, pulling wagons, lifting lumber, digging holes, helping in emergencies and performing daily jobs for the needs of people.

Gretz, Susanne. **Teddy Bear's Moving Day**. Four Winds, 1981.

Gretz's colorful fuzzy bears get into all kinds of mischief on moving day, but finally settle in their new quarters.

Harrison, David. **Let's Go, Trucks!** Illustrated by Bill Dugan. Golden Press, 1973.

Pictures of various types and sizes of trucks are accompanied by brief descriptions of their use.

Hughes, Shirley. **Moving Molly**. Prentice Hall, 1978.

Molly is lonely after her family moves from the city to the country, but her new next door friends help her adjust.

Kessler, Ethel, and Leonard Kessler. **Night Story**. Macmillan, 1981.

A truck driver who takes his haul at night sees things people don't see in the day — nighttime animals, freight trains, ambulance and police and fire fighters on emergencies, and all night cafes.

Mathieu, Joe. **Big Joe's Trailer Truck**. Random House, 1974.

Simple text tells the daily events of a truck driver's job from reporting to the dispatcher and the service garage to leaving the truck terminal and hauling his trailer load to its destination hundreds of miles away.

O'Brien, Anne Sibley. **Where's My Truck?** Holt, Rinehart, and Winston, 1985.

Jason cannot find his truck until he puts his toys away in this simple board book.

Petrie, Catherine. **Joshua James Likes Trucks**. Illustrated by Jerry Warshaw. Childrens Press, 1982.

This beginning reader shows all the trucks a little boy likes.

Quackenbush, Robert. **City Trucks**. Albert Whitman, 1981.

How trucks work to help the city and the city people will fascinate even country children.

Sharmat, Marjorie. **Mitchell Is Moving**. Illustrated by Jose Aruego and Ariane Dewey. Macmillan, 1978.

Moving sounds like a good idea until the little dinosaur realizes he will miss his best friend next door.

Siebert, Diane. **Truck Song**. Illustrated by Byron Barton. Crowell, 1984.

Rhyming and rhythmic text convey the mood and experience of driving a big rig. Bold, bright illustrations perfectly suit the words.

Spier, Peter. **Bill's Service Station**. Doubleday, 1981.

This board book is cut in the shape of the service station where the day's activities take place.

Thompson, Graham. **Cars and Trucks**. G. Stevens Publishing, 1986.

Large print text for the beginning reader identifies about a dozen work vehicles from tractors to car transporters and briefly describes their purpose.

Tobias, Tobi. **Moving Day**. Illustrated by William Péne du Bois. Random House, 1976.

In the midst of all the confusion of moving, a little girl finds security in keeping her toy bear close by.

Wolfe, Robert. **The Truck Book.** Carolrhoda, 1981.

Photographs and brief text describe thirteen kinds of trucks including fuel tankers, cement trucks, telephone trucks, and eighteen-wheelers (tractors and trailers).

Wood, Leslie. **Bump, Bump, Bump.** Oxford University Press, 1986.

Brief text and brightly colored pictures tell a tale of a moving van that slowly loses everything it is carrying.

Related Activities for Trucks

Terry and His Tow Truck
(A Flannel-board Story)

Make felt shapes of a tow truck, a bus, a station wagon, and a sports car. Use two pieces of yarn to outline the road on the board. (See illustrations on pages 108 and 109.)

Terry the Turtle drove a tow truck. An old, slow tow truck. Terry's tow truck wasn't shiny and it wasn't fast, but it always got Terry to places where he wanted to go.

Now, one fine shiny day, Terry was driving down the highway in his tow truck. His old, slow tow truck. Goin' about forty miles an hour when—

Zoom! Bertha Bear's big bus pulled right up behind him.

"What a hunk of junk!" bellowed Bertha. "Get that old, slow tow truck out of my way. I'm going places today!"

Well, Terry slowed down so Bertha's big bus could pass by.

Before long Sam Snake's skinny station wagon pulled up behind Terry's tow truck.

"What a hunk of junk!" hissed Sam. "Get that old, slow tow truck out of my way. I'm going places today!"

Well, Terry slowed down so Sam's skinny station wagon could pass by. Terry kept on goin' down the highway, slow and easy when—

Zoom! Clyde the Cool Cat cruised up in his oh-so-cool and classy sports car.

"Man, what a hunk of junk!" called Clyde. "Get that old, slow tow truck out of my way. I'm going places today!"

And Terry once again slowed down so Clyde the Cool Cat could cruise by in his cool and classy sports car.

Now all the cars and station wagons and the buses were speeding by when all of a sudden the bright shiny day turned dark. It started to rain. It rained and it rained. It rained so hard that the roads and the highway started to get slippery. And when roads and highways get slippery, cars and wagons and buses start to slip and slide around.

It rained and it rained. The cars and the wagons and the buses tried to slow down, but they were all goin' so fast that they slipped and they slid right off the highway. They slipped off the highway and they got stuck deep down in the ditch. Nobody was going anyplace. Nobody except Terry and his old, slow tow truck.

Terry drove up hills and down hills, slow and easy. He stopped by the first ditch. He hooked his tow truck to Clyde's cool and classy sports car. Terry pulled and he pulled and he pulled Clyde's car slowly out of the ditch.

Then Terry drove up another hill and down another hill, slow and easy. He stopped by another ditch. He hooked his tow truck to Sam's skinny station wagon. Terry pulled and he pulled and he pulled Sam's wagon slowly out of the ditch.

(Text continues on page 110.)

TERRY AND HIS TOW TRUCK

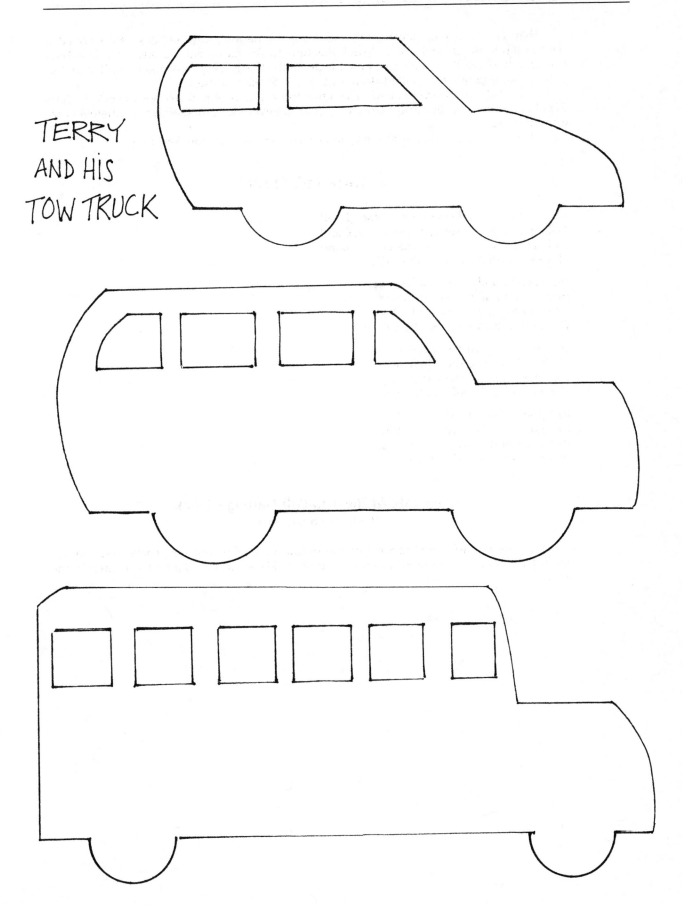

TERRY
AND HIS
TOW TRUCK

Then Terry drove up another hill and down another hill, slow and easy. He stopped at the last ditch. He hooked his tow truck this time to Bertha's great big bus. This time Terry had to pull and pull (let's all give him a little help—this is a big job), and he pulled and he pulled and, finally, Terry pulled Bertha's bus out of the last ditch.

After that nobody ever called Terry's tow truck a hunk of junk. Nobody ever told Terry to get out of the way. Because Terry's tow truck got everybody on their way—wherever they wanted to go.

Then Terry drove up another hill and down another hill, slow and easy.

Truck Talk Chant

Talking to the truckers on the citizen band.
Talking to the truckers on the citizen band.
Talking to the truckers on the citizen band.
This here's Book Lady on the CB!

Hey, good buddy, how's it looking.
Hey, good buddy, how's it looking.
Hey, good buddy, how's it looking.
This here's Book Lady on the CB!

You're all clear to the windy city.
You're all clear to the windy city.
You're all clear to the windy city.
This here's Book Lady on the CB!

10-4 good buddy have a nice trip.
10-4 good buddy have a nice trip.
10-4 good buddy have a nice trip.
This here's Book Lady on the CB!

The Tale of the Too-Full Garbage Truck
(A Flannel-board Story)

For this story you will need cutouts of the following objects: four egg shells, two banana peels, five onions, and a large green garbage bag. Place on the board as indicated in the story.

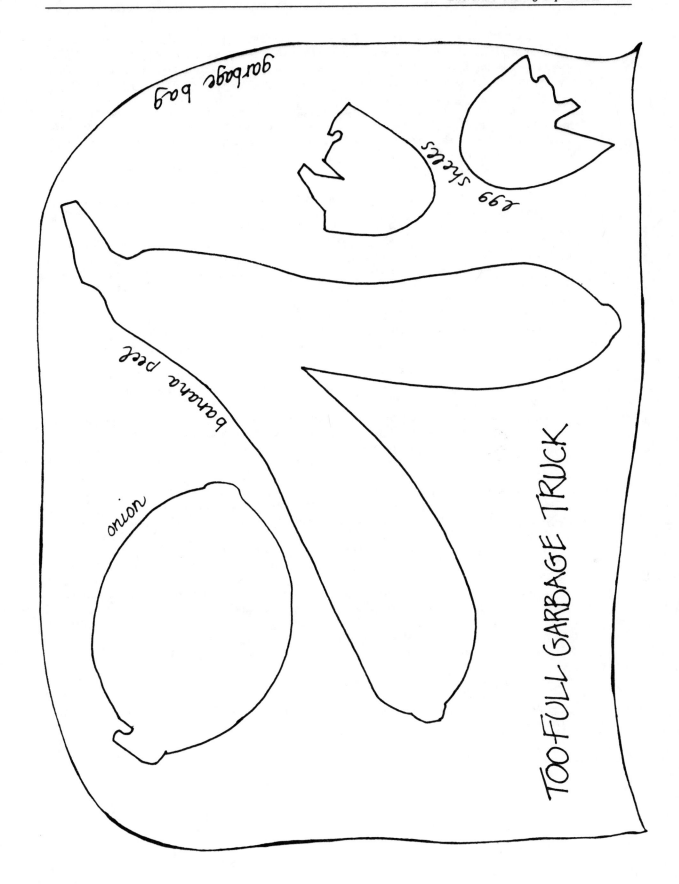

garbage bag

egg shells

banana peel

onion

TOOFULL GARBAGE TRUCK

Gregory drove a garbage truck. Gregory liked to drive a garbage truck because he liked to help keep the town clean and neat. Each morning Gregory drove to a street in town. There were overflowing garbage cans. Gregory loaded each one carefully into his garbage truck. By the end of the day the street was nice and neat again, and Gregory took his garbage to the dump.

The people in the town liked Gregory and his truck. They liked the way the street looked after Gregory cleaned it up. The only thing about Gregory they did not like was the smell of his truck when it had all the garbage inside. They called a meeting at the town hall to talk to Gregory about the smell.

When they told him the problem, Gregory just shrugged. "That is how it is with garbage," he said simply.

"Not my garbage!" snapped Mrs. Johnson. "I only cook omelets made with fresh new eggs. Nothing smells bad about eggs."

"Eggs smell bad in garbage," said Gregory. "That is how it is with garbage."

"Not my garbage!" snapped Mrs. Northern. "I only cook banana cream pie made with fresh new bananas. Nothing smells bad about bananas."

"Bananas smell bad in garbage," said Gregory. "That is how it is with garbage."

"Not my garbage!" snapped Mrs. Smithers. "I only cook liver and onions made with fresh new onions. Nothing smells bad about onions."

"Onions smell bad in garbage," said Gregory. "That is how it is with garbage."

Well the people in the town would not believe their garbage smelled that bad. They still thought it was Gregory's truck that made the smell. Then for one week Gregory and his truck went on vacation.

"Good," said all the people in town. "Now we won't have to smell that horrible truck anymore. We'll just pile all our garbage in one pile so it won't make a mess, but none of the things we make smells bad."

On Monday Mrs. Johnson made an omelet. She put the egg shells out on the garbage pile. (*Place egg shells on board.*) On Tuesday Mrs. Northern made banana cream pie. She put the banana peels on the garbage pile. (*Place banana peels on board.*) On Wednesday Mrs. Smithers made liver and onions. She put the onions on the garbage pile. (*Place onions on board.*)

On Thursday, Mrs. Johnson smelled something bad. "That smells like Gregory's old garbage truck!" she said. Mrs. Northern and Mrs. Smithers smelled it, too. They looked and looked for Gregory and his garbage truck, but all they found was ... their pile of garbage.

"Oh," said Mrs. Johnson. "I guess there are times when old eggs do smell bad."

"Oh, yes," said Mrs. Northern. "There are times when old bananas smell bad."

"Oh, my, yes," said Mrs. Smithers. "And even times when old onions smell bad."

On Friday, Gregory pulled into town in his garbage truck.

Everyone met him at the town hall. "We are sorry we thought your truck smelled. Please take the garbage away so our street will be nice and neat again."

Gregory smiled and got out of his truck. "I brought something new from my vacation." And out of the truck he pulled a green plastic garbage bag. "Put all your eggs and bananas and onions in this and your garbage won't smell anymore." (*Place green bag over garbage pile.*)

From then on, everyone set out green garbage bags instead of overflowing garbage cans. Gregory loaded them in his truck and the street looked nice and neat. Best of all, Gregory's truck always smelled just fine. Gregory just smiled and said, "That's how it is with garbage."

Dump Truck Song
(To the tune of "Ten Little Indians")

On the last line of each verse, touch hands to shoulders and lower slowly to sides as you "dump" the load. After the children know the format, let them suggest items to put in the dump truck.

> Bumpity-bumpity comes the dump truck
> Bumpity-bumpity comes the dump truck
> Bumpity-bumpity comes the dump truck
> Duuuu-uuuump out the load.
>
> I've got oranges in my dump truck
> I've got oranges in my dump truck
> I've got oranges in my dump truck
> Duuuu-uuuump out the load.
>
> I've got boxes in my dump truck
> I've got boxes in my dump truck
> I've got boxes in my dump truck
> Duuuu-uuuump out the load.
>
> I've got garbage in my dump truck
> I've got garbage in my dump truck
> I've got garbage in my dump truck
> Duuuu-uuuump out the load.

April Fool Monkey Shines
(A Story with Masks)

For this story make simple masks of a monkey, elephant, camel, penguin, pig, and hippo. Give each child a mask as the character is mentioned in the story. Wrap boxes in brown paper for Monkey to deliver.

elephant

pig

Attach shape to front or side of paper bag

monkey

hippo

MONKEY SHINES
APRIL FOOL

camel

penguin

Monkey had a new job. He was working for Goldflats and Hobnob Department Store. Goldflats and Hobnob's motto was "Give the customers what they want." Monkey's job was to drive the delivery truck that took the things to the customers who wanted them.

The morning of April Fool's Day Monkey woke up feeling silly. He felt like playing one April Fool's trick after another all day long. "I know," he said. "I'll mix up all the orders as I deliver them. Goldflats and Hobnob won't give the customers what they want today!"

Monkey's first delivery was to Elephant. "Let's see," said Monkey as he drove the delivery truck up to Elephant's house. "Elephant ordered a hot tub. Well, I think I'll deliver him a mudpack." Monkey put the mudpack on Elephant's porch, rang the bell, and drove away in the delivery truck very fast. He laughed, "April Fool, Elephant. Goldflats and Hobnob did not give the customers what they wanted this time."

Monkey's next delivery was to Camel. "Let's see," said Monkey as he drove the delivery truck up to Camel's house. "Camel ordered a pair of sandals. Well, I think I'll deliver him the hot tub." Monkey put the hot tub on Camel's porch, rang the bell, and drove away in the delivery truck very fast. He laughed, "April Fool, Camel. Goldflats and Hobnob did not give the customers what they wanted this time."

Monkey's next delivery was to Penguin. "Let's see," said Monkey as he drove the delivery truck up to Penguin's house. "Penguin ordered a tuxedo. Well, I think I'll deliver him a pair of sandals." Monkey put the sandals on Penguin's porch, rang the bell, and drove away in the delivery truck very fast. He laughed, "April Fool, Penguin. Goldflats and Hobnob did not give the customers what they wanted this time."

Monkey's last delivery was to Pig. "Let's see," said Monkey as he drove the delivery truck up to Pig's house. "Pig ordered a mudpack. Well, all I have left in the delivery truck is a tuxedo. That is what Pig gets." Monkey put the tuxedo on Pig's porch, rang the bell, and drove away in the delivery truck very fast. He laughed, "April Fool, Pig. Goldflats and Hobnob did not give the customers what they wanted this time."

When Monkey got back to Goldflats and Hobnob's Department Store, the phone was ringing off the hook. The secretary, Miss Hippo, said, "Monkey, it is all your fault the customers are calling! The first call I got was from Elephant."

Monkey laughed. "He was supposed to get a hot tub and I left him a mudpack. He did not get what he wanted."

"No," said Miss Hippo. "And he was delighted. He said the mudpack took all his wrinkles away and has made him much more handsome than the hot tub would have. He said it was just what he wanted. Then I got a call from Camel."

Monkey laughed. "He was supposed to get a pair of sandals and I left him a hot tub. He did not get what he wanted."

"No," said Miss Hippo. "And he was delighted. He said the hot tub was so nice and warm that he took his first bath in a year and is off to the opera. He said it was just what he wanted. Then I got a call from Penguin."

Monkey laughed. "He was supposed to get a tuxedo and I left him a pair of sandals. He did not get what he wanted."

"No," said Miss Hippo. "And he was delighted. He said the sandals put him in the mood to get away and he is off to Palm Beach for the vacation of a lifetime. He said it was just what he wanted. Then I got a call from Pig."

Monkey laughed. "He was supposed to get a mudpack and I left him a tuxedo. He did not get what he wanted."

"No," said Miss Hippo. "And he was delighted. He said the tuxedo made him remember his old tap shoes he had not had on in years. It started his whole career in show business over again. It made him much younger than the mudpack ever could. He said it was just what he wanted. I think the April Fool is on you, Monkey. All of Goldflats and Hobnob's customers got just what they wanted!"

Monkey thought about that as he climbed back into his delivery truck. He was glad all the customers were happy with their deliveries, but he couldn't wait for next year to play more April Fool's tricks.

Ice Cream Truck Song
(To the tune of "Three Blind Mice")

Ting-a-ling, ting-a-ling.
Ice cream truck, ice cream truck.
Fudgesicle, Popsicle, Eskimo Pie,
Ice cream sandwiches—give them a try.
When it's so hot, it's such fun to buy
From the ice cream truck.
Ting-a-ling.

Everything and the Kitchen Sink
(An Object Story)

For extra interest, bring in boxes, a garbage bag, a nest, a work glove, and a faucet from the sink to show as you tell the story.

Kevin and his family were moving to a new house in a new town. Kevin's mother said, "Kevin, in the new house you will have the same bed and same toy box and same bookshelves as you have in your old yellow room, but they will be in a new blue bedroom." Kevin was excited to go to the new house and see his new blue room.

For weeks Kevin's mother packed boxes for the moving van to take to the new house in the new town. One box was filled with blankets. One box had pots and pans. One box had books and records. Kevin's mother gave him his very own box to pack his toys. Soon everything was packed for the moving van to take to the new house in the new town. Kevin was excited to go to the new house and see his new room.

On the morning of moving day, the big red moving van came very early. Chuck, the moving man, got out of the truck and called, "Is this the family that is moving to a new house in a new town?"

"Yes," said Kevin. "When can we go?"

"We will go after everything is packed in the big red moving van," said Chuck.

"Well, I've been packing for weeks," said Kevin's mother. "I feel like I've packed everything but the kitchen sink!" They all laughed and laughed. Kevin's mother found a special place for him to sit where he could see everything, but not be in the way.

Kevin watched as Chuck carried out the box filled with blankets and the box filled with pots and pans and the one filled with books and records.

"When can we go?" asked Kevin.

"We will go after everything is packed in the big red moving van."

Then Chuck carried out Kevin's bed. Suddenly Kevin did not want to go anymore. He wanted his bed in his old yellow room. Then Chuck carried out Kevin's toy box. Kevin wanted his toy box in his old yellow room. When Chuck carried out Kevin's bookshelves, Kevin asked in a little voice, "When can we go?"

Chuck smiled. "We'll go after everything is packed in the big red moving van."

"Everything?" asked Kevin.

"Everything," said Chuck.

Kevin climbed down from his special place. He went to the next door neighbors and got a bag full of garbage. He put the bag in his room.

"What's this?" asked Chuck. "I thought this room was empty. Well, we are not going until everything is packed into the big red moving van." And he carried the bag of garbage to the big red moving van.

Kevin ran to the back yard. He found the old bird's nest the birds had not used since last spring. He put the old bird's next in his room.

"What's this?" asked Chuck. "I thought this room was empty. Well, we are not going until everything is packed in the big red moving van." And he carried the old bird's nest to the big red moving van.

Kevin ran to the garden. He found a work glove there. He put the work glove in his room.

"What's this?" asked Chuck. "I thought this room was empty. Well, we are not going until everything is packed into the big red moving van." And he carried the work glove to the big red moving van.

Kevin ran to the kitchen. He pulled and pulled and pulled on the kitchen sink. That is where his mother found him. "Kevin, what are you doing?" she asked.

"We can't go until we pack the kitchen sink in the big red moving van. I don't want to move to the new house," said Kevin. "I want my bed and toy box and bookshelves in my old yellow room."

Just then Chuck came in. "I think we are finally all packed," he said. "Say Kevin, did I tell you that your new house has a swing set in the back yard and a porch to play on and little boy next door who is just your age?"

Kevin's mother smiled at him. "Your father and I are going to live in the new house in the new town with a new kitchen sink. Let's just leave this kitchen sink here and you come with us."

"All right," said Kevin.

And by the time Kevin had been on the swing set and played on the porch and met the new little boy next door who was just his age, Chuck had Kevin's bed and toy box and book-shelves all moved in to the new blue room.

And they looked just fine.

Scoop and Dump

(To the tune of "Skip to My Lou")

Scoop! goes ditch digger in the dirt (*Bend low, then raise arms high.*)
Scoop! goes ditch digger in the dirt
Scoop! goes ditch digger in the dirt
Scoop up all the dirt.

Reach up so high with the crane (*Cup hand, hold up high.*)
Reach up so high with the crane
Reach up so high with the crane
Hold the dirt up high

Dump the dirt into the truck (*Reach high, drop hand to knees.*)
Dump the dirt into the truck
Dump the dirt into the truck
Haul it all away

Good-bye! (*Wave.*)

Books for Tractors and Other Helpers

Aylesworth, Jim. **Siren in the Night.** Illustrated by Tom Centola. Albert Whitman, 1983.

On a quiet evening walk, a happy family is disturbed by the sirens of a fire truck. When the little boy cries and the dog barks, the parents reassure them that "fire fighters help people." Any young child who has been frightened by fire sirens should be similarly soothed by this book.

Barbaresi, Nina. **Firemouse.** Crown, 1987.

Mack the Mouse leaves his home in a body shop when it burns to the ground. He takes refuge at the fire station where he organizes a group of mice into a fire fighting squad. The fire house cat thinks the "Brooklyn Blazers" are absurd until they put out a fire at the fire station all on their own. Note that the names of the Blazers have special meaning for fire fighters: for example, "Halligan" is a metal tool for forcing open doors, "Spanner" is a wrench for tightening leaky hose couplings.

Barton, Byron. **Machines at Work.** Crowell, 1987.

What a busy day at the construction site! Lots of different work machines knock down one building and begin to construct another.

Baynton, Martin. **Fifty and the Great Race**. Crown, 1987.

Fifty the tractor must win the race at the annual fair or risk being scrapped for junk.

Bundt, Nancy. **The Fire Station Book**. Text by Jeff Linzer. Carolrhoda, 1981.

Clear photographs show all the action at a fire station, including a fire.

Burton, Virginia Lee. **Katy and the Big Snow**. Houghton Mifflin, 1943, 1971.

Katy, the tractor, had a bulldozer and a snowplow and was the pride of the highway department of Geoppolis. She isn't allowed to plow most snows because she is so strong, but when the big snow threatens to cripple the city, Katy plows the roads so the police, fire department, water department, doctors and postal workers can all keep the city functioning.

Burton, Virginia Lee. **Mike Mulligan and His Steam Shovel**. Houghton Mifflin, 1939, 1967.

This classic story of Mike Mulligan and Mary Anne, his beloved steam shovel, who dig the cellar of a town hall, continues to be a favorite read aloud. Burton's syncopated text perfectly captures the rhythms of the steam shovel racing to finish its work before the sun goes down.

Bushey, Jerry. **Building a Fire Truck**. Carolrhoda, 1981.

Photographs and text describe the process of making fire trucks, a custom built and painstaking operation.

DeWitt, Jamie. **Jamie's Turn**. Illustrated by Julie Brincklow. Raintree, 1984.

This true adventure written by a 12-year-old farm boy describes an accident with farm machinery when he and his stepdad are picking corn. In addition to the cornpickers, tractors and an ambulance are important vehicles in this story about care and concern.

Fast Rolling Fire Trucks. Illustrated by Carolyn Bracken. Grosset & Dunlap, 1986.

Wheels on the covers of this book add to the fun of the fire truck and its activities—pumping water, raising fire fighters in a snorkel truck and using foam to put out airport fires.

Gibbons, Gail. **Fire! Fire!** Crowell, 1984.

Bold illustrations depict fire fighters in the city, the country, in the forest, and on the waterfront.

Gibbons, Gail. **New Road!** Crowell, 1983.

Children will enjoy watching the planning and construction of a new road.

Greene, Grahame. **The Little Fire Engine**. Illustrated by Edward Ardizzone. Doubleday, 1973.

Replaced by modern equipment Sam Trolley, the fireman, wonders what will become of him, the little horse-drawn fire engine, and Toby, the fire horse.

Haddad, Helen. **Truck and Loader**. Illustrated by Donald Carrick. Greenwillow, 1982.

Truck and loader, working together, help to build roads, remove trees, and dam a pond for a swimming pool with a sandy beach.

Nichols, Paul. **Big Paul's School Bus**. Illustrated by William Marshall. Prentice Hall, 1981.

Paul, the school bus driver, is careful to follow all the rules and watch over his passengers in a day on the school bus.

Rayner, Mary. **Garth Pig and the Ice Cream Lady**. Atheneum, 1977.

When Garth Pig is sent to the ice cream truck to get treats for all the piglets, he is kidnapped by the wolf disguised as the ice cream lady and the other piglets must rescue him. And the ice cream!

Spier, Peter. **Fire House, Hook & Ladder Company Number Twenty-four**. Doubleday, 1981.

Heavy board book about exciting things that happen at a fire station including getting a cat out of a tree and putting out a fire.

Thompson, Graham. **Diggers and Loaders**. G. Stevens Publishing, 1986.

Large print text with brightly-colored illustrations for beginning readers identifies such work vehicles as bulldozers, cranes, and fork lifts.

Thompson, Graham. **Tractors**. G. Stevens Publishing, 1986.

Large print text for the beginning reader identifies and describes the functions of the following kinds of tractors: plow, disk harrow, seed planter, hay loader, crop sprayer, mower, baler, baler stacker combine, harvester, and snow plow.

Wilson, Rodger. **Where's the Fire?** Prentice Hall, 1976.

Children are introduced to all kinds of vehicles—bike, truck, car—as they follow an old-fashioned hook and ladder to a fire.

Related Activities for Tractors and Other Helpers

Cement Mixer Chant

Do the actions indicated in the first two lines. On the last two lines roll one hand over the other.

> Cement mixer comes (*Pretend to drive truck.*)
> Cement mixer comes
> With a rumble, rumble, rumble rub
> Rumble, rumble, rub.
>
> Shovel in the sand (*Pretend to shovel.*)
> Shovel in the sand
> With a rumble, rumble, rumble rub
> Rumble, rumble, rub.
>
> Add the cement (*Pretend to carry heavy bag.*)
> Add the cement
> With a rumble, rumble, rumble rub
> Rumble, rumble, rub.
>
> Mix water in (*Stir.*)
> Mix water in
> With a rumble, rumble, rumble rub
> Rumble, rumble, rub.
>
> Keep the mixer turning (*Roll hands one over other faster.*)
> Keep the mixer turning
> Keep the mixer turning
> Or concrete will get hard! (*Freeze in place.*)

Can't Be Too Clean
(A Flannel-board Story)

Prepare two-sided felt figures (dirty on one side) of the following: lawn chair, car, dog. Also prepare a dirty boy, a small pig, a middle-sized pig, and a big pig. Add these to the flannel board as indicated in the story.

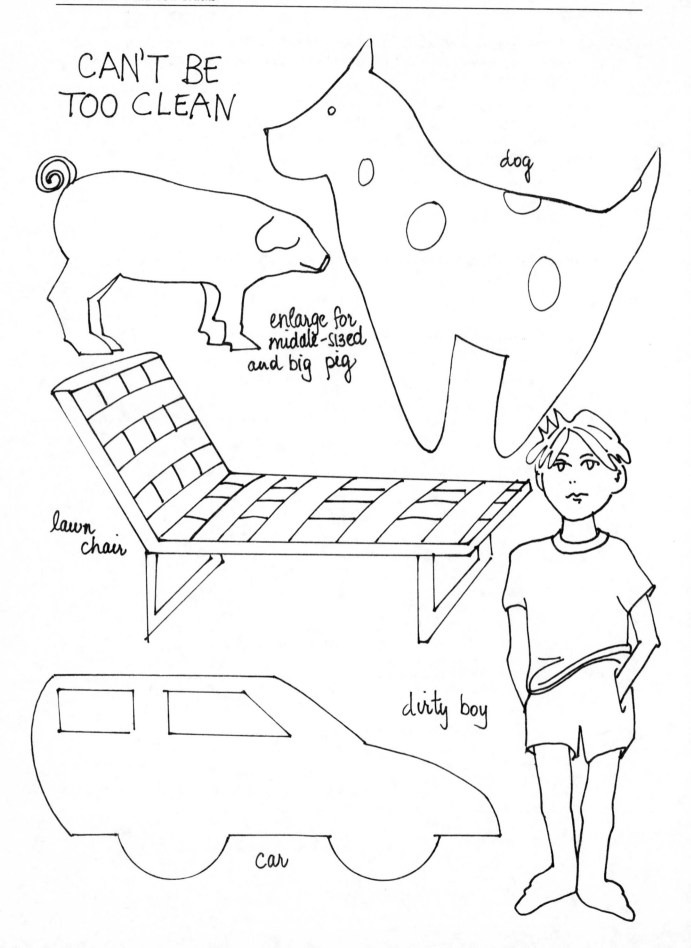

CAN'T BE
TOO CLEAN

dog

enlarge for
middle-sized
and big pig

lawn
chair

dirty boy

car

Sam liked his job. He drove a big white truck with two blue brushes. His job was to sweep the streets clean. After Sam finished, he looked back. "Clean and neat," said Sam. "Can't be too clean."

On Monday as Sam was running his big white truck with the two blue brushes, he saw a dirty lawn chair. Sam drove over to the dirty lawn chair and ran his brushes over it. When Sam finished, he looked back at the clean lawn chair and the clean street. "Clean and neat," said Sam. "Can't be too clean."

On Tuesday as Sam was running his big white truck with the two blue brushes, he saw a dirty car. Sam drove over to the dirty car and ran his brushes over it. When Sam finished, he looked back at the clean car and the clean lawn chair and the clean street. "Clean and neat," said Sam. "Can't be too clean."

On Wednesday as Sam was running his big white truck with the two blue brushes, he saw a dirty dog. Sam drove over to the dirty dog and ran his brushes over it. When Sam finished, he looked back at the clean dog and the clean car and the clean lawn chair and the clean street. "Clean and neat," said Sam. "Can't be too clean."

On Thursday as Sam was running his big white truck with the two blue brushes, he saw a dirty little boy. Sam drove over to the dirty little boy and tried to run his brushes over him. That was when the people in town decided there was such as thing as *too* clean. They met that night in town hall and finally decided the ones to help them were the three dirty pigs.

So on Friday as Sam was running his big white truck with the two blue brushes, he saw a very big dirty pig. Sam drove over to the big dirty pig and ran his brushes over it. When Sam finished, he looked back. But while Sam wasn't looking the clean big pig hid and the dirty middle-sized pig took his place. "Oh, no," said Sam. "There must be something wrong with the soap. It is not working. The pig is still dirty, but smaller. I have to get him clean. Can't be too clean."

Sam drove back over to the middle-sized dirty pig and ran his brushes over it. When Sam finished, he looked back. But while Sam wasn't looking the clean middle-sized pig hid and the dirty little pig took his place. "Oh, no," said Sam. "There must be something wrong with the soap. The pig is still dirty but smaller. I have to get him clean. Can't be too clean."

Sam drove back over to the little dirty pig and ran his brushes over it. When Sam finished, he looked back. But while Sam wasn't looking the clean little pig hid. "Oh, no," said Sam. "There must be something wrong with the soap. The little pig is gone. Maybe there is such a thing as being too clean. After this I'll only clean the streets."

And from then on that is just what he did.

Fast and Loud
(To the tune of "Are You Sleeping")

You may wish to divide the children into two groups and let one make quiet siren sounds while the other sings. Be sure to switch groups!

> Red lights flashing.
> Red lights flashing.
> Sirens blast.
> Sirens blast.
> Ambulance, police cars,
> Fire trucks in a hurry.
> Fast, fast, fast.
> Fast, fast, fast.

Fire Truck Song
(To the tune of "Farmer in the Dell")

Ding goes the bell (*Clap hands.*)
Ding goes the bell
Get set to fight the fire!
Ding goes the bell

Jump into your boots (*Jump.*)
Jump into your boots
Get set to fight the fire!
Jump into your boots

Zip your yellow coat (*Run thumb from belt to chin.*)
Zip your yellow coat
Get set to fight the fire!
Zip your yellow coat

Slide down the pole (*Reach high, then squat.*)
Slide down the pole
Get set to fight the fire!
Slide down the pole

Run to the truck (*Run in place.*)
Run to the truck
Get set to fight the fire!
Run to the truck

Drive to the fire (*Pretend to drive.*)
Drive to the fire
Get set to fight the fire!
Drive to the fire

(*Make loud siren noises.*)

Put Out the Fire
(To the tune of "Good Night Ladies")

Drive the fire truck (*Pretend to drive.*)
Drive the fire truck
Drive the fire truck
Let's all put out the fire.

Sound the siren (*Make siren noise.*)
Sound the siren
Sound the siren
Let's all put out the fire.

Squirt the hoses (*Pretend to hold hose.*)
Squirt the hoses
Squirt the hoses
Let's all put out the fire.

Climb the ladder (*One hand over the other as if climbing.*)
Climb the ladder
Climb the ladder
Let's all put out the fire.

Fire is all out (*Wipe forehead — Whew!*)
Fire is all out
Fire is all out
We'll all drive home again.

Drive the fire truck (*Sing softly, pretend to drive.*)
Drive the fire truck
Drive the fire truck
We'll all drive home again.

Farm Work
(To the tune of "The Farmer in the Dell")

The tractor plows the soil
The tractor plows the soil
It helps to grow the food we eat
The tractor plows the soil

The combine picks the beans
The combine picks the beans
It helps to grow the food we eat
The combine picks the beans

Three Tractors and Buba
(A Story with Props)

Hang pictures of three tractors around the necks of three children. On the fourth, place pig ears and nose. Have three pieces of rope to use as indicated in the story. Have all children make oinking sound when you mention the word "squealed."

THREE TRACTORS and BUBA

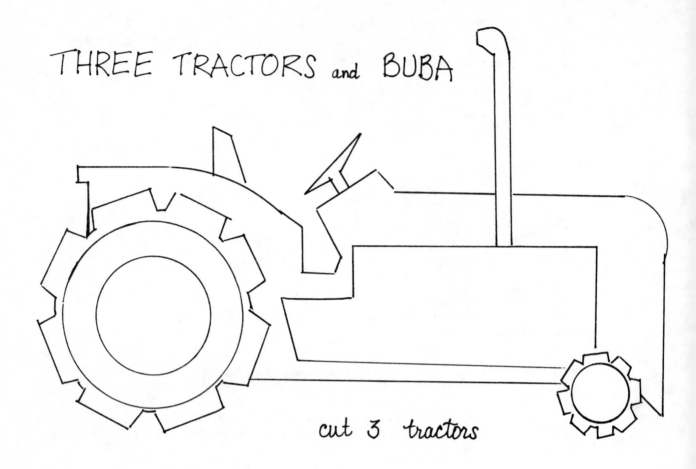

cut 3 tractors

half mask for BUBA

(*Line up three children with tractors.*)

Stan, Dan, and Fran were brothers who lived on a pig farm together in Iowa. Of all the farms in the area, the brothers always raised the biggest, fattest, loudest pigs. Everyone waited each year at the county fair to see what Stan, Dan, and Fran would show in the pig judging contest.

Well, this year the brothers had a big surprise. They had raised a bigger, fatter, louder pig than ever. They had named her Buba and were keeping her a big secret until time for the county fair. They built the biggest mud hole they could and hid their pig behind the barn. (*Have pig child enter and sit on floor.*)

The morning of the pig show, the brothers got up early and went to get Buba out of the mud hole. But big, fat, loud Buba had a surprise for the brothers. She was in no mood to go to a county fair, and she would not budge an inch no matter how they coaxed and begged and called her to come get in the truck. She just sat in the mud and squealed. (*Oink.*)

"All right," said Stan. "Buba, if you won't come out, I'll pull you out!" He hitched his tractor to a long rope and tied the other end around Buba. (*Hand one rope to pig and first tractor child.*) Then he pulled and he pulled and he pulled, but Buba just sat in the mud and squealed. (*Oink.*)

"All right," said Dan when he could see his brother needed help. "Buba, if you won't come out, I'll pull you out!" He hitched his tractor to a long rope and tied the other end around Stan's tractor whose rope was tied to Buba. (*Hand second rope to first and second tractors.*) Then they pulled and pulled and pulled, but Buba just sat in the mud and squealed. (*Oink.*)

"All right," said Fran when he saw both his brothers could not do it. "Buba, if you won't come out, I'll pull you out!" He hitched his tractor to a long rope and tied the other end around Dan's tractor whose rope was tied to Stan's tractor whose rope was tied to Buba. (*Hand rope to second and third tractors.*) Then they all pulled and pulled and pulled, but Buba just sat in the mud and squealed. (*Oink.*)

Now there was one more brother named Jeremy. The older brothers never paid too much attention to Jeremy because he never won prizes for big, fat, loud pigs. In fact Jeremy did not raise pigs at all. He raised bees and sold their honey at the county fair. When he heard all the squealing Buba was doing he came running and offered to help.

Well that made Stan and Dan and Fran laugh and laugh and laugh. Finally Stan wiped the tears from his eyes and said, "Now, Jeremy, how can you possibly get a pig out of the mud that three tractors could not?" He and the other brothers laughed some more. Buba sat in the mud and squealed. (*Oink.*)

But Jeremy knew a lot about bees. He picked an armful of the biggest, sweetest smelling honeysuckle he could find and threw them on Buba's head.

Now it was not long before the bees noticed the flowers on Buba's head and began to swarm around her ears and fly past her eyes to get the good nectar out of that honeysuckle. (*Wiggle fingers by head of pig child.*) Not many minutes after that Buba decided that going to the county fair was better than staying and being stung by bees. So she let out one last good squeal, shook off the flowers and walked right past those tractors into the pickup truck. (*Help pig child stand up.*)

Stan drove the truck while Dan and Fran washed Buba and tied her tail with a big red bow. Jeremy carried the basket of honey. They arrived just in time for the pig judging where, of course, Buba won first place. Jeremy's honey won first place, too, and they put both trophies in Jeremy's room.

Vendor Cart

Divide the children into groups representing the street vendors. Teach each group the two lines for that street vendor so they can chant back to you. You may wish to give each group an umbrella like the street vendors carry.

Street vendors calling
To come and to see
What does the vendor cart
Have there for me?

Hot dogs, hot dogs.
Come and buy a hot dog!

Street vendors calling
To come and to see
What does the vendor cart
Have there for me?

Pretzels, pretzels
Eat a nice warm pretzel.

Street vendors calling
To come and to see
What does the vendor cart
Have there for me?

Ices, ices.
Try some chocolate ice cream.

Street vendors calling
To come and to see
What does the vendor cart
Have there for me?

Puppies, puppies
Come and love a puppy.

Street vendors calling
To come and to see
The vendor with puppies
Is the one for ME!

Kids That Wiggle, Machines That Work

Start the action rhyme out slowly, getting faster with each verse until all the wiggles are out and the children are ready to listen.

Bulldozers push (*Push.*)
Cranes reach (*Reach high.*)
Tractors pull (*Pull.*)
Police cars screech (*Hands over ears.*)

GAMES FOR TRACTORS AND TOW TRUCKS

The Crane

Play this game like "London Bridge Is Falling Down." Sing the words to that tune and have the children walk under the crane. After two children have been caught, they may form another crane for the rest to walk under.

Lift the dirt up in a crane
In a crane, in a crane
Lift the dirt up in a crane
Dump into the dump truck. (*Drop hands to catch child.*)

Truck Talk Game

Expand children's knowledge of the kinds of trucks that help us in our daily lives by playing this game. It will be especially effective after you introduce *Trucks* by Gail Gibbons. First, recite the chant below, then ask children to name as many different kinds of trucks as they can. If you wish to direct the brainstorming, suggest categories of trucks such as "delivery trucks" or "emergency trucks." Try to get children to become fairly specific in this game. For example, delivery trucks might include bread trucks, refrigerated trucks, cattle trucks, armored trucks (delivering money), and bookmobiles.

Truck Talk Chant:

Some trucks push.
Some trucks pull.
Some trucks carry
A load brimful.
How many trucks
Can you name
In this truck talk
Listing game?

I Loaded My Moving Van

Play this variation of the traditional game "I unpacked my Grandmother's Trunk" by substituting the line "I loaded up my moving van and took along a (an)...." The leader names an article that begins with the letter A, then invites the next person in the group to add an object beginning with the letter B. Here are a few examples to get you going: armchair, basket, couch, dog.

Work Machine Workout

All kinds of machines help us get our work done. Suggest kinds of machines for kids to be. Some examples might be a street sweeper, a road grader, a tractor. Perhaps several kids can work together to become one machine. Then at a given signal—gong, alarm clock—the machines perform various actions such as "sweep," "lift," "tug," "pick up" or "push."

CRAFTS FOR TRACTORS AND TOW TRUCKS

Moveable Parts Trucks

Using the illustrations below of a tow truck and a dump truck, make vehicles form old file folders (or lightweight cardboard). The various parts of the trucks are connected with brad fasteners so the parts can move. Use this craft as a followup to the story "Terry and His Tow Truck" and the "Dump Truck Song."

(Text continues on page 130.)

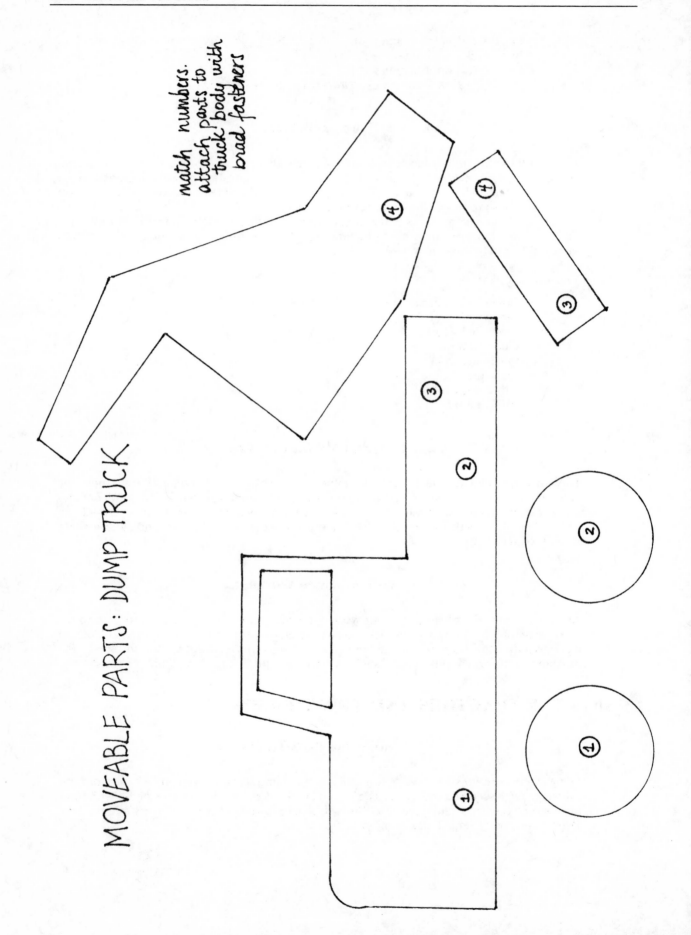

MOVEABLE PARTS: DUMP TRUCK

match numbers.
attach parts to
truck body with
brad fasteners

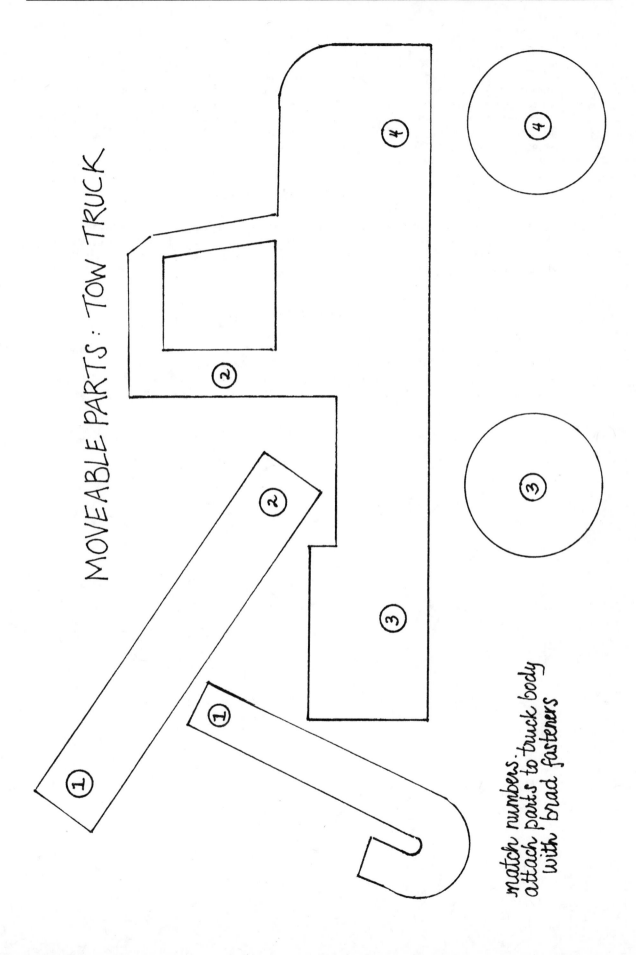

MOVEABLE PARTS : TOW TRUCK

match numbers.
attach parts to truck body
with brad fasteners

Fire Fighter Helmet

This kind of firefighter's equipment is so popular to make with young people that it is probably already part of your program, but don't forget to include it when you read fire truck stories and do the activities in this chapter. It is simple to make. Cut out a large oval from a sheet of red construction paper. Then cut out one-half of an oval as shown in the following illustration. Push this cut-out portion forward and place the hat on the head. A shield may be added for authenticity. (See illustration on next page.)

Garbage Truck Collage

Give each child an outline of a garbage truck, then provide different materials for them to glue on in a collage. Examples of materials might be egg shells, small seeds, bits of paper. Use this activity as a followup to the story "The Tale of the Too-Full Garbage Truck." (See illustration on page 132.)

On the Move Craft

Fold a piece of construction paper lengthwise and cut out the moving van according to the illustration below. Write the child's name on the side and stand it up as a place card. Children can cut out pictures from catalogs and magazines of items they would put in a moving van and paste them on the inside of the truck. (See illustration on page 133.)

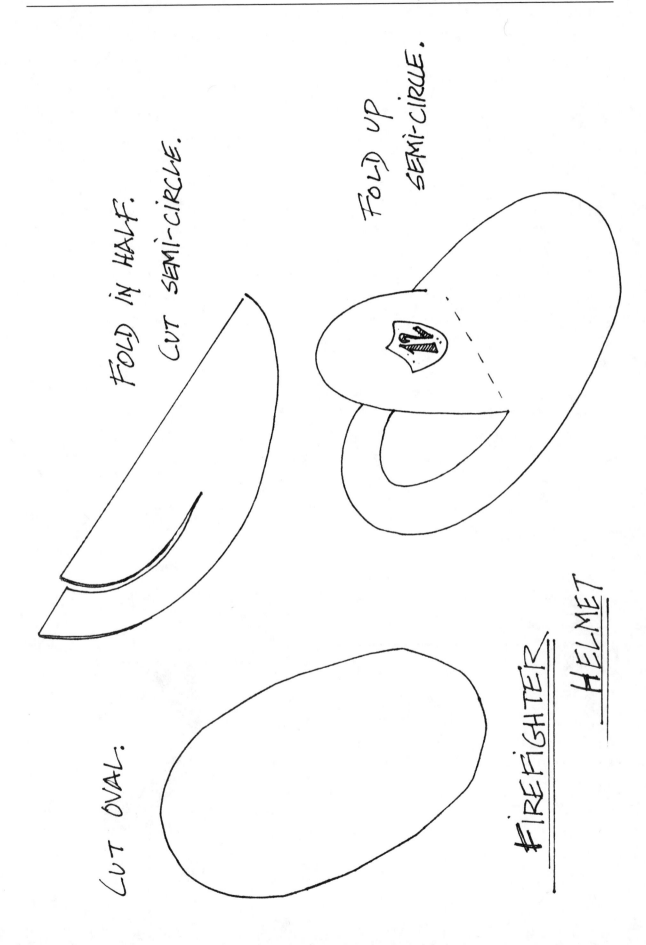

FOLD IN HALF.
CUT SEMI-CIRCLE.

FOLD UP
SEMI-CIRCLE.

CUT OVAL.

FIREFIGHTER
HELMET

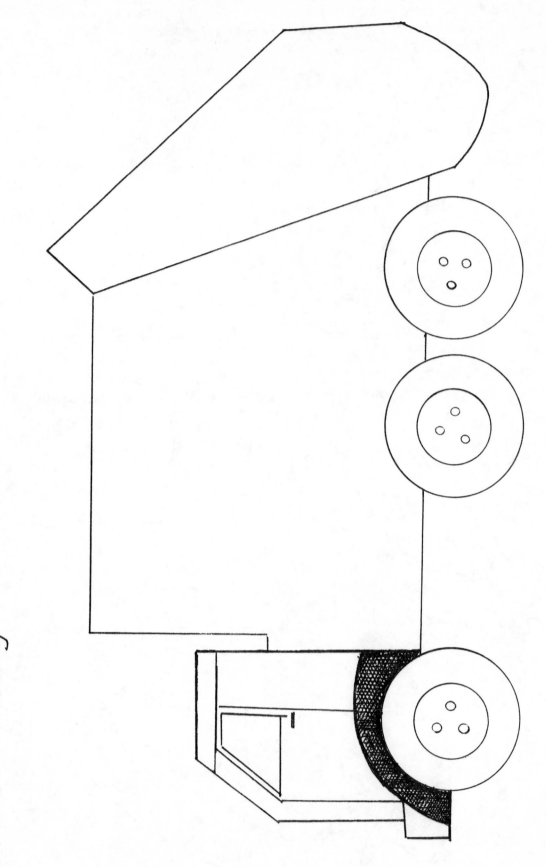

Garbage Truck
Collage

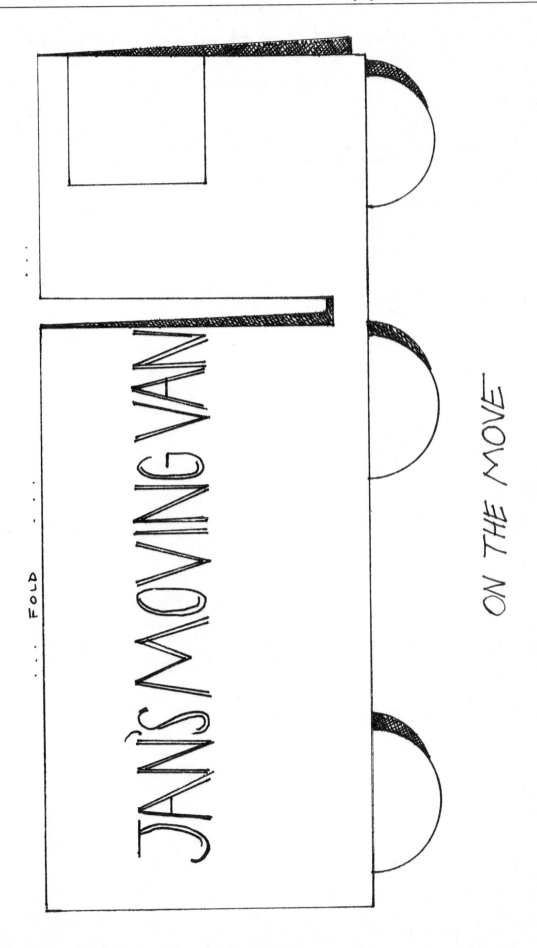

FOLD

JAN'S MOVING VAN

ON THE MOVE

TAKE-HOME ACTIVITY FOR TRACTORS AND TOW TRUCKS

Truck Talk Take-Home Game

Encourage families to look for different kinds of trucks that you have mentioned in your school or library. This game is a perfect activity for long car trips or for shorter journeys across town. Provide a starter list for members of the family to check off as they see the different kinds of trucks. Here are some examples:

Trucks for Building Up and Tearing Down

> Wrecking cranes
> Cement truck
> Steam roller
> Digger loader
> Bull dozer

Other categories could be "Trucks for Keeping Our Town Clean," "Trucks for Treats," and "Trucks with Sirens."

6

Up in the Air

INTRODUCTION

The ancient Greek myth of Icarus who tries his wings and Leonardo da Vinci's early flying machine remind us of our human aspiration to travel "up in the air." Some of these mythical and fantasy stories appear in chapters 7 and 8. Certainly, the bridge between fantasy and reality is not always a fixed place. This chapter, then, ranges from everyday airplane and helicopter transportation to the more incredible feats of space travel.

The first theme of the chapter covers airplane travel. Stories and activities begin on the ground with preparation for takeoff. Young children will know what to expect on their first flight after you read Jill Krementz's *Jamie Goes on an Airplane*, and many will identify with the little boy and his anxious bear in David McPhail's *First Flight*. Our stories extend the scope of these books by taking a humorous look at some potential frustrations—lost luggage, closed airports, and schedule delays—situations even children will become familiar with today.

The second theme includes hot air balloons and helicopters—modes of air transportation fewer children actually experience first hand, but the subject of such outstanding books as Wegen's *Balloon Trip* and Calhoun's *Hot-Air Henry*.

The third theme of space travel becomes the most fanciful part of this chapter. Russell Hoban's *They Came from Aargh* and Ezra Jack Keats' *Regards to the Man in the Moon*, show the ease with which children create their own space travel fantasies. "Willie's Space Ship" and "Out of This World Vacation" extend this wish fulfillment into your own setting with the next generation of astronauts.

INITIATING ACTIVITY

Welcome Aboard

As each child says his or her name, go around the room and pin wings to the children's shirts. You can use plastic pins from airlines or make your own version from cardboard. In any case, children will be ready to "take off" with you to enjoy the stories in this chapter about flight and air travel.

Leader: Welcome aboard
                Our big jet plane.
                Fasten your seat belt
                And tell me your name.

LITERATURE-SHARING EXPERIENCES

Books for Planes

Barton, Byron. **Airplanes**. Crowell, 1986.

Clear text and pictures describe all kinds of air craft.

Barton, Byron. **Airport**. Crowell, 1982.

Bright colors and sparse text describe how people come to airports and what preparations are made before the airplane lifts off.

Crews, Donald. **Flying**. Greenwillow, 1986.

An airplane takes off, flies and lands after passing over cities, countryside, and lakes.

Florian, Douglas. **Airplane Ride**. Crowell, 1984.

Sailing the skies across the United States, a pilot takes us on a series of loops and dives.

Garelick, May. **Runaway Plane**. Illustrated by Jozef Sumichrast. O'Hara, 1973.

A robbery is foiled when two little boys chase a toy airplane into a grocery store.

Gay, Michel. **Little Plane**. Macmillan, 1985.

A little book describes a little plane's adventures and antics.

Gramatky, Hardie. **Loopy**. Putnam, 1941.

A classic book about an animated little plane and his aerial excitement.

Keats, Ezra Jack. **The Trip**. Greenwillow, 1978.

Louie makes a diorama complete with an airplane. Then he pretends to fly the plane in the scene and gives rides to his friends.

Kremetz, Jill. **Jamie Goes on an Airplane**. Random House, 1986.

A big board book for toddlers and preschoolers who will enjoy a detailed account of taking an airplane trip. Such experiences as checking carry-on luggage through security and enjoying a meal on the plane are shown.

McPhail, David. **First Flight**. Little, Brown, 1987.

A little boy masters all the steps of an airplane flight by himself. His teddy bear seatmate has a less relaxed first trip!

Provensen, Alice, and Martin Provensen. **The Glorious Flight across the Channel with Louis Bleriot July 25, 1909**. Viking, 1983.

Fascinated by flying machines, Louis Bleriot finally invents a model that flies over the English Channel in thirty-seven minutes. It was a glorious flight!

Rockwell, Anne. **Planes**. Dutton, 1985.

Simple text and colorful pictures show many different kinds of air transportation.

Ross, Pat, and Joe Ross. **Your First Airplane Trip**. Lothrop, Lee and Shepard, 1981.

Line drawings and text explain the steps involved in taking an airplane trip. Such details as going through security, locating air vents and tray tables on the plane are explained so children will be prepared for their first airplane trip.

Snoopy's Facts and Fun Book about Planes. Random House, 1979.

> Charles Schultz's characters introduce planes, their construction and use.

Spier, Peter. **Bored—Nothing to Do!** Doubleday, 1978.

> Two bored boys construct their own airplane out of "Wheels, wood, seat, nails, glue, cloth, hinges, windshields, rope, and ... stuff" and it flies! Their frustrated parents later discover the TV and car won't work and the household gadgets seem to be missing essential parts. The angry (but obviously proud) parents send the boys to their rooms upon the plane's landing. The boys, once again, declare they are "bored" with "nothing to do!"

You Can Fly a Jet Plane. Illustrated by Carolyn Bracken. Western, 1983.

> A "drive away" board book places young readers at the controls of a jet plane. Various scenes from the runway to the mountain view are shown.

Young, Miriam. **If I Flew a Plane**. Illustrated by Robert Quackenbush. Lothrop, Lee and Shepard, 1970.

> A youngster dreams of adventures in the skies as an airplane pilot.

Related Activities for Planes

Going Flying
(To the tune of "Good Night Ladies")

This song will recall the experiences many young children have had in getting ready to take an airplane trip, and it will be a followup activity after you've read Barton's *Airport* or Krementz's *Jamie Goes on an Airplane*.

> Going flying,
> Going flying,
> Going flying,
> Let's pack up our bags.
>
> Here's the airport,
> Here's the airport,
> Here's the airport,
> Take me to my gate.
>
> Show your tickets,
> Boarding passes,
> Through the checkpoint,
> Now it's time to board.
>
> Take your places,
> By the window.
> Fasten seat belts—
> Now it's time to go!

The Great-Full-Service-with-Everything-You-Ever-Wanted Airport
(A Story to Generate Discussion)

Most of us have had at least one really awful airport experience these days. This story was inspired by such an experience we had so we decided to give you an opportunity to do a little brainstorming with your students or the children in your library about what the dream airport might be like. After you read or tell this story, encourage children to tell you what services and goods might be provided in an airport. This might be a creative writing experience you could do with the group or you could ask children to draw a picture of the dream airport.

Donkey Donkey was no dumb dumb. For a plain-looking animal, she had had a world of experience. She had sung on national television. She had met the Queen of England. And she had flown around the world on a concert tour. Donkey Donkey loved her work, but she was getting tired of traveling on airplanes because much of her time was spent on the ground, waiting in airports for the airplanes.

One night so much rain fell that the little planes and the big jets couldn't take off. Taxicabs and buses couldn't drive to the airport or take anyone into the hotels in the city because the roads were all flooded. Thousands were stranded in the world's busiest airport with no place to go and nothing to do for the night. People started to get angry. Not Donkey Donkey. Donkey Donkey was not a dumb animal.

First Donkey Donkey took over the loudspeaker. (The airport personnel were delighted to have somebody else take over.) Donkey Donkey asked the flight crews to take the blankets and pillows off the airplanes and take them all to Terminal One. Anyone who was sleepy could head to Terminal One. There was going to be a big slumber party! Any spare life preservers found on the planes were filled with rain water—some people even got waterbeds!

Then Donkey Donkey asked the flight attendants to take the peanuts and beverages down to the baggage claim area and serve them on the conveyor belts to anyone who wanted a little midnight snack.

And then Donkey Donkey herself went into Terminal Two to give a bluegrass and folk song concert to anyone who couldn't go to sleep in all the excitement.

By the next morning the rain had stopped enough for the planes to fly again. Grateful passengers cheered when Donkey Donkey got on her flight. But Donkey Donkey promised to come back one day to build a great-full-service-with-everything-you-ever-wanted-airport. As far as I know, she hasn't done it yet. But won't it be exciting when she does? No one will ever mind having to wait for an airplane in an airport again. What do you suppose the great-full-service-with-everything-you-ever-wanted-airport will be like?

Carry On

(A Flannel-board or Object Story)

Tell this story with flannel-board pictures for the various objects the animals carry on the plane, or bring in actual objects to show as they appear in the story. In either case, children should enjoy the exaggeration and ridiculous outcome that may not be too farfetched after all.

Flight 4-3-2-1 was a small plane. It had just room enough for four passengers but not much room for carry-on luggage.

Rabbit was the first passenger to board the plane. He was carrying a big shopping bag of baskets.

"What are you trying to carry on?" asked Penguin the Stewardess.

"Just a few things for Easter," said Rabbit. "I thought I'd save myself a few steps this year."

"Well, all right, but there is not much room. All carry-ons must fit under the seat," said Penguin.

So Rabbit shoved his shopping bag under the first seat of the airplane.

Walrus was the second passenger to board the plane. He was carrying a yard-long submarine sandwich.

"What are you trying to carry on?" asked Penguin.

"Just a little something to sink my teeth into," said Walrus. "I get so hungry on long flights."

"Well, all right, but there is not much room. All carry-ons must fit under the seat," said Penguin.

So Walrus stuffed his yard-long submarine sandwich under the second seat of the airplane.

Kangaroo was the next passenger to board the plane. He was carrying boxing gloves and training weights.

"What are you trying to carry on?" asked Penguin.

"Just a few little things to help me get ready for the heavyweight championship of the whole world," said Kangaroo.

"Well, all right, but there is not much room. All carryons must fit under the seat," said Penguin.

So Kangaroo pushed and shoved her boxing gloves under the third seat and she pushed and shoved her training weights under the fourth seat.

The last passenger to board the plane that day was Hippo. Now Hippo was very fat, but she was not carrying anything at all. Hippo was riding her exercise bike down the aisle of the plane.

"What are you trying to carry on?" asked Penguin the Stewardess.

"I am not trying to carry on anything at all!" said Hippo.

"Well, it's not all right. There is too much carrying on around here. Get that bicycle off of this plane. All carry-ons must fit under the seat," said Penguin.

"I could fit this under the seat," said Hippo, "if someone could make some room."

So Kangaroo picked up her training weights and boxing gloves and put them in her own pouch and made some room. Then Walrus pulled out his yard-long submarine sandwich and shared it with everyone so there was more room. And Rabbit took out his shopping bag and sent it on ahead by special delivery. Then Hippo was able to fit her exercise bike under the seats after all.

And then Flight 4-3-2-1 was ready for takeoff.

Take-Off Chant

Capture the excitement of an airplane takeoff with this hand-clapping chant. This would be a good followup activity after you've read *Airport* by Barton.

Warm up
Engines!
Propellers
Roll
Down the runway
Here we go!
Hold your ears
Makes you want
To give a cheer!
Faster
Faster
Up so high!
Don't you just
Love to fly?

In My Plane

(To the tune of "She'll Be Comin' 'Round the Mountain")

I'll be roarin' down the runway in my plane.
I'll be roarin' down the runway in my plane.
I'll be roarin' down the runway,
I'll be roarin' down the runway,
I'll be roarin' down the runway in my plane.

I'll be soaring above the clouds in my plane.
I'll be soaring above the clouds in my plane.
I'll be soaring above the clouds,
I'll be soaring above the clouds,
I'll be soaring above the clouds in my plane.

I'll be flying through rain and thunder in my plane.
I'll be flying through rain and thunder in my plane.
I'll be flying through rain and thunder,
I'll be flying through rain and thunder,
I'll be flying through rain and thunder in my plane.

I'll be landing at the airport in my plane.
I'll be landing at the airport in my plane.
I'll be landing at the airport,
I'll be landing at the airport,
I'll be landing at the airport in my plane.

Puddlestop Express Mess

(An Object Story with Masks)

Pack four suitcases with the different objects mentioned in the story and distribute them to four different children as you tell this story. Before you begin, give the children paper bag masks for the characters of Pig, Hippo, Opossum, and Lion.

PUDDLESTOP EXPRESS MESS

MS. HIPPO

PAPER BAG MASKS
cut out eyes
to fit child's face

MR. LION

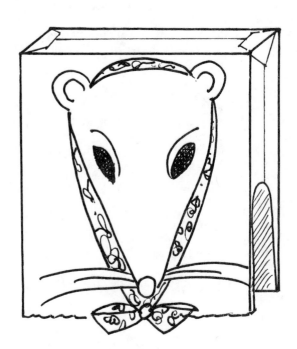

GRANDMA OPOSSUM

fit over
shoulder
→

MS. PIG

Puddlestop Express Airlines always ran late. Sometimes the planes didn't run at all. And, when they did get to where they were going, they often made mistakes. This is a story about one of those mistakes.

At the height of the tourist season when everyone wants to go on vacation by airplane, Puddlestop Express Airlines was running late. When the flight crew loaded up the baggage compartment of the last flight, somebody got the luggage tags all mixed up. But there was no time to straighten things out.

Puddlestop Express touched down at the first town on its route—Puddle Town. It let out Ms. Pig and left her luggage on the runway. (*Give first bag to Ms. Pig. This bag really belongs to Ms. Hippo.*)

The Puddlestop Express then made a hasty getaway and took off again. Before long it came to its next destination, the town of Downandout. There it let out Grandma Opossum and dumped her luggage out of the back of the plane, nearly hitting Grandma on the head. (*Give second bag to Grandma. This is really Mr. Lion's bag.*)

Next the Puddlestop Express took off for the sleepy little town of Shut Eye. It was just before dark when the plane landed. The stewardess hurried Ms. Hippo down the aisle and out the plane. The flight crew just remembered to find her luggage in the nick of time. (*Give third bag to Ms. Hippo. This is really Ms. Pig's bag.*)

At last Puddlestop Express reached its final destination—the famous town of Rut-in-the-Road. Mr. Lion picked up his luggage and started to descend from the aircraft when he noticed something was wrong. (*Give fourth bag to Mr. Lion. This is really Grandma's bag.*)

"This is NOT my luggage!" he shouted.

"Are you certain?" asked the stewardess. "Just open it up and take a look inside."

So Mr. Lion opened up the luggage and inside he found Grandma Opossum's pink nightgown and bed pillow.

"This is certainly not MY luggage!" repeated Mr. Lion.

"Oh dear!" sighed the stewardess. "I'm afraid we have a mess on the Puddlestop Express. We'll just have to backtrack to straighten things out."

So the Puddlestop Express took off again and headed back to Shut Eye. There was Ms. Hippo with a suitcase full of workout records and extra large sweat shirts.

"This is not MY luggage!" she shouted.

"Oh dear!" sighed the stewardess. "I guess we have a mess on the Puddlestop Express. We'll just have to backtrack again to straighten things out."

So the Puddlestop Express took off again. This time it landed at Downandout. There was Grandma Opossum with a bag full of movie magazines and videotapes of old movies.

"This is not MY luggage!" she shouted.

"It's MY luggage," shouted Mr. Lion.

"Good, now we're getting to the bottom of this," said the stewardess.

"But I still don't have my luggage!" shouted Ms. Hippo.

"Oh dear!" sighed the stewardess. "I guess we still have a mess on the Puddlestop Express. We'll just have to backtrack again to straighten things out."

So the Puddlestop Express took off again. Finally it landed at Puddle Town. There was Ms. Pig with a suitcase full of swimming suits and beach towels.

"This is not MY luggage!" shouted Ms. Pig.

"But it's MY luggage!" shouted Ms. Hippo.

Ms. Pig and Ms. Hippo exchanged bags. And Ms. Pig ended up with her workout records and extra large sweat shirts. Ms. Hippo got back her swimming suits and beach towels.

"Give me back MY luggage!" shouted Grandma Opossum. So Mr. Lion gave Grandma her bag with the pink nightgown and pillow. And Mr. Lion ended up with his bag of movie magazines and videotapes of old movies.

In the end everyone got back the right luggage, but they were so angry they never flew Puddlestop Express again. It was not worth the mess!

Wings on My Feet

(An Action Rhyme)

I've got wings!
　　(*Arms extended out.*)
I can fly!
　　(*Flap arms like wings.*)
Higher and higher
　　(*Arms over head.*)
Up in the sky.

Am I an eagle?
　　(*Flap arms up and down.*)
Am I a plane?
　　(*Hold arms level at shoulders.*)
A helicopter?
　　(*turn with arms above head.*)
Or a whooping crane?
　　(*Flap arms.*)

No! I'm me
　　(*Shake head.*)
I walk on the street
　　(*Walk in place.*)
But I can pretend
　　(*Point to self.*)
I've got wings on my feet!
　　(*Jump high.*)

I Made a Little Airplane

Just as soon as children are old enough to fold paper, they are eager to make paper airplanes to fly. Recite this little poem with the children, then pass out the paper for them to make airplanes so everyone will have one to fly when you say the poem together again.

> I made a little airplane
> To fly around my room
> It wasn't very fancy,
> But it sure could take off—Zoom!

Books for Helicopters and Balloons

Adams, Adrienne. **The Great Valentine's Day Balloon Race.** Scribners, 1980.

　　Rabbits Orson and Bonnie decorate a hot air balloon to enter the Valentine's Day Balloon Race and win the prize heart in the end.

Calhoun, Mary. **Hot-Air Henry.** Illustrated by Erick Ingraham. Morrow, 1981.

　　Henry, the Siamese Cat takes off in a hot air balloon and ends up maneuvering through a squadron of geese, scares off an eagle, and lands the craft to the admiration of the man and child who were preparing for their own flight.

Coerr, Eleanor. **The Big Balloon Race.** Illustrated by Carolyn Croll. Harper & Row, 1981.

　　Ariel at first is not happy to have a famous mother, but in the end helps her win the big hot air balloon race.

Douglass, Barbara. **The Great Town and Country Bicycle Balloon Chase**. Illustrated by Carol Newsom. Lothrop, Lee and Shepard, 1984.

Gina and her grandpa join the bicycle balloon chase—a race between a hot air balloon and bicycles. They take short cuts through the country on their bikes and almost win, but decide to chase the balloonists runaway parrot instead.

Gay, Michel. **Little Helicopter**. Macmillan, 1986.

Little Helicopter isn't big enough to help during large disasters, but he is just the right size to hear a small drowning kitten. After the rescue, they enjoy a merry-go-round ride.

Hughes, Shirley. **Up and Up**. Lothrop, Lee and Shepard, 1979.

After many tries, a little girl succeeds in flying with a handful of balloons.

Johnson, Crockett. **Harold's Trip to the Sky**. Harper & Row, 1957.

Harold travels to the sky with the help of his purple crayon.

Lamorisse, Albert. **The Red Balloon**. Doubleday, 1956.

A young boy finds a red balloon with a mind of its own floating across the skies of Paris.

Patience, John. **Brock the Balloonist**. Derrydale, 1983.

In this Fern Hollow tale, Brock Gruffy the Badger sets off in a hot air balloon only to cause havoc around the village. But when he is imprisoned for damages, Monty and Spud, two mischievous mice, take the balloon and find a fortune in gold to pay off all the debts.

Quin-Harkin, Janet. **Benjamin's Balloon**. Illustrated by Robert Censoni. Parents, 1978.

A runaway balloon with Benjamin on board has high flying adventures.

Wegen, Ron. **Balloon Trip**. Clarion, 1981.

In this wordless picture book, large illustrations tell the story of a boy and girl climbing aboard a hot air balloon with their father to travel from the countryside, across New York Bay to get a bird's-eye view of the Statue of Liberty and the Empire State Building. As they move out into the country, storm clouds form and they descend safely.

Wildsmith, Brian. **Bear's Adventure**. Pantheon, 1981.

When two men land their hot air balloon in the mountains Bear climbs inside, falls asleep, and wakes to find himself floating off in a "forest" of skyscrapers. The balloon is punctured and Bear joins a costume parade, is interviewed on television, and given a ride on a helicopter before he is given another ride in a hot air balloon by the first two balloonists.

Willard, Nancy. **The Well-Mannered Balloon**. Illustrated by Haig Shekerjian and Regina Shekerjian. Harcourt Brace Jovanovich, 1976.

What do you do when your normally well-mannered balloon suddenly begins to eat everything in sight? That is the problem James faces in the middle of the night.

Related Activities for Helicopters and Balloons

Uplifting Experience
(An Action Rhyme)

I know a way you sit on the ground,
    (*Squat on ground.*)
Then rise to the sky with a zzzzzip.
    (*Stand, saying "zzzzzip."*)
You can ride in the basket of a hot air balloon,
    (*Touch fingertips over head.*)
Or go on a helicopter trip.
    (*Cross wrists overhead, wave hands.*)

Whirlybird to the Rescue
(A Participatory Story)

Select six children to help you tell this story. Four children stand in front of the group to become a traffic jam, a forest of trees, and the driveway. Have these children hold their arms as the directions indicate. One child is Barney Beagle. You may wish to make a mask for this character. The other child is Whirlybird the Helicopter. For an added touch, give this child a beanie with a propeller or a pinwheel to hold. Teach all children the Whirlybird call.

WHIRLYBIRD TO THE RESCUE!

BARNEY BEAGLE

paper plate mask

It was a busy time in Metropolis. The police department, the fire department and the hospital staff were working day and night to keep people safe and sound. They were doing their best, but sometimes that just wasn't enough. Sometimes they had to call on Whirlybird the Helicopter. Whirlybird always came to the rescue.

At 7:45 A.M. the traffic jammed up at the intersection of First Street and Main Street. The police couldn't get through the line of cars and buses and trucks and vans to help. (*Have line of children criss-cross their hands in front of them so they form an overlapping line of traffic jam.*) So the police called, "Whirlybird! Whirlybird! We're in a fix! Whirlybird! Whirlybird! Please come quick!" And Whirlybird flew up in the air, and came straight down in that traffic jam. (*Move Whirlybird child through line.*) Whirlybird got that traffic jam unstuck so the cars and trucks and buses and vans could go on their way. Whirlybird came to the rescue!

At noon a fire began to roar out of control in the city park. The fire department couldn't get their hoses through the trees to put out the fire. (*Have line of children raise their arms above their heads.*) So the fire department called, "Whirlybird! Whirlybird! We're in a fix! Whirlybird! Whirlybird! Please come quick!" And Whirlybird flew up in the air and with its skyhooks it laid down firehoses in the forest of trees. (*Move Whirlybird child through the line.*) Whirlybird put out the fire in the city park. Whirlybird came to the rescue!

At 8:00 P.M. Barney Beagle swallowed a whole skein of Mrs. Brown's knitting yarn. Mrs. Brown called the hospital. But the hospital ambulance was gone. So the hospital staff called, "Whirlybird! Whirlybird! We're in a fix! Whirlybird! Whirlybird! Please come quick!" Whirlybird flew up in the air and landed right down on the Brown's driveway. (*Have line of children hold hands as if forming a driveway. Move Barney child down the line to the end.*) Then Whirlybird took Barney to the hospital where the doctors operated on him. Before long Barney recovered just because of Whirlybird's quick work. Whirlybird always came to the rescue!

Final chant:

> Whirlybird! Whirlybird! You come quick!
> Whirlybird! Whirlybird! You are slick!

Helicopter Song
(To the tune of "I'm a Little Tea Pot")

As you sing, the children may move in a circle, crossing wrists overhead and waving hands like helicopter blades.

> In my helicopter I can rise
> Off the ground, straight to the skies.
> I can see the people far below.
> Spin my blades and up I go.

Balloon to Zanzibar
(A Flannel-board Story)

Make circles for the balloons of red, blue, yellow, green, purple and pink. Place them on the board as indicated in the story.

Stevie's mother called, "The library is having a balloon launch. Do you want to go?"
"Sure," said Stevie. "What is a balloon launch?"
Stevie's mother explained. "Everyone gets a balloon. We all write our names on cards and tie the cards onto the balloon strings. Then we let the balloons go up into the sky. The balloons may land nearby or go far away. If a card is found it is sent back to the library. We can see whose went the farthest."

"Mine will go farthest," said Stevie. "Up and up and up! My card is going all the way to ..." he stopped to think what place was far away his older sister had mentioned. "... to Zanzibar!"

When Stevie got to the library, the other boys and girls were each holding a card ready to tie onto a balloon. Stevie got a red balloon. All the other boys and girls got balloons. Even the babies and the mothers got balloons. Everyone went outside to send the balloons up into the sky. Everyone but Stevie.

Stevie noticed there was an extra blue balloon. A blue balloon no one wanted to send up in the sky. So Stevie tied a red and a blue balloon onto his card. "Up and up and up. All the way to Zanzibar!" said Stevie.

Stevie noticed there was an extra yellow balloon. A yellow balloon no one wanted to send up in the sky. So Stevie tied a red and a blue and a yellow balloon onto his card. "Up and up and up. All the way to Zanzibar!" said Stevie.

Stevie noticed there was an extra green balloon. A green balloon no one wanted to send up in the sky. So Stevie tied a red and a blue and a yellow and a green balloon onto his card. "Up and up and up. All the way to Zanzibar!" said Stevie.

Stevie noticed there was an extra purple balloon. A purple balloon no one wanted to send up in the sky. So Stevie tied a red and a blue and a yellow and a green and a purple balloon onto his card. "Up and up and up. All the way to Zanzibar!" said Stevie.

Stevie noticed there was an extra pink balloon. A pink balloon no one wanted to send up in the sky. So Stevie tied a red and a blue and a yellow and a green and a purple and a pink balloon onto his card. "Up and up and up. All the way to Zanzibar!" said Stevie.

Stevie started out the door with all those balloons, but before he could let them go, the button on his sweater got caught in all those strings, and Stevie launched a red and a blue and a yellow and a green and a purple and a pink balloon—and himself—into the air. "Up and up and up. All the way to Zanzibar!" said Stevie.

"Call the police!" cried one of the fathers. "He might fall into traffic!"

"Call the airport!" cried the librarian. "Low flying balloons coming! Boy attached!"

"Call Grandma!" cried Stevie's mother. "Stevie is going to land in her yard!"

And that is just what happened. The balloons let Stevie down with a gentle "thump" in his grandma's yard—right across the street from the library.

"My card didn't go very far, Grandma, did it?" asked Stevie. "My card didn't go to Zanzibar."

"How about this instead?" asked Grandma. She gave him two warm peanut butter cookies and a big hug.

And Stevie decided that was better than all the balloons in Zanzibar.

The Only Way to Fly
(To the tune of "Yankee Doodle")

In my dreams I like to soar
High in my balloon,
Gliding, coasting in the sky,
And sailing toward the moon
Nibbling on a bit of cloud,
Polishing the stars,
In my pretty dream balloon
I'm on my way to Mars!

Books for Rockets

Asch, Frank. **Mooncake.** Prentice Hall, 1983.
    When Bear wants to taste the moon, he builds a rocket to get there.

Hoban, Russell. **The Flight of Bembel Rudzuk.** Illustrated by Colin McNaughton. Philomel Books, 1982.
    Bembel Rudzuk, a wizard, bothers the princess with his strange creature, the squidgerino squelcher.

Hoban, Russell. **They Came from Aargh**. Illustrated by Colin McNaughton. Philomel Books, 1981.

Three children dressed as outer space aliens in funnel hats and packing box space suits blast off in their homemade spaceship (constructed of chairs, vacuum cleaner hoses, and bicycle tires) to enjoy mummosaurs' lunch on the planet Earth before roaring back to Aargh. McNaughton's illustrations capture the whimsy in Hoban's text of children playing at space travel in their own home.

Keats, Ezra Jack. **Regards to the Man in the Moon**. Four Winds, 1981.

Louie uses some junk scraps and his imagination to take his friends on a trip through space.

Minarik, Else. **Little Bear**. Illustrated by Maurice Sendak. Harper, 1957.

One of Little Bear's easy-to-read adventures takes him on a trip to the moon, but back in time for lunch.

Moncure, Jane. **Skip Aboard a Space Ship**. Illustrated by Helen Endres. Child's World, 1978.

Skip and Eric spend the night in a tree house that becomes a spaceship for their imaginative flight to the moon.

Sadler, Marilyn. **Alistair in Outer Space**. Illustrated by Roger Ballen. Prentice Hall, 1984.

One day when Alistair is returning his library books, a spaceship picks him up and whisks him off in outer space. Alistair is more concerned with getting his books back than in having an adventure.

Ungerer, Tomi. **Moon Man**. Harper & Row, 1967.

Bored with his life, Moon Man catches the tail of a comet to make a crash landing to earth. He is imprisoned as an invader, but starts to fade and disappear. When he is in his first quarter again, he reappears in the outside world. He briefly enjoys himself, but discovers life is too risky on earth, so he boards a test rocket (resting on a castle turret launching pad) to return to space.

Yolen, Jane. **Commander Toad and the Big Black Hole**. Illustrated by Bruce Degen. Coward, McCann, 1983.

When a Black Hole threatens the spaceship Star Warts, Commander Toad must save the ship and crew.

Yolen, Jane. **Commander Toad and the Dis-asteroid**. Illustrated by Bruce Degen. Coward, McCann, 1985.

A strange call for help from a flooded asteroid brings Commander Toad and the crew of the Star Warts to the rescue.

Yolen, Jane. **Commander Toad and the Intergalactic Spy**. Illustrated by Bruce Degen. Coward, McCann, 1986.

Commander Toad and his Star Warts crew travel to the planet Eden to discover Cousin Tip Toad, an Intergalactic Spy among spies on a spy convention.

Yolen, Jane. **Commander Toad and the Planet of Grapes**. Illustrated by Bruce Degen. Coward, McCann, 1982.

Commander Toad and his crew fly the Star Warts through "deep hopper" space to find new worlds when they discover the Planet of Grapes.

Related Activities for Rockets

Blast Off
(A Participatory Story)

Have children repeat each line after leader. Set an even rhythm by tapping knees.

Ready?
We're going on a moon walk.
We are all set to go!
Climb up to the spaceship.
Count backwards:
10-9-8-7
WAIT!
Have you got your moon gloves?
Here—put them on.
Ready?
We're going on a moon walk.
We are all set to go!
Count backwards:
10-9-8-7-6-5
WAIT!
Have you zipped your space suit?
Altogether—ZIP.
Ready?
We're going on a moon walk.
We are all set to go!
Count backwards:
10-9-8-7-6-5-4
WAIT!
Have you got on your moon boots?
Here—put them on.
Left.
Right.
Ready?
We're going on a moon walk.
We are all set to go!
Count backwards:
10-9-8-7-6-5-4-3-2
WAIT!
Have you got your helmet?
Here—put it on.
NOW we are ready!
Count backwards:
10-9-8-7-6-5-4-3-2-1-0
BLAST OFF!

Star Ship Crew Song
(To the tune of "Old MacDonald")

"Old MacDonald" has always been a favorite add-on song, so this spacecraft version should have an immediate appeal. In this case, the add-ons are the names of the children in your group. Everyone gets to join the crew of the Star Ship in this jolly sing-a-long. Be sure to clap when the song dictates so each child will feel especially welcomed to the crew. The last two lines are sung after everyone has been added to the song.

> Captain Starquest had a ship.
> Star ship was its name.
> And on that ship
> He had a mate.
> (Amy) was her name. (*Sing name of first child.*)
> With a clap-clap here!
> And a clap-clap there!
> Here a clap, there a clap,
> Everywhere a clap-clap!
> Captain Starquest had a ship.
> Star Ship was its name.

(Repeat as you add other children, then, when you are finished with last child, sing these last two lines:)

> Welcome to the Star Ship crew!
> You and you and you!
> Yahoo!! (*spoken*)

Space Shot
(An Action Rhyme)

This is an adaptation of a fingerplay in *Starquest*, edited by Robin Currie for the State Library of Iowa in 1983. Substitute the name of each child in your group. It is so short that it could be repeated many times for a warm up activity.

Johnny looked at the moon.	(*Circle arms over head*)
Johnny looked at the stars.	(*Wiggle fingers*)
He jumped in a rocket,	(*Palms together, waist high*)
And set off for Mars!	(*Palms together, quick over head*)

Willie's Space Ship
(A Flannel-board Story)

To tell this story, prepare the following shapes: a brown felt rectangle for the refrigerator carton, a foil-covered rectangle, a foil covered disc with a center hole cut out for the hub cap, a coil shape for the telephone cord, a digital clock face, a triangle for the megaphone. Place these figures on the board as they are mentioned in the story. Then find a slide whistle to blow at the end of the story when the spaceship takes off.

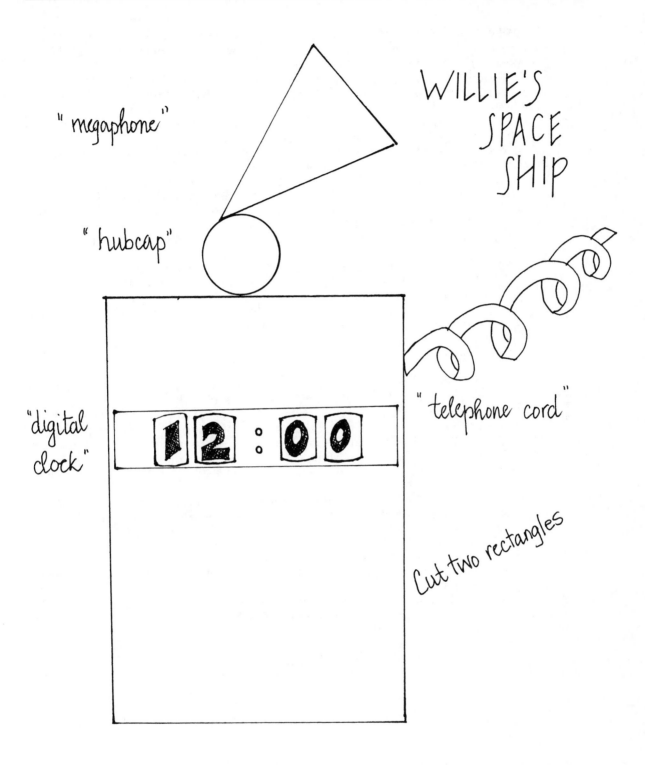

"megaphone"

WILLIE'S
SPACE
SHIP

"hubcap"

"digital
clock"

"telephone cord"

Cut two rectangles

Willie wanted a spaceship of his very own. Not a small plastic model of a spaceship. But a spaceship big enough to climb inside. A spaceship that was shiny with lots of thing-a-ma-bobs. A spaceship that would go whoooosh!

Willie told his dad, "I want a spaceship of my own. A spaceship big enough to climb inside. A spaceship that is shiny with lots of thing-a-ma-bobs. A spaceship that will go whooooosh!"

"Well," said his dad. "I don't know about all that, but I do know something that is big enough to climb inside."

Dad gave Willie a big refrigerator carton. Willie climbed inside the carton. But it wasn't shiny. It did not have lots of thing-a-ma-bobs. And it didn't go whooooooosh!

"I have something to help make spaceships to...." said Willie's little brother, Sam.

"Oh, no you don't," said Willie. "You don't know anything about spaceships."

Willie told his mom, "I want a spaceship of my own. A spaceship that is shiny with lots of thing-a-ma-bobs. A spaceship that will go whooooosh!"

"Well," said his mom. "I don't know about all that, but I do know something that is shiny."

Mom gave Willie a roll of aluminum foil. (*Put silver rectangle over plain one.*) Now it was shiny. But it did not have lots of thing-a-ma-bobs. And it didn't go whooooooosh!

"I have something to help make spaceships to...." said Willie's little brother, Sam.

"Oh, no you don't," said Willie. "You don't know anything about spaceships."

Willie told his big brother, "I want a spaceship of my own. A spaceship with lots of thing-a-ma-bobs. A spaceship that will go whooooosh!"

"Well," said his big brother. "I don't know about all that, but I do have one thing-a-ma-bob."

His big brother gave Willie a hubcap. (*Put shiny disc on top of the rectangle.*) A hubcap was one thing-a-ma-bob. Not lots. And it didn't go whooooooosh!

"I have something to help make spaceships to...." said Willie's little brother, Sam.

"Oh, no you don't," said Willie. "You don't know anything about spaceships."

Willie told his big sister, "I want a spaceship of my own. A spaceship with lots of thing-a-ma-bobs. A spaceship that will go whooooosh!"

"Well," said his big sister. "I don't know about all that, but I do have these things. Maybe they will help."

His big sister gave Willie an old telephone cord, an old digital clock, and a cheerleader's megaphone. Willie put all these on his spaceship. Now Willie's spaceship was big and shiny and had lots of thing-a-ma-bobs. But it still didn't go whooooooosh!

"I have something to help make spaceships to...." said Willie's little brother, Sam.

"O.K., Sam," said Willie. "What do you have to help?"

"I have something to help make spaceships go whoooosh!" said Sam. And he pulled out his supersonic slide whistle.

So Willie and Sam climbed inside the shiny spaceship with all the thing-a-ma-bobs. And they took off together—whoooooosh! (*Blow slide whistle.*)

Ten Little Spaceships
(To the tune of "Ten Little Indians")

Robin Currie did the original version of this as a fingerplay for the State Library of Iowa's 1983 summer programming manual, *Starquest*. We're redone it for this chapter and added the musical part.

One little, two little
Three little spaceships;
Four little, five little,
Six little spaceships,
Seven little, eight little,
Nine little spaceships,
Ten little spaceships go.

(*Hold up 1 finger for each ship.*)

(*Spoken:*)
Countdown? Ready?
10-9-8-7-6-5-4-3-2-1-0   (*Everyone crouches down lower and lower during the count*)

BLAST OFF!   (*Jump up, thrust arms above head*)

Out of This World Vacation
(A Participatory Story)

Teach children the chant in this story and suggest actions for the different compass directions (for example, wiggle fingers to suggest the snowstorm in the North; undulate hand to suggest a heat wave in the South; cross arms in front of chest to suggest the traffic jams in the East and West). Another action might be a motion with your hands similar to the way a stewardess indicates positions of exit signs over wings of the plane. Ask children if they have seen a stewardess do this. Now children will be ready to join into the storytelling as you tell the story.

Goosey Goosey Gander loved to travel. She especially liked to fly to the far corners of the world. So she bought a ticket on Orbit Airlines to fly all around the world on her vacation. Orbit Airlines had a snazzy motto. It went like this:

North, South
East, West
Take Orbit Airlines—
We're the best!

Goosey arrived at the airport, boarded the Early Bird Special plane and took off before dawn. The plane headed North.

North, South
East, West
Take Orbit Airlines—
We're the best!

Just as the Early Bird approached the far North, a terrible snowstorm began. All the airports closed down so the Early Bird Special flew on to the South.

North, South
East, West
Take Orbit Airlines—
We're the best!

But, just as the Early Bird approached the South, a terrible heat wave began. It was so hot that all airports in the South shut down. The Early Bird Special flew on to the East.

North, South
East, West
Take Orbit Airlines—
We're the best!

When the Early Bird approached the East, the pilot saw a terrible traffic jam. So many planes were circling the airports that he didn't even try to land. Well, there was just one direction left for the Early Bird to go and that was West. So the Early Bird headed West to get away from it all.

North, South
East, West
Take Orbit Airlines—
We're the best!

Now, when the Early Bird approached the West it was so busy with other planes trying to get away from it all that the pilot called back to the passengers to say there was just no place left to go. Orbit Airlines had gone North, South, East, and West all right, but no place was a good place to land for vacation that year.

"But this is my vacation," said Goosey Gander. "I always go somewhere on my vacation. Let's just keep on going...."

"But, Madame," said the pilot, "there's no place left in the world to go!"

"Well," said Goosey Gander. "Orbit Airlines is the best. I'm sure you can do something."

"All right. I'll do my best!" said the pilot.

So the pilot radioed to the control tower. Then the pilot pressed a big silver button on the control panel. The wings of the Early Bird closed up, right up to the body of the aircraft.

Then the pilot pressed another button—a big red button—in the middle of the control panel. And the Early Bird swerved around until it was straight up. The Early Bird became a supersonic rocketship shooting into outer space. So Goosey Goosey Gander got to go on her vacation after all. It was a trip out of this world!

The Way to Go Home
(A Circle Story)

Cut two circles from posterboard. Cut a wedge from one and opposite the wedge draw or paste a picture of a rocketship. On the other circle draw or paste pictures of a planet with rings, star, moon, space creature, and another rocketship. Make sure these pictures will show through the wedge cut. Place the circle with the wedge on top of the one with the pictures and put a brad through the center of both circles. As you tell the story, turn the circles so the appropriate picture shows through the opening.

(Text continues on page 157.)

THE WAY TO GO HOME

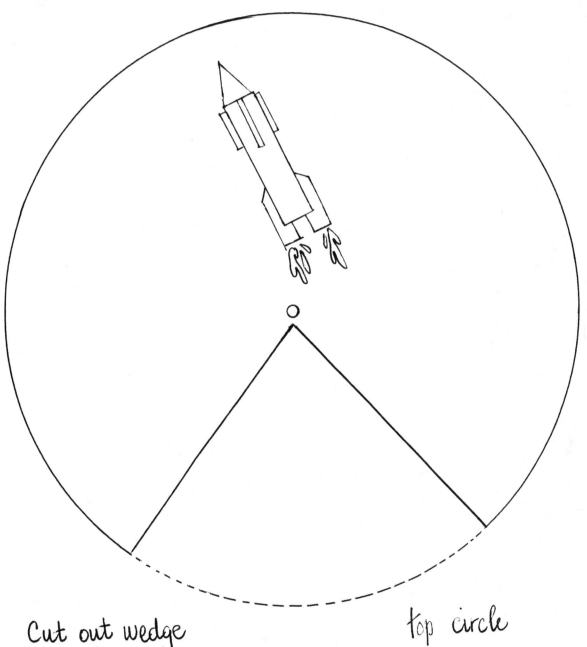

Cut out wedge

top circle
attach to bottom circle at center
with brad

THE WAY TO GO HOME

bottom
circle

It had been a twenty-five year journey for the Starship Wayward, but at last the crew's exploring was over and they were ready to go home. Captain Wrongway studied the maps and the star charts and set the course, but he could not figure out how to get home.

Luckily they saw a planet and stopped to ask directions. "We are lost," said Captain Wrongway. "Can you show us the way to go home?"

"Certainly," said the planet. "I know I am home when I see rings. If you just fly in circles, you will be home in no time." (*Have children make large circles with arms*.)

So Captain Wrongway and the Starship Wayward spent another two years flying in circles, (*stop actions*) but they still did not get home.

Luckily they saw a star and stopped to ask directions. "We are lost," said Captain Wrongway. "Can you show us the way to go home?"

"Certainly," said the star. "I know I am home when I see twinkling lights. If you just blink your lights on and off, you will be home in no time." (*Have children blink eyes*.)

So Captain Wrongway and the Starship Wayward spent another two years blinking the lights on and off, (*stop actions*) but they still did not get home.

Luckily they saw a moon and stopped to ask directions. "We are lost," said Captain Wrongway. "Can you show us the way to go home?"

"Certainly," said the moon. "I know I am home when I hear a humming sound from the lunar oceans. If you just make a humming sound, you will be home in no time." (*Have children hum*.)

So Captain Wrongway and the Starship Wayward spent another two years making a humming sound, (*stop noise*) but they still did not get home.

Luckily they saw a space creature and stopped to ask directions. "We are lost," said Captain Wrongway. "Can you show us the way to go home?"

"Certainly," said the space creature. "I know I am home when my antenna beep. If you just beep your antenna, you will be home in no time." (*Have children put fingers to top of heads and beep*.)

So Captain Wrongway and the Starship Wayward spent another two years beeping the antenna, (*stop action*) but they still did not get home.

Captain Wrongway had just about given up ever seeing home again, when they saw another spaceship and stopped to ask directions. "We are lost," said Captain Wrongway. "Can you show us the way to go home?"

"Certainly," said the other spaceship. "I know I am home when I am back where I started from. Put your engines in reverse and you will be home in no time."

So Captain Wrongway put the engines of the Starship Wayward in reverse and traveled back past the space creature with the beeping antenna (*Show space creature, have children repeat beeping action*), past the moon with the humming oceans (*Show moon, have children hum*), past the star with the twinkling lights (*Show star, have children blink eyes*), past the planet with the circling rings (*Show planet, have children make large circles with arms*). Then Captain Wrongway kept on flying backwards and in no time, the Starship Wayward was back home.

GAMES FOR UP IN THE AIR

Rocket, Rocket, Blast Off

Play this game by seating the children in a circle. One child is the astronaut and walks around the outside touching children's heads and saying:

Rocket, Rocket, Rocket,
Blast off!

When he says "blast off," the child touched chases him around the circle. The first one to "splash down" in the empty space becomes the astronaut and the game continues.

Great Galaxies

Use the book *They Came from Aargh* by Russell Hoban (p. 148) to stimulate a creative dramatics experience. Gather a box of accessories such as strange hats and kitchen items. Each child chooses space gear from this box. Move as a group from one part of the room to the next as if exploring planets. It is fun to hang a posterboard in each area with a planet or a funny space creature on it. At each stop, help the children name the planet, tell one thing they eat there, one thing they wear there, and how they move. (Challenge older children to have all these items begin with the same letter of the alphabet. For example, if the planet is Saturn, they will eat squash, wear sun glasses, and slither from place to place.) Use the movement selected to travel to the next planet. Don't forget to splash down at the end!

Friendly Skies

In this adaptation of London Bridge, everyone is involved and all are winners as they become part of two rocket ships that then travel around the room.

Teach the following words to the tune of "London Bridge Is Falling Down."

> Let's go on a rocket trip,
> Rocket trip, rocket trip.
> Let's go on a rocket trip,
> Zero ... BLAST OFF!

Have two children form the traditional arch. The child caught when arms are dropped on the words "blast off" chooses which rocket (person in the arch) to travel in and stands behind the other child. When all are safely on board (lined up in two lines behind the people forming the arch), everyone puts hands on waist of the person in front, and they travel around the room to the next activity.

Mind Flight
(A Quiet Listening Game)

On long flights passengers are given head sets so they can enjoy listening to music. Give children an opportunity to listen to mood music inspired by science fiction films such as *2001* and *Star Wars* or to Holtz's *The Planets*. Tell them to imagine they are listening with head sets on their ears, but they should close their eyes to imagine the journey to the stars.

Fly Me to the Moon Game

For this variation of "Pin the Tail on the Donkey" make a picture of the moon on a posterboard and provide shapes of rocket ships from construction paper for each child. Play in the manner of the traditional game by blindfolding each child as he or she places a rocket on the moon. Rather than designate a winner or a few winners, pass out moon rocks to everyone at the end. (Chunks of swiss cheese will do nicely.)

Gravity Walk Game

This variation of "Simon Says" introduces children to the concept of gravity. Older children may enjoy another experience. After you have tried moving around as if there were very little gravity, tell them to imagine they are moving on Jupiter, where they would be almost three times as heavy as on earth. Vary directions and movements to suit the ages and abilities of your group. This basic set of directions will get you going.

Captain Quest says we have just landed on the moon. On the moon there is very little gravity and we don't weigh much at all. It's much easier to move here. You almost fly when you walk. But don't get carried away or you might go right out into outer space.
When Captain Quest says "Jump!", you jump. But when I say "Jump!" you just stand still. (Proceed with different actions, some preceded by saying "Captain Quest" and some actions given without saying "Captain Quest." The last set of instructions should encourage sitting down, such as "Captain Quest says splash back down to earth.")

CRAFTS FOR UP IN THE AIR

Design Your Own Satellite Craft

Thousands of satellites orbit around our earth so you can invite children to make their own versions. Some basic materials to supply include paper plates covered with foil, and paper cups to attach to the plates with glue or tape. Small paper parasols and plastic drinking straws can be poked into the basic structure to function as probes and antenna. Colored dot stickers, pipe cleaners, paper curls, and lightweight metal springs (from old pens) can be added to make your satellite more spectacular. (See illustration on page 160.)

Rocket Roundup

We call this craft "rocket roundup" because you can make rockets from just about anything you can round up around the house. Paper towel and toilet paper tubes are the main body sections of the craft. Smaller paper cups (3 oz.) will fit easily into the towel tubes. Then make nose sections for the craft from cardboard circles (slit circle to center and overlap). Glue the tent-shaped section to end of paper cup. Make rudders from cardboard patterns (see illustration on page 161) and then make two slits to slide into the towel tube. Your rocket will stand up. Add red and orange flames from construction paper or tissue paper and tape or glue to the bottom of the rocket if you wish. Blast off!

Refrigerator Carton Rocket

Refrigerator cartons make wonderful rocket ships that children can design themselves. You may wish to cut the top into a pointed shape and cut out a few porthole windows. The "windows" can be covered with colored acetate or pictures of planets. Cover the entire carton with butcher paper so children can have a hand in decorating their spacecraft with dials and gears and gauges. Punch a few holes on the inside of the craft and tie strings with paper cups attached to simulate microphones. Children may wish to cover the microphone with foil. This activity will make use of an odd assortment of household items, from egg cartons to Christmas tree ornaments. Dig through your bottom drawers and tool sheds for inspiration. (See illustration on page 162.)

(Text continues on page 163.)

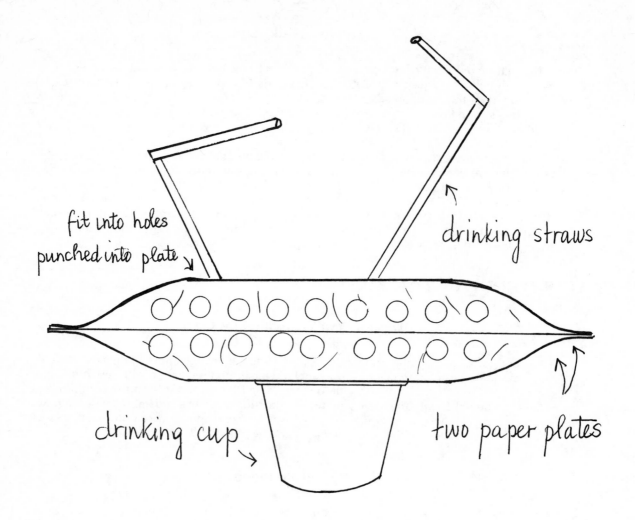

fit into holes
punched into plate

drinking straws

drinking cup

two paper plates

JATELLITE CRAFT

ROCKET ROUNDUP

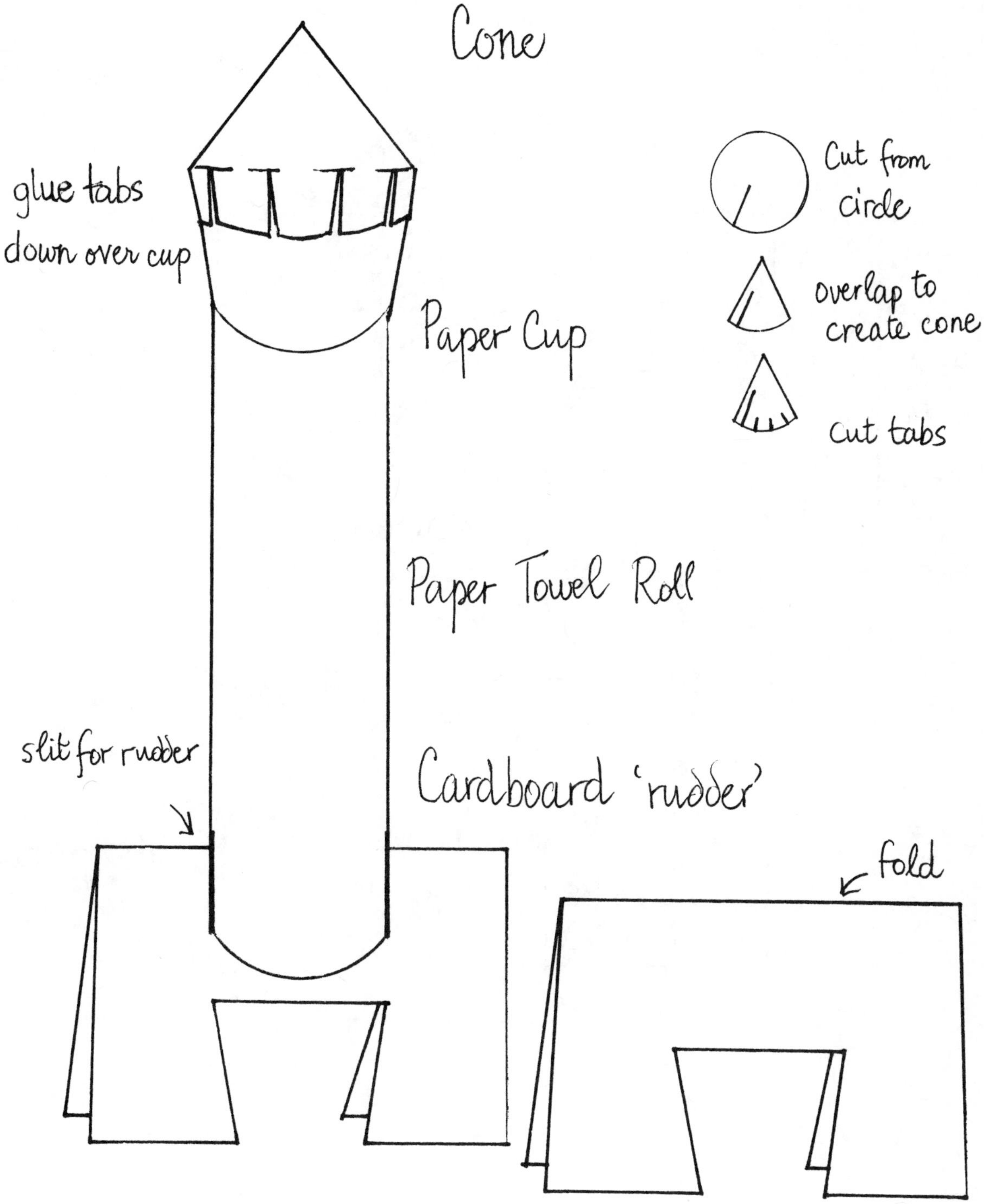

Cone

glue tabs
down over cup

Paper Cup

Paper Towel Roll

slit for rudder

Cardboard 'rudder'

Cut from circle

overlap to create cone

cut tabs

fold

REFRIGERATOR CARTON ROCKET

Cut out porthole

paper cup micro-phones

egg carton dials

paper plate gauges

Add painted details

SPACESHIP GALAXY

12:00 TIME

SPEED

ALTITUDE

FOOD

PEACE

USSA

Extra Special Extraterrestrial
(A Carry-Home Craft)

Provide trays of cut up raw vegetables for fruits for children to turn into strange space creatures or vehicles. Carrots may be transformed into rockets, oranges into satellites or an oddball extraterrestrial. Toothpicks may be used to assemble parts (raisin eyes, radish slice mouths, etc.). Curly endive and leaf lettuce make attractive hair. Just let your imagination soar with this craft.

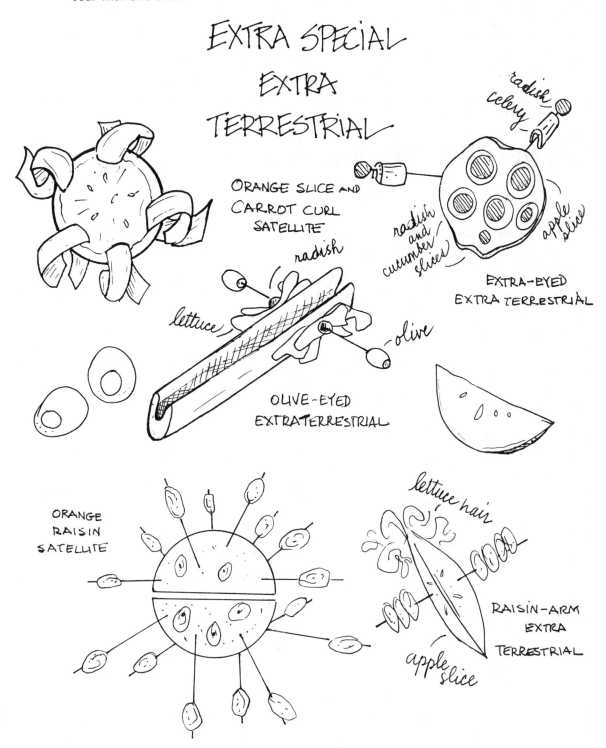

Send home this recipe for Moon Crater Dip so parents can watch their children become vegetable lovers right before their very eyes. They will love you for your inspiration!

Moon Crater Dip

    1 12-ounce carton cottage cheese
    1 tablespoon lemon juice
    1 teaspoon paprika
    ½ teaspoon garlic powder
    Dash pepper

Blend all ingredients until smooth in a blender or mixer. Dip raw veggie extraterrestrials in this concoction to turn children into vegetable lovers.

(This is an adaptation of the "Food Quest" activity from *Starquest* published by the State Library of Iowa in 1983 and compiled by Robin Currie.)

TAKE-HOME ACTIVITY FOR UP IN THE AIR

Flight Bag Take-Home Activity

Provide children with paper bags (plain ones so that children can decorate the outside and big enough to stash lots of materials. Have sticker, star cutouts, pictures of airplanes available for them to glue on the bags. Fill the bag with maps so the children can plan "let's pretend" trips, "play" airplane tickets, boarding passes, travel brochures. This will be a fun project to put together at home, school, or in the library. It may be enjoyed again and again as young travelers re-enact taking an airplane trip.

7

Magic Carpets and Merry-Go-Rounds

INTRODUCTION

The unlikely vehicles in this chapter will take you to unexpected places along uncharted courses. When Max climbs into his private boat to sail to *Where the Wild Things Are*, we are all passengers on the voyage. Since the world of childhood is the world of make-believe journeys, children will respond to the stories in this chapter quite naturally.

The first theme, "Circus Rides and Carousels," introduces fun rides children experience first hand. After you read *Carousel* by Drews or *The Longest Float in the Parade* by Carrick, invite children to join in the action rhymes: "Circus Parade" and "Horse of a Different Color Merry-Go-Round." Rhyming and rhythmical skills will be learned readily through "The Ferris Wheel" and "Roller Coaster Ride" action rhymes.

The second theme, "Incredible Dream Machines," moves from the everyday world of escalators and elevators into the fantastic. Children may build their own dream machines out of ordinary cartons or enjoy the humorous results of a contemporary genie's wish fulfillment in the flannel-board story "Into the Wild Blue Yonder."

The third theme, "Fairy Tales and Fantastical Journeys," ranges from traditional tales such as *Sunflight* to the modern fantasy *The Polar Express*. Authors of picture books are continually retelling the old and seeking new perspectives on the traditional. In a similar vein, we have retold the Cinderella story with a focus on the golden coach in "A Bumpkin in a Pumpkin." Invite children to participate in their own "Flights of Fantasy" with this enrichment activity after you share some of the suggested stories.

The fourth theme of the chapter, "Silly Spare Parts," pulls together the prehistoric and supersonic. Stories and activities will teach children cooperation and exercise, imaginative thinking through "Brontosaurus Bump," encourage artistic ventures with a stegosaurus craft to take home. As a final game, invite children to climb on "The Witch's Broom" and all zoom off together!

INITIATING ACTIVITY

Magic Carpet Ride

Many schools, child care centers, and libraries use carpet squares for storytime. These carpets (or a large throw rug) can be transformed into magic carpet rides with the following verse (and a little magic of your own!), to begin magical journeys into fantasy transportation.

> Come sit on my carpet
> Sit on my rug
> Curl up close
> So you can be snug
> Close your eyes
> Think lovely things
> You can fly
> on magic wings!

LITERATURE-SHARING EXPERIENCES

Books for Circus Rides and Carousels

Bonzon, Paul. **The Runaway Flying Horse**. Parents, 1976.

A little wooden merry-go-round horse decides on a grand adventure off the merry-go-round platform.

Brenner, Barbara. **The Snow Parade**. Crown, 1984.

When Andrew Barclay parades through the snow, he is joined by people and animals of all kinds.

Brown, Marcia. **The Little Carousel**. Scribners, 1946.

Anthony thinks the day will be boring until a carousel visits his street.

Carlson, Nancy. **Harriet and the Roller Coaster**. Carolrhoda, 1982.

When George challenges Harriet to ride the scary roller coaster, she finds she is really the brave one.

Carrick, Carol. **The Longest Float in the Parade**. Greenwillow, 1982.

Jimmy is excited when he wins the special prize for longest float in the parade.

Crews, Donald. **Carousel**. Greenwillow, 1982.

Brief text describes a carousel ride. The accompanying illustrations are paintings and photographs of the paintings with the camera moved to simulate the carousel's motion.

Crews, Donald. **Parade**. Greenwillow, 1983.

The "vehicles" that make parade preparations (street sweeper and vending carts) begin this picture book. Other modes of parade transportation shown are marching bands, floats, old-time bicycles, antique cars, and a fire engine. In the end the remnants of the parade are left for the street sweeper once more.

Freeman, Don. **Bearymore**. Viking, 1976.

When Bearymore the circus bear cannot fall asleep in the fall for hibernation, he thinks of a plan for a new act using a unicycle and umbrella.

Leigh, Oretta. **The Merry-Go-Round**. Illustrated by Kathryn E. Shoemaker. Holiday House, 1985.

Animals go up and down and children enjoy the ride on the merry-go-round.

Levenson, Dorothy. **The Magic Carousel**. Illustrated by Ati Forbert. Parents, 1967.

Dana and her younger sister Lisa love to ride the carousel in New York City, but one day their horses ride off the carousel to take them on a magical ride through the park, past the zoo, down the avenue, and on to Washington Square before they return to the carousel.

McCrady, Lady. **The Perfect Ride**. Illustrated by Dennis Kendrick. Parents, 1981.

What is the perfect ride? The dog family visits Play Land to find out.

Peet, Merle. **The Balancing Act**. Clarion, 1987.

In this counting book little elephants—one by one—balance on a tightrope until there gets to be ten and—oops!—the string breaks. Music is included for the story-song and an author's note suggests ways to use the song as a game, too.

Related Activities for Circus Rides and Carousels

Circus Parade
(An Action Rhyme)

Invite children to march to the beat of this action rhyme. Add actions and make props of circus wagons if you wish to turn this into a full-fledged procession.

> The circus is coming to town, to town!
> Here come the wagons! Here come the clowns!
> Teams of elephants raise the Big Top.
> Horses and ponies clippety-clop!
> Brass bands come marching by with their drums—
> Drum-a-dee, drum-a-dee, drum-a-dee, drum!
> Come join the parade.
> Dance to the beat—
> On wagon or horseback
> Come march down the street!

With Flying Colors
(A Story for Puppets or Flannel-board)

This story may be told with simple jointed stick puppets, a unicycle made from cardboard and attached to a stick, and with two people holding a length of string for the tightrope. If you choose this method, put pieces of Velcro™ on the chimpanzees' hands so they can balance the colored balloons. An alternative storytelling method uses felt figures for Ching, Chang, and Chong, and colored circles of felt for the red, yellow, blue, green, orange, and purple balloons. Pin a length of string across the flannel-board to represent the tightrope and make a unicycle out of felt, too.

WITH FLYING COLORS

orange

red

blue

yellow

green

purple

cut unicycle shape
from cardboard

attach to dowel

The star attraction of the Tingaling Brothers Circus was the Chimpanzee Family—Ching, Chang, Chong. Every day high above the center ring of the circus, Ching, Chang, and Chong would climb on their unicycle and ride it across a tightrope. The crowds would clap and cheer.

First the ringmaster would blow his whistle. (*Blow a whistle or let a child do this.*) Then the trained elephants Allie and Ellie would raise the tightrope high above the center ring. (*Stretch the string or let two children do this.*) Then Ching would climb on the unicycle and ride it across the tightrope. (*Let child move unicycle and another child move Ching or place felt figures on board.*)

Then Chang would climb on Ching's shoulders and Ching and Chang would ride the unicycle across the tightrope. (*Let another child place Chang on top of Ching and all move their "puppets" across the string or move the felt figures.*)

Then Chong would climb on Chang's shoulders and Ching and Chang and Chong would ride the unicycle across the tightrope. (*Let another child place Chong on top of Chang and all move their "puppets" across the string or move the felt figures.*)

The crowds would clap and cheer. (*Urge all children to clap.*)

Every day it was the same. The ringmaster would blow the whistle. Allie and Ellie would raise the tightrope. Ching would climb on the unicycle and ride it across the tightrope. Chang would climb on Ching's shoulders. Then Ching and Chang would ride the unicycle. Then Chong would climb on Chang's shoulders and Ching and Chang and Chong would ride the unicycle across the tightrope. (*Motion for each child to perform these stunts again as the story directs.*) The crowds would clap and the crowds would cheer. Every day it was the same.

One day the crowds got tired of clapping and cheering. Day after day they had seen the same old act. Ching, Chang, Chong, Ching, Chang, Chong, Ching, Chang, Chong, all day long. It got boring.

"Give us something new," said the crowds.

"Give us something exciting," said the crowds.

"Give us lights and colors and action," said the crowds.

"All right," said the ringmaster to Ching, Chang, and Chong. "You had better come up with something new and exciting or you will be replaced. Tomorrow is your last chance."

"What a dark day," cried Ching.

"What a rainy day," sighed Chang.

"What a dark and rainy day. We are really down and out," moaned Chong.

And they began to cry so hard that they tumbled down from their tightrope. (*Drop string and place them on the ground.*)

Just then Bubbles the Clown came by with a rainbow of brightly-colored balloons. Ching, Chang, and Chong put their heads together and stopped crying immediately.

"Lights!" shouted Ching.

"Color!" shouted Chang.

"Action!" shouted Chong.

Now the next day when the ringmaster blew his whistle, (*Blow whistle.*) Allie and Ellie raised the tightrope high above the center ring. (*Stretch string again.*)

Ching climbed on the unicycle and rode it across the tightrope. (*Move unicycle and Ching.*) Then Ching tossed up in the air two balloons—one red balloon, and one yellow balloon. (*Attach colored circles to Ching's hands.*)

The crowds cheered!

Then Chang climbed on Ching's shoulders and Ching and Chang rode the unicycle across the tightrope. (*Move Ching, Chang and unicycle.*) Then Ching tossed up the red and yellow balloons and Chang tossed up a blue and a green balloon. (*Attach these colored circles.*)

The crowds clapped!

Then Chong climbed on Chang's shoulders and Ching and Chang and Chong rode the unicycle across the tightrope. (*Move Ching, Chang, Chong and the unicycle.*) Then Ching tossed up the red and yellow balloons, and Chang tossed up a blue and a green balloon, and Chong tossed up an orange and a purple balloon. (*Attach these colored circles.*)

The crowds clapped and the crowds cheered!

"Hooray!" cheered the ringmaster. "That was new and exciting. That had lights and color and action! You are the star attraction of the Tingaling Brothers Circus once again. You were a huge success."

And they were a success—Ching, Chang, and Chong and the red-yellow-blue-green-orange-and-purple flying balloons on the unicycles high above the center ring—you might even say that they had come through with flying colors.

Horse of a Different Color Merry-Go-Round
(An Action Rhyme with Puppets)

This action rhyme will teach children colors and give them a chance to stretch and move like horses on a merry-go-round. It's a perfect "wiggle" after you've read *The Runaway Flying Horse* or *The Magic Carousel*.

In preparation, make horses of many colors from colored paper and mount them on dowels so the children can hold the horses as if they are on a merry-go-round.

Arrange the children in a circle and practice the chant together. Children will move up on toes, then bend knees on the word "down," then move around clockwise on the words "round and round." Everyone pauses on the last line when the horse of a different color is named and the new horse is handed to a child in the merry-go-round. The verse is repeated until all children are holding horses. Then repeat the chant one last time using the final stanza. (See illustration next page.)

Chant:
 Up and down,
 Round and round
 A bright (pink, green, red, blue, etc.) horse
 On a merry-go-round!

Final stanza:
 Up and down,
 Round and round
 Merry go, merry go,
 Merry-go-round!

Carousel Ride Song
(To the tune of "Did You Ever See a Lassie?")

Oh, climb aboard the carousel,
The carousel, the carousel.
Oh, climb aboard the carousel,
This horse is for you!

The music is beginning,
We'll soon all start spinning,
Oh, climb aboard the carousel.
We're waiting for you!

HORSE OF A DIFFERENT COLOR

The Ferris Wheel
(An Action Rhyme)

Mime appropriate actions with children, raising arms high over head at the top of the ferri
wheel. Then move to a squatting position as the wheel brings you down as you do this
rhyme.

> Up, up, over the top,
> Down on the other side.
> Up, up, over the top,
> The ferris wheel we ride.
>
> Up, up, up in the air,
> Slowing when we reach the top.
> This is the scariest part of it all:
> Up at the top we stop!
>
> Up, up, up at the top
> We can see far and wide.
> "Bump" goes the wheel, let out a squeal!
> Down on the other side.

Bumper Car Bump
(To the tune of "Jingle Bells")

Bumper cars, bumper cars,
Racing round the track.
Going slow, going fast,
Oops! We're gonna crash!
That's OK, bumper cars
Are made of bouncy stuff.
Bump me here or bump me there—
I'll never get enough!

Roller Coaster Ride
(An Action Rhyme)

Up and down, up and down
   (*Raise hands overhead, slide them down to the floor.*)
The roller coaster ride.
Up and down, up and down,
   (*Raise hands overhead, slide them down to the floor.*)
Keep your hands inside
   (*Put hands in lap.*)
Up and up and up and up
   (*Raise hands high over head.*)
Close your eyes—don't peek
   (*Cover eyes.*)
Down and down and down and down
   (*Slide hands to ground.*)
And don't forget to SHREEEEEEK!
   (*SHREEEEEEK!*)

Books for Incredible Dream Machines

Castle, Caroline. **Herbert Binns and the Flying Tricycle**. Illustrated by Peter Weevers. Dial, 1987.

Herbert Binns, a small mouse and a brilliant inventor, is nearly thwarted in his plan to fly a green tricycle by three jealous characters who steal a vital part of the machine.

Farber, Norma. **Up the Down Elevator**. Illustrated by Annie Gusman. Addison-Wesley, 1979.

As the elevator fills with all kinds of people working and selling things, children learn the numbers one to ten.

Hutchins, Pat. **Changes, Changes**. Macmillan, 1971.

Two toy people arrange and rearrange a series of blocks to make vehicles from a firetruck to a tugboat in this wordless picturebook of motion and change.

Keeping, Charles. **Willie's Fire-Engine**. Oxford University Press, 1980.

Willie dreams of rescuing a princess in a castle while driving a brilliantly colored fire engine. In so doing, he becomes a "hero among his heroes."

Moncure, Jane. **The Four Magic Boxes**. Illustrated by Helen Endres. Child's World, 1978.

What fun when packing boxes can become a train, fire engine, airplane and ship for Jim and his friends.

Slepian, Jan, and Ann Seidler. **Alfie and the Dream Machine**. Illustrated by Richard E. Martin. Follett, 1964.

Alfie, the youngest of the dream people, learns how to collect dream wishes and send them through the dream machine after several mishaps and threats from the Bad Dream Man.

Related Activities for Incredible Dream Machines

Listen to a Dream Machine
(A Participatory Chant)

You may have the children add the sounds to this chant as a group or divide into four groups and have each add a sound. Older children will enjoy making all the different noises at once!

Have you heard my dream machine?
It makes a sound like this:
Zip, zip, zippity zip.

Have you heard my dream machine?
It makes a sound like this:
Zip, zip, zippity zip.
Plinkety, plinkety, plink.

Have you heard my dream machine?
It makes a sound like this:
Zip, zip, zippity zip.
Plinkety, plinkety, plink.
Tick, tock, tick, tock.

Have you heard my dream machine?
It makes a sound like this:
Zip, zip, zippity zip.
Plinkety, plinkety, plink.
Tick, tock, tick, tock.
Sssssssss-boom!

Elevator Song

(To the tune of "London Bridge")

Elevator going up
Going up, going up
Elevator going up
Get in please.

Turn around and face the front
Face the front, face the front
Turn around and face the front
Door is closing.

Elevator going up
Going up, going up
Elevator going up
Get in please.

Hold your breath in so there's room
So there's room, so there's room
Hold your breath in so there's room
Please don't sneeze!

Elevator going down
Going down, going down
Elevator going down
Get in please.

Swallow or your ears will pop
Ears will pop, ears will pop.
Swallow or your ears will pop
Bend your knees.

Elevator going down
Going down, going down
Elevator going down
Get in please.

At the bottom, watch your step
Watch your step, watch your step
At the bottom, watch your step,
Best foot forward.

Escalator: A Moving Experience

(To the tune of "I'm a Little Teapot")

On the escalator we can ride:
All the stairs go up this side.
Then we can get off and turn around—
On that side they come back down.

Into the Wild Blue Yonder

(A Flannel-board Story)

Tell this story with the following pieces cut from felt: a plain blue car, a large horn, two wings, a television set and antenna, and a stack of burgers. Place these objects on the flannel-board as the story directs. Then, when Sam wishes his car to go into the wild blue yonder, remove all the pieces from the board.

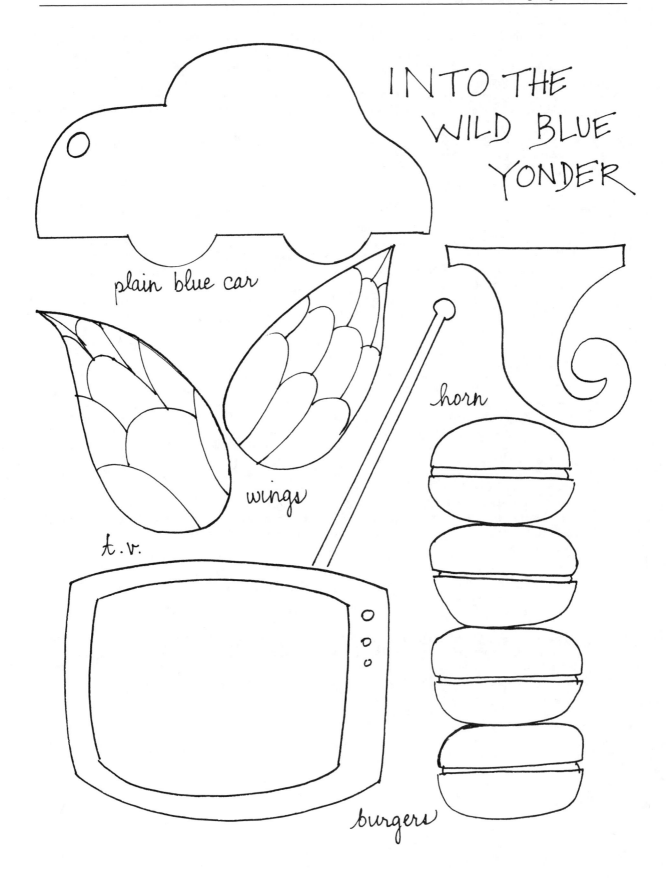

INTO THE WILD BLUE YONDER

plain blue car

wings

t.v.

horn

burgers

Sam was a plain, ordinary-looking man. He lived in a plain, ordinary house. And he lived a plain, ordinary life. One day he bought a plain, ordinary-looking car. (*Place car on flannel-board.*) He bought the car from Mr. Aladdin's Used Car Shoppe. After that, Sam's life began to change.

When Sam got his plain blue ordinary-looking car home, he decided to give it a super wax all over the hood of his car. Suddenly, there was a puff of smoke, and a green genie flew out of the radiator.

"I am a genie. Your wish is my command. What wild and crazy wish do you want?" asked the green genie.

Now Sam had never seen a genie before in his life, especially a green genie. You see, Sam had always lived a plain, ordinary life. For the first time in his life, he began to think wild and crazy thoughts.

"Well," said Sam, "I am a plain, ordinary man, but if I had a big fancy horn on my car, I would feel important when I rode down the street. Get me a big fancy horn."

So the genie put a big fancy horn on the front of Sam's plain blue car. (*Put horn on the car.*) Sam sounded the horn as he whizzed off down the street.

"My, I feel important," he said. "But I would feel really important if my car could take off over seas and in the air. Get me some wings."

So the genie put two wings on the back of Sam's not so plain blue car. (*Put wings on the car.*) Sam took off in his car—over seas and in the air.

"My, I feel really important," he said, "but I am missing all the comforts of home. Bring me a giant television set and an antenna and a year's supply of super burgers to eat when I get hungry!" ordered Sam.

So the genie put a television and television antenna on Sam's blue car. (*Put television and antenna on top of the car.*) Then the genie stuffed the car with a year's supply of burgers. (*Put burgers on the car.*)

"My, I feel really important AND I have all the comforts of home," said Sam, "but I still have one wild and crazy wish!"

"This better be good," said the genie. "You've already used up three wishes. This is the last one you are going to get."

"I wish," said Sam, "I wish to go faster than the speed of sound, faster than the speed of light. And, I wish to go off into the wild blue yonder."

"Your wish is my command," smiled the genie.

There was a puff of smoke. Sam's car went into the wild blue yonder. (*Remove car and accessories from board.*) Nobody knew if Sam felt important anymore. He was never seen or heard of again.

The Incredible Dream Machine
(A Participatory Story)

Jan Irving did the original version of this as a promotional skit for the *Incredible Library Dream Machine* in 1984 for the State Library of Iowa. This version suggests building a dream machine with children from your group. The leader is Professor Ima Wizard. Teach the entire group the dream machine chant to get the action going.

Chant:
> Input
> Speed Up
> Run
> Stop
> Dream Up
> Brainstorm
> Output
> Stop!

Greetings! I am Professor Ima Wizard. Today, we're going to build an incredible dream machine. All we need are a few spare parts and a little imagination. Is there anyone out there who would like to take part in this invention? Good!

First we need a pilot, co-pilot, and a co-co-pilot! (*Select three kids and ask them to sit down in chairs in front of the group. You may hand them props such as a steering wheel, headphones, balloons, and umbrellas.*)

I think we're ready to take off. No, I guess we need a few more parts. Here are some gizmos. Who could get these into gear? (*Select a few more kids to join the original crew. You can name them other props or ask them to use their arms and make sounds like machine parts.*)

O.K. Ready for take off! Oops! Wait a minute! I almost forgot the whatchamacallits! Here they are! (*Pull more props out of a box or bag. Give these to other kids.*)

Now we're ready! Oops! One more thing! A Switcheroo! Here it is! (*Pull another contraption such as a light switch out of a bag and hand it to another kid.*)

And, of course, we'll need a little inspiration. (*Hand several bottles of soap bubbles to children to come up in front and blow bubbles.*)

Everybody ready? Let's crank up the engines (*do big cranking motion*), and....

How silly of me! I forgot that we need fuel. I'll need everyone to repeat after me:

Input
Speed Up
Run
Stop
Dream Up
Brainstorm
Output
Stop!

Good, say that again. (*Repeat chant.*) And again—(*repeat chant a third and louder time.*)

Thank you all very much and here we go! (*Each part of the dream machine goes into motion. Children may be encouraged to make appropriate actions and sounds for each part of the machine. The machine may move in place or around the room as you wish. The chant may be spoken again to stop the action of the dream machine.*)

Super Dooper Dream Machine

(A Participation Story)

Jan Irving did this story originally for the State Library of Iowa's summer programming manual, *The Incredible Library Dream Machine* in 1984. You can add your own dreams and schemes to make an even more incredible journey with your group of children.

We're going through a Super Dooper Dream Machine. Everybody ready? Let's go....
Bend down, the door is low.
See that button off to the right?
If everyone's set, I'll just press it IN—Generator generating!
Let's see, help me turn the dial. It's a BIG one.
Good! Activators activating!
And, now, the throttle—ooommmfff. Everybody's got to PULL HARD. P-O-W-E-R!
Everyone crouch down. There's going to be a bump.
And now, jump, jump, jump (little low jumps) three times.
Look at that! We've all become frogs!
Now, everyone do one big Leapfrog Jump. Good! But, look, that was so big, we've all become Kangaroos!
OK, everyone do one big Kangaroo Jump. Whoa! That was so big, we just jumped over the moon.
We're the cow who jumped over the moon! Can you all make one big MOO! That was good.
But, we're all in outer space now! And we're falling....

Whew! We've landed on a cloud. A marshmallow cloud! We're bouncing. Wheee! Fun! Oops! Too much fun. The cloud has sprung a leak.

Now it's raining. It's raining so hard it's raining cats and dogs. Stick in your head so you won't get wet. Wow! Wasn't that lucky? We've all become turtles. And we've got shells to keep us dry. Let's just wait inside our shells until the rain stops.

OK, rain's over. We can go out again. But keep down low, remember the door out is low.

Look at that! What do I see?
I see you. Do you see me?
Back the way we used to be.
Wasn't that a super dream machine ride?

Ride on a Dream Machine
(An Action Rhyme)

Jan Irving did this little action rhyme for the State Library of Iowa's summer programming manual *The Incredible Library Dream Machine* in 1984. Use it to accompany any of the picture books in this chapter about fantastic journeys.

Ready to ride on a dream machine?
Here's some fairy dust,   (*Toss out imaginary dust*)
Now you've got wings!   (*Fling out arms*)
Higher and higher   (*Stretch arms wider*)
What do you know
We've landed on
The Rainbow   (*Arch arms overhead*)
Everyone ready?
Down we slide—   (*Sit down on floor*)
Wasn't that a happy ride?

Books for Fairy Tales and Fantastical Journeys

Duncan, Lois. **Horses of Dreamland.** Illustrated by Donna Diamond. Little, Brown, 1985.

Poetic text describes a child's dream journey on a horse over starlit trails of deserts, hillsides, cities, and seas. She encounters wolves, but overcomes the nightmare and crosses the horizon to the comfort of her own bed—only to dream again of the horse in her dreamland.

Faulkner, Matt. **The Amazing Voyage of Jackie Grace.** Scholastic, 1987.

While Jackie is taking his bath, a crew of sailors join him. In search of their ship, they enlist Jackie's help to defeat pirates on the high seas in this tale of a fantastic journey.

Field, Eugene. **Wynken, Blynken and Nod.** Illustrated by Susan Jeffers. Dutton, 1982.

Field's well-known bedtime poem of three fishermen who sail through the night in a wooden shoe to catch stars in their nets of silver and gold takes on a new meaning with Jeffer's illustrations of children taking the fanciful voyage.

Hague, Kathleen. **The Legend of the Veery Bird.** Illustrated by Michael Hague. Harcourt Brace Jovanovich, 1985.

When the quiet youth needs help, the Keeper of the Forest gives the world a bird with a beautiful voice.

Jeffers, Susan. **All the Pretty Horses.** Macmillan, 1974.

Mother sings the beautiful traditional lullaby and the little girl dreams of the wonderful magical horses.

Lynn, Janet. **The Twelve Dancing Princesses: A Fairy Story**. Illustrated by Laszlo Gal. Methuen, 1979.

When twelve princesses wear out their shoes every night, the king hires the gardner's boy to find the secret.

McDermott, Gerald. **Sunflight**. Four Winds, 1980.

Daedalus fashions wings for himself and his son Icarus to escape from King Minos' labyrinth. Although he is warned by his father not to fly too high, Icarus flies too near the sun and perishes.

Perrault, Charles. **Cinderella**. Retold by Amy Ehrlich. Illustrated by Susan Jeffers. Dial Books for Young Readers, 1985.

Beautiful retelling and magic pictures enhance this version of the classic tale. The pumpkin turned into a coach is a favorite dream ride. Older children will enjoy the language, younger ones may need the story abbreviated slightly for shorter attention spans.

Prater, John. **The Gift**. Puffin Books, 1985.

In this wordless adventure two children climb inside a carton that they have received and go on many fantastic flights—through tunnels, to the beach, deep undersea, down waterfalls in the tropics and back home until their father discards the box.

Price-Thomas, Brian. **The Magic Ark**. Crown, 1987.

A young boy goes on a fantastic flight in Mr. Antrobus' magical flying Noah's Ark.

Small, Ernest. **Baba Yaga**. Illustrated by Blair Lent. Houghton Mifflin, 1966.

Baba Yaga pursues Marusia and Dimitri, two Russian children, in her flying mortar which she steers with a pestle. In the end, the children are rescued by a horseman in a magical flight.

Van Allsburg, Chris. **The Polar Express**. Houghton Mifflin, 1985.

A beautiful jingle bell is all that is left of a boy's fanciful trip to the North Pole on Christmas Eve to meet Santa Claus.

Van Allsburg, Chris. **The Wreck of the Zephyr**. Houghton Mifflin, 1983.

A boy, obsessed with the desire to be the greatest sailor, sails his boat in the air one night only for it to wreck. The wreck of the Zephyr remains on the edge of a cliff for passersby to speculate about.

Wynne-Jones, Timothy. **Zoom Away**. Illustrated by Ken Nutt. Douglas & McIntyre, 1985.

Zoom the Cat sets off on high adventure with Maria and Uncle Roy to rescue Uncle Roy's boat, the Catship, that is stuck on the Arctic ice in the North Pole. The dream voyage ends when Zoom awakes on the wing chair in Maria's cozy sitting room.

Yolen, Jane. **Rainbow Rider**. Illustrated by Michael Foreman. Crowell, 1974.

When seeking friends, the sand, tumbleweed and cactus are not suitable, but Rainbow Rider flings his tears to the sky and magic happens.

Related Activities for Fairy Tales and Fantastical Journeys

Flights of Fantasy

Children probably know Captain Hook and Santa Claus. Introduce them to Apollo, the ancient Greek god who, as the gleaming sun god, rode a golden chariot across the sky each day.

If I were Apollo
Ruling the sky,
I'd ride in a chariot
Higher than high.

If I were Captain Hook
In Never Never Land,
I'd rule a flying galleon
With the hook on my hand.

If I were Santa Claus
With toy bags all full,
I'd drive a red sleigh
With reindeer to pull.

Most of the time
I ride on my bike,
But in my wild dreams
I can ride what I like.

Butterflight
(To the tune of "Twinkle, Twinkle Little Star")

Think of all the different types of fantasy transportation. Thumbelina rides a bird; James in *James and the Giant Peach*, uses butterflies and other insects to embark on flights of fancy. How many others can you and the children remember? What kind of fantasy would you choose for yourself?

Riding on a butterfly,
Sailing up into the sky.
Touch the stars, and see the moon
Gliding like a big balloon.
Up above the world so high,
Riding on a butterfly.

Fairy Dust Wanderlust

Want some magic? Well, you must
Sprinkle on some fairy dust.
Sprinkle some on your wagon,
And roll over the clouds.
    (*Roll hands.*)

Want some magic? Well, you must
Sprinkle on some fairy dust.
Sprinkle some on your skateboard,
And do some loop-the-loops.
    (*Move arms in a figure 8.*)

Want some magic? Well, you must
Sprinkle on some fairy dust.
Sprinkle some on your sled,
And slide down a rainbow.
    (*Reach high, then scoop hands to the ground.*)

Want some magic? Well, you must
Sprinkle on some fairy dust.
Sprinkle some on your bed,
And be carried away to the land of dreams.
　　(*Pretend to sleep on hands.*)

A Bumpkin in a Pumpkin

This version of the Cinderella story focuses on the pumpkin coach rather than on the glass slipper and fancy ball, and, because it is an updated story, Cinderella doesn't wait around for the prince, but takes matters in her own hands.

The two-sided pumpkin/coach storytelling device can be used to focus on the magic transformation. Cut two pumpkin shapes from construction paper. Cut window as indicated in illustration. Glue two pumpkin shapes together. Open window and draw fuzzy dice inside. Decorate this side as coach. Attach the wheels with brad fasteners so they can be pulled down as indicated in the story.

You might try this story as a kit or with hand puppets. Good for all ages!

　　Once upon a time, when girls found fairy godmothers in the garden along with the radishes, there lived a girl whose name was Cinderella. Cinderella had no mother, but she had two older sisters who were supposed to look out after her. Well, they didn't care one hoot about that! Instead they took off every night for the bright lights of the city. And there they had a fine time riding around in fast and fancy vehicles.
　　In the meantime, Cindi was not living life in the fast lane. One night the sisters frisked off to the city for a fancy masked ball. Of course they left Cindi at home to do all the work. While Cindi was out weeding the garden, a fairy godmother rose up out of the parsley.
　　The fairy godmother said, "My dear, I can see you need a little magic in your life. With a whoosh of my wand you, too, can be off and on your way. If you just bring me a vegetable, we can get things off the ground."
　　Cindi said, "Well, what kind of vegetable do you have in mind?

> A potato?
> A tomato?
> A cabbage?
> A pea?
> What kind of magic
> Is this going to be?"

Fairy Godmother thought for a minute and said, "Well, that's not what I had in mind. Let's try again."
　　So Cindi suggested,

> "A zucchini?
> An eggplant?
> A broccoli stalk?
> Please tell me exactly
> What you want."

BUMPKIN IN A PUMPKIN

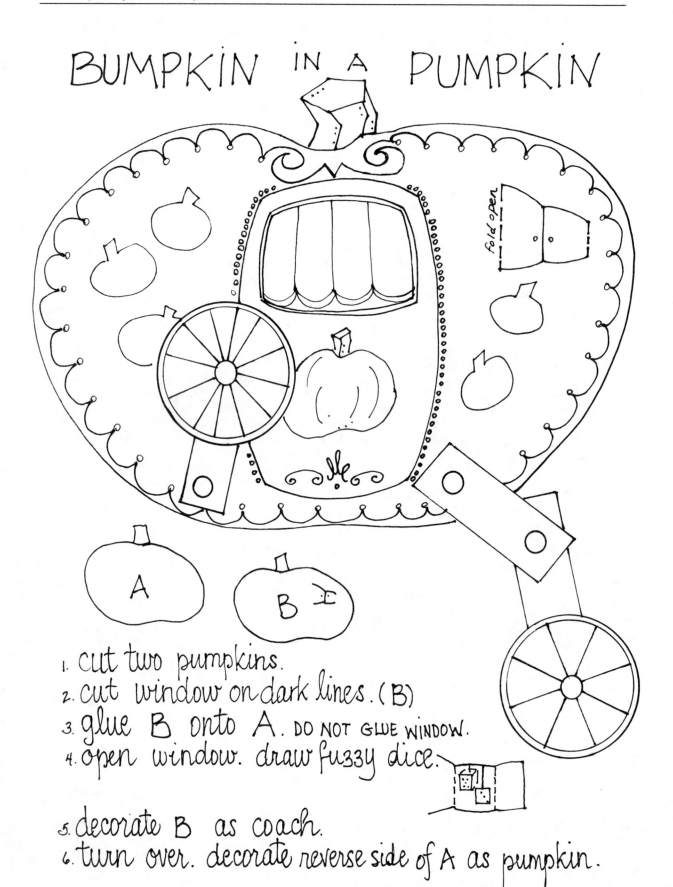

Fold open

1. cut two pumpkins.
2. cut window on dark lines. (B)
3. glue B onto A. DO NOT GLUE WINDOW.
4. open window. draw fuzzy dice.

5. decorate B as coach.
6. turn over. decorate reverse side of A as pumpkin.

Fairy Godmother thought for a minute more. "I'm not quite certain myself," she said. "But I don't think a flying tomato would make the proper splash."
Cindi said,

> "I'm fresh out of squash
> Lettuce and beans.
> Cantaloupe, watermelon
> And you said—no peas.
> But what about this:
> Here's a little something
> A round, fat
> Golden yellow pumpkin."

Fairy Godmother thought for a quick minute and exclaimed,

> "A pumpkin, a pumpkin!
> Yes, that's the thing!
> Now, whoosh, whoosh, whoosh,
> And zing a zing zing."

Fairy Godmother whooshed her magic wand over the pumpkin and before you could say "pumpkin pie in the sky" right there before Cindi's eyes appeared a gleaming golden yellow pumpkin coach with silver wheels and velvet curtains at the windows.
But before Cindi could say "I'm on my way" Fairy Godmother said,

> "Now, quick! Bring six
> Little mice.
> I'll whoosh my wand
> Now close your eyes.
> Whoosh, whoosh, whoosh.
> Surprise! Surprise!"

And the little mice turned into six beautiful white horses.
Well, the fairy godmother was really rolling now. She was winding up her wand and said, "What do we have here to make a nice coachman? Then we'll need two footmen, and we'll have to do something about the way you look. For the masked ball you need the proper attire. I think a baby blue chiffon formal with maybe some glass slippers?"
But Cindi said, "Whoa, there! That is some snazzy coach, and I love all the horse power. Where I'm going I won't need footmen or a baby blue rag! I thought glass slippers went out with high button shoes! Just let me in the driver's seat myself, and I'm off to the rock concert."
Fairy Godmother looked doubtful. "Well, if you are sure that is what you want, I'll be on my way."
Cindi said, "Oh, before you go, could you whoosh up enough magic to change those silver wheels to radials? I can live with the velvet curtains, but I'd love a pair of those fuzzy dice hanging from the rear view mirror."
Fairy Godmother looked doubtful. "Well, if you are sure that is what you want." Once more she whooshed her magic wand.
"Out of sight," said Cindi. She hopped into the pumpkin and took off for the rock concert. She even made a little music of her own along the way. If you listen very closely I think you can hear her singing,

> "Don't want no city lights
> No fancy show.
> Just give me my wheels
> And I'm ready to go!
> Just a whoosh of magic
> And a garden patch,
> What do you get?
> Just a bumpkin
> In a pumpkin,
> Natch!"

Roller Derby Reindeer

Santa Claus, Santa Claus
Can it be right?
Do you fill the stockings
In just one short night?
How can you travel
So far and so fast?
Are the reindeer all tired
When you finish at last?
I bet I know how
You keep them so fleet:
You put roller skates
On all thirty-two feet!

Books for Silly Spare Parts

Bang, Betsy. **The Old Woman and the Red Pumpkin: A Bengali Folk Tale**. Illustrated by Molly Garrett Bang. Macmillan, 1975.

A colorful retelling of an old woman who outwits a jackal, bear and tiger to avoid being eaten.

Barton, Byron. **Wheels**. Crowell, 1979.

Clear line drawings and easy text trace the development of wheels from rocks to their use on carts, chariots, wagons and more complex kinds of transportation including motor cars, cycles, and buses.

Calhoun, Mary. **Cross-country Cat**. Illustrated by Erick Ingraham. Morrow, 1979.

It is an unusual cat that can walk on two legs—even more unusual is one who can ski and make it home after being out in the snowy woods.

Drescher, Henrik. **The Yellow Umbrella**. Bradbury, 1987.

Monkeys and a yellow umbrella add up to wordless picturebook fun.

Freeman, Don. **Space Witch**. Viking Press, 1959.

Tilly Ipswitch, Queen of Halloween, takes fanciful trips to other planets to scare up some new frights.

Hayes, Barbara. **The Magic Horse**. Illustrated by Gerry Embleton. Rourke Enterprises, 1984.

A magic flying horse plays a key role in the quest of Prince Firuz to capture Princess Dura for his bride.

Hughes, Shirley. **Up and Up**. Lothrop, Lee and Shepard, 1979.

Using a handful of balloons, a little girl finally succeeds in flying.

Lyon, David. **The Runaway Duck**. Lothrop, Lee and Shepard, 1985.

Egbert the pull-toy duck has an exciting adventure when his pull cord is wrapped around the bumper of his owner Sebastian's father's car.

McPhail, David. **Pig Pig Rides**. Dutton, 1982.

Pig Pig's wonderful transportation adventures, from leaping 500 elephants on his motorcycle to flying to the moon, are a little too much for his mother.

Mayer, Mercer. **A Special Trick**. Dial, 1970.

Elroy begins pronouncing the strange words in the magician's dictionary to calls forth all kinds of creatures, including a winged pony to get him out of the mess.

Pinkwater, Daniel. **Roger's Umbrella**. Illustrated by James Marshall. Dutton, 1982.

When Roger's umbrella threatens all kinds of bad behavior, three old ladies teach him how to control it.

Ransome, Arthur. **The Fool of the World and the Flying Ship**. Illustrated by Uri Shulevitz. Farrar, Straus & Giroux, 1968.

This story, based on a Russian folk tale, tells the adventures of a young man, the fool of the world, who sets out to marry the princess by bringing the Czar a flying ship. Aided by an ancient old man, the lad gets his ship, and along the journey, picks up a merry crew of peasants who help him perform seemingly impossible tasks. The "fool" wins over the Czar, marries the princess and becomes so clever "all the court repeats everything he says," as the tale ends happily ever after.

Sendak, Maurice. **Where the Wild Things Are**. Harper & Row, 1963.

Max travels by boat to the strange land of the wild things, then returns to where "someone loves him best of all."

Related Activities for Silly Spare Parts

Brontosaurus Bounce

Since piggy back rides are so much fun, try this new and updated way to go for a ride. The leader is the head of the brontosaurus. Invite a child to come by pointing to him on the word "you."

> There's a brontosaurus down at the zoo.
> I'm going for a ride. You come, too.

The child should put his hands on your waist. Both should bend and straighten knees to these words:

> Bumpin' along on a dinosaur,
> Let's move over for just one more.

Stop bouncing and repeat the first rhyme, pointing to another child to join the line. When everyone is in line walk and bounce around the room on the dinosaur and back to places for another activity.

An Awesome Sight

> There once was a boy named Roberto Bernini
> Who juggled everything, even zucchini.
> His brother's baseball, his mother's hat,
> His father's pizza, the family cat.
>
> When setting the table,
> He balanced the cups
> On stacks of saucers
> Then tossed them up.
>
> They didn't come crashing,
> They caused no disaster,
> They didn't touch
> The ceiling plaster.
>
> Cups spun out the window,
> And into the sky,
> Saucers kept spinning—
> And no one knew why.

They kept right on going
Up, up and away,
Til they circled the edge
Of the Milky Way.

Now you may not believe me
But those saucers and cups
Scooped up some stardust
As they travelled up.

They lit up the skies
As they blinked through the night—
Newspapers called it
An awesome sight!

A flying saucer?
A new satellite?
An extraterrestrial
Travelling at night?

But you know how it started—
It was Roberto Bernini—
The kid who juggled
Even zucchini!

The Witches Broom

(To the tune of "Farmer in the Dell")

Play this game during Halloween or any other magical time of the year. Place the children in a circle and invite one at a time to be in the center like the traditional "Farmer in the Dell" song.

A witch rides a broom
A witch rides a broom
Heigh ho we've got more room
On the witch's broom

The witch takes a cat
The witch takes a cat
Heigh ho we've got more room
On the witch's broom

The cat takes a bat
The cat takes a bat
Heigh ho we've got more room
On the witch's broom

The bat takes a rat
The bat takes a rat
Heigh ho we've got more room
On the witch's broom

The rat takes a hat
The rat takes a hat
Heigh ho we've got more room
On the witch's broom

The hat has a gnat
And that's the end of that!
Heigh ho we're out of room
On the witch's broom!
ZOOOOOM!

Arm Chair Travelers

(To the tune of "A Hunting We Will Go")

A traveling we will go.
A traveling we will go.
We'll stay at home, but let's pretend
A traveling we will go.

A climbing we will go.
A climbing we will go.
We ride up cliffs in mountain lifts
    (*Raise arms slowly.*)
A climbing we will go.

A sailing we will go.
A sailing we will go.
We paddle on a river boat
    (*Roll hands.*)
A sailing we will go.

A flying we will go.
A flying we will go.
We parachute out of a plane
    (*Arms overhead, bend knees slowly to ground.*)
A flying we will go.

A puffing we will go.
A puffing we will go.
We speed through tunnels on a train
    (*Say, "Tooooot-toot."*)
A puffing we will go.

We travel with our books.
We travel with our books.
Books can help us to pretend!
We travel with our books.

Come Home Now

This poem will make a fun followup for *Pig Pig Rides* by McPhail (p. 184).

Little child, little child, come right in!
Where in the world do you think you have been?

I rode a camel across the sand
Gallumpa, gallumpa, gallumpa.
I took a tide in a Model-T
Rumbley, rumbley, bumpa.

I rode a huge whale under the sea
Blubada blubada swoosh
I soared in a rocket ship to the moon
Whoooosh.

Little child, little child, I have a hunch
You are hungry now for your lunch!

GAMES FOR MAGIC CARPETS AND MERRY-GO-ROUNDS

Magical Musical Chairs

Play circus music. Have one chair for each child. When the music stops, a child seated in a certain chair gets to pick what he or she will be in the circus. That child may act out how the character would move—such as a tightrope walker or horseback rider. The others may imitate. Choose the "special chair" each time so all get a chance to be part of the circus fun. At the end, all the children can do their own movement for a real three-ring circus!

The Big Parade

Line the children up in two lines facing each other as if watching a parade. Use a handful of pennants. When you give one to a child he or she may walk between the lines as in a parade: marching, swinging an elephant trunk, driving a car or circus wagon. Sing these words to the tune of "The Farmer in the Dell" as each child joins the parade.

> Come join the big parade
> Come join the big parade
> It's your turn so get in line!
> Come join the big parade

Those with pennants stand at the end of the respective lines and wave them until everyone has had a turn. Then lead the whole parade around the room.

Unicorn Catch

Sing these words to the tune of "London Bridge Is Falling Down" and play the game in the traditional way.

> Come and catch a unicorn,
> Unicorn, unicorn.
> There is magic on its horn.
> Come and catch one!

The unicorns should hold one finger in front of their foreheads for horns. The two forming the bridge can be a prince and princess and wear tin foil crowns. Unicorns choose prince or princess after being caught. At the end of the game, the royal pair leads their unicorns to a safe place for the next activity.

Magic Rings and Unicorns

Borrow or make a simple ring toss game. Have the children work as a group to see how many rings they can toss onto the unicorn's horn.

CRAFTS FOR MAGIC CARPETS AND MERRY-GO-ROUNDS

Stegosaurus Standup

After you've enjoyed the "Brontosaurus Bounce" (p. 185), invite children to make another prehistoric creature. (Just imagine what a bouncy ride you would have on a stegosaurus!)

Fold a sheet of construction paper in half so you have a folded-over piece that measures 9x6 inches. Lay your hand on the paper with the palm on the open edge. Draw around your hand with your middle finger on the fold. Cut out the stegosaurus (see illustration on page 190). Notice that the three longest fingers become the spikes of the creature's back and should not be cut through so your stegosaurus will stand up.

Elephant Parade Craft

One of the most fun kinds of transportation for kids is an elephant ride. What could be more fun than a whole parade of elephants?

Make your own stand-up elephant parade by using a piece of construction paper 12 x 4 1/4 inches. Fold the paper again lengthwise to get a folded strip that is 12 x 2 1/4 inches. Now draw around the pattern and cut out your elephant chain. Be certain you leave part of each elephant's head uncut on the fold line so the elephants will stand up. Use the scraps to make ears for your elephants. You may draw on eyes if you wish. (See illustration on page 191.)

Circus Wagons

Use individual serving size cereal boxes. The children may make circus wagons by gluing on animal shapes and cut out bars. Or you may cut out portions for them to fill with shapes of animals. Attach wheels or cut out cardboard circles to either circus wagon with brad fasteners. (See illustration on page 192.)

Dream Machine

Use a large refrigerator box to build a dream machine as a group project. Adults begin by cutting out porthole windows and doors. Children add the finishing touches any way they wish. Supply them with a variety of hardware, shiny and brightly colored papers. Some of our favorite materials include baking cups, styrofoam cups, egg carton sections, paper coils, and pipe cleaners. (See illustration on page 193.)

Magic Fairy Wands

Supply children with dowels for the handle and craft felt in bright colors to make a soft sculpture end to the fairy wand. They may trace and cut two identical shapes of moons or stars. Glue edges with fabric glue leaving a small part at the bottom. Stuff with old pillow stuffing or fiberfill. Put glue on the end of the dowel and insert into the hole in the soft sculpture. Glue the opening shut around the dowel. Ribbons tied onto the wand will make it even more magical. (See illustration on page 194.)

(Text continues on page 195.)

STEGOSAURUS STAND-UP

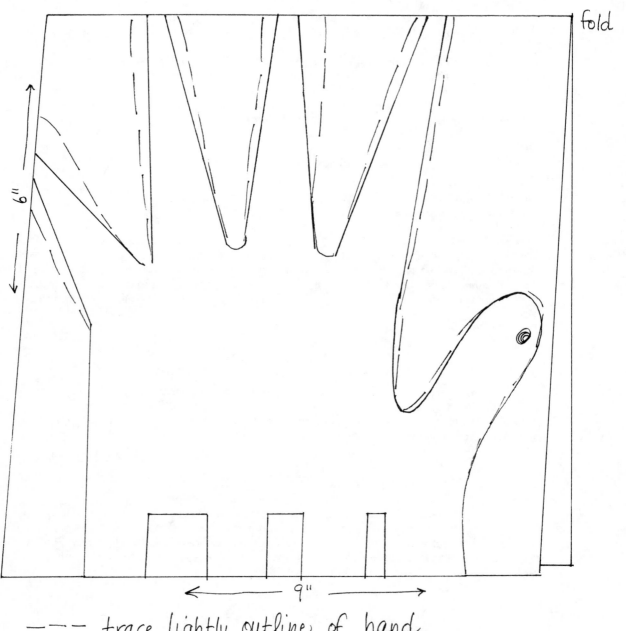

fold

6"

9"

- - - - trace lightly outline of hand
———— cut on straight lines to suggest spikes on back

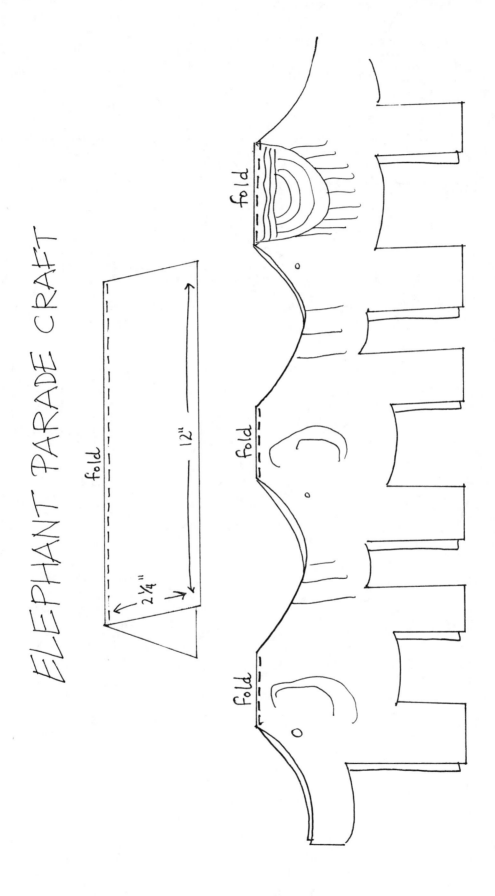

CIRCUS WAGONS

DREAM MACHINE

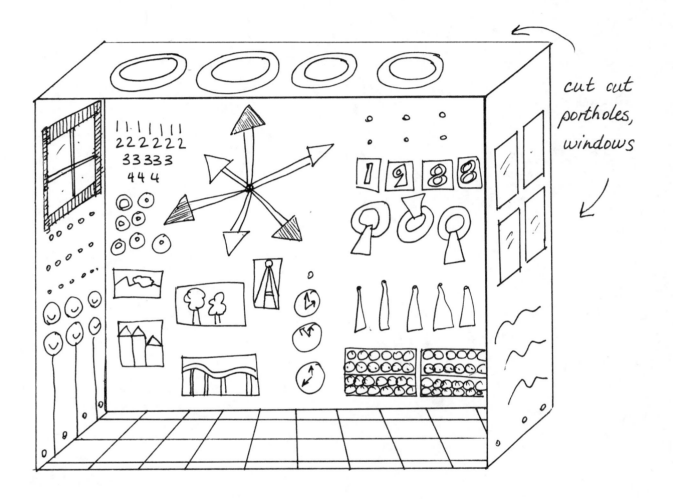

cut out
portholes,
windows

Add pictures, streamers, paper and styrofoam
cups and shapes, egg cartons, paper & fabric scraps...

MAGIC FAIRY WANDS

Cut two felt shapes

stuff

Glue edges

dowel

Glue onto dowel

Add ribbons

A Horse of a Different Color

Children might enjoy taking home their favorite horse of a different color after you have done the chant with them (p. 171). They can trace the horse shape, and cut out of colored paper or trace onto white paper and paint with bright rainbow colors. Allow to dry before cutting out. Attach with glue or tape to a straw. Use the horses to review the names of colors and do the chant as a closing activity.

TAKE-HOME ACTIVITY FOR MAGIC CARPETS AND MERRY-GO-ROUNDS

Dream Trip Take-Home Activity

The best kind of family trips are planned together. Encourage children to plan unusual dream trips with their families by sending home scrapbooks. A few pages of folded paper can be provided. Label the page with such lines as: "This summer we're dreaming about going on a trip to ... (the moon, a black hole, the North Pole, an amusement park)." "Our favorite kind of vehicle to get there will be ... (a time machine, Santa's sleigh, a roller coaster, a dinosaur)." "For a souvenir we will bring back ... (moon rocks, a pet reindeer, a flying carpet, a stuffed wish bear)."

8

Trolley Cars and Rickshaws
Long Ago and Far Away

INTRODUCTION

In this final chapter we provide an overview of the development of transportation through the ages and around the globe. Stories and activities focus on the major inventions that have helped people move on — the wheel, wagon, boat, and steam power — rather than provide a strict chronological record. Picture books show culturally diverse vehicles from Chinese junk boats in Flack's *The Story about Ping* to carts in Lewin's *Jafta — the Journey*. This chapter has not been subdivided between long-ago and far-away because modes of transportation used in some parts of the world today such as horse carts would be considered historical vehicles in other parts of the world. But the past and present exist side by side even in the United States. Maybelle the cable car still runs up hills in San Francisco along with taxis and buses.

Here is the opportunity to recreate the past through participatory stories and games. Stagecoaches, covered wagons, and the Pony Express are all vehicles children love to learn about. Films and television series have heightened the drama of these historical ways to travel. Now make them first-hand experiences for your children with our "Pull Them into a Circle" initiating activity or capture the rhythm of a covered wagon rumbling over the land with "Wagons, Ho!"

Children will learn skills from sequencing and classification to rhyme and rhythm and group cooperation. Historical accuracy and current information have been provided in the introductions to many activities, but the overall tone is lighthearted and whimsical enough to take a new look at the invention of the wheel in the flannel-board story "Reinventing the Wheel" or to join a crazy octopus on the "Double Double Double Decker Bus." Children respond to the imaginative nonsense of *The Owl and the Pussycat* in Lear's "pea green boat" just as they linger over the historical account of flight in the Provensens' *The Glorious Flight*. The scope, then, of this chapter is as wide as the world and as diverse as past and present developments in the story of transportation.

INITIATING ACTIVITY

Pull Them into a Circle

Pull your wagons into a circle so you won't get ambushed. Each wagon on the wagon train contained an individual family. Have the children roll hand over hand during first two lines. Leader points to a child on the last two lines so each can tell his or her name.

> Westward wheels a rollin'
> On the wagon train.
> Who's inside your wagon?
> Tell me, what's your name.

LITERATURE-SHARING EXPERIENCES

Books for Trolley Cars and Rickshaws

Anno, Mitsumasa. **Anno's Journey**. Collin World, 1977.

Anno's journey by horseback in a not clearly defined past age pictures characters and events from literature and art. Transportation from horse carts to stage coaches and railroads tell this unusual story of a journey through times past in a Northern European setting.

Brenner, Barbara. **Wagon Wheels**. Illustrated by Don Bolognese. Harper & Row, 1978.

An easy-to-read history in four short chapters, tells the story of a Black family who travel by wagon after the Civil War to Kansas in order to homestead.

Brown, Marcia. **Felice**. Scribners, 1958.

A little boy who is learning to be a gondolier in Venice wants a cat to go along with him and finds one who stows away in the gondola one night.

Burton, Virginia Lee. **Maybelle the Cable Car**. Houghton Mifflin, 1952.

The competition between Maybelle the cable car and Big Bill the new bus takes place in San Francisco. They discover there is a need for both kinds of transportation.

Byars, Betsy. **The Golly Sisters Go West**. Illustrated by Sue Truesdell. Harper & Row, 1985.

It's a rollicking west journey for the Golly sisters as they sing and dance their way across the frontier.

Cox, David. **Tin Lizzie and Little Nell**. Bodley Head, 1982.

A race of the new Tin Lizzie Car versus Little Nell the horse pulling the family in a sulky takes place in Australia. Nobody remembers who won!

Crowley, Arthur. **The Wagon Man**. Illustrated by Annie Gusman. Houghton Mifflin, 1981.

When children are lured away from home by the Wagon Man, one of the boys challenges him to a riddle game to save the children from Tarry Town.

Emberley, Barbara. **One Wide River to Cross**. Illustrated by Ed Emberley. Prentice Hall, 1966.

Bold woodcuts illuminate the American folk song based on the story of Noah and the ark.

The Erie Canal. Illustrated by Peter Spier. Doubleday, 1970.

The words to the familiar folk song and history of the canal are included at the back of this book that depicts not only travel on the canal but life in the small towns nearby.

Flack, Marjorie, and Kurt Weiss. **A Story about Ping**. Viking Press, 1933.

Boats on the Yangtze River provide an oriental setting for Ping as he arrives too late to get on board his boat one night.

Goble, Paul. **Death of the Iron Horse**. Bradbury, 1987.

Based on a true incident in 1867 in Nebraska, this story relates the derailment of a train by the Cheyenne who consider the "Iron Horse" a threat to their lives.

Hall, Donald. **Ox Cart Man**. Illustrated by Barbara Cooney. Viking, 1979.

Carefully detailed and lyrical account of a nineteenth century New England man and his family who fill the ox drawn cart to take to market where all the goods—including the ox and cart—are sold as the cycle begins all over again.

Krasilovsky, Phyllis. **The Cow Who Fell in the Canal**. Illustrated by Peter Spier. Doubleday, 1957.

Children who have not seen a canal will be enchanted with the cow who floats down the narrow waterway like we would drive down the street.

Kraus, Robert. **The Gondolier of Venice**. Illustrated by Robert Byrd. Windmill Books, 1976.

Will Venice sink? It is up to Gregory the gondolier to make sure that does not happen.

Levinson, Riki. **I Go with My Family to Grandma's**. Illustrated by Diane Goode. Dutton, 1986.

In this turn of the century setting, five cousins and their families go to visit Grandma in Brooklyn in a bicycle built for two, a trolley, a horse-drawn wagon, a train, and a ferry boat.

Lewin, Hugh. **Jafta—the Journey**. Illustrated by Lisa Kopper. Carolrhoda, 1983.

In this story of South Africa, Jafta and his mother go by cart to the city where his father works.

McDermott, Gerald. **The Voyage of Osiris**. Windmill, 1977.

The ancient Egyptian myth of Osiris comes to life with McDermott's fluid illustrations that tell the story of the god who is cast out to sea in a chest and dismembered by the evil Set. The final journey to the underworld ends triumphantly in a river barge ritualistically as the Nile floods give new life to the desert each year.

Provensen, Alice, and Martin Provensen. **The Glorious Flight across the Channel with Louis Bleriot July 25, 1909**. Viking, 1983.

Fascinated by flying machines, Louis Bleriot finally invents a model that flies over the English Channel in thirty-seven minutes. It was a glorious flight!

Rees, Ennis. **Windwagon Smith**. Illustrated by Peter Plasencia. Prentice Hall, 1966.

A fanciful covered wagon with a sail takes Windwagon Smith sailing across the prairie.

Scott, Geoffrey. **Egyptian Boats**. Carolrhoda, 1981.

This easy-to-read nonfiction book describes the importance of boats to the ancient Egyptians and describes various kinds including the ambatch, sailboats, merchantment, the barge, and the funeral boat.

Spier, Peter. **Noah's Ark**. Doubleday, 1977.

Almost wordless, but delightfully-detailed pictures recount the story of Noah and the flood.

Steele, Philip. **Land Transport around the World**. Dillon Press, 1986.

Large photographs and a sparse text introduce fourteen different kinds of transportation, from the more traditional horsecarts in Paraguay to a modern monorail in Germany.

Steig, William. **Farmer Palmer's Wagon Ride**. Farrar, Strauss & Giroux, 1974.

A wild ride in Farmer Palmer's wagon leaves the pig, donkey, and even the farmer in fear of their lives.

Related Activities for Trolley Cars and Rickshaws

Round the World Different Ways
(To the tune of "Good Night Ladies")

Add appropriate actions for each verse (holding reins, pulling, pedaling, chugging motion with hands). Use this song as an opportunity to discuss different kinds of transportation. A "trishaw" may be a new word to many children, for example. It is a mixture of a bicycle and a carriage, and somewhat similar to a rickshaw.

Drive a horse cart.
Drive a horse cart.
Drive a horse cart.
We're in Paraguay.

Pull an ox cart.
Pull an ox cart.
Pull an ox cart.
We're in India.

Pedal a trishaw.
Pedal a trishaw.
Pedal a trishaw.
We're in Thailand.

Take a railway,
In the mountains.
Take a railway.
We're in Switzerland.

Round the world
Lots of places
People going
So many different ways.

Reinventing the Wheel—A Rock and Roll Story
(A Flannel-board Story)

For this flannel board story, cut shapes of a triangle, rectangle, six-sided hexagon, and a circle. Place on the board as directed in the story.

People say the invention of the wheel by Cave Man was the greatest thing to happen to transportation. But it was the reinventing of the wheel that tells the whole story.

Cave Man was inventing things. He had been working on creating fire for several days, but he was not warm yet. He decided to take a break from that and begin on his next invention: the wheel.

"Wheel will be easy," said Cave Man, "I'll take a big rock and cut off the sides. Then wheel will roll like this. (*Roll hands*.) Why, I'll have wheel done in time for lunch."

So Cave Man got a big rock and he chipped away at one side and another and another and pretty soon he had a shape that had three points. (*Place triangle on the board*.) It was a nice shape, but it didn't look very much like a wheel and it didn't act very much like a wheel. It didn't roll like this. (*Roll hands*.)

So Cave Man took the big rock and he chipped away some more at one side and another and another and pretty soon he had a shape that had four points. (*Place rectangle on the board*.) It was a nice shape, but it didn't look very much like a wheel and it didn't act very much like a wheel. It didn't roll like this. (*Roll hands*.)

So Cave Man took the big rock again and he chipped away at one side and another and another and pretty soon he had a shape that had six points. (*Place hexagon on the board*.) It was a nice shape, but it didn't look very much like a wheel and it didn't act very much like a wheel. It didn't roll like this. (*Roll hands*.)

Cave Man was just about to give up when Cave woman came in. "Here is wheel," said Cave Man. "What do you think?"

Cave Woman shook her head. "You have missed the whole point of the wheel," she said. "A wheel has no points at all." And she took out her nail file and shaved off all the points on wheel. (*Place circle on board*.)

Cave Man was impressed. This looked like wheel and best of all it acted exactly like wheel should. It rolled just fine. (*Roll hands*.)

"Thanks," said Cave Man.

"Think nothing of it," said Cave Woman. "But now that I have reinvented the wheel, could you please finish working on fire so we can have lunch?"

Horse Power
(A Participatory Story)

Make ten grocery bag masks of horses. Select children to wear them in the story and one more child to play the part of Sam who holds a poster board stagecoach, as shown. Have the children in costume participate as indicated in the story. Have all children slap on knees, increasing speed as the horses trot, gallop and run.

In Colonial America, stagecoaches were the finest way to travel long distances. Most of them were pulled by teams of two horses. The horses ran fast and pulled hard. After awhile, the horses got tired, the horses got hungry. The driver had to change the team in New York and Boston and Philadelphia and Richmond.

(*Give child the stagecoach to hold.*) One day Sam started out from New York to Boston to Philadelphia to Richmond, Virginia. In New York he hitched up a team of horses named Abigail and Adam. (*Line up two horses in front of the stagecoach.*) Out on the road they trotted. Then they galloped. Then they ran. By the time they got to Boston, Abigail and Adam were tired. They were hungry. Sam had to change the team. (*Have children playing horses sit down.*)

In Boston, he hitched up a team named Betsy and Benjamin. (*Line up next two horses in front of the stagecoach.*) Out on the road they trotted. Then they galloped. Then they ran. By the time they got to Philadelphia, Betsy and Benjamin were tired. They were hungry. Sam had to change the team. (*Have children playing horses sit down.*)

In Philadelphia, he hitched up a team named Charles and Constance. (*Line up next two horses in front of the stagecoach.*) Out on the road they trotted. Then they galloped. Then they ran. By the time they got to Richmond, Charles and Constance were tired. They were hungry. Sam had to change the team. (*Have children playing horses sit down.*)

But Richmond was the end of the line. Sam had to go all the way back to New York and it was a long trip. One team could not go that far. Sam thought and thought. Then he said, "Whoa! What I need is more horse power!" So he hitched up two horses named David and Debra. (*Line up next two horses in front of the stagecoach.*) Then he hitched up two more horses named Ebenezer and Elizabeth. (*Line up next two horses in front of those horses.*) He had four-horse power. Out on the road they trotted. Then they galloped. Then they ran. They got to Philadelphia, but they were not tired. They trotted. Then they galloped. Then they ran. They got to Boston, but they were not tired. They trotted. Then they galloped. Then they ran. They got all the way to New York before they were tired and hungry. (*Have horses sit down.*)

Colonial stagecoaches were the finest way to travel. With a four-horse power stagecoach, they became the fastest, too. They still stopped in New York and Boston and Philadelphia and Richmond, but only because those were fun places to visit.

cut out eyes to fit child's face

HORSE POWER

STICK FOR HANDLE

Wagons, Ho!

One of the important ways to travel during the settlement of the West was the covered wagon. Give children a chance to recreate this adventure by practicing this chant several times until children are able to experience the rhythm and feel of the rolling wagons.

Let's go
Across the country
Like folks did
So long ago.
Hitch up the team
Let's pack
The covered wagon.
Get inside.
Wagons, ho!

Roll on
across the prairie
Tall grass
Swishing by—
Swish, swish
Swish, swish

Roll on
Through the river.
Water splashing
at our wheels—
Splash, splash
Splash, splash

Roll on
Over mountains
Foot hills
Rumble by
Rumble, rumble
Rumble, rumble

Roll on
to the new land.
Clear the forest.
Build a home.
Journey's
ended.
We are
settlers.
This was
wilderness.
Now
we're
home!

Trolley Car Song
(To the tune of "Jingle Bells")

Trolley car,
Trolley car,
Painted red and black.
Ding, ding,
Ding, ding,
Ding, ding, ding.
Come on, everyone stand back!
Trolley car,
Trolley car,
Better stay on track.
If you try to jump the rails,
You will just get out of whack!

Double Trouble
(To the tune of "If You're Happy and You Know It")

Introduce this British vehicle by singing this silly song with children. Many cities have adopted the English double decker bus for sight-seeing. If you wish to act out this song, let children become the various characters. For example, two children seated back to back can wiggle arms and legs to be the octopus.

On the double, double, double decker bus,
It was driven by a crazy octopus
He drove up to see the queen
She served green tea and sardines
On the double, double, double decker bus.

On the double, double, double decker bus,
The Bobby Bulldog made an awful fuss
When he found it double parked
You could hear him growl and bark,
"You're in trouble with your double decker bus."

On the double, double, double decker bus,
Said the Queen, "You're sounding much too furious.
Bobby Bulldog, join the ride
Tea and sardines on the side
On the double, double, double decker bus."

Out of Steam
(To the tune of "Row, Row, Row Your Boat")

Along with the wheel and the sailboat, the steam engine was one of the biggest developments in the history of transportation. Steam engines criss-crossed the country by the late 1800s transporting freight and passengers.

Engine puffing down the track,
Whistle starts to scream. (Whoooo!)
Slower, slower, slower,
Running .. out .. of .. steam
Sssssssss ....

Mush, Dogs—Go!
(A Flannel-board Story)

In preparation, make felt shapes of the following: red sweater, green sweater, blue and black snowshoes, two cooking pots, two sacks of potatoes, and a sack of dog food. Add to the sled and remove the pieces as indicated in the story.

(Text continues on page 206.)

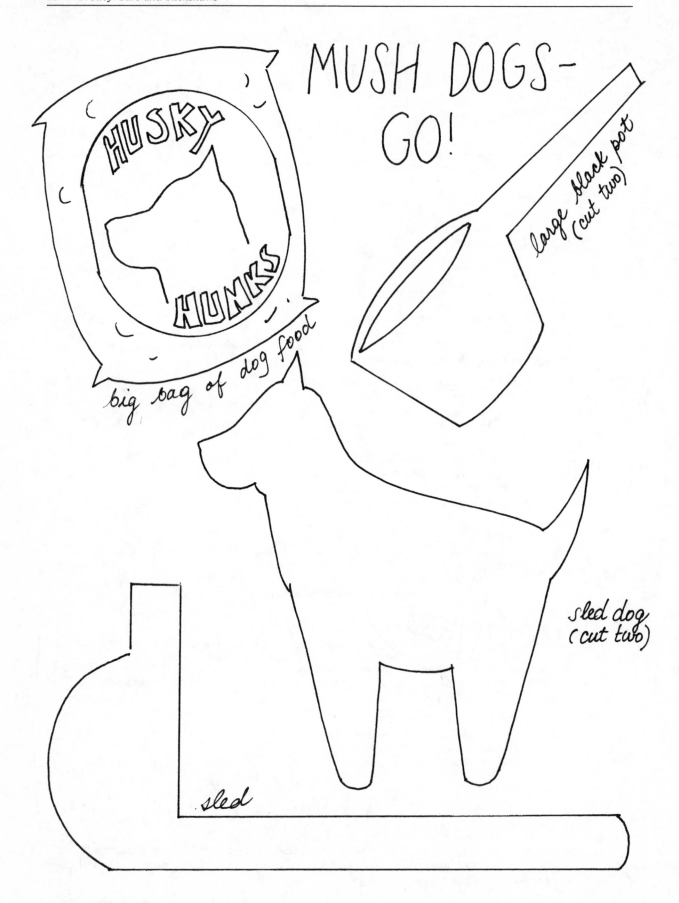

MUSH DOGS-
GO!

big bag of dog food

large black pot
(cut two)

sled dog
(cut two)

sled

MUSH DOGS—
GO!

snow shoes
(cut two)

U.S.
CHOICE
No.1
POTATO

potatoes
(cut two)

sweater
(cut two)

Eric lived in Greenland in a cabin far from everyone else. He was a scientist doing experiments in the cold weather. Eric could not just run to the store whenever he needed something. He only went every six months and then he bought lots and lots of things to last him. Eric did not drive a car or a truck into cold snow. He had a sled with two dogs to pull it. The dogs pulled fast and could carry heavy loads.

One January Eric came to town in his dog sled to get supplies for six months. He bought all the food he would need and started back out of town. But as he went down the street, he saw a sign that said: "Two-for-One After Christmas Special." Eric thought that paying for one and getting two sounded like a fine idea so he went into the store. It was a clothing store and the sale was on warm wooly sweaters. Eric picked a red one he paid for—and got a green one for free! He brought out the sweaters and said to the dogs:

> One for the money
> Two in the snow
> Load up the sled
> Mush, dogs—go!

And the dogs said, ARF!

Eric went a little further out of town and saw another sign. This one said: "Going out of Business. Everything Two-for-One Today Only." "What luck," thought Eric, and he went inside. The things that were on sale in this sports store were snowshoes. Eric bought a blue pair—and got a black pair free. He brought out the snowshoes and said to the dogs:

> One for the money
> Two in the snow
> Load up the sled
> Mush, dogs—go!

And the dogs said, ARF!

Eric went not much further and saw a sign that said, "We Overbought! Everything two-for-one until it is gone!" Eric was very excited about all the bargains he was getting so he went into that store, too. What was on sale in the kitchen wares store were large cooking pots. Eric bought a large black pot—and got another black pot free. He brought out the pots and said to the dogs:

> One for the money
> Two in the snow
> Load up the sled
> Mush, dogs—go!

And the dogs said, ARF!

Eric was almost out of town when he saw the last sign. It said: "While Supplies Last. All Two-for-One." Eric could hardly wait to see what other bargains he could get on his trip to town. The things on sale in the grocery store were twenty-five-pound sacks of potatoes. Eric bought twenty-five pounds of potatoes and got another twenty-five pounds free. He brought out the potatoes and said to the dogs:

> One for the money
> Two in the snow
> Load up the sled
> Mush, dogs—go!

And off they set for the cabin in the wilderness.

The dogs were strong, but this time Eric had loaded the sled so full they could just barely pull it over the snow. Eric could see the dogs would not make it to the cabin with the load. So when he saw a reindeer in the forest he had an idea. He gave one of the heavy wool sweaters to the reindeer to keep him warm. Then he called out to the dogs:

> One for the money
> Two in the snow
> Sweater for Reindeer
> Mush, dogs—go!

And all the dogs said, ARF!

Giving the sweater away helped some, but it was still a heavy load for the dogs. Eric could see the dogs would not make it to the cabin with the load. So when he saw a bear in the forest he had an idea. He gave one pair of snowshoes to the bear so he would not sink in the snow. Then he called out to the dogs:

> One for the money
> Two in the snow
> Bear gets the snowshoes
> Mush, dogs—go!

And all the dogs said, ARF!

Giving the snowshoes away helped some, but it was still a heavy load for the dogs. Eric could see the dogs would not make it to the cabin with the load. So when he saw a walrus in the forest he had an idea. He gave one cooking pot to the walrus to keep the fish he caught. The walrus carried the pot away with his tusk! Eric laughed and called out to the dogs:

> One for the money
> Two in the snow
> Pot for a walrus
> Mush, dogs—go!

And all the dogs said, ARF!

Giving the cooking pot away helped some, but it was still a heavy load for the dogs. Eric could see the dogs would not make it to the cabin with the load. So when he saw a seal in the forest he had an idea. He gave one bag of potatoes to the seal to feed her family. Eric called out to the dogs:

> One for the money
> Two in the snow
> Seal gets potatoes
> Mush, dogs—go!

And all the dogs said, ARF!

Now the sled was light enough for the dogs to pull easily and they were back to the cabin in no time. Eric unloaded the sled and took all the things inside. The last thing he took off was a big bag of Husky Hunks, the dog treats. He gave each dog a treat for being such good workers.

And all the dogs said, ARF!

Canal Cat

(A Flannel-board Story)

In preparation, make felt shapes of the following: a gondola, red rooster, green frog, yellow canary, blue bird, and a black cat. Add to and remove from the board as the story indicates.

(Text continues on page 210.)

CANAL CAT

Blue Bird

Puccinella

Red Rooster

Yellow Canary

CANAL CAT

Green Frog

Gondola

Puccinella was a cat who lived in Venice, Italy. He had a fancy name, but he was not a fancy cat. He was a plain alley cat. But he was a fine singer and he grew tired of singing his serenades down dark alleys and passageways. One day, Puccinella looked out to the canals where the beautiful gondola boats waited. Soon the gondoliers would float the boats out on the Grand Canal and they would sing and serenade all day and all night.

"Today," said Puccinella, "I will hide in one of the gondolas. And I will go out to sea. That is the life for me! O sole-a-meow!"

So Puccinella waited until Mario, one of the gondoliers, lay down for a siesta in his gondola. Then, the eager cat hid way down in the gondola. And he also fell asleep.

After awhile, Mario woke up and the passengers came to the canal. They started to climb in the gondolas.

First came Red Rooster. "Please, may I float in your boat? I want to go to sea," he said.

"Just come with me," said Mario.

So Red Rooster got into the gondola.

Next came Green Frog. "Please, may I float in your boat? I want to go to sea," he said.

"Just come with me," said Mario.

So Green Frog got into the gondola.

Next came Yellow Canary. "Please, may I float in your boat? I want to go to sea," he said.

"Just come with me," said Mario.

So Yellow Canary got into the gondola.

Next came Blue Bird. "Please, may I float in your boat? I want to go to sea," he said.

"Just come with me," said Mario.

So Blue Bird got into the gondola.

Then Mario pushed the gondola with his long oar, and he began to sing, "O sole-a-mia!" And Puccinella woke up! He started to sing and howl at the top of his lungs, "O sole-a-meow!"

Then Blue Bird started to sing. The gondola began to swing.

That made Yellow Canary start to sing. The gondola began to sway.

That made Green Frog start to croak. The gondola began to roll.

That made Red Rooster start to crow. The gondola began to rock.

Mario was frantic. "Don't rock the boat!" he cried.

But it was too late. The gondola rolled over. And out came Blue Bird. Out came Yellow Canary. Out came Green Frog. Out came Red Rooster. And out came Mario. Everyone was floating into the Grand Canal. All except Puccinella. He was hanging on to the side of the gondola.

Then the gondola rocked and rolled again and turned right side up. Puccinella jumped inside and sang his finest serenade "O sole-a-meow! This is the life for me!"

After that Puccinella rode up and down the canals singing his serenades. He never rocked the boat again. But he became a fine canal cat.

Shipped Out
(To the tune of "My Bonnie Lies Over the Ocean")

In China they sailed on a junk boat
With cotton sails on bamboo masts
Clipper ships sailed back in England
They clipped along ever so fast
Sailing, sailing to when ships were in their heyday,
Heyday
Hoist the mainsail
To long ago and far away.
HEY!

The kayak they used in Alaska
Had room for just one in the crew
In Spain they sailed on a big galleon
Out over the ocean so blue
Sailing, sailing
To when ships were in their heyday,
Heyday
Hoist the mainsail
To long ago and far away.
HEY!

Mayflower Voyage
(Finger Play)

Hold up one finger for each pilgrim mentioned.

Five little pilgrims	(*Five fingers extended.*)
Needed a ship.	
They found the Mayflower	
To make the long trip.	
The first little pilgrim	(*Hold up thumb.*)
waved England good by,	
Then looked ahead	(*Shade eyes with hand.*)
at the sea and sky.	
The second small pilgrim	(*Hold up index finger.*)
looked into the pools,	
There were fish swimming there	(*Palms together, wiggle wrists.*)
In hundreds of schools.	
The third little pilgrim	(*Hold up middle finger.*)
cried out, "Mercy, me!	
All I can see is the sea,	(*Hands to head, wag head.*)
the sea, the sea!"	
The fourth little pilgrim	(*Hold up ring finger.*)
Looked up in the air.	
He saw a sea gull	(*Flap elbows.*)
Flying there.	
The fifth little pilgrim	(*Hold up smallest finger.*)
Was the first one to know	
The journey was over.	(*Point straight ahead.*)
He cried out, "Land ho!"	
The Pilgrims gave thanks	(*Fold hands.*)
For lands to explore	
As the Mayflower rested	
On America's shore.	

Ports of Call: A Tale of Circumnavigation
(A Circle Story)

Teach this whopper of a word in this circle story. "Circum" means around and "navigation" means travel. So in this story there is a trip around the world—told with a circle poster, of course!

Make two circles of poster board. On one put a picture of a bear and a duck to the left of the center. Cut a wedge to the right side of center.

PORTS OF CALL

HOME SWEET HOME

TOP CIRCLE ↑

(Connect circles with brad)

BOTTOM CIRCLE ↑

On the other circle show the following modes of transportation: subway, double decker bus, camel, rickshaw, kangaroo, cable car. Finally, show a sign reading "Home Sweet Home."

You may wish to teach the four-line refrain to the children before the story begins so they can repeat it with you.

Commodore Beary had been on his ship the SS *Ursa Major*, for twenty-one years, seven days, and ten hours when he said,

> "Enough of the water,
> Enough of this boat.
> I want to be where
> I don't have to float.
>
> "Give me some dry land
> So I won't be sea sick.
> A camel or cab
> Will just do the trick!"

His First Mate, Mallard, had done a lot of traveling and knew about dry land as well as the water. The two friends set off to find some dry land and another way to travel. The first place they docked was New York City. "What can I ride here?" asked Commodore.
  "Try the subway," said First Mate Mallard. "That is what I always ride in New York."
  So Commodore Beary and First Mate Mallard went down the steps into the subway tunnel. They bought tokens and waited for the subway train. Rumble-rumble-rumble. The subway train made a lot of noise.
  "Too much noise," said Commodore Beary. "You won't find this much noise on my ship." So they went back to the SS *Ursa Major* and sailed on for seven more days and ten hours until the Commodore said,

> "Enough of the water,
> Enough of this boat
> I want to be where
> I don't have to float."

This time Commodore Beary and First Mate Mallard docked in London. "What can I ride here?" asked Commodore.
  "Try the double decker bus," said First Mate Mallard. "That is what I always ride in London."
  So they waited at the bus stop until a double decker bus came along. The only seats left were on the top deck. Commodore Beary knew he would get dizzy on the top deck.
  "Too high," he said. "You won't find seats this high on my ship." They went back to the SS *Ursa Major* and sailed on for seven days and ten hours when the Commodore said,

> "Enough of the water,
> Enough of this boat
> I want to be where
> I don't have to float."

This time Commodore Beary and First Mate Mallard docked in Egypt. "What can I ride here?" asked Commodore.
  "Try the camel," said First Mate Mallard. "That is what I always ride in Egypt."
  So Commodore Beary and First Mate Mallard stood on the desert sand and waited for a caravan to come by. When the caravan came, there was a camel with no one riding. The camel kicked up lots and lots of sand with his big flat feet.
  "Too much sand," said Commodore Beary. "You won't find this much sand on my ship." They went back to the SS *Ursa Major* and sailed on for seven days and ten hours when the Commodore said,

> "Enough of the water,
> Enough of this boat
> I want to be where
> I don't have to float."

This time Commodore Beary and First Mate Mallard docked in Japan. "What can I ride here?" asked Commodore.

"Try the rickshaw," said First Mate Mallard. "That is what I always ride in Japan."

So Commodore Beary and First Mate Mallard stood on a corner and waited for a rickshaw. Pretty soon one came down the street. Commodore Beary started to step into the rickshaw, but it creaked and cracked and he was afraid it would not hold him.

"Too rickety," said Commodore Beary. "My ship is much more solid than this." They went back to the SS *Ursa Major* and sailed on for seven days and ten hours when the Commodore said,

> "Enough of the water,
> Enough of this boat
> I want to be where
> I don't have to float."

This time Commodore Beary and First Mate Mallard docked in Australia. "What can I ride here?" asked Commodore.

"Try the kangaroo," said First Mate Mallard. "That is what I always ride in Australia."

So Commodore Beary and First Mate Mallard stood in the outback and waited for a kangaroo with an empty pouch to come by. Pretty soon one came along, hopping and jumping and leaping across the bush. Commodore Beary did not like all that hopping and leaping and jumping.

"Too bumpy," said Commodore Beary. "My ship is much more stable than this." They went back to the SS *Ursa Major* and sailed on for seven days and ten hours when the Commodore said,

> "Enough of the water,
> Enough of this boat
> I want to be where
> I don't have to float."

This time Commodore Beary and First Mate Mallard docked in San Francisco. "What can I ride here?" asked Commodore.

"Try the cable car," said First Mate Mallard. "That is what I always ride in San Francisco."

So Commodore Beary and First Mate Mallard stood by the cable car tracks and waited for a cable car to come along. Pretty soon one came along, but it was full of people. They waited for another one, but it was full of people. They waited for another one, but when it was full, too, Commodore Beary said, "Too full. My ship always has plenty of room." They went back to the SS *Ursa Major* and sailed on. Commodore Beary said,

> "Enough of the land.
> I like my own boat.
> I want to be where
> I am free and can float."

First Mate Mallard hung a sign over the porthole that said, "Home Sweet Home." The friends had a lot more adventures after that, but they always come back to their ship in the end.

GAMES FOR TROLLEY CARS AND RICKSHAWS

Four Corners of the World

Set up four corners of the room as different parts of the world, country or state—north, south, east and west. These may be areas you have studied or places pictured in travel posters or books. At each place the group will come up with the names of four items found in that region. Sing this little jingle as you travel from corner to corner to the tune of "Row Your Boat."

North, south, east, and west—
How much do you know?
Name me something you would see
As 'round the world we go.

Chariot Song

Sing these words to the tune "Pop Goes the Weasel" as the children circle the leader. On the word "come" point to one child to join the leader in the center. That child gets to choose the next one to come to the center and so on until everyone is in the winner's circle.

Round and round the Roman roads
The chariots are racing.
Rumble, rumble go the wheels
Come join the winners!

Pony Express

The Pony Express carried mail across country by handing it off from one carrier to another at designated points between St. Joseph, Missouri, and Sacramento, California. The mail went on to San Francisco by boat.

Recreate the Pony Express experience for your children. Mark a paper bag MAIL BAG and fill with treats. Children sit in a long line, as far apart as possible. The mail must go through. Set the bag by one seated child who must get it to the next child without using hands or feet. The last one in line can open the bag and share.

Wagon Train

Scatter children throughout the room. The wagon master walks to one child as all sing the following words to the tune of "If You're Happy and You Know It."

Won't you come along and join the wagon train?
Won't you come along and join the wagon train?
We will blaze the trail before us
And will sing this Western chorus
Won't you come along and join the wagon train?

That child places hands on shoulders of the wagon master and they both head for another child. Each adds on to the line until all the children are in the train. Pull the wagons into a circle and be seated for the next activity.

CRAFTS FOR TROLLEY CARS AND RICKSHAWS

Chuck Wagon

Cut a simple covered wagon from paper. Children can cut pictures of favorite food and paste on their ideas of a hearty meal at the end of the trail.

Who's on the Ark?

Use a file folder. Cut the shape of an ark from the folder, leaving the bottom fold intact. Children decorate the outside and draw water along the bottom. Inside they paste pictures of animals.

CRAFTS FOR TROLLEY CARS AND RICKSHAWS

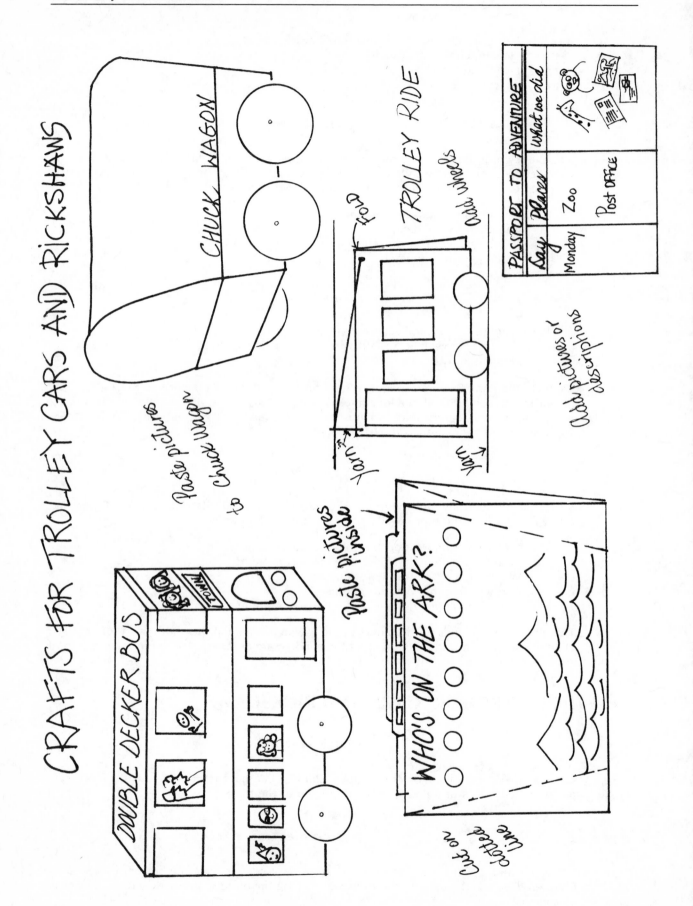

CHUCK WAGON

Paste pictures to Chuck Wagon

TROLLEY RIDE

fold

Yarn

Add wheels

Add pictures or descriptions

PASSPORT TO ADVENTURE		
Day	Places	What we did
Monday	Zoo	
	Post Office	

DOUBLE DECKER BUS

Paste pictures inside

WHO'S ON THE ARK?

Cut on dotted line

Double Decker Bus

For each child, cover two shoe boxes with red wrapping paper. Attach the boxes one on top of the other with strong two-sided tape, the kind used for carpets or fabric. Decorate the outside of the boxes with windows and cut out people looking out, destination sign on front, wheels and headlights cut from cardboard. Another good box to use for a smaller bus are the kind bank checks come in.

Trolley Ride

Copy the illustration that is designed to be a stand-up trolley car. Children can color the trolley, cut out on the solid lines and fold on the dotted line. The children may add yarn for the tracks and line.

TAKE-HOME ACTIVITY FOR TROLLEY CARS AND RICKSHAWS

Passport to Adventure

Use the outlined chart for each child and family to record their travels. Write specific places in your community that families visit such as post office, bus station, airport, car dealer, garage. Families can write the name of the exact place visited and date to record their adventures. Completed charts can be displayed at the library or classroom.

DATE   PLACES WE VISITED   MY FAVORITE PART

Day 1

Day 2

Resource Bibliography

Blocksma, Mary, and Dewey Blocksma. **Easy to Make Spaceships That Really Fly**. Illustrated by Marisluna Russo. Prentice Hall, 1983.

Materials for these easy to make spaceships include paper plates, straws, styrofoam cups and fast food cartons. Results are satisfying and fun.

Blumberg, Rhoda. **The First Travel Guide to the Moon**. Illustrated by Roy Doty. Four Winds, 1980.

A jaunty guide for the 21st century traveller to the moon. Fun for older guides or for a teacher resource book.

Brown, Walter R., and Norman D. Anderson. **Ferris Wheels**. Pantheon, 1983.

This resource book provides the history of pleasure "wheels" with many old photographs and drawings as well as present day pictures.

Cars and Boats. Illustrated by Louise Nevett. Consultant Caroline Pitcher. Franklin Watts, 1983.

Instructions for making such projects as a milk carton bus, steamroller, tank truck, Viking long-ship and match box train use pictures and a minimum of text so children who are new readers will be able to complete the vehicles with little help.

Cobblestone, Vol. 8, no. 7, July 1987.

This issue entitled "Cobblestone Hits the Road: The Automobile in History" includes articles on Henry Ford, famous automobile races, and early recreational vehicles.

Conaway, Judith. **Things That Go: How to Make Toy Boats, Cars and Planes**. Illustrated by Renzo Barto. Troll Associates, 1987.

Illustrated directions show how to make seventeen vehicles including a kooky car from an animal cookie box, an oatmeal box tank truck, and a toothpaste box airplane.

Larrick, Nancy. **The Wheels on the Bus Go Round and Round**. Illustrated by Gene Walton. Golden Gate Junior Books, 1972. Music arranged by Patty Zeitlin.

School bus songs and chants are designed to make the miles fly by.

Linsley, Leslie. **Air Crafts: Playthings to Make and Fly**. Photographed by Jon Aron. Lodestar, 1982.

Craft projects that use air to move include whirley copters, distance gliders, and valentine kite. All use materials found around the home and instructions are clear.

Planes and Space. Illustrated by Louis Nevett. Consultant, Caroline Pitcher. Franklin Watts, 1983.

A yogurt container satellite, egg carton moon buggy, and potato jet are just a few of the unusual creations described in this craft resource book. Clear and brightly-colored illustrations with a minimum of text can be followed easily by younger children.

Quackenbush, Robert. **Along Came the Model T**. Parents, 1978.

This biography of the developer of the first lightweight, inexpensive automobile may be read by middle grade elementary children or used as a teacher resource for younger children. The brightly colored cartoon illustrations and craft project of a styrofoam "tin lizzie" might be enjoyed by younger and older children.

Raffi. **The Raffi Singable Songbook**. Illustrated by Joyce Yamamoto. Crown, 1980.

A collection of fifty-one songs from the popular song maker includes several favorites on transportation—"Bumping Up and Down," "Jig Along Home," "Listen to the Horses," "New River Train," "Who Built the Ark," and "Workin' on the Railroad."

Readers on the Move. I READ program manual. Illinois Library Association, 1986.

This guide to programming provided Illinois libraries with a summer full of movement related activities. It is available from the Illinois Library Association, Chicago, Illinois.

Shactman, Tom. **Parade!** Macmillan, 1985.

A brief history of parades begins this book that focuses on the preparations and behind the scenes experiences of the Annual Thanksgiving Day Macy's Parade. This resource book is fine background for the stories in chapter 7 of this book.

Simon, Seymour. **How to Be a Space Scientist in Your Own Home**. Illustrated by Bill Mornson. Lippincott, 1982.

A collection of scientific experiments for teachers or older children explores principles of space flight.

Thomas, Art. **Merry-Go-Rounds**. Illustrated by George Overlie. Carolrhoda, 1981.

An easy-to-read text traces the history of merry-go-rounds from 900 years ago in Arabia with men riding horses and playing a game of catch at the same time. Later they became machines with wooden horses—the first operated by people, then by steam engines with pipe organs.

Tunis, Edward. **Frontier Living**. Crowell, 1961.

This illustrated history of the frontier provides background on freight wagons, coach lines, early railroads, and stage coaches for the teacher or older child.

Van Steenwyk, Elizabeth. **Behind the Scenes at the Amusement Park**. Whitman, 1983.

This history of present day maintenance of many well known amusement parks such as Disneyland and Disneyworld are included as well as basic information about roller coasters and carousels.

West, Robin. **Far Out: How to Create Your Own Star World**. Photographs by Bob Wolfe and Diane Wolfe. Drawings by Priscilla. Carolrhoda, 1987.

Space creatures and vehicles are created from such household items as toilet paper tubes, drinking cups, and egg cartons. Brightly colored construction paper details will inspire kids to add stellar touches to their own constructions.

Williams, J. Alan. **The Interplanetary Toy Book**. Macmillan, 1985.

Step-by-step instructions for flying machines, space vehicles, and creatures are included. Materials needed range from cardboard boxes to plastic bottles and containers.

Wyler, Rose. **Science Fun with Toy Boats and Planes**. Illustrated by Pat Stewart. Julian Messner, 1986.

Experiments with boats that float, are propelled by paddles or propellers, and simple paper planes teach children the principles of floating and flying as they make their own boats and planes.

Skills List

Self-Awareness Skills
Gross Motor Skills
Directional Orientation Skills
Health and Safety Skills
Color Recognition Skills
Size and Shape Skills
Rhythm and Rhyming Skills
Following Directions Skills
Group Cooperation Skills
Musical Skills
Artistic Skills
Role and Dialogue Invention Skills
Sequencing Skills
Classification Skills
Word Recognition Skills

Breakdown
of Activities
by Skills Area

Refer to Alphabetical Index of Activities for page numbers.

Self-Awareness Skills

Arm Chair Travelers
Balancing Act
Come Home Now
Dream Trip Take-Home Activity
Everybody Rides
Flight Bag Take-Home Activity
Flights of Fantasy
Fly Me to the Moon Game
Magical Musical Chairs
Mind Flight
Mini Olympics
Off to a Silly Start
On-the-Go Bingo
Park Your Car
Passport to Adventure
Pony Express
Pull Them into a Circle
Stegosaurus Standup
Too Many Training Wheels
Walk with Your Eyes Diary
Welcome Aboard
Wings on My Feet
Your Kind of Town

Gross Motor Skills

1-2-3-4 Moose
All Aboard
Animal Parade
Arm Chair Travelers

Baby Buggy Chant
Balancing Act
Bicycle Built for Everybody
Big Parade
Blast Off
Bouncity-Bounce
Brontosaurus Bounce
Camper Caper
Captain Says
Cement Mixer Chant
Chariot Song
Chuck Wagon
Circus Parade
Crane
Double Trouble
Dream Machine
Dump Truck Song
Elevated or Underground
Fairy Dust Wanderlust
Family Trip Tricks
Ferris Wheel
Fire Truck Song
Flippity-Flop
Four Corners of the World
Friendly Skies
Gas Station Song
Gravity Walk Game
Great Galaxies
Great Train Chain Game
Helicopter Song
Horse of a Different Color Merry-Go-Round

Horse Power
How Do They Do It?
I Made a Little Airplane
Incredible Dream Machine
Kids That Wiggle, Machines That Work
Magic Rings and Unicorns
Magical Musical Chairs
Mayflower Voyage
Mind Flight
Mini Olympics
Moving Around
Not for the Birds
Off to a Silly Start
Out of This World Vacation
Particular Penguins
Pony Express
Pull Them into a Circle
Put on the Brakes
Put Out the Fire
Ride on a Dream Machine
Roller Coaster Ride
Round the World Different Ways
Row Your Boat Some More
School Bus Song
Scoop and Dump
Sea Worthy Craftable Craft
Slow and Fast
Snow Time
Space Shot
Star Ship Crew Song
Stilts
Strut Your Stuff
Super Dooper Dream Machine
Things That Help Us Work
Three Tractors and Buba
Train Tales Game
Tumbling Tricks
Unicorn Catch
Uplifting Experience
Vendor Cart
Wagon Train
Whirlybird to the Rescue
Who Will Save the Day?
Who's Moving Outside?
Wings on My Feet
Winter Wonderland
Work Machine Workout

Directional Orientation Skills

Camper Caper
Cheap Skates
Four Corners of the World
Long Walk Home

Out of This World Vacation
Park Your Car
Your Kind of Town

Health and Safety Skills

Bicycle Built for Five
Elevator Song
Higher, Daddy
Just Enough Ice for the Mice
Mini Olympics
No Fuss on the Bus
Put on the Brakes
Road Hog
Roller Coaster Ride
Seat Belt Song
Skateboards—Be Careful!
Stilt Walk
Stilts
Traffic Lights
Whirlybird to the Rescue

Color Recognition Skills

Balloon to Zanzibar
Bicycle Built for Everybody
Bicycle Built for Five
Blast Off
Boxcar Countdown
Canal Cat
Christmas on the Scooter Limited Express
Design Your Own Sportscar
Family Trip Tricks
Hopscotch Song
Horse of a Different Color Merry-Go-Round
Horse of a Different Color
Horse Power
Just Enough Ice for the Mice
Kangaroo Countdown
Mayflower Voyage
Mush, Dogs—Go!
Parking Meter Rhyme
Rainbow Express
School Bus Match
Ship Shape
Shoe Shoe Choo Choo Train Cars
Ten Little Space Ships
Too Many Training Wheels
Traffic Lights
Trolley Ride
Walk with Your Eyes Diary
Who's Moving Outside?
With Flying Colors

Size and Shape Skills

Assembly Line Game
Bicycle Built for Five
Bumpkin in a Pumpkin
Can't Be Too Clean
Can't Miss
Carry On
Christmas on the Scooter Limited Express
Double Decker Bus
Elephant Parade Craft
Extra Special Extraterrestrial
Fans of the Foot
Fred's Sled
Gingerbread Kid
Great Race
Horse of a Different Color
I Made a Little Airplane
Magic Fairy Wands
Moveable Parts Trucks
Oatmeal and Shoebox Train Engine
Paper Snail and Turtle Craft
Picture This School Bus Craft
Refrigerator Carton Rocket
Reinventing the Wheel
Round and Round
Row, Row, Row Your Boat Craft
Ship Shape
Slightly Stilted
Smooth Sailing
Stegosaurus Standup
Three Tractors and Buba
What Big Feet You Have!
With Flying Colors

Rhythm and Rhyming Skills

At the Station
Awesome Sight
Baby Buggy Chant
Blast Off
Bouncity-Bounce
Boxcar Countdown
Brontosaurus Bounce
Bumper Car Bump
Bumpkin in a Pumpkin
Butterflight
Canal Cat
Chariot Song
Circus Parade
Come for a Ride
Come Home Now
Dancer
Dog Hunt
Double Trouble

Escalator: A Moving Experience
Fairy Dust Wanderlust
Ferris Wheel
Four Corners of the World
Great Race
Hare and Tortoise Retold
Helicopter Song
Home in the Van
Horse of a Different Color Merry-Go-Round
How Do They Do It?
I Made a Little Airplane
Ice Cream Truck Song
Just Enough Ice for the Mice
Kangaroo Countdown
Kids That Wiggle, Machines That Work
Listen to a Dream Machine
Magic Carpet Ride
Movin' and Groovin' at the Zoo
Moving Around
Mush, Dogs—Go!
No Fuss on the Bus
Off to a Silly Start
Only Way to Fly
Out of Steam
Packing the Car
Parking Meter Rhyme
Particular Penguins
Ports of Call
Pull Them into a Circle
Ride on a Dream Machine
Roller Coaster Ride
Roller Derby Reindeer
Sea Worthy Craftable Craft
Seasonal Walks
See Saw Chant
Shipped Out
Skateboards—Be Careful!
Sled Song
Slightly Stilted
Space Shot
Star Ship Crew Song
Subway Ride
Swing Song
Take-Off Chant
Terry and the Tow Truck
Truck Talk Chant
Truck Talk Game
Uplifting Experience
Wagons, Ho!
Welcome Aboard
Whirlybird to the Rescue
Who Will Save the Day?
Wings on My Feet
Witch's Broom

Following Directions Skills

1-2-3-4 Moose
All Aboard
All Hands on Deck
All Hands on Deck Craft
Assembly Line Game
Balancing Act
Bicycle Built for Everybody
Bicycle Built for Five
Big Parade
Blast Off
Brontosaurus Bounce
Camper Caper
Captain Says
Chariot Song
Chuck Wagon
Circus Wagons
Design Your Own Satellite Craft
Design Your Own Sportscar
Dog Hunt
Double Decker Bus
Elephant Parade Craft
Everybody Rides
Extra Special Extraterrestrial
Family Trip Tricks
Fans of the Foot
Fast and Slow
Fire Fighter Helmet
Flight Bag Take-Home Activity
Four Corners of the World
Friendly Skies
Garbage Truck Collage
Gravity Walk Game
Great Galaxies
Great Train Chain Game
Horse of a Different Color Merry-Go-Round
Horse of a Different Color
I Loaded My Moving Van
Ice and Mice
Incredible Dream Machine
Listen to a Dream Machine
Magic Carpet Ride
Magic Rings and Unicorns
Magical Musical Chairs
Mind Flight
Mini Olympics
Moveable Parts Trucks
Moving Around
Oatmeal and Shoebox Train Engine
On the Move Craft
On-the-Go Bingo
Paper Snail and Turtle Craft
Park Your Car
Passport to Adventure

Picture This School Bus Craft
Pony Express
Put on the Brakes
Real Swingers
Refrigerator Carton Rocket
Round and Round
Row Your Boat Some More
Row, Row, Row Your Boat Craft
Sea Worthy Craftable Craft
Shoe Shoe Choo Choo Train Cars
Simple Gas Pump
Smooth Sailing
Snow Time
Stegosaurus Standup
Stilts
Strut Your Stuff
Super Dooper Dream Machine
Swing Things
Take Along Bag
Things That Help Us Work
Tracks and Trails
Trolley Ride
Truck Talk Game
Truck Talk Take-Home Game
Tumbling Tricks
Wagon Train
Way to Go Home
Welcome Aboard
What Big Feet You Have!
Who Will Save the Day?
Who's on the Ark?
Winter Wonderland
Witch's Broom
Work Machine Workout
Your Kind of Town

Group Cooperation Skills

1-2-3-4 Moose
All Aboard
Animal Parade
Assembly Line Game
At the Station
Bicycle Built for Everybody
Big Parade
Blast Off
Brontosaurus Bounce
Captain Says
Chariot Song
Chuck Wagon
Come for a Ride
Crane
Dream Machine
Dream Trip Take-Home Activity

Everybody Rides
Fast and Loud
Four Corners of the World
Friendly Skies
Gravity Walk Game
Great Galaxies
Great Train Chain Game
Great-Full-Service-with-Everything
Horse of a Different Color Merry-Go-Round
I Helped Pack the Trunk
I Loaded My Moving Van
Incredible Dream Machine
Listen to a Dream Machine
Magic Rings and Unicorns
Magical Musical Chairs
Mini Olympics
Moving Around
Off to a Silly Start
On-the-Go Bingo
Passport to Adventure
Pony Express
Put on the Brakes
Race for Three Wheels
Refrigerator Carton Rocket
Rocket, Rocket, Blast Off
Roller Rink Round
School Bus Match
Super Dooper Dream Machine
Swing Things
Traffic Jam
Train Tales Game
Truck Talk Game
Truck Talk Take-Home Game
Unicorn Catch
Vendor Cart
Wagon Train
Way to Go Home
Who's Moving Outside?
Winter Wonderland
Witch's Broom
Work Machine Workout

Musical Skills

All Aboard
Baby Walk
Bicycle Built for Everybody
Big Parade
Bumper Car Bump
Butterflight
Carousel Ride Song
Chariot Song
Chuck Wagon
Crane

Dancer
Double Trouble
Dump Truck Song
Elevated or Underground
Elevator Song
Escalator: A Moving Experience
Farm Work
Fast and Loud
Fire Truck Song
Fly Me to the Moon Game
Friendly Skies
Gas Station Song
Going Flying
Helicopter Song
Home in the Van
Hopscotch Song
Ice Cream Truck Song
In My Plane
Let's Take a Taxi
Movin' and Groovin' at the Zoo
Only Way to Fly
Out of Steam
Put Out the Fire
Roller Rink Round
Round the World Different Ways
Row Your Boat Some More
Sailing on the Ocean in Our Boat
School Bus Song
Scoop and Dump
Seasonal Walks
Seat Belt Song
Shipped Out
Skateboard Song
Skateboards — Be Careful!
Sled Song
Slow and Fast
Star Ship Crew Song
Stilt Walk
Subway Ride
Swing Song
Ten Little Space Ships
Traffic Lights
Trolley Car Song
Unicorn Catch
Very Best Bike
Wagon Song
Wagon Train
Witch's Broom

Artistic Skills

All Hands on Deck
All Hands on Deck Craft
Circus Wagons

Design Your Own Satellite Craft
Design Your Own Sportscar
Double Decker Bus
Dream Machine
Elephant Parade Craft
Everybody Rides
Extra Special Extraterrestrial
Fans of the Foot
Fire Fighter Helmet
Garbage Truck Collage
Horse of a Different Color
Ice and Mice
Magic Fairy Wands
Moveable Parts Trucks
Oatmeal and Shoebox Train Engine
On the Move Craft
Paper Snail and Turtle Craft
Park Your Car
Picture This School Bus Craft
Real Swingers
Refrigerator Carton Rocket
Round and Round
Row, Row, Row Your Boat Craft
Shoe Shoe Choo Choo Train Cars
Simple Gas Pump
Smooth Sailing
Snow Time
Stegosaurus Standup
Stilts
Take Along Bag
Tracks and Trails
Trolley Ride
What Big Feet You Have!
Who's on the Ark?
Your Kind of Town

Role and Dialogue Invention Skills

April Fool Monkey Shines
Come for a Ride
Double Trouble
Flights of Fantasy
Horse Power
Incredible Dream Machine
No Fuss on the Bus
Not for the Birds
Puddlestop Express Mess
Road Hog
Rocket, Rocket, Blast Off
Stuck in a Rut
Super Dooper Dream Machine
Three Tractors and Buba
Vendor Cart
Whirlybird to the Rescue

Who's Moving Outside?
With Flying Colors

Sequencing Skills

April Fool Monkey Shines
Baby Walk
Balloon to Zanzibar
Bicycle Built for Everybody
Bicycle Built for Five
Blast Off
Boxcar Countdown
Bumpkin in a Pumpkin
Camper Caper
Can't Be Too Clean
Can't Miss
Canal Cat
Carry On
Cement Mixer Chant
Cheap Skates
Come for a Ride
Dog Hunt
Everything and the Kitchen Sink
Family Trip Tricks
Fast and Slow
Fred's Sled
Gingerbread Kid
Going Flying
Great Race
Great-Full-Service-with-Everything
Hare and Tortoise Retold
Higher, Daddy
Hopscotch Song
Horse Power
I Helped Pack the Trunk
Into the Wild Blue Yonder
Just Enough Ice for the Mice
Kangaroo Countdown
Long Walk Home
Mayflower Voyage
Mr. Bumpenrumble's New Car
Mush, Dogs—Go!
No Fuss on the Bus
Not for the Birds
Out of This World Vacation
Parking Meter Rhyme
Passport to Adventure
Race for Three Wheels
Rainbow Express
Reinventing the Wheel
Road Hog
Sandy Claws
School Bus Match
School Bus Song

Sea Worthy Craftable Craft
Ship Shape
Skis, Please
Smooth Sailing
Stuck in a Rut
Swing Things
Take-Off Chant
Tale of the Too-Full Garbage Truck
Ten Little Space Ships
Terry and the Tow Truck
There's No Place Like Home
Three Tractors and Buba
Too Many Training Wheels
Traffic Jam
Traffic Lights
Train Tales Game
Walk with Your Eyes Diary
Way to Go Home
What Do I Do?
Whirlybird to the Rescue
Who Will Save the Day?
Willie's Space Ship
With Flying Colors

I Helped Pack the Trunk
Kids That Wiggle, Machines That Work
Mind Flight
Mr. Bumpenrumble's New Car
Not for the Birds
On-the-Go Bingo
Ports of Call
Puddlestop Express Mess
Rainbow Express
Rocket, Rocket, Blast Off
Round the World Different Ways
School Bus Match
Seasonal Walks
Shipped Out
Strut Your Stuff
Things That Help Us Work
Train Tales Game
Truck Talk Game
Truck Talk Take-Home Game
Walk with Your Eyes Diary
What Do I Do?
Who's on the Ark?
Work Machine Workout

Classification Skills

April Fool Monkey Shines
Assembly Line Game
Dream Trip Take-Home Activity
Elevated or Underground
Fast and Slow
Four Corners of the World
How Do They Do It?

Word Recognition Skills

Family Trip Tricks
Four Corners of the World
I Helped Pack the Trunk
Put on the Brakes
Swing Things
Traffic Jam
Train Tales Game

Alphabetical Index
of Activities Showing
Associated Skills

This index is designed so that it can be used in two ways: All the activities in the book—games, songs, crafts, projects, etc.—are listed alphabetically, each with its page number. Thus we have an activities index. In addition, the skills enriched by the activities in *Full Speed Ahead* are listed across the top of each two-page column, and for each activity *X*'s mark the associated skills. Thus we have a chart for immediate skill identification.

ACTIVITY	Self-Awareness Skills	Gross Motor Skills	Directional Orientation Skills	Health and Safety Skills	Color Recognition Skills	Size and Shape Skills	Rhythm and Rhyming Skills	Following Directions Skills	Group Cooperation Skills	Musical Skills	Artistic Skills	Role and Dialogue Invention Skills	Sequencing Skills	Classification Skills	Word Recognition Skills
1-2-3-4 Moose (p. 29)		X						X	X						
All Aboard (p. 81)		X						X	X	X					
All Hands on Deck (p. 98)								X			X				
All Hands on Deck Craft (p. 100)								X			X				
Animal Parade (p. 28)		X							X						
April Fool Monkey Shines (p. 113)												X	X	X	
Arm Chair Travelers (p. 187)	X	X													
Assembly Line Game (p. 71)						X		X	X					X	
At the Station (p. 78)							X		X						
Awesome Sight (p. 185)		X					X								
Baby Buggy Chant (p. 70)							X								
Baby Walk (p. 6)										X			X		
Balancing Act (p. 50)	X	X			X			X							
Balloon to Zanzibar (p. 146)				X	X										
Bicycle Built for Everybody (p. 49)		X			X		X	X	X	X			X		
Bicycle Built for Five (p. 38)						X	X	X					X		
Big Parade (p. 188)		X			X		X	X	X	X			X		
Blast Off (p. 148)		X						X	X						
Bouncity-Bounce (p. 48)		X			X										
Boxcar Countdown (p. 84)							X	X					X		
Brontosaurus Bounce (p. 185)		X					X	X	X						

ACTIVITY	Self-Awareness Skills	Gross Motor Skills	Directional Orientation Skills	Health and Safety Skills	Color Recognition Skills	Size and Shape Skills	Rhythm and Rhyming Skills	Following Directions Skills	Group Cooperation Skills	Musical Skills	Artistic Skills	Role and Dialogue Invention Skills	Sequencing Skills	Classification Skills	Word Recognition Skills
Extra Special Extraterrestrial (p. 163)						X		X			X				
Fairy Dust Wanderlust (p. 180)		X					X								
Family Trip Tricks (p. 77)		X			X			X					X		X
Fans of the Foot (p. 29)						X		X			X				
Farm Work (p. 123)										X					
Fast and Loud (p. 121)															
Fast and Slow (p. 29)								X	X	X			X	X	
Ferris Wheel (p. 172)		X					X								
Fire Fighter Helmet (p. 130)								X			X				
Fire Truck Song (p. 121)		X								X					
Flight Bag Take-Home Activity (p. 164)	X							X							
Flights of Fantasy (p. 179)	X											X			
Flippity-Flop (p. 29)		X													
Fly Me to the Moon Game (p. 158)	X									X					
Four Corners of the World (p. 214)		X	X				X	X	X					X	X
Fred's Sled (p. 44)						X							X		
Friendly Skies (p. 158)		X						X	X	X					X
Garbage Truck Collage (p. 130)								X			X				
Gas Station Song (p. 60)		X								X			X		
Gingerbread Kid (p. 9)						X									

ACTIVITY	Self-Awareness Skills	Gross Motor Skills	Directional Orientation Skills	Health and Safety Skills	Color Recognition Skills	Size and Shape Skills	Rhythm and Rhyming Skills	Following Directions Skills	Group Cooperation Skills	Musical Skills	Artistic Skills	Role and Dialogue Invention Skills	Sequencing Skills	Classification Skills	Word Recognition Skills
Mini Olympics (p. 50)	X	X						X							
Moveable Parts Trucks (p. 127)		X		X				X	X						
Movin' and Groovin' at the Zoo (p. 19)						X	X	X			X				
Moving Around (p. 32)		X					X			X					
Mr. Bumpenrumble's New Car (p. 58)								X	X						
Mush, Dogs—Go! (p. 203)					X		X						X	X	
No Fuss on the Bus (p. 81)				X			X					X	X		
Not for the Birds (p. 4)		X											X		
Oatmeal and Shoebox Train Engine (p. 102)											X	X	X	X	
Off to a Silly Start (p. 1)	X	X				X	X	X	X		X				
On the Move Craft (p. 130)								X			X				
On-the-Go-Bingo (p. 103)	X							X	X					X	
Only Way to Fly (p. 147)							X			X					
Out of Steam (p. 203)							X			X					
Out of This World Vacation (p. 153)		X	X										X		
Packing the Car (p. 55)						X	X	X							
Paper Snail and Turtle Craft (p. 73)	X	X	X					X			X				
Park Your Car (p. 53)					X		X	X			X				
Parking Meter Rhyme (p. 63)							X						X		

ACTIVITY	Self-Awareness Skills	Gross Motor Skills	Directional Orientation Skills	Health and Safety Skills	Color Recognition Skills	Size and Shape Skills	Rhythm and Rhyming Skills	Following Directions Skills	Group Cooperation Skills	Musical Skills	Artistic Skills	Role and Dialogue Invention Skills	Sequencing Skills	Classification Skills	Word Recognition Skills
Shoe Shoe Choo Choo Train Cars (p. 102)					X			X			X				
Simple Gas Pump (p. 73)								X			X				
Skateboard Song (p. 34)		X								X					
Skateboards—Be Careful! (p. 34)				X			X			X					
Skis, Please (p. 46)													X		
Sled Song (p. 46)							X			X					
Slightly Stilted (p. 47)		X				X	X								
Slow and Fast (p. 25)		X					X								
Smooth Sailing (p. 102)		X				X		X		X	X		X		
Snow Time (p. 52)		X						X			X				
Space Shot (p. 150)							X								
Star Ship Crew Song (p. 149)		X					X								
Stegosaurus Standup (p. 189)	X					X		X		X					
Stilt Walk (p. 47)		X		X											
Stilts (p. 52)		X		X				X			X				
Strut Your Stuff (p. 29)								X						X	
Stuck in a Rut (p. 56)							X	X		X		X	X		
Subway Ride (p. 81)								X	X						
Super Dooper Dream Machine (p. 177)		X								X		X			
Swing Song (p. 49)							X			X					

ACTIVITY	Word Recognition Skills	Classification Skills	Sequencing Skills	Role and Dialogue Invention Skills	Artistic Skills	Musical Skills	Group Cooperation Skills	Following Directions Skills	Rhythm and Rhyming Skills	Size and Shape Skills	Color Recognition Skills	Health and Safety Skills	Directional Orientation Skills	Gross Motor Skills	Self-Awareness Skills
Who's Moving Outside? (p. 26)				X			X				X			X	
Who's on the Ark? (p. 215)		X			X			X							
Willie's Space Ship (p. 150)			X											X	X
Wings on My Feet (p. 143)									X					X	
Winter Wonderland (p. 58)							X	X							
Witch's Broom (p. 186)						X	X	X	X	X	X				
With Flying Colors (p. 167)			X	X											
Work Machine Workout (p. 127)		X					X	X						X	
Your Kind of Town (p. 52)					X			X					X		X

Literature Index

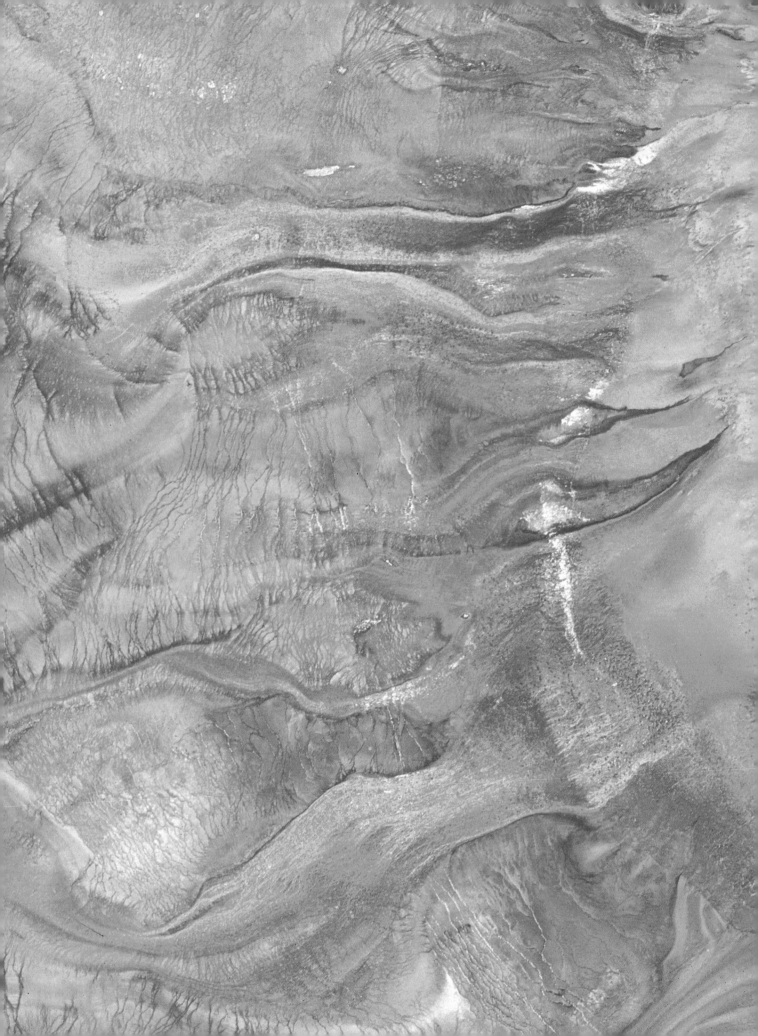

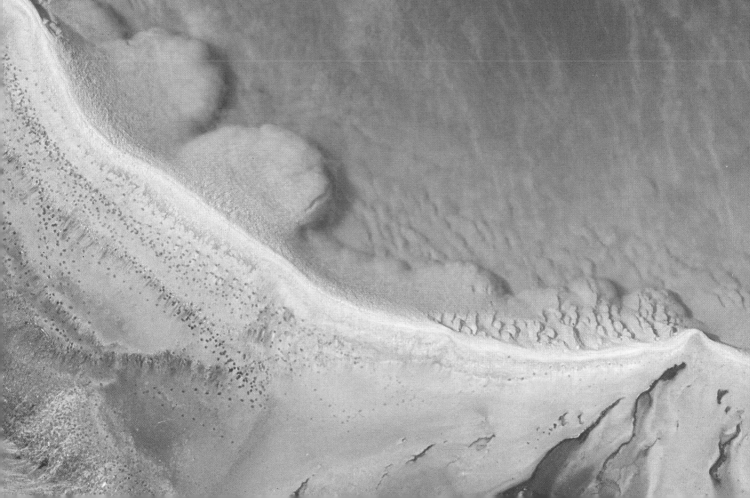

THE USBORNE
INTERNET - LINKED
ENCYCLOPEDIA OF
PLANET
EARTH

THE USBORNE
INTERNET - LINKED
ENCYCLOPEDIA OF
PLANET
EARTH

Anna Claybourne, Gillian Doherty and Rebecca Treays
Designed by Laura Fearn and Melissa Alaverdy

Consultant: Dr. William Chambers
Managing designer: Stephen Wright
Managing editors: Felicity Brooks and Jane Chisholm
Cover design: Zoe Wray and Sarah Cronin
Digital images: John Russell and Nicola Butler
Picture Research: Ruth King

Page 1: aerial view of the Grand Prismatic Spring,
Yellowstone National Park, U.S.A.
Pages 2-3: the Chicago skyline, U.S.A.
This page: computer-enhanced image of an iceberg

CONTENTS

Some words in this book have an asterisk after them.
*This means that you can find out more about them on
the page listed in the footnote.*

Internet links

Throughout this book, we have recommended websites where you can find out more. To visit the recommended
sites, go to the Usborne Quicklinks Website at **www.usborne-quicklinks.com** and enter the keywords "planet earth".
There you will find links to click on to take you to all the recommended sites. Pictures marked in this book with a ★
symbol can be downloaded for free for your own personal use from Usborne Quicklinks. When using the Internet,
please make sure you follow the Internet safety guidelines displayed on the Usborne Quicklinks Website. For more
information on using Usborne Quicklinks and the Internet, see page 155.

PLANET EARTH

THE EARTH IN SPACE

The Earth may seem enormous, but it's actually just a tiny speck in a universe made up of billions of stars and planets. Its position in relation to the Sun is very important. The Sun provides the heat and light which we need to survive.

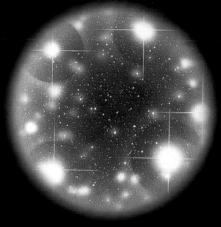

The universe is everything; not just the billions of stars and planets, but the vast spaces in between.

The Sun

Mercury

Venus

Earth

Mars

This picture shows the nine planets in our solar system in the correct order, although they are not to scale.

Jupiter

Saturn

Neptune

Uranus

Pluto

Our solar system

Stars are huge balls of hot gas which give off heat and light. Most stars look tiny, but that's just because they are far away. The nearest star to Earth is the Sun.

A planet is an object that travels around, or orbits, a particular star. As each planet moves, it also spins around on its own axis (an imaginary line running through the planet). The Earth is one of nine planets that orbit the Sun. Together they make up our solar system.

The Earth spins around on its axis as it orbits the Sun.

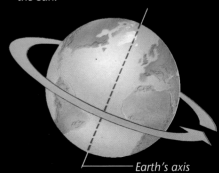

Earth's axis

The Moon

Most of the planets in our solar system have moons. A moon orbits a planet in the same way that a planet orbits a star. Earth has just one moon, but some planets, such as Saturn, have several. It takes almost 28 days for the Moon to orbit the Earth.

As the Moon orbits the Earth, it rotates. It takes exactly the same amount of time to spin around once as it does to travel around the Earth. This means that when we look at the Moon from the Earth, we always see the same side of it.

This picture of the Moon was taken from the Apollo 11 satellite*.

Living Earth

Earth is the third planet from the Sun. It is the only known planet with the right conditions to support living things, although scientists are searching for life on other planets.

The Earth's distance from the Sun means that it receives just the right amount of heat and light. Its combination of gases enables plants, animals and people to breathe, and it is warm enough for water to exist as a liquid. All of these things are essential for life on Earth.

Galaxies

Our solar system is part of a galaxy called the Milky Way. A galaxy is a cluster of millions of stars. Galaxies are so big that it can take a ray of light thousands of years to travel across one. There are 6,000 million known galaxies in the universe, but there could be many, many more.

The Milky Way galaxy

*Satellites, 11

LOOKING AT THE EARTH

We now have a more accurate picture of the world than ever before. Modern technology has meant that scientists can monitor vast areas of the Earth from space. Even inaccessible places, such as deserts, ocean floors and mountain ranges, have been mapped in detail.

A map showing the layout of streets in Manhattan, New York, U.S.A.

Maps of the Earth

A map is a diagram which gives information about a particular area. Maps can show anything from road layouts to the shape of the land. Some focus on small areas, but others show the whole of the Earth's surface. The size of a map in relation to the area it represents is called its scale. If a map's scale is 1:100, it shows an area 100 times its size.

Flattening the Earth's surface

Because the Earth is roughly spherical, the best way to represent it accurately is as a globe. In order to produce flat maps of the Earth's surface, cartographers (map-makers) have to stretch some areas and squash others. Different kinds of maps give the countries slightly different shapes and sizes. These different views of the Earth's surface are called projections*.

The most accurate flat map of the world looks like pieces of orange peel.

Dividing lines

On maps, imaginary lines are used to divide up the Earth. These help us to measure distances and find where places are. The lines that run horizontally are called lines of latitude and the lines that run vertically are known as lines of longitude. The distance between the lines is measured in degrees (°).

Some of the lines used to divide up the Earth have special names. The most important ones are shown on this globe.

Arctic Circle

Tropic of Cancer

The Equator

Tropic of Capricorn

*Projections, 147

Satellite observation

Artificial satellites are man-made devices which orbit the Earth, moons, or other planets. They observe the Earth using a technique called remote sensing. This means that instruments on the satellite monitor the Earth without touching it. Some satellites orbit the Earth at a height of between 5km (3 miles) and 1500km (930 miles), providing views of different parts of the Earth. Others stay above the same place all the time, moving at the same speed as the Earth to give a constant view of a particular area. These are called geostationary satellites. They travel at a height of around 36,000km (22,370 miles).

Sensing

Satellites use a range of remote sensing techniques. One useful type is radar. It can provide images of the Earth even when it is dark or cloudy. Radar works by reflecting radio waves off a target object. The time it takes for a wave to bounce back indicates how far away the object is.

Cameras are used to photograph the Earth's surface. The images are converted into electrical pulses and beamed to Earth. Some cameras use a form of radiation known as infrared. Different types of surfaces reflect infrared light differently, so it's possible to obtain images of the Earth which show the varieties of land surfaces. This can be useful for monitoring vegetation.

Prime Meridian line

This ERS-1 satellite is used to collect information to help scientists study climate change.

Satellite uses

Information provided by satellites enables experts to produce accurate maps, predict hazards such as volcanic eruptions or earthquakes, and record changes in land use around the world. Sensors can also reveal day-to-day changes, such as whether soil is wet or dry, and there are even satellites especially for monitoring weather.

This satellite image of the Earth shows its different types of land surfaces.

THE SEASONS

The Earth takes just over a year to orbit the Sun. As it makes its journey, different parts of the world receive different amounts of heat and light. This causes the seasons (spring, summer, autumn and winter).

Tilting Earth

The Earth is tilted at an angle as it travels around the Sun. This means that one hemisphere is usually closer to the Sun than the other. The hemisphere that is nearer the Sun receives more heat and light energy than the one that is tilted away. So in this half it is summer, while in the other it is winter.

As the Earth orbits the Sun, the half that was nearer the Sun gradually moves further away, so that eventually it becomes winter in this hemisphere and summer in the other. In June the Sun's rays are most concentrated at the Tropic of Cancer and in December they are most concentrated at the Tropic of Capricorn.

In June, it is summer in the Arctic. The summer only lasts for six to eight weeks.

Most of the year, it is winter in the Arctic because it is tilted away from the Sun.

The diagram below shows how the seasons change as the Earth orbits the Sun.

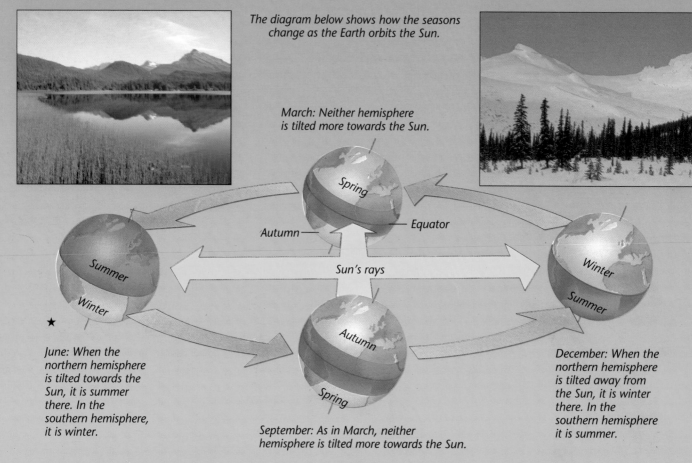

March: Neither hemisphere is tilted more towards the Sun.

Spring

Autumn — — Equator

Summer

Winter

Sun's rays

Winter

Summer

Autumn

Spring

June: When the northern hemisphere is tilted towards the Sun, it is summer there. In the southern hemisphere, it is winter.

September: As in March, neither hemisphere is tilted more towards the Sun.

December: When the northern hemisphere is tilted away from the Sun, it is winter there. In the southern hemisphere it is summer.

Internet link *Watch an animation of Earth's changing seasons.*

The heat and light that the Sun gives out are essential for life on Earth.

Leap years

The time it takes for the Earth to orbit the Sun is called a solar year. A solar year is 365.26 days, but as it is more convenient to measure our calendar year in whole days, we round the number down to 365. In order to make up the difference, every four years we have to add an extra day to our calendar year, making it 366 days. These years are called leap years*. The additional day is February 29th. However, this does not make up the difference exactly, so very occasionally the extra day is not added.

Equatorial seasons

The Earth is hottest where the Sun's rays hit its surface full on. But because the Earth's surface is curved, in most places rays hit the ground at an angle. This causes them to spread out over a larger area, which makes their effect less intense.

However, at areas near the Equator, rays hit the Earth almost at a right angle throughout the year. This means that the temperatures there are high all year round. Temperatures are also affected by the distance the Sun's rays have to travel through the Earth's atmosphere. This distance is less for areas near the Equator than it is at the poles, which means that less heat energy is absorbed by the atmosphere.

This picture shows how the Sun's rays spread out as they reach the Earth's surface.

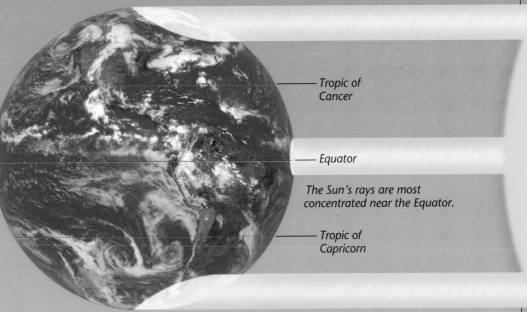

Tropic of Cancer

Equator

The Sun's rays are most concentrated near the Equator.

Tropic of Capricorn

The Sun's rays spread out at the poles and have further to travel through the Earth's atmosphere.

Near the poles, the midday Sun is low on the horizon, making temperatures cool.

Near the Equator, the midday Sun is high in the sky and its rays are very intense.

13

*Leap years, 148

DAY AND NIGHT

When it's daytime in Australia, it's night-time in South America. This is because the Earth spins around on its axis as it orbits the Sun, so the part of the Earth that faces the Sun is constantly changing.

Day and night

It takes 24 hours, or one day, for the Earth to spin around once. As it rotates, a different part of the world turns to face the Sun. The part of the Earth that is turned towards the Sun is in the light (daytime), but as it turns away from the Sun it becomes dark (night-time).

This diagram follows the change from day to night in one place (marked by the flag) as the Earth spins.

Path of orbit around the Sun

Sunrise and sunset

In the morning, you see the Sun "rise" in the sky. This is only an illusion. In fact, the Sun doesn't move at all, but as your part of the Earth turns to face it, the movement of the Earth makes it seem as though the Sun is rising. When your part of the Earth turns away from the Sun at night, it looks as if the Sun is sinking in the sky until eventually it disappears over the horizon. This is called a sunset.

In the morning, the Sun looks as though it's rising, as your part of the Earth gradually turns to face it.

In the evening, the Sun seems to sink down in the sky, as your part of the Earth turns away from it.

Daylight hours

Everywhere in the world, apart from places that are on the Equator, days are longer in the summer than in the winter. This is because the hemisphere where it is summer receives more sunlight than the hemisphere where it is winter.

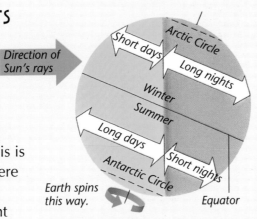

This diagram shows how the length of day and night varies depending on the time of year and where you are on the Earth.

Midnight Sun

The area north of the Arctic Circle is known as the Land of the Midnight Sun, because during the summer it is daylight there all the time. Because the northern hemisphere tilts towards the Sun in summer, the Arctic Circle doesn't turn away from the Sun, even at night. In winter, by contrast, it is dark there all the time because the northern hemisphere tilts away from the Sun. The same thing happens in the southern hemisphere, in the areas south of the Antarctic Circle.

This shows the Sun in the Arctic Circle in the middle of the night. During the summer, the Sun is visible there all the time.

Moon shapes

The Moon doesn't give out any light of its own. It looks bright to us because we see the Sun's rays reflected off its surface. During the day, we can't usually see the Moon because the Sun is brighter.

As the Moon orbits the Sun and we see different amounts of its sunlit side, its shape seems to change as shown in these diagrams.

The pictures below show what the Moon looks like from Earth when it is in each of the positions numbered above.

1. New moon		5. Full moon	
2. Crescent		6. Waning	
3. Half moon		7. Half moon	
4. Waxing		8. Crescent	

INSIDE THE EARTH

The Earth is not solid. It has a solid surface, but inside it is made up of different layers, some of which are molten, or liquid. If you sliced through the Earth, you would see three main layers: a hard outer shell called the crust, the mantle and the core.

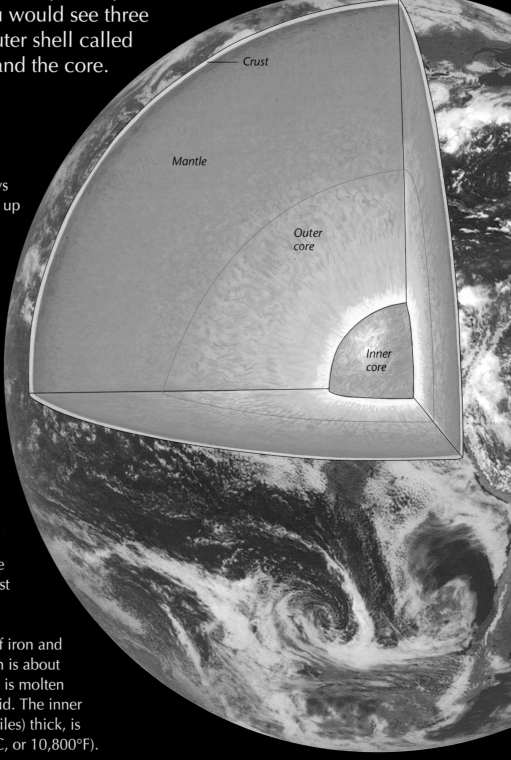

The cutaway section of this globe shows the structure of the Earth.

Crust

Mantle

Outer core

Inner core

The structure of the Earth

The picture on the right shows the different layers that make up the Earth, though the layers are not drawn to scale.

The thinnest layer is the crust. It is between 5km (3 miles) and 70km (43 miles) thick. Below this is the mantle which is made of silicon and magnesium. The mantle is about 3,000km (1,900 miles) thick.

The upper and lower parts of the mantle are solid rock, but the middle layer is so hot that the rock has melted to form a thick substance called magma. The solid upper layer and the crust float on this liquid layer.

The core is probably made of iron and nickel. The outer core, which is about 2,200km (1,400 miles) thick, is molten whereas the inner core is solid. The inner core, about 1,300km (800 miles) thick, is extremely hot (about 6,000°C, or 10,800°F).

The Earth's crust

There are two different types of crust. Thick continental crust forms land, and much thinner oceanic crust makes up the ocean floors. Continental crust is made of granite, which is a light rock. Oceanic crust is made of a heavier rock called basalt.

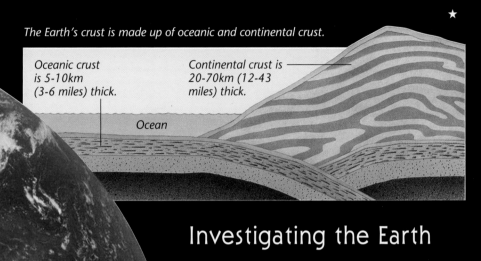

The Earth's crust is made up of oceanic and continental crust.

Oceanic crust is 5-10km (3-6 miles) thick.

Continental crust is 20-70km (12-43 miles) thick.

Ocean

Investigating the Earth

It's difficult to find out about the inside of the Earth. Geologists, who study rocks, find out about areas near the surface by drilling holes into the crust and collecting rock samples. But they can only drill a short distance below the surface.

Volcanic eruptions provide some information about material deep inside the Earth. But the main way that geologists find out about the Earth's structure is by studying earthquakes. During an earthquake, vibrations called seismic waves travel through the Earth. As they pass through different materials, they change speed and direction. By studying records of earthquakes, called seismograms, geologists try to determine what rocks are at different depths.

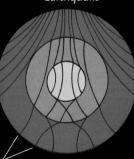

Earthquake

Paths of waves

This diagram shows how seismic waves change direction as they pass through the Earth.

Magnetic Earth

The Earth is magnetic. This may be caused by molten iron in its core. It is as if the Earth has a huge magnetic bar in the middle. The ends of this "magnet" are called the magnetic poles. These are not in exactly the same place as the geographic North and South poles.

This diagram shows the Earth's magnetic field: the area affected by its force. The lines show the direction of the magnetic field.

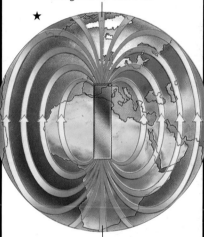

Magnetic North Pole

Magnetic South Pole

You can see this magnetic force at work when you use a compass. The compass needle, which is magnetic, always points north. This is because it is pulled, or attracted, by the magnetic north pole.

A compass's magnetic needle always points north.

THE EARTH'S CRUST

The Earth's crust is broken up into large pieces which fit together like a giant jigsaw puzzle. The pieces are called plates. Many of the Earth's most spectacular features have been formed, over many thousands of years, by the movement of these plates.

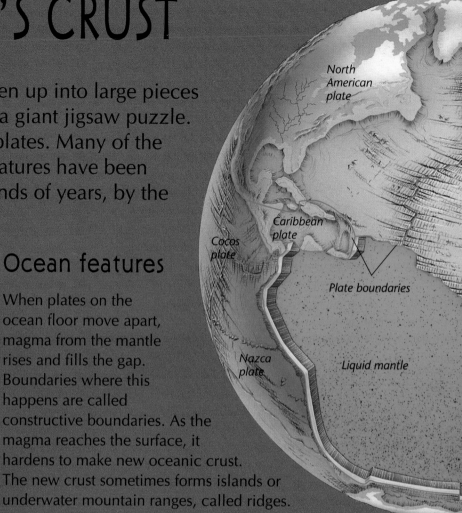

North American plate

Caribbean plate

Cocos plate

Nazca plate

Plate boundaries

Liquid mantle

A moving surface

The Earth's crust is divided into seven large plates and several smaller plates. Each one is made up of either continental or oceanic crust, or both. The edges of the plates, where they meet, are called plate boundaries.

The plates float on the liquid mantle and are constantly moving. Their movement is usually slow, an average of 5cm (2in) a year, which is roughly the rate at which your fingernails grow. They can move towards one another, spread apart or shift sideways. Because all the plates fit together, movement of one plate affects all the others.

Ocean features

When plates on the ocean floor move apart, magma from the mantle rises and fills the gap. Boundaries where this happens are called constructive boundaries. As the magma reaches the surface, it hardens to make new oceanic crust. The new crust sometimes forms islands or underwater mountain ranges, called ridges.

Oceanic crust ★ | Ridge | Trench | Currents of hot magma | Plate boundaries

When plates push together, underwater trenches form as one plate is forced below another. These boundaries are called destructive boundaries. The deepest trench, the Marianas Trench in the Pacific Ocean, is deeper than Mount Everest is tall.

This diagram shows how ridges and trenches form.

Shifting continents

As plates shift, the position of the oceans and continents on the Earth's surface changes. The maps on the right show how geologists think the continents may have shifted.

Geologists think that there was once a single supercontinent, which we call "Pangaea".

As new rock formed at plate boundaries, the floor of the Atlantic Ocean probably widened.

Today, South America and Africa are drifting apart at a rate of 3.5cm (1.5in) each year.

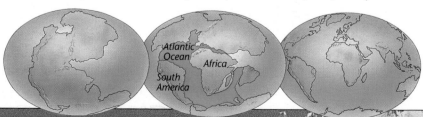

Atlantic Ocean

Africa

South America

★

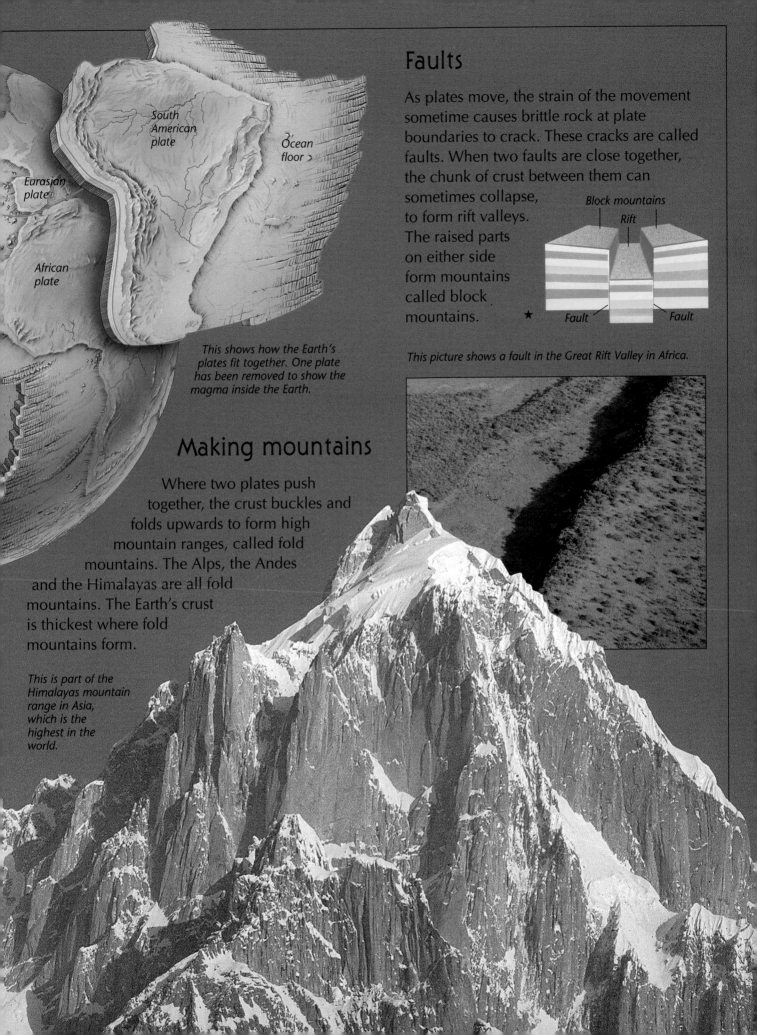

South
American
plate

Ocean
floor >

Eurasian
plate

African
plate

This shows how the Earth's plates fit together. One plate has been removed to show the magma inside the Earth.

Faults

As plates move, the strain of the movement sometime causes brittle rock at plate boundaries to crack. These cracks are called faults. When two faults are close together, the chunk of crust between them can sometimes collapse, to form rift valleys. The raised parts on either side form mountains called block mountains.

Block mountains

Rift

★

Fault

Fault

This picture shows a fault in the Great Rift Valley in Africa.

Making mountains

Where two plates push together, the crust buckles and folds upwards to form high mountain ranges, called fold mountains. The Alps, the Andes and the Himalayas are all fold mountains. The Earth's crust is thickest where fold mountains form.

This is part of the Himalayas mountain range in Asia, which is the highest in the world.

ROCKS, MINERALS & FOSSILS

The Earth's crust is made up of rock. There are three kinds of rocks: igneous, sedimentary and metamorphic. Over many years, rocks are sometimes transformed from one kind to another.

Igneous rock

Igneous rock gets its name from the Latin word for "fire", because it is formed from hot molten rock from inside the Earth. When this molten rock, or magma, cools, it forms solid igneous rock. The way that the magma cools determines the kind of igneous rock that is formed.

Tuff is an igneous rock made from pieces of volcanic rock and crystals compressed together.

Obsidian is a shiny igneous rock formed when magma cools quickly.

Sedimentary rock

Sedimentary rock is made from tiny pieces of rocks and the decayed remains of plants and animals. These fragments, called sediment, are usually blown by winds, or carried by rivers or landslides, to the sea, where they sink. The water and upper layers of sediment press down on the lower layers, until eventually they form solid rock.

Chalk is a sedimentary rock made from tiny sea creatures.

Sandstone is a sedimentary rock made up of sand grains.

The Grand Canyon, U.S.A., is a gorge formed by the Colorado River. You can see the layers of sandstone. Layers of rock like this are called strata.

Metamorphic rock

Metamorphic rock is rock that has been changed by heat or pressure. It can be formed from igneous, sedimentary or other metamorphic rocks. Its name comes from a Greek word meaning "transformation". The texture, appearance and chemical composition of the rock can be altered by heat from magma or pressure caused by plate movements.

Marble is a metamorphic rock formed from limestone.

Mica schist is a layered metamorphic rock.

Minerals

Rocks are made from substances called minerals, which in turn are made up of simple chemical substances called elements. If you look at a rock with a magnifying glass, you can sometimes see the different minerals it contains. Some minerals are cut and polished to be used as gemstones.

These pictures show minerals in rocks and as gemstones.

Opal can be milky white, green, red, blue, black or brown.

Turquoise runs through rock in the form of veins.

Carnelian is a dark red stone.

Fossils

The shapes or remains of plants and animals that died long ago are sometimes preserved in rocks. They are called fossils.

Fossils are formed when a dead plant or animal is buried by sediment which turns to sedimentary rock. Usually the remains decay, although hard parts such as teeth, shells and bones can sometimes survive. The space left by the plant or animal fills up with minerals which preserve its shape.

The fossil of an ammonite (an extinct sea creature)

THE EARTH'S RESOURCES

★ Iron is extracted from its ore in a blast furnace.

T he Earth provides all sorts of useful rocks, minerals and other materials. We quarry stone and sand for building and glassmaking, extract over 60 types of metal, and mine hundreds of useful chemicals and compounds such as salt, talcum and silicon.

Iron ore, coke (a type of coal) and limestone go in here.

Metals

Metals are among the most important materials we get from the Earth. They are strong, yet they can be beaten out into flat sheets or drawn out to make wire. They also conduct electricity and heat well. They have a range of properties: some, such as iron, are very strong;

some, including calcium and lithium, have medical uses; and precious metals, such as silver and gold, are used to make necklaces, bracelets and other decorative items.

Most metals are found in ores, types of rocks that contain a metal in the form of a chemical compound. Metals are extracted from ores by mixing them with other chemicals to cause a reaction.

The furnace is over 30m (100ft) tall.

Iron ore, coke and limestone react with each other in a blast furnace to make new chemicals, leaving the iron free.

Molten iron flows out here.

Hot air is blasted into the furnace.

Waste called slag comes out here.

People have used precious metals for centuries as attractive settings for precious stones like these.

More minerals

As well as metals and stone, the Earth provides many other chemicals and elements which have thousands of uses, often depending on how hard they are (see the scale of hardness opposite). For example, corundum is used to make sandpaper and silicon is used in electronic circuits.

The Mohs scale

The hardness or softness of minerals is measured on a scale of 1 to 10, called the Mohs scale. Soft minerals, such as talc, crumble easily into powder. On the other end of the scale are the hardest minerals, such as diamonds, which are used in cutting tools.

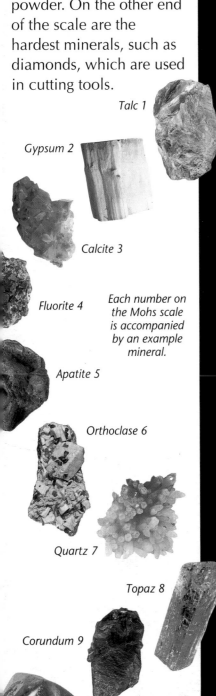

Talc 1

Gypsum 2

Calcite 3

Fluorite 4

Each number on the Mohs scale is accompanied by an example mineral.

Apatite 5

Orthoclase 6

Quartz 7

Topaz 8

Corundum 9

Diamond 10

Silicon chips

Silicon comes from a rock called quartz. It has become very important in modern society, because it is used to make the electronic chips that run computers, digital watches, mobile phones and millions of other everyday appliances.

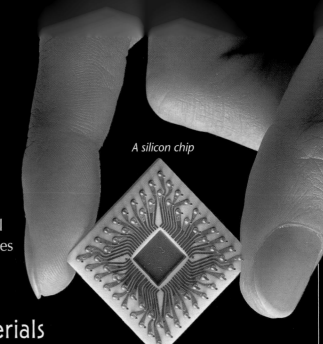

A silicon chip

Building materials

Rocks and minerals from the Earth are used to make bricks, cement, glass and other building materials. Stone for building is usually extracted from the ground in quarries. It's often so hard and heavy that explosives have to be used to blast it apart first.

Sand is made of rocks, minerals and sometimes seashells, ground down to fragments by the action of water (which is why it is usually found near the sea). Concrete and glass are both made using sand.

The Taj Mahal is a huge Indian tomb built from marble.

ENERGY FROM THE EARTH

The Earth's rocks, minerals and fossils contain energy which we can extract and use. Oil, gas and coal, which can be converted into heat and electricity, all come from the Earth. So do other forms of energy, such as nuclear energy.

This huge structure is the top part of an oil platform, which sticks out above the sea's surface. It contains equipment for processing the oil, and living quarters for the workers.

NORTH CORMORAN

Fossil fuels

Coal, oil and natural gas are fossil fuels. They are called this because, like fossils*, they form in the ground over many years from the bodies of dead plants and animals.

Coal is formed from trees and other plants that died thousands of years ago. Layers of sand and clay gradually settled on top of them, and compressed them slowly into thick, underground layers, or seams, of coal.

Oil is formed in the same way, but from the bodies of tiny sea creatures. It is found under the seabed, or underground (because some areas that were once sea are now land). Under certain conditions, natural gas is formed from dead plants and animals.

Extracting fuels

The coal we use comes from underground mines, or opencast mines, which are huge, open holes dug in the ground. To extract oil and gas, a drill, supported by a structure called a rig, bores a hole into the ground or seabed. Sometimes the fuel flows out naturally, but usually water is pumped into the hole to force the oil or gas out.

Coal being extracted from a mine at the surface of the ground, called an opencast mine

*Fossils, 21

24

Using fossil fuels

When a fossil fuel is burned, it releases energy, which is used to heat buildings and to run vehicle engines. In power stations, heat from fossil fuels is converted into electricity.

The world depends on fossil fuels. They provide more than three-quarters of the energy we use. But we use them up more quickly than they can form, so they are running out. In around 200 years, humans will need to get most of their energy in other ways.

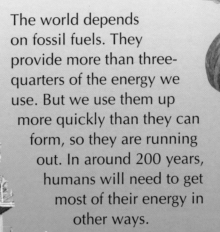

As well as providing energy, oil is used to make plastic, which is made into thousands of things, from drinks bottles to polyester clothing.

Radiation

Some minerals found in the ground are radioactive. This means their atoms (the tiny particles they are made of) are unstable.

Instead of staying as they are, unstable minerals break up and send out particles or rays, known as radiation. As they break up, a type of energy called nuclear energy is released. Uranium, a metal, is the main radioactive mineral used to produce nuclear energy.

Like many metals, uranium doesn't exist naturally, but is found bonded together with other minerals in an ore*. After being mined from the ground, the uranium is extracted from the ore using chemical reactions.

This diagram shows how atoms of uranium produce nuclear energy.

A tiny particle called a neutron is fired at the uranium nucleus.

This is the nucleus, or middle, of a uranium atom.

The nucleus splits, giving off heat.

More neutrons fly off the nucleus and split other uranium atoms.

*Ore, 22

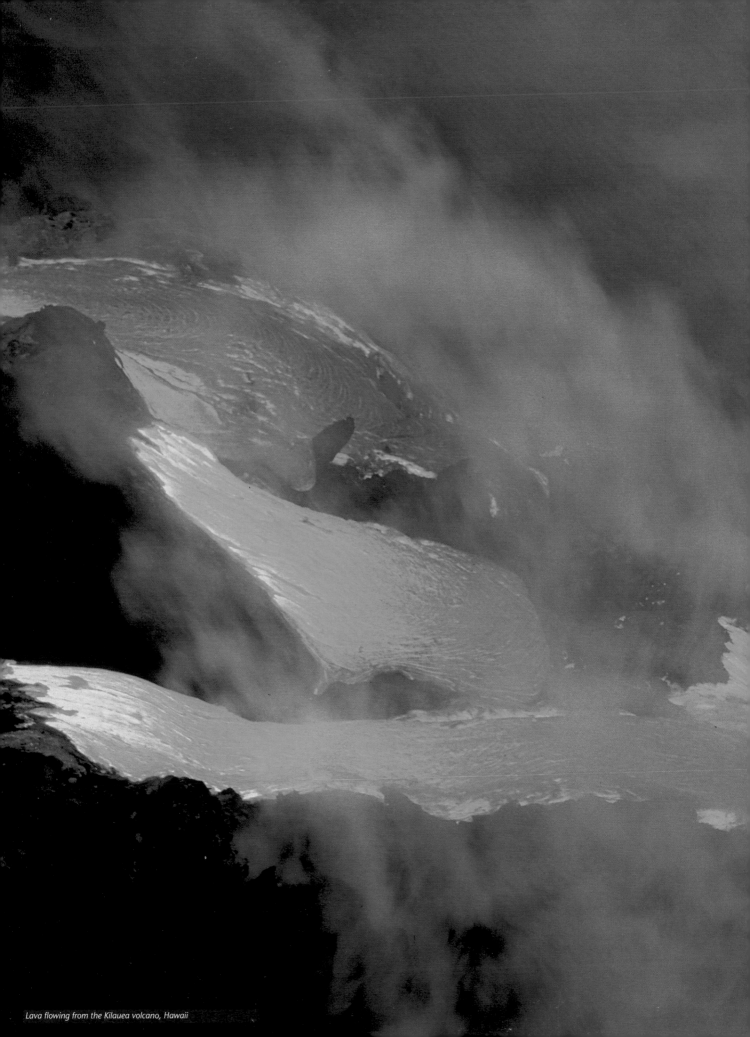

Lava flowing from the Kilauea volcano, Hawaii

EARTHQUAKES AND VOLCANOES

THE EXPLODING EARTH

An erupting volcano is one of the most dramatic sights in the natural world. Bubbling hot lava spews out of a hole in the Earth's crust and engulfs the land. Ash, dust and poisonous gases pour into the air and chunks of rock are hurled high into the sky.

Volcanoes

Volcanoes erupt when red-hot molten rock, called magma, in the Earth's mantle rises towards the surface. Eventually it builds up enough pressure to burst through the Earth's crust. Once magma has reached the surface of the Earth it is called lava.

Growing

When a volcano erupts, the lava and ash it throws out eventually set as a solid layer of volcanic rock. As the layers build up, the volcano grows. Thick lava flows only a short way before setting, so it forms steep-sided cone volcanoes. Thinner lava flows further before setting hard, so it forms shield volcanoes that have gently sloping sides.

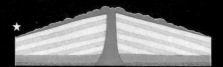

A cross-section through a shield volcano

A cross-section through a cone volcano

Dust, ash and gases —

Crater ~ the hole at the top of a volcano

Volcanic bomb

Layers of volcanic ash ~ tiny particles of lava

Vent ~ the main pipe up the middle of a volcano

Dyke ~ a pipe leading from the vent to the surface

Magma chamber ~ place where magma collects below the Earth's crust

Bombs and blocks

Volcanic bombs and blocks are thick lumps of molten lava which are blasted into the air as a volcano erupts. They start to cool and harden as they travel through the air. Blocks tend to be angular whereas bombs are more rounded.

Some blocks are the size of trucks.

As they twist through the air, some bombs form a "tail".

Tiny bombs shaped like drops form from very runny lava.

Dead or alive?

Volcanoes that erupt regularly are known as active volcanoes. Volcanoes that won't ever erupt again are called extinct volcanoes. Sometimes, people think a volcano is extinct when actually it is only dormant (sleeping). In 1973, on an island near Iceland, a volcano that was believed to be extinct erupted, destroying 300 buildings. It hadn't erupted for over 5,000 years.

Danger

Lava destroys everything it engulfs. But, because it usually flows quite slowly, it rarely kills people. There is more danger from the hot gas, bombs and ash which can sweep down a volcano's slopes at speeds of 200km/h (120 mph). In AD79, when Mount Vesuvius in Italy erupted, the people of Pompeii were wiped out by poisonous gas and ash.

A plaster cast made from the hollow of a body left in the ash in Pompeii.

VOLCANIC VARIATIONS

Most volcanoes occur at weak spots on the Earth's crust, where it is easiest for magma to burst through. Volcanoes erupt in different ways, depending on how thick their lava is.

Hot spots

Some volcanoes are found in the middle of plates. They may be caused by especially hot patches in the Earth's mantle, called hot spots. Scientists think that currents of extra-hot magma shoot up and burn through the Earth's crust to erupt on the surface.

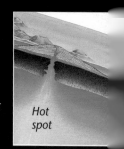

Hot spots in the Earth's mantle may cause volcanoes in the middle of plates. ★

Hot spot

Volcanoes with runny lava, like this, erupt gently.

Subduction zones

Volcanoes also occur at subduction zones. These are places where two plates collide head on and one plate is pushed down beneath the other. As the plate is forced deeper and deeper underground, it begins to melt, forming magma. This newly formed magma rises up through cracks in the surface and explodes in a volcano.

Spreading ridges

Whole mountain ranges of volcanoes can form at underwater boundaries where two plates are moving apart. These are called spreading ridges. As the plates move apart, magma from the mantle rises to the surface. Most of it solidifies on the edge of the plates to make new crust, but some works its way up to the seabed, where it erupts as volcanoes.

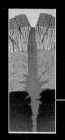

Spreading ridges form when plates move apart.

— *Rising magma*

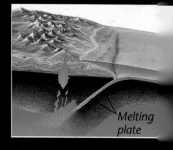

At subduction zones, one plate is forced underground where it starts to melt.

★

Melting plate

★

Thick or thin lava

Not all volcanoes erupt in the same way. Some throw clouds of ash high into the air, while others have a gentle lava fountain. The way a volcano erupts depends on the thickness and stickiness of the lava. The thicker and stickier the lava, the more gases are trapped within it. It is these gases that cause the build-up of pressure which makes a volcano erupt explosively.

When lava is thin and runny, gases can escape more easily. This makes an eruption less violent, because the gases can just bubble out of the top of the volcano. Many of the different types of eruptions are named after particular volcanoes that have erupted in that way.

Hawaiian-type eruptions are usually gentle. They occur when lava is runny, so trapped gases bubble out easily.

Plinian-type eruptions are the most explosive. Trapped gases cause massive explosions as they escape and huge amounts of volcanic ash are thrown high into the air.

NATURAL HOT WATER

In areas where volcanoes are found, there are often other dramatic natural features and events as well as volcanic eruptions. Hot springs rich in minerals*, jets of steaming hot water which shoot into the air, and underwater chimneys which belch out black water can also be caused by volcanic activity.

Hot rock

In volcanic areas, when magma rises into the Earth's crust, it heats the rock around it. This rock might contain groundwater. Groundwater is rain or sea water which has seeped down into the Earth's crust through cracks in the surface. As the rock heats up, it heats the groundwater that comes into contact with it, producing a natural supply of hot water.

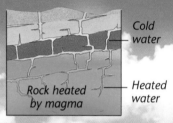

Cold water

Rock heated by magma

Heated water

Hot rock heats up groundwater. ★

Hot springs

Groundwater heated by hot rock sometimes bubbles to the surface as a hot, or thermal, spring. The water usually contains minerals which have been dissolved from the rock below. Minerals from the water often build up around the edge of the springs.

This is the Morning Glory pool, one of many hot springs in Yellowstone National Park, U.S.A. The park has over 10,000 features, such as hot springs and geysers, which have been caused by hot volcanic rock.

*Minerals, 21

Black smokers

Around volcanic mountain ranges under the sea, hot springs sometimes emerge through holes in the seabed called hydrothermal vents.

Some vents, called black smokers, look like chimneys and puff out plumes of hot, cloudy black water. The water is cloudy because of the minerals it has dissolved from the hot rock. As minerals are deposited around the vent, the sides of the chimney build up. Some unusual creatures live near black smokers, such as tubeworms and blind spider crabs. They feed on bacteria which live on the minerals given out by the vents.

Black smokers form on the seabed and puff out clouds of hot, black water. Some are as tall as 6m (20ft).

Geysers

A geyser is a jet of hot water and steam which shoots into the air from a hole in the ground. Geysers occur when heated groundwater gets trapped in a network of cracks under the Earth's surface. Because the water is trapped, it continues to heat up until it boils and forms steam. The pressure builds up until it forces the water to find a way out of the ground. This results in occasional bursts of hot water.

"Old Faithful" is a geyser in Yellowstone National Park, U.S.A. A fountain of hot water like this spurts out once every hour or so.

Internet link *For a link to a website about the Hawaiian Island volcanic chain, go to www.usborne-quicklinks.com*

VOLCANIC ISLANDS

A volcanic island called White Island, off the coast of New Zealand

If a volcano on the seabed erupts enough times, it may become tall enough to reach the surface of the sea and begin to form an island. As ash and lava from repeated eruptions pile up around the vent, the island grows.

Hot spot islands

Hot spot volcanoes* under the sea sometimes grow into volcanic islands. Over thousands of years, a hot spot can produce a chain of volcanic islands. Scientists think that hot spots remain in a fixed position inside the Earth, while the crust above moves. Over a long period of time, a volcanic island is carried away from the hot spot that caused it.

When an island moves away from a hot spot, the volcano becomes extinct as it loses its supply of magma. A new volcano then forms on the part of the plate lying above the hot spot. Eventually a chain of islands is formed.

The Hawaiian island chain is made up of hot spot volcanic islands.

Kauai
Oahu
Molokai
Maui
Hawaii

Hot spot

*Hot spots, 30

Island arcs

Curved chains of volcanic islands, known as island arcs, sometimes form above subduction zones* where magma rises through cracks in the seabed. Scientists are not sure why they form an arc, but it may be connected with the way the plates move, or the spherical shape of the Earth.

An island is born

This picture shows steam and ash billowing from Surtsey, a volcanic island near Iceland.

In 1963, fishermen off the coast of Iceland saw smoke rising from the sea. They thought it must be a boat on fire. In fact, it wasn't smoke, but ash and steam from a volcano just below the water's surface.

During the next four years, the volcano erupted many times. As it emerged above the water, the eruptions became more explosive as water pressure decreased. Lava and ash built up, until eventually they formed a volcanic island. The island was named Surtsey after Surt, the Nordic giant of fire.

Black beaches

Some volcanic islands have black sandy beaches. This is because they are formed from basalt lava which is black. When the lava runs down to meet the sea, it cools instantly. The change in temperature makes the lava shatter into tiny pieces which form the grains of sand.

A black sandy beach in Tahiti

*Subduction zones, 30

LIVING WITH VOLCANOES

Despite the danger that active volcanoes present, many people choose to live on their slopes. Scientists have found ways to help predict when eruptions will happen, so they are sometimes able to warn those at risk.

Monitoring volcanoes

Before a volcano erupts, the ground may change shape. This kind of change can be measured by instruments such as tiltmeters and geodimeters. The ground may also begin to tremble. This is known as volcanic tremor. It can be detected by seismometers.

Such instruments were used to monitor the Mount St. Helens volcano, Washington, U.S.A., in early 1980. They recorded a bulge swelling by 1.5m (5ft) per day. The area around the volcano was evacuated shortly before it erupted.

A group of experts monitoring the Mount St. Helens volcano were in a plane flying over it when the volcano began to shudder. This photograph of the eruption was taken as the pilot turned the plane to escape the blast.

The area around Mount St. Helens after the eruption. Despite the evacuation of the area, 61 people died.

A bulge on the side of Mount St. Helens swelled to 90m (295ft) before a massive eruption blasted away the side of the volcano.

Using volcanoes

Although volcanoes are usually a destructive forcè, they can also be put to productive uses.

The ash from volcanoes contains minerals which make soil very fertile. As a result, the land around volcanoes is very good for farming. This is one of the reasons why people choose to live in such dangerous places.

Engineers have discovered how to use the heat energy in volcanic rock to produce electricity. When groundwater seeps into the cracks in volcanic rock, it gets hot. (Sometimes cracks are created artificially to produce the same effect.) The hot water is then pumped up to the surface where it is converted into steam. The steam is used to turn machines called turbines which make electricity.

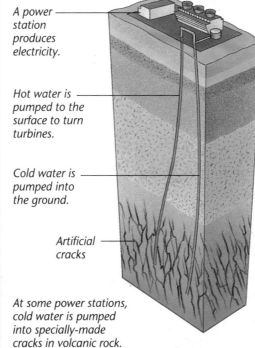

A power station produces electricity.

Hot water is pumped to the surface to turn turbines.

Cold water is pumped into the ground.

Artificial cracks

At some power stations, cold water is pumped into specially-made cracks in volcanic rock.

EARTHQUAKE EFFECTS

An earthquake is a sudden release of energy which makes the ground tremble. The effects of a large earthquake can be devastating: the ground lurches violently and buildings sway from side to side, or may even collapse. However, earthquakes only occur in certain parts of the world and most earthquakes are not felt by people at all.

An apartment block in San Francisco, U.S.A., which has been damaged by an earthquake

Damaging effects

Earthquakes cause most damage when they occur in large towns and cities. During severe earthquakes, buildings and bridges collapse, and cracks called fissures may appear in the ground. There are also threats from hazards such as fire and flooding. These may be caused when underground gas pipes or water pipes crack during an earthquake.

The power of earthquakes

Over 800,000 earthquakes occur each year, but only around 1,000 of these cause significant damage. Their power and effects are measured by seismologists, scientists who study earthquakes.

There are two scales for measuring earthquakes: the Richter scale and the Mercalli scale. The Richter scale measures the power of vibrations called seismic waves, that travel through the ground when an earthquake happens. These vibrations are registered using a device called a seismometer. Then a chart of the vibrations, known as a seismogram, is produced.

Earthquakes are rated between 1 and 10 on the Richter scale. With each step up the scale, the energy released is about 30 times greater than at the step below.

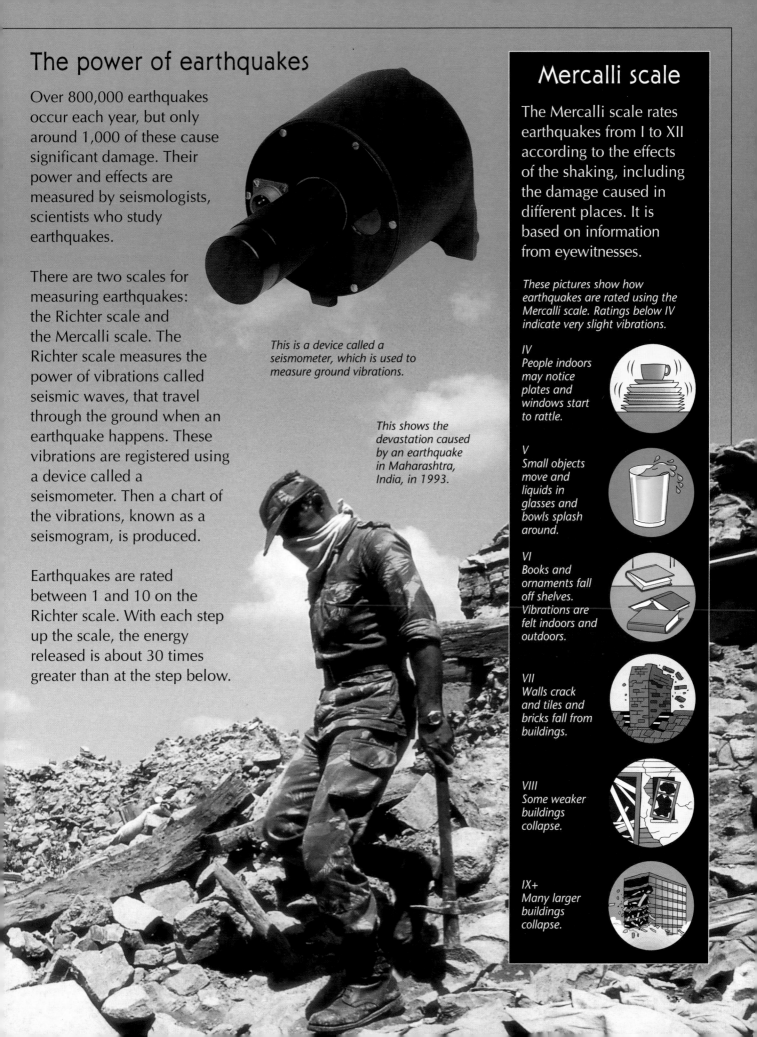

This is a device called a seismometer, which is used to measure ground vibrations.

This shows the devastation caused by an earthquake in Maharashtra, India, in 1993.

Mercalli scale

The Mercalli scale rates earthquakes from I to XII according to the effects of the shaking, including the damage caused in different places. It is based on information from eyewitnesses.

These pictures show how earthquakes are rated using the Mercalli scale. Ratings below IV indicate very slight vibrations.

IV
People indoors may notice plates and windows start to rattle.

V
Small objects move and liquids in glasses and bowls splash around.

VI
Books and ornaments fall off shelves. Vibrations are felt indoors and outdoors.

VII
Walls crack and tiles and bricks fall from buildings.

VIII
Some weaker buildings collapse.

IX+
Many larger buildings collapse.

HOW EARTHQUAKES HAPPEN

Earthquakes are most common near plate boundaries*. The movement of the plates causes stress to build up in certain areas of rock. When this stress is suddenly released, the surrounding rock vibrates, causing an earthquake.

Fault lines

Earthquakes occur along cracks in the Earth's crust called faults. Faults can be tiny fractures or long cracks stretching over vast distances. They occur when plates slide against each other, causing the rock to be twisted, stretched or squeezed until it splits. Boundaries where plates slide past each other in the same or in opposite directions are called conservative margins.

San Francisco

The North American plate moves 1cm a year.

San Andreas fault

The Pacific plate moves 6cm a year.

Los Angeles

San Diego

Mexico

Earthquakes regularly occur along the San Andreas fault, along the west coast of America. These plates slide in the same direction, but move at different speeds.

This diagram shows how some plates slide past each other in opposite directions.

An overhead view of the San Andreas fault

Releasing energy

If the jagged edges along a fault become jammed, energy builds up as the two edges strain against one another. Eventually, the stress becomes so great that one side is suddenly forced to give way, causing a jerking movement. The energy that has built up is released, making the surrounding rock vibrate in an earthquake.

A fault running through rock

Energy builds up at the point where the rocks become jammed.

*Plate boundaries, 18

The focus

The point where the rock gives way is called the focus. This is where an earthquake starts. The focus is usually about 5-15km (3-9 miles) underground. The point on the surface directly above the focus is called the epicentre. Seismic waves travel outwards from the focus in all directions. The strength of an earthquake depends on the amount of energy released. However, waves from even a small earthquake can be detected on the other side of the world.

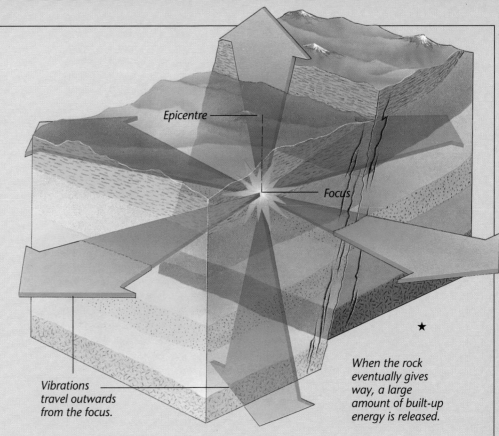

Epicentre

Focus

Vibrations travel outwards from the focus.

★

When the rock eventually gives way, a large amount of built-up energy is released.

Seismic waves

Seismic waves are at their strongest nearest the focus and become weaker as they travel out. There are different types of seismic waves, each of which makes the rock it travels through vibrate in a different way.

Different types of seismic waves travel by distorting rock in different ways.

 Direction of waves

 Vibrations of the rock particles as the waves pass through

Stretching and squeezing movement

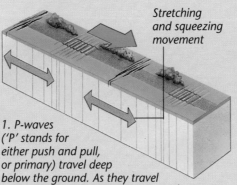

1. P-waves ('P' stands for either push and pull, or primary) travel deep below the ground. As they travel through rock, they stretch and squeeze the rock particles. ★

2. S-waves ('S' stands for either shake or secondary) make the rock move up and down and from side to side. They travel deep underground. ★

Vertical and horizontal movement

Circular movement

3. L-waves ('L' stands for long) only travel along the surface. Most earthquake damage is caused by this type of wave. ★

Aftershocks

Sometimes, not all of the energy that has built up is released during an earthquake. This may mean that after the main earthquake there are smaller tremors, known as aftershocks, as the remaining energy is released. Small amounts of energy may also be released before an earthquake occurs. This produces tremors known as foreshocks.

EARTHQUAKE SAFETY

By monitoring faults, scientists can sometimes predict when and where earthquakes are likely to occur. This means that they can take steps to limit the damage caused by an earthquake or even prevent an earthquake from happening.

Seismic gaps

Stress that builds up at fault boundaries is often released gradually by slow movement known as fault creep. Earthquakes are less likely to happen in areas where fault creep occurs, because stress is being released. They are most likely to occur at sections of a fault where there has been no movement for many years. These sections are known as seismic gaps.

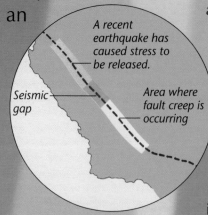

A recent earthquake has caused stress to be released.

Seismic gap

Area where fault creep is occurring

By identifying seismic gaps, scientists can carefully monitor areas where earthquakes are most likely to occur.

Monitoring faults

If the surface of the Earth suddenly starts to tilt, it may be a sign that an earthquake is about to happen. Devices called tiltmeters can measure tiny changes in the level of the ground.

Horizontal movement along faults can be monitored using lasers. A laser beam is bounced off a reflector, which then reflects it back. A computer records the time it takes the beam to travel this distance. If the time changes, it shows that movement has taken place.

Scientists use lasers like these to detect ground movements. They can detect shifts as slight as 1mm (0.04in).

Preventing earthquakes

Earthquakes can be prevented by releasing jammed plates before too much stress builds up. This can be done by conducting a small explosion to shift the plates. Alternatively, drilling deep holes and injecting water into rocks reduces friction, enabling smoother movement along a fault.

Keeping safe

During an earthquake, if you are indoors, the safest place to be is under a solid table or desk. You should cover your eyes to protect them from flying glass and hold on tightly to the leg of the table. If you are outside, it's better to be in an open space, away from buildings, trees and power lines.

Animal instincts

Animals have sometimes been reported as behaving strangely shortly before an earthquake. For example, shortly before an earthquake in Haicheng, China, in 1975, snakes that had been hibernating emerged unexpectedly. Scientists think this may be because animals' highly developed senses can detect slight vibrations, changes in electrical currents in rocks, or the release of gases. In San Francisco, U.S.A, zoo animals are monitored in case the way they behave provides clues that an earthquake is about to happen.

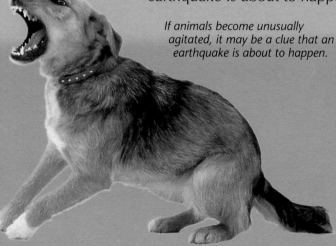

If animals become unusually agitated, it may be a clue that an earthquake is about to happen.

Safe buildings

In areas where there is a high risk of earthquakes happening, more buildings are being designed so that minimum damage is caused if there is an earthquake. The foundations of some buildings are constructed to absorb vibrations and reduce the effects of shaking. Steel frames can be used to strengthen buildings, so that a building may sway but will not collapse when the ground trembles.

The Transamerica skyscraper in San Francisco, U.S.A., is designed to withstand earth tremors.

GIANT WAVES

An earthquake or a volcanic eruption under the sea or near the coast can cause giant waves called tsunami. These waves surge across the sea in all directions. Just before a tsunami crashes onto the shore, it slows down suddenly and may swell to an enormous height.

A tsunami hit Papua New Guinea in 1998, causing incredible devastation. This is a still from a video taken there. It shows steel roofing wrapped around a tree by the force of the water.

Tsunami

Tsunami begin when an earthquake or volcano causes ground movement on the seabed or near the sea. This jolt shifts the water, causing waves to form. Out at sea, tsunami are a similar height to ordinary waves, although the distance between the top, or crest, of one tsunami and the next can be more than 100km (62 miles). What makes tsunami so dangerous is their speed. They race across the sea at speeds of up to 800km/h (500mph). As a tsunami reaches the shore, the friction of the seabed against the water acts like a brake, forcing it to slow down suddenly. The height of the tsunami increases to form a wall of water which towers above the shore and then crashes down, rushing inland and flooding the coast.

Tsunami travel out rapidly in all directions from the place where they initially form.

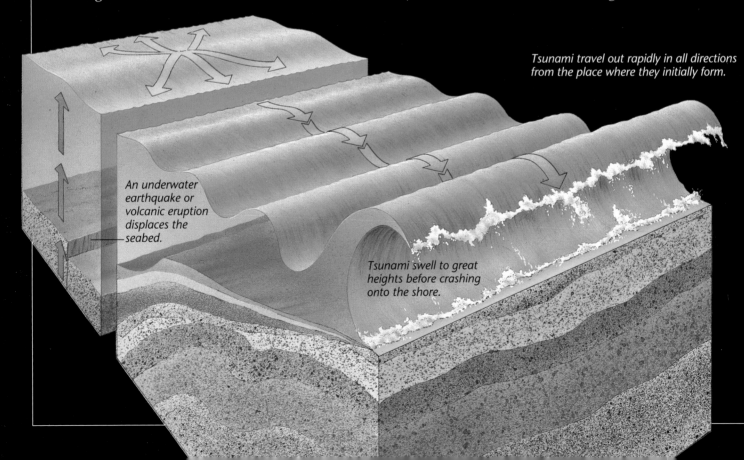

An underwater earthquake or volcanic eruption displaces the seabed.

Tsunami swell to great heights before crashing onto the shore.

Tsunami warning system

Most tsunami occur in the Pacific Ocean. For this reason, there are observation stations throughout the Pacific to monitor earthquakes. If an earthquake is large enough to generate tsunami, warnings are issued to coastal towns, so that they can prepare for it. Tide stations along the coast then monitor the arrival of the tsunami.

Observation and tide stations in the Pacific monitor tsunami.

Tsunami look like a huge wall of water. They can reach heights of up to 50m (165ft).

★

North America

PACIFIC OCEAN

Central Pacific
tsunami warning
station

South America

Australia

○ Tide stations
● Observation
  stations

Autumn in the Cache National Forest, Idaho, U.S.A.

CLIMATE

THE EARTH'S ATMOSPHERE

Surrounding the Earth is a blanket of gases which make up its atmosphere. The atmosphere contains the air we need to breathe. It also affects weather and climate and protects us from extremes of temperature and from the Sun's harmful rays.

The troposphere

The troposphere is the layer of the atmosphere nearest to the Earth's surface. As well as a mixture of gases, this layer contains clouds, dust and pollution. It extends to between 10km (6 miles) and 20km (12 miles) from the Earth. Temperatures are high near the Earth because the air is heated from below by the Earth's surface, which is warmed by the Sun. Higher up, the air is thinner and can't hold as much heat, so temperatures decrease.

The troposphere is the layer where the weather is produced. It gets its name from the Greek word *tropos* which means "a turn". This is because the air there is constantly circulating*.

The atmosphere's structure

The gases surrounding the Earth are held by gravity, a force which attracts things to Earth. The atmosphere is divided into layers according to the temperature of these gases. The diagram below shows the different layers.

This diagram shows some of the layers in the Earth's atmosphere. The outermost layer, the exosphere, is not marked; it is around 400km (250 miles) from Earth.

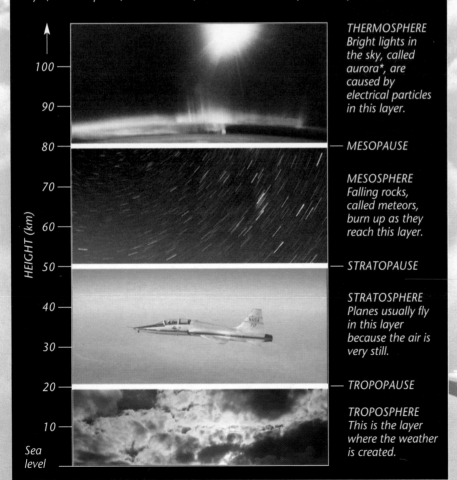

HEIGHT (km)

100
90
80
70
60
50
40
30
20
10
Sea level

THERMOSPHERE
Bright lights in the sky, called aurora, are caused by electrical particles in this layer.*

— MESOPAUSE

MESOSPHERE
Falling rocks, called meteors, burn up as they reach this layer.

— STRATOPAUSE

STRATOSPHERE
Planes usually fly in this layer because the air is very still.

— TROPOPAUSE

TROPOSPHERE
This is the layer where the weather is created.

*Air currents, 50; aurora, 90

The stratosphere

The upper limit of the stratosphere is around 50km (30 miles) from the Earth's surface. When you fly in a plane, you fly in this layer, just above the clouds.

The stratosphere contains a concentration of ozone gas which absorbs ultraviolet rays from the Sun. This causes the stratosphere to heat up. This layer of ozone gas is very important, as it helps to shield the Earth from harmful ultraviolet rays, which can cause skin cancer and damage to the eyes.

The mesosphere

The mesosphere reaches a height of around 80km (50 miles). Temperatures here are the coolest in the atmosphere because the mesosphere contains no ozone, dust or clouds, which absorb energy from the Sun. It is hottest at the bottom due to the warmer stratosphere layer below.

The thermosphere

Temperatures in the thermosphere can be extremely high, reaching up to 1,500°C (2,732°F). This is because there is a high proportion of a gas called atomic oxygen. This absorbs ultraviolet rays from the Sun in the same way that ozone does.

The ozone layer

The layer of ozone gas in the stratosphere is being damaged by chemicals called chlorofluorocarbons (CFCs), which are used in some spray cans and refrigerators. At certain times of year, a hole in the ozone layer appears over Antarctica, and in other areas the ozone layer becomes very thin. This damage means that more of these harmful ultraviolet rays reach the Earth's surface.

The bright pink areas in this picture show a hole in the layer of ozone gas over Antarctica.

When you fly in a plane in the stratosphere you can often see the clouds in the troposphere below.

PH-BFO

AIR AND OCEAN CURRENTS

As the Sun heats the Earth, it causes air and water to move around in the form of currents. As particles of air and water are heated, they expand and rise and then cool and fall, producing patterns of circulating air and water, which are crucial in determining climate.

The circular shapes on the satellite image in the background are called spiral eddies. They are swirls of water which have separated from the main band, or current, of water.

Moving air

The air around us is constantly pushing in every direction. The force that it exerts as it does is known as atmospheric pressure.

The movement of air is affected by temperature. The Sun heats up the land and oceans, which in turn heat the air directly above in the troposphere*. As the air is heated, it rises and moves off, leaving behind an area of low pressure. When the air cools, it sinks down on the Earth's surface in a different area, causing high pressure.

Because the Sun doesn't heat up the world evenly, there are differences of pressure. Where there is a difference, air rushes from high to low pressure areas in order to even out the pressure. This moving air is wind. As the air moves, the spinning of the Earth causes it to be deflected into fast spirals. This deflection is known as the Coriolis effect*.

Global winds

Air is constantly circulating between the tropics* and the poles as global winds. Warm air flows from the tropics and pushes out the cold air at the poles, which then flows back towards the tropics. The Westerlies and trade winds are examples of global winds.

Global winds form because areas near the Equator receive more heat from the Sun than other areas. As the air is heated, it rises and spreads out. When it cools, it sinks at around 30° north and south of the Equator, causing pressure at the Earth's surface to increase. This forces the air outwards in the direction of both the Equator and the poles.

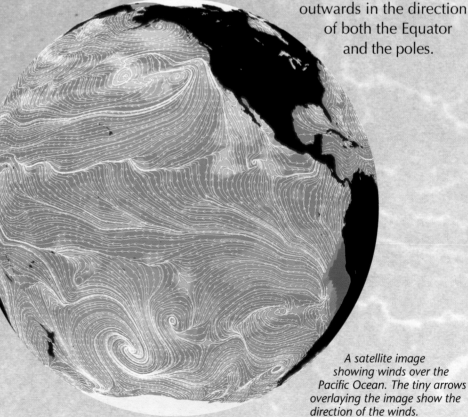

A satellite image showing winds over the Pacific Ocean. The tiny arrows overlaying the image show the direction of the winds.

*Coriolis effect, 84; tropics, 146; troposphere, 48

Moving water

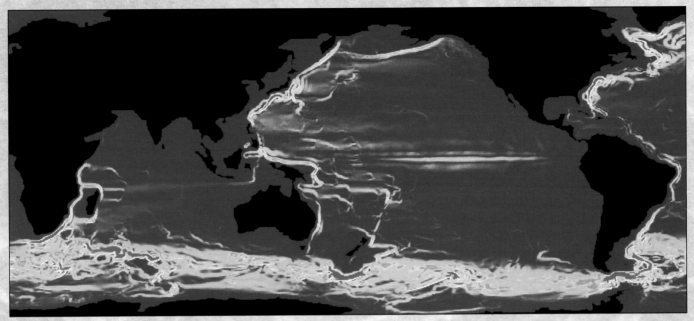

This image shows ocean currents around the world. The red areas are fast currents and the light blue areas are slow currents.

Ocean currents are wide bands of water, like rivers that flow in the world's oceans. They sweep around the oceans, moving water between hot and cold places.

Just as heat from the Sun causes the movement of air, it also causes the movement of water in the form of currents. However, in the oceans, the temperature difference between the poles and the

A satellite picture of part of the Gulf Stream, a current of water that flows in the Atlantic Ocean.

Equator is greater than it is on land. Near the Equator, the Sun's rays penetrate far below the ocean's surface. At the poles, the Sun's rays hit the water at a shallow angle. This causes the water to act like a mirror, reflecting rather than absorbing the Sun's rays.

Effects of currents

Currents vary in temperature and move at different speeds. If a current is much warmer or cooler than the surrounding water, it can dramatically affect the climates of the coastal areas that it flows near. A current called the Gulf Stream, which runs between the Gulf of Mexico and Europe (where it becomes the North Atlantic Drift), brings a mild climate to northwest Europe. The Labrador current

is a cold current which runs from the Arctic Ocean along the northeast coast of North America, bringing a cold climate to Newfoundland.

El Niño

The incredible effect that the warming of the ocean can have on weather and climate is illustrated by a phenomenon known as El Niño. Every few years, a current of water in the Pacific, off the northwest coast of South America, suddenly becomes warmer. Scientists are not sure why this happens, but it sets in motion a chain of climatic changes, including floods, droughts and severe storms.

NATURAL CYCLES

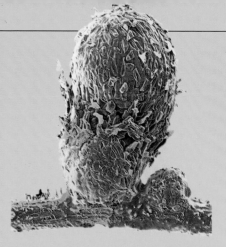

This magnified part of a pea plant contains bacteria which convert nitrogen from the air into a form the plant can use.

Some substances, such as nitrogen and carbon, are constantly changing form as they move around in huge cycles. This exchange of substances is essential to life on Earth. The air, land, water, plants, animals, and even your own body, all form a part of these cycles.

Keeping a balance

Living things take in substances such as oxygen, nitrogen, carbon and water from the world around them through food, soil and air. They use them to live and grow. When a plant or animal dies and decays, its body is broken down and gases are released into the air. The cycle continues, with these substances being used again and again. This process maintains the balance of gases in the air.

The nitrogen cycle

This diagram shows some of the different forms that nitrogen takes.

Plants take in nitrogen from the air.

Plants are eaten by animals.

Bacteria convert ammonia in the soil into nitrates, which are then taken in by plants.

As dead plants and animals decay, nitrogen is released into the soil.

Nitrogen (chemical symbol ~ N) makes up 78% of the air. Plants and animals need it for growth. Plants take in nitrogen from the air and the soil. Bacteria convert the substance into a form the plants can use. Animals obtain nitrogen by eating plants or by eating animals that have eaten plants. When plants and animals die and decay, fungi and bacteria break down their remains and nitrogen is released back into the soil.

This dung beetle is feeding on animal dung. Insects like this help to break down plant and animal matter.

One form that carbon can take is charcoal, as shown here. Charcoal can be burned as a fuel. When it is burned, it gives out carbon dioxide.

The carbon cycle

Carbon forms part of the gases in the air, mainly as carbon dioxide (chemical symbol ~ CO_2), which is a compound of carbon and oxygen. Plants take in CO_2 from the air and use it to make food. At night, they give out CO_2.

Animals obtain carbon by eating plants. They release carbon in their waste and when they breathe out. CO_2 is also released when plants and animals die and decay. Carbon can be stored in the form of fossilized remains. Eventually these form fossil fuels* such as coal and oil, which release CO_2 when burned.

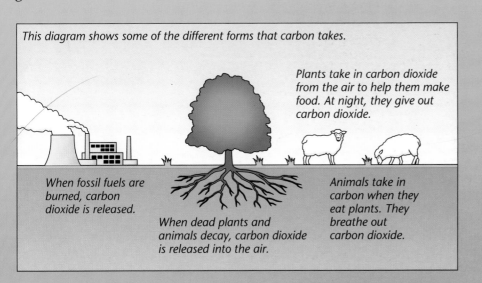

This diagram shows some of the different forms that carbon takes.

Plants take in carbon dioxide from the air to help them make food. At night, they give out carbon dioxide.

When fossil fuels are burned, carbon dioxide is released.

When dead plants and animals decay, carbon dioxide is released into the air.

Animals take in carbon when they eat plants. They breathe out carbon dioxide.

Upsetting cycles

Left alone, these cycles create a natural balance of gases. However, human activities are interfering with this balance by adding waste and pollution to the atmosphere. The effects of human disruption on the carbon cycle are described on pages 54 to 55.

One of the major factors that affects the nitrogen cycle is farming. When farmers harvest crops, they remove plants which have taken in nitrates from the soil. Because the plants are not allowed to decay naturally, the nitrogen is not returned to the soil, and the cycle is broken.

The algae in this canal is thriving because of excess nitrates running into it from fertilizer used on nearby farmland.

Farmers often use chemical fertilizers* to replace nitrates in soil. But this can also upset the balance, as it's difficult to judge the right amount of nitrates. If too much is added, it can seep through the soil into rivers, where it can affect plants and animals.

*Fertilizer, 114; fossil fuels, 24

GLOBAL WARMING

Some of the gases in the atmosphere help to keep the Earth warm. They trap heat from the Sun in the same way that a greenhouse traps heat. This process is known as the greenhouse effect. But, as these gases increase, the Earth could be becoming too warm.

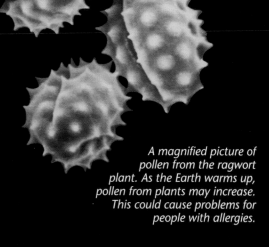

A magnified picture of pollen from the ragwort plant. As the Earth warms up, pollen from plants may increase. This could cause problems for people with allergies.

Greenhouse gases

The Earth's surface absorbs some of the heat from the Sun, but the rest is bounced back into the atmosphere. Most of it escapes into space, but some is trapped in the atmosphere by gases known as greenhouse gases. The main greenhouse gases are carbon dioxide and water in the form of clouds. As the amount of greenhouse gases increases, more heat is trapped.

Most greenhouse gases occur naturally, but industrial processes and other pollution are increasing the amount of greenhouse gases in the atmosphere. Scientists think that this may be causing the Earth to become warmer. This process is known as global warming.

Plants are important for the balance of greenhouse gases because they take in carbon dioxide.

Balance of gases

Whenever we burn oil, coal or wood, carbon dioxide is released. For example, when forests are burned to make room for farming, they release carbon dioxide. This also reduces the number of plants available to absorb carbon dioxide, upsetting the natural balance of the carbon cycle*. Factories, power stations and cars also give out pollution which may contribute to global warming.

Huge roads like this one are useful for car drivers. But the pollution from cars could be contributing to global warming.

McArthur Blvd
n Wayne Airport
NEXT EXIT

Venice, Italy, is a city built on over 100 tiny islands in the Lagoon of Venice. If the sea level rises, it may eventually disappear under the sea.

Rising sea level

As temperatures rise, so will the sea level. This will eventually result in the flooding of low-lying areas. Scientists estimate that the sea level is rising at a rate of 1-2mm (0.04-0.08ins) each year. It may rise by a further 0.25-1m (0.8-3.3ft) by the year 2100. There are two main reasons for the increased volume of water. Firstly, as the oceans heat up, the water expands. The sea level rises because the water is taking up more space. Secondly, the higher temperatures may cause glaciers and polar icecaps to melt. This water will then flood into the sea.

Changing climate

If temperatures rise, climates all over the world will be affected. Scientists predict that the average temperature will increase by around 2°C (3.6°F) in the next century. The effect this will have is not known. Some areas may become warmer and drier, and others wetter. There may also be an increase in extreme weather such as strong winds and rainstorms.

Changes in climates will also affect the habitats* of plants and animals. This could help some species to thrive, while others may be forced to move in search of food and water if they are to survive.

Shifting the balance

People have already begun to take steps to reduce the emission of gases that contribute to global warming. The main ways that this can be achieved are by looking at alternative energy sources and reducing pollution levels.

Carbon cycle, 53; habitats, 100

WORLD CLIMATES

The long-term or typical pattern of weather in a particular area is known as its climate. Climates vary enormously in different parts of the world. They determine the character of an area, affecting the plants, animals and people that live there.

This map of the Earth's surface contains information from several different satellites*. It shows some of the main climate types around the world.

Maple trees grow in temperate regions, which have lots of vegetation.

Temperate and tropical regions are green. They contain lots of vegetation.

Tropical grasslands and deserts are yellow and brown. They are dry, with little vegetation.

Snowy regions are light blue or white. The swirling white masses are clouds.

Climate types

Areas can be grouped into several main climate types, such as polar, temperate and tropical. These are also known as biomes*. The most important factor in determining an area's climate is its latitude*, because this affects the amount of heat received from the Sun. This in turn has a crucial effect on the vegetation and animals which give each climate zone its distinctive characteristics.

The map above shows how areas at the same latitude share broadly similar climates. The different climate zones are described in more detail on the following pages.

Other factors, such as height and distance from the ocean, are also very important in determining the climate of a particular area.

*Biomes, 101; latitude, 10; satellites, 11

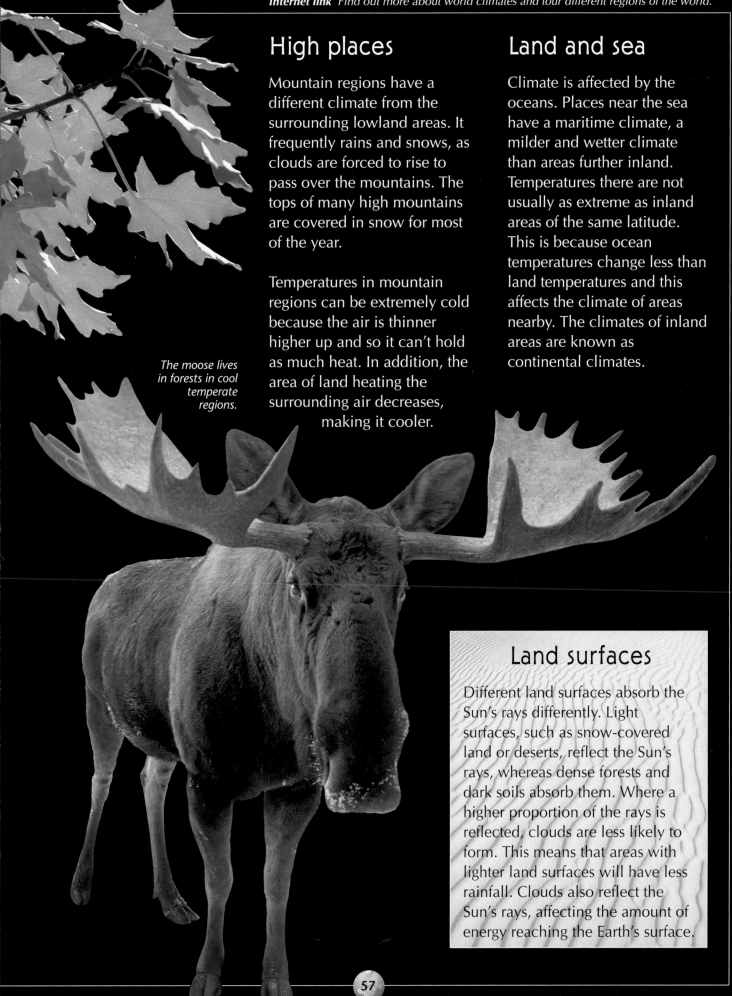

High places

Mountain regions have a different climate from the surrounding lowland areas. It frequently rains and snows, as clouds are forced to rise to pass over the mountains. The tops of many high mountains are covered in snow for most of the year.

Temperatures in mountain regions can be extremely cold because the air is thinner higher up and so it can't hold as much heat. In addition, the area of land heating the surrounding air decreases, making it cooler.

The moose lives in forests in cool temperate regions.

Land and sea

Climate is affected by the oceans. Places near the sea have a maritime climate, a milder and wetter climate than areas further inland. Temperatures there are not usually as extreme as inland areas of the same latitude. This is because ocean temperatures change less than land temperatures and this affects the climate of areas nearby. The climates of inland areas are known as continental climates.

Land surfaces

Different land surfaces absorb the Sun's rays differently. Light surfaces, such as snow-covered land or deserts, reflect the Sun's rays, whereas dense forests and dark soils absorb them. Where a higher proportion of the rays is reflected, clouds are less likely to form. This means that areas with lighter land surfaces will have less rainfall. Clouds also reflect the Sun's rays, affecting the amount of energy reaching the Earth's surface.

Internet link For a link to a website that takes you on a virtual expedition of the Earth's rainforests, go to **www.usborne-quicklinks.com**

RAINFORESTS

This is a tropical rainforest in Bali, Indonesia. The tallest trees tower above the canopy. They are called emergents.

In the tropics*, it rains nearly every day and is hot throughout the year. Large areas are covered in thick, lush forests called tropical rainforests.

Rainy places

Tropical rainforests receive more than 4,000mm (160in) of rain each year. The intense heat causes water to evaporate quickly, making the air very moist, or humid.

Inside the rainforests it is dark and damp. As trees compete to reach the light, they grow quickly, spreading out their branches to absorb the light. Their leaves form a thick green canopy which blocks out most of the Sun's rays.

This map show where the tropical rainforests are.

In places the canopy can be up to 7m (23ft) thick. The area between the canopy and the ground is called the understorey.

*Tropics, 146

58

Rainforest people

Many traditional groups, or tribes, of people living in tropical rainforests survive by hunting animals and gathering plants, or by small-scale farming. However, recently other settlers have moved into these areas for commercial reasons. They chop down trees and burn them in order to clear land, which is then used for growing crops or grazing cattle.

These rainforest trees are being burned to create space for farming.

Animal life

Rainforests are home to over half the world's plant and animal species. Different kinds of animals have adapted to living at different levels in the rainforest. Many animals live in the branches of trees. They need to be good at climbing and able to move easily from tree to tree by swinging, jumping or gliding.

On the forest floor, the tangled vegetation makes it difficult for some animals to move around. The larger animals tend to be sturdy so that they can easily force their way through. There are also many insects on the forest floor.

Colugos, or flying lemurs, climb trees to eat leaves and fruit. They use the flaps of skin between their arms and legs to help them glide between trees.

Forests in danger

Every year, huge areas of rainforest are chopped down or burned. The disappearance of so many trees affects the balance of gases in the atmosphere. This may cause an increase in global warming*. Due to the destruction of their natural habitat, many rainforest plants and animals have died out and many others are endangered.

Golden lion tamarins are an endangered species of monkey.

TROPICAL GRASSLANDS

The tropical grasslands are flat, open plains in the central parts of continents. They occur between 5° and 15° north and south of the Equator and get their name from the grasses that make up the majority of the vegetation.

This map shows where the tropical grasslands are.

Acacia trees in the Taragire National Park, Tanzania, Africa. Acacias are among the few trees that can survive in the dry tropical grasslands.

Two seasons

The tropical grasslands have two seasons: a dry season, when the vegetation is dry and brown, and a rainy season, when the grasses become tall and green.

The rainy season in an area occurs when the Sun is directly overhead and the trade winds* meet there. As the warm moist air is forced to rise, it rains heavily. When the Sun is no longer directly overhead, the point where the trade winds meet shifts and the dry season begins. The trade winds are dry because they have already shed any moisture on the coast.

Vegetation

Only a few trees grow in the tropical grasslands, for example the acacia tree whose thick trunk is resistant to the fires that sometimes rage during the dry season. However, there are around 8000 species of grasses, which are well adapted to surviving the dry season. Their long roots can reach out in search of the little water that is available.

*Trade winds, 50

Grassland animals

The tropical grasslands are home to large numbers of herbivores (plant-eating animals). These attract large hunting animals, such as lions and cheetahs, that feed on them. Because the land is so exposed, many animals live in large groups, so that some animals can watch out for predators while others feed or rest.

Some of the fastest animals, such as cheetahs, gazelles and ostriches, live in grasslands. Speed is important for survival, both for the hunters and the hunted. With so few hiding places, a hunt for food often results in a chase.

During the dry season, wildebeest move away, or migrate, to find food and water. Many thousands of wildebeest migrate together for protection.

Cheetahs are the fastest land mammals, reaching speeds of up to 110km per hour (68mph).

The tsetse fly

Many grassland areas are now used for farming. However the largest grasslands, in Africa, are almost untouched. This is because of a parasite, carried by an insect called the tsetse fly, which infects humans and animals. In humans, it causes sleeping sickness, the effects of which are sluggishness, fever and sometimes death. In animals, it causes a similar disease called nagana.

A close-up of a tsetse fly feeding on a human arm.

MONSOONS

At certain times of year, some areas of the tropics have a period of torrential rain known as a monsoon. The heavy rain can cause severe flooding, but people rely on the rain for survival. In fact, the start of the rainy season is often welcomed with celebrations.

Three seasons

Monsoons occur in certain parts of the tropics, particularly in Southeast Asia. Monsoon regions have three seasons ~ a long cool dry season, a hot humid season when the land is very dry, and a rainy season when there are thunderstorms on most days.

During the rainy season, it rains very heavily and there are strong winds. You can see how strong the winds are by the way the trees are blowing.

Changing winds

The word *monsoon* comes from an Arabic word which means "season". It refers to the rainy season and to the seasonal winds that cause it. During the dry season, the land is cooler than the ocean, and so dry winds blow from the land to the ocean. The rainy season occurs when the Sun is almost directly overhead. The land is hotter than the ocean, so moist winds rush in from the ocean. As the winds rise and cool, they shed their moisture as heavy rain.

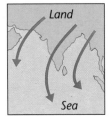

In the dry season, winds blow from the land to the sea.

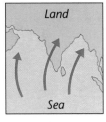

In the rainy season, moist winds rush in from the sea.

Farming

Around a quarter of the world's people live in monsoon areas. Many of them rely on growing their own food. The main crops are rice and tea, which grow well in wet conditions.

A rice farm in China. The field has been flooded with water, as rice plants grow well in waterlogged soils.

Rice in particular needs lots of water to grow. The seedlings are planted during the monsoon season in flooded fields called paddy fields. Rice is an important food for many poor nations, because it can be grown cheaply and in large quantities. Too little rain in the monsoon season can be disastrous, resulting in crop failure and possibly famine.

When trees are cut down for wood and to clear space for farming, it means that there are no more roots to hold the soil* together. In monsoon regions, this can cause problems, because heavy rains will then wash away soil that is important for farming.

Diseases

A magnified mosquito. These insects thrive in monsoon regions.

A number of serious diseases spread easily after the monsoon season, because stagnant floodwater provides an ideal breeding ground for the bacteria that cause them. Typhoid and cholera are particularly common. Mosquitoes, insects which can carry diseases such as malaria and yellow fever, also thrive in the warm, wet conditions of monsoon regions.

*Soil erosion, 115

TROPICAL DESERTS

The tropical deserts are the hottest and driest places in the world. With so little water or shelter, only a few animals and plants are able to survive in the burning heat of the day. Very few people live in tropical deserts.

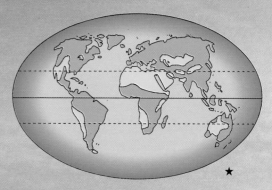

Tropical deserts exist mainly between 15° and 30° north and south of the Equator.

This is a fertile area, called an oasis, in the Thar Desert, Rajasthan, India. These people are collecting water there.

Desert climate

Most deserts are hot during the day and cold at night. During the day, the heat is intense because there are few clouds to block the Sun's rays. Temperatures can reach over 52°C (126°F). At night, the lack of clouds allows heat to escape, so temperatures can drop to below freezing.

Less than 250mm (10in) of rain falls on deserts each year. When it rains, it is usually in short, violent storms. If the land has been baked by the heat of the Sun, these brief rainstorms can cause floods because the rain is not absorbed quickly enough by the dry ground.

Oases

There is water in the desert, but most of it is stored underground in types of rocks called porous rocks*. In a few places, where these rocks are at the surface, moist areas called oases are formed. Birds, animals and people gather at oases to drink and most desert plants grow near them.

*Porous rocks, 128

Desert landscapes

Only 25% of the world's deserts are sandy. Most deserts consist of bare rock or stone. Some even have dramatic rocky mountains. In sandy deserts, sand often collects together to form hills called dunes, which move and change shape as the wind blows the sand across the desert.

Strong winds sometimes sweep across deserts, causing sand-storms which can wear away the rocks in their path. Over many years, this "sand-blasting" effect can produce some unusually-shaped rocks. The process of wearing away rocks in this way is known as erosion*.

This is a sand dune in the Sahara Desert, Africa, the biggest desert in the world. The man is one of the Tuaregs, a group of people who live in the Sahara.

Adaptation

In order to survive in the desert, those plants and animals that live there have adapted so that they are able to cope with the heat and limited supplies of water.

Some desert plants can store water in their stems or can access water deep in the ground through long tap roots. Others can reduce water loss by rolling up their leaves.

Usually animals lose lots of water in their droppings, but many desert animals have dry droppings. This helps them to save water, so that they can last longer without water.

Camels can drink gallons of water in a few minutes and then last days without any.

Desert expansion

The world's deserts are increasing in size. This process, known as desertification, is caused by the destruction of the vegetation near the edges of deserts. People living in these dry areas need grass for their animals to eat and wood from trees to burn as fuel. This destruction of vegetation means that the soil is easily washed or blown away and the water cycle* is disrupted. Once this has happened, it is very difficult for vegetation to grow there.

*Erosion, 118; water cycle, 80

MEDITERRANEAN CLIMATES

Mediterranean climates are warm temperate* climates. They get their name from the regions bordering the Mediterranean Sea. However, other parts of the world, such as small areas around Cape Town (South Africa), Perth (Australia), San Francisco (U.S.A.) and Valparaíso (Chile) also share this climate.

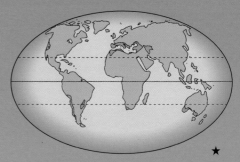

★

This map shows those areas with a Mediterranean climate.

Warm and dry

Mediterranean climates cover only a small part of the world. They are found on the west coasts of continents between 30° and 40° north and south of the Equator. The winters are warm and wet and the summers are hot and dry.

During the summer, warm, dry winds blow from the tropics*, bringing dry conditions. In the winter, the steady rainfall transforms the parched, brown landscape into a rich green one.

In the Mediterranean region itself, the Mediterranean Sea (an inland sea) has a crucial effect on the climate of the surrounding countries. In the summer, the sea is cooler than the land, so the air sinks down over the sea and the surrounding area. This means that there is very little rain. The lack of cloud cover also means that temperatures are high. In winter, the relative warmth of the sea causes mild winters, and warm, moist air from the sea brings rain.

In other parts of the world which have a Mediterranean climate, cold offshore currents* have a similar effect on the local climate as the Mediterranean Sea has on southern Europe.

This town in the south of France overlooks the Côte d'Azur, a stretch of coastline by the Mediterranean Sea which is a popular spot for vacations.

Oranges grow well in Mediterranean climates.

Vegetation

There are two main types of vegetation in Mediterranean regions: trees such as cork oaks and olives, and low woody plants, or scrub. The vegetation is well adapted to the dry summer climate, with thick, waxy leaves which reduce the amount of water the plant loses and long roots which enable them to reach water deep underground.

Farming

Those places with Mediterranean climates are home to some of the world's most important wine producers. Grape vines are particularly well adapted to the climate, as they have long roots and tough bark.

Tourism

People sunbathing on a beach in the Côte d'Azur, southern France

The hot, dry summers in Mediterranean countries such as Greece, Spain, Italy and southern France have made them popular vacation destinations for North Europeans from cooler climates searching for summer sunshine. This has meant that tourism has become an important part of the economy of these countries. Resorts tend to be developed in strips along the coast, where closeness to the sea and pleasant beaches are also major attractions.

A vineyard in the Douro Valley, Portugal. The grapes are being hand-picked to make wine.

The Mediterranean climate is good for growing citrus fruits, such as oranges, lemons and grapefruit. The summers are hot, which means that the fruit ripens quickly. Citrus fruits also have thick skins which help them to retain moisture so that they can survive the dry conditions.

Because Mediterranean summers are so dry, many farmers have to water the land artificially to help their crops grow. This is called irrigation.

*Ocean currents, 51; temperate, 68; tropics, 146

TEMPERATE CLIMATES

The area between the Arctic and Antarctic Circles (the Frigid Zone) and the tropics (the Torrid Zone) is called the Temperate Zone. As the term temperate suggests, temperatures are never very extreme, but this vast area contains a wide range of climates and landscapes.

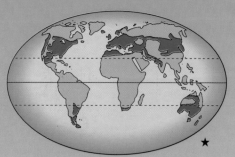

The purple areas of this map show the parts of the world with temperate climates.

Varied climates

The vegetation in the Temperate Zone ranges from forests to dry grasslands. However, all the different areas have four seasons*: spring, summer, autumn and winter. This is because of the Earth's tilt and the way that each hemisphere faces the Sun and then faces away from it.

Green lands

The mid-latitudes (between 40° and 60° north and south of the Equator) have a rainy climate, which is usually described as cool temperate. The steady rain throughout the year is the result of cool air from the poles meeting warm air from the tropics*. The warm air is forced upwards, causing swirling patterns of clouds and rain known as depressions.

The moderate temperatures in cool temperate regions mean that vegetation has a long period of uninterrupted growth, so the landscape is very green. Most trees are deciduous trees, which means that they lose their leaves in winter.

This region, which includes most of Europe, contains the richest farmland areas. The fertile soil and rainfall throughout the year make it suitable for a wide variety of crops, including grains, green vegetables and deciduous fruits.

In temperate regions, many of the trees are deciduous. This means that they lose their leaves in winter.

Before the leaves on deciduous trees fall, they change from green to orange, red and yellow.

Grasslands

A view of the huge grasslands, or prairies, of North America

The prairies of North America and the steppes of Russia are huge temperate grasslands which lie in the middle of continents. Their summers are hot and sunny, but their winters can be quite harsh because they are away from the warming effects of the ocean*.

These areas receive too little rainfall for trees to grow, so the main vegetation is grasses. In the vast, treeless prairies of North America, winter frosts break up the rich soils, but summer days are long and warm. Wheat is suited to these conditions and is grown extensively.

Seasonal life

The lives of many animals and plants in temperate regions closely follow the cycle of the seasons.

Annual plants complete their life's cycle in a year. They produce seeds which begin growing in spring and then flower in summer. In autumn, they produce seeds and fruit. At the end of the year the plants die. Perennial plants last for several years, but still produce new growth in the spring. During autumn, deciduous trees start to lose their leaves and by winter, they are bare.

In the winter, the ground often freezes, leaving few plants for animals to feed on.

Many animals prepare for the winter by storing up food. Some, such as the dormouse, cope with the lack of food by going into a deep sleep known as hibernation. During hibernation, an animal's breathing and heartbeat slow down and it does not need to eat. There are also animals that avoid the cold weather altogether by moving, or migrating, to warmer places.

A dormouse hibernating in its nest during the winter months

*Maritime climates, 57

POLAR REGIONS

The Arctic, the area around the North Pole, and the Antarctic, the area around the South Pole, are known as the polar regions. The temperatures there are usually below freezing and huge expanses of land and sea are covered in ice and snow.

This map shows the Antarctic from above. The imaginary line around it is called the Antarctic Circle.

Antarctic

In the middle of the Antarctic Ocean is a land mass, or continent, known as Antarctica, which is covered in a thick layer of ice. Temperatures are so low that when snow falls it doesn't melt, but builds up with each snowfall. The weight of the snow on top presses down on the lower layers to form ice.

No land mammals live permanently in Antarctica because it is so cold, but some animals, such as seals, go there to breed. A number of sea birds, including penguins, live there permanently.

The emperor penguin is one of seven different species of penguins that live in the Antarctic.

This map shows the Arctic from above. The imaginary line around it is called the Arctic Circle.

Arctic

The Arctic is mainly made up of the Arctic Ocean, but its edges are bordered by several countries, including Greenland, Canada and Alaska. The land here, called the tundra, is just warm enough for animals and plants to survive.

In the summer, the ice on the tundra melts and the surface of the ground thaws. The ground often becomes boggy, because deeper down it is still frozen and the water cannot seep through. This frozen layer is called permafrost.

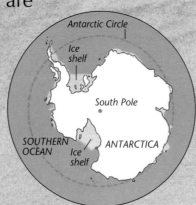

Keeping warm

Some polar animals have adapted to living in the sea, as icy winds make it difficult to survive on land. For example, penguins cannot fly and seals move awkwardly on land, but both are good swimmers. Other animals have adapted to cope with the cold in different ways. Polar bears have a thick layer of fat under their skin which keeps them warm. Musk oxen have thick, shaggy coats. Many polar animals have small ears, which help to reduce heat loss.

These penguins are huddling together for warmth. They take turns standing on the outside.

The Arctic fox's white winter coat means that it doesn't stand out against the snowy background.

Blending in

A number of animals in the Arctic have different winter and summer coats. As the snow falls in the winter, their coats change and become white. This enables them to camouflage themselves, or blend in with their backgrounds. During the summer a brown coat helps them to blend in more easily with the grass. Their ability to change with their environment helps these animals to hide from predators or to sneak up on their prey without being seen.

In summer, the Arctic fox's brown coat enables it to blend in with rocks and plants.

Arctic shelters

Some animals that live in the Arctic build burrows or dens in the snow to protect themselves from the cold winds. For example, polar bears build dens, with many chambers in the snow, for their cubs to take shelter.

MOUNTAINS

About 5% of the world's land surface is covered by high mountains and mountain ranges. Mountain areas have more than one type of climate because, as you go up a mountain, there are fewer particles in the air and the temperature falls.

The Great Basin Desert in Nevada, U.S.A., lies on the sheltered side, or rain shadow, of the Sierra Nevada mountains.

Mountain ranges

Most mountains are formed when the plates that make up the Earth's crust push together, forcing the land into fold mountains*. This is why mountains often occur in long lines, or ranges.

When air is blown from the sea onto a mountain range, it is forced to rise. The tiny water droplets in the air cool down, condense and turn into clouds. Rain or snow then falls on the mountainside. The sheltered land on the other side of the mountain, called the rain shadow, gets very little rain, and may become a desert.

Mountain peaks in the Andes, on the border between Chile and Argentina

Mountain levels

The higher up a mountain you go, the colder it gets. This is because the air higher up is thinner, so it can store less heat. There are different types of weather, vegetation and animal life at different heights up the mountain. Few species live on the windy peaks, but mountain goats and sheep graze on the grassy, rocky slopes below. Farther down, below a line called the treeline, it is warm enough for trees to grow. Animals such as cougars and hares live in mountain forests.

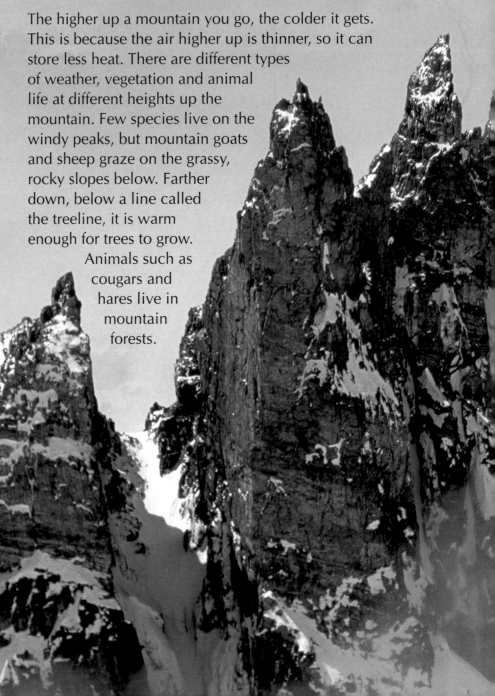

Adaptation

Mountain species are adapted to surviving in cold temperatures and strong winds. Mountain plants grow close to the ground and have deep roots, so they don't get blown away. Many mountain animals have large lungs for extracting enough oxygen from the thin air, and thick fur which keeps them warm.

The alpine forget-me-not flower is adapted to mountain climates. It has shorter, thicker stems and deeper roots than the common forget-me-not.

This shepherd from the Basque region of France is holding two baby goats. Goats are well-suited to the mountain climate.

Mountain people

Like mountain animals, people who live in high mountain areas have bigger lungs than lowlanders, to help them breathe more easily in the thin air. Mountain people may also be cut off from other cultures. For example, the Basque people, who have lived in the Pyrenees mountains between France and Spain for thousands of years, have a very unusual language which is unlike any other on Earth. This is because their mountain home meant that, for centuries, they rarely mixed with other peoples.

*Fold mountains, 19

CHANGING CLIMATES

Ever since the Earth was formed, its climate has been changing. Volcanic eruptions, collisions with asteroids, and the path of the solar system through space may all have caused climate changes that affected the atmosphere, the landscape and living things.

The red outline on this map shows the areas of the Earth that were covered in ice during the last Ice age. The white areas are those places that are still covered in ice today.

Long ago, widespread volcanic activity could have caused fires which damaged habitats, wiping out various species.

Ice ages

Throughout its history, the Earth has gone through several Ice ages, when the climate was colder than it is now, and glaciers* spread across much of the globe. Sea levels were lower as well, because a lot of the world's water was frozen into ice.

Within each Ice age, there have been slightly warmer periods called interglacials. Several thousand years ago, the Earth was in an Ice age. Then the climate got warmer and most of the ice melted. But the Ice age may not be over. Some experts think that we are now in an interglacial period.

Ice ages have several causes. As the galaxy spins, the Earth may enter magnetic fields which shield it from the Sun's heat. It may also sometimes change its orbit, move away from the Sun and get cooler

Explosions

Long-term climate patterns can be affected by sudden events, such as huge volcanic eruptions, or asteroids (lumps of rock from space) hitting the Earth. Events like this in the past could have filled Earth's atmosphere with smoke and dust which blocked out the sunlight, making the climate cold and dark and killing plants

Geological evidence

We can tell the Earth's climate has changed by looking at rocks and fossils. Many rocks form gradually in layers. These layers provide a record of what happened, called the fossil record. In warmer periods of the Earth's history, more plants and animals were alive and more fossils were preserved. Layers with fewer fossils show colder periods, when there were fewer living things.

Landscapes also hold clues about the past. For example, a U-shaped valley shows where a glacier gouged out a channel during an Ice age.

Fossils found in stone, such as this well-preserved bird fossil, can reveal which types of animals lived in which places long ago.

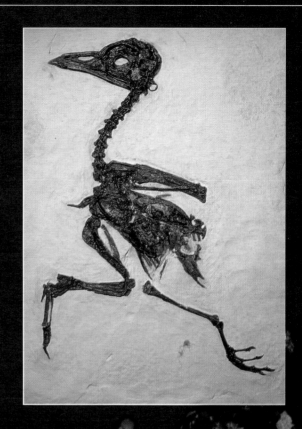

As well as blocking out vital sunlight with smoke and ash, volcanic eruptions can destroy plant life by smothering the land with lava, hot molten rock that burns everything in its path.

Moving continents

As the plates* that make up the Earth's crust have slowly changed position, the climate of each continent has altered. For example, what is now West Africa was once at the South Pole. As it got nearer the Equator, its climate warmed up as it received more sunlight. Climates are also affected by ocean currents*. As the continents separated from each other, currents could flow between them, bringing cold or warm water from other parts of the Earth.

*Glaciers, 130; ocean currents, 51; plates, 18

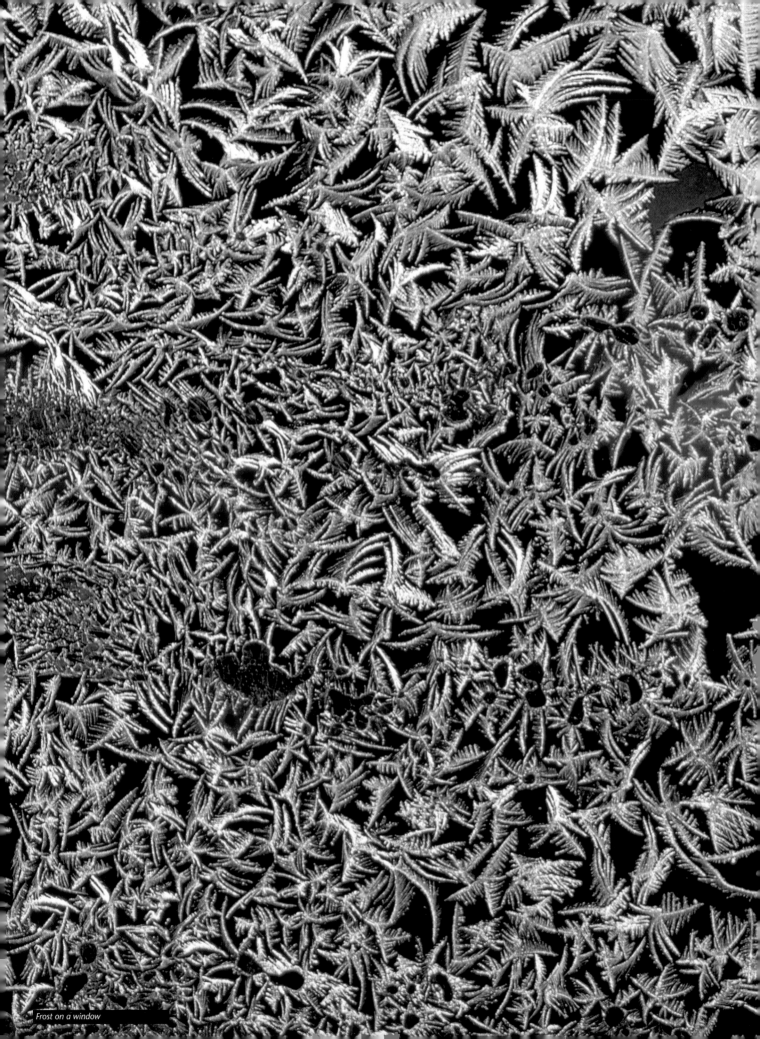
Frost on a window

WEATHER

WHAT IS WEATHER?

Weather is the way the Earth's atmosphere* behaves, whether it is hot or cold, windy or still, raining, snowing or hailing. Climate* means the overall temperature and patterns of weather in a particular place. But weather itself changes from day to day, and is much harder to predict.

The importance of weather

Weather affects everyone's life. Crops rely on the right weather conditions to grow properly. Summer vacations and trips to ski resorts may be ruined if the weather behaves unexpectedly. Weather is also a factor in many of the world's worst disasters, such as floods, landslides, ice storms, droughts and famines.

The right weather is so important that, for thousands of years, people have worshipped weather gods and used rituals to try to affect it. But, even with modern technology, it is almost impossible to control the weather.

This Japanese dancer wears a special costume and waves a large feather as part of traditional dance which is meant to make the rain fall.

*Atmosphere, 48; climate, 56; cumulus clouds, 81; evaporation, 80

What weather is

Weather is made up of three main ingredients: temperature, the movement of the air, and the amount of water in the air.

Hot weather is caused by the Sun heating up the land and the atmosphere*. If the Sun is hidden by clouds, or if a cold wind is blowing, the temperature is cooler.

Wind is also caused by the Sun. As air gets hotter, it expands, gets less dense, and rises. A mass of colder, heavier air, called a cold front, rushes in to replace it, making wind.

Finally, the Sun's heat makes water from plants, soil, rivers and seas evaporate* into the air. The water forms clouds, and may then fall as rain, snow or hail.

These three factors are always changing and affecting each other. They combine to make complicated patterns, known as weather systems. You can find out more about them on the next few pages.

Umbrellas have been used for hundreds of years to protect people from the weather. These paper umbrellas, called parasols, help to protect people from the Sun.

Traditional signs

Cumulus clouds usually appear when the weather is warm and sunny.

The way bees behave could help us predict the weather.

Today, scientists can predict the weather using satellites and computers. But before these were invented, people predicted the weather by observing signs, such as the way the clouds look, and the way animals behave. For example, cumulus clouds* usually mean sunny weather, and bees usually go home to their hives before a storm.

Weather facts

• The heaviest hailstones, weighing up to 1kg (2lb 3oz), fell in Gopalganj, Bangladesh, in 1986.

• The wettest place in the world is Tutunendo, Colombia. It gets nearly 12m (40ft) of rain a year.

• The biggest recorded snowflakes were 38cm (15in) across and fell on Fort Keogh, Montana, U.S.A., in 1887.

• The driest place in the world is Calama, Chile. Until 1971, there had been no rain there for 400 years.

WATER AND CLOUDS

The amount of water on Earth doesn't change. But water changes its state as it moves around in a huge cycle. It exists as a liquid (water) in seas and rivers, freezes into a solid (ice) which makes snow and hail, and floats in the air as clouds.

Snowflakes form when water droplets freeze into ice crystals. These snowflakes have been tinted so you can see their six-sided shapes more clearly.

The water cycle

When water is heated up, it changes from a liquid into tiny invisible water droplets that float in the air. This process is called evaporation.

The Sun's heat causes water to evaporate from rivers, lakes and seas. Plants suck up water from the ground and it escapes from their leaves as tiny droplets. People and animals breathe out water droplets in their breath.

When water droplets in clouds become heavy, they fall as rain, snow or hail.

Water flows down to the sea in streams and rivers.

Water droplets in the air rise, cool down and form clouds.

Water evaporates from rivers and seas in the heat of the Sun.

Plants and animals take in water that has fallen as rain.

This diagram shows how the water cycle works.

As water droplets rise, they get cooler, because the air is cooler higher up. This makes the water condense, or turn into liquid again, to form bigger droplets which can be seen as clouds. As clouds get colder, the water droplets join together and grow bigger. When they are heavy enough they fall as rain, and flow back into rivers, lakes and seas. This process is known as the water cycle.

Clouds

The way clouds look depends on how fast they have formed and how much water is in them. When clouds form slowly and steadily, they spread out across the sky in sheets. On hot days, clouds grow faster and puff up into heaps. Clouds full of big droplets look darker.

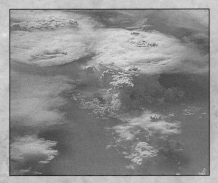

Cumulus clouds look like white, puffy heaps. They often form high in the sky in warm sunny weather.

Stratus clouds form low, flat layers and often block out the sunshine.

Cirrus clouds are high and wispy. (The word cirrus *means "like wispy hair" in Latin.)*

These tall, piled-up cumulonimbus clouds were photographed over the Gulf of Mexico. A cumulonimbus cloud is freezing at the top, but warmer at the bottom.

Precipitation

Water that falls onto the Earth's surface is called precipitation. Rain is the most common kind. There are many types of rain, from light drizzle to heavy downpours and monsoon rains*. Rain is vitally important for plants and animals, and too much or too little can be disastrous.

In freezing weather, precipitation sometimes takes the form of snow or hail instead of raindrops. The diagram on the right shows how hailstones are formed.

Hail begins as ice crystals in giant cumulonimbus clouds.

Air currents push the crystals up and around inside the cloud.

As they move, the crystals bump into water droplets, which freeze around them in layers, like the layers of an onion.

The layers of ice build up until they form heavy hailstones, which fall to Earth.

*Monsoons, 62

THUNDERSTORMS

Sometimes in warm weather, huge storm clouds form very quickly. These clouds are full of water and fast-moving air currents. They can build up a store of electricity powerful enough to make lightning and thunder.

Electric clouds

In hot, damp weather, lots of tiny invisible water droplets rise very fast. When they hit the colder air above, they make a tall, piled-up cloud called a cumulonimbus cloud.

Inside the cloud, water droplets and ice crystals rub together in the swirling air. This rubbing causes the crystals and droplets to build up a strong electric charge. Some have a negative charge (-) and some have a positive charge (+). Negative charges collect at the bottom of the cloud, making a huge energy difference between the cloud and the ground, which has a positive charge.

The difference builds up so much that it has to be equalized. A giant spark jumps between the bottom of the cloud and the ground, allowing the different charges to even out. The spark appears as a flash of lightning.

The satellite photograph on the left shows piled-up cumulonimbus storm clouds viewed from above.

Lightning zigzags through the air as it finds the easiest path from the cloud to the ground.

Ball lightning is a very rare kind of lightning which appears as a small, floating ball of bright light. It can travel through walls and has been seen inside buildings and aircraft.

Lightning

When lightning strikes, it travels first downwards, then upwards. The first stroke, called the leader stroke, is invisible. It jumps from the cloud to the ground. This creates a path for the main stroke, which sparks from the ground back up to the cloud.

The main stroke contains so much energy that it heats up the air around it. The heat makes the air expand quickly, causing an explosion. This is the loud noise of thunder.

Struck by lightning

Lightning always travels the shortest distance it can between the cloud and the ground. So it usually strikes high places, tall buildings or prominent objects such as trees or people.

Lightning quickly heats up whatever it strikes. When a tree is struck, the water in the tree boils instantly and turns into steam, which makes the trunk explode. But although lightning is dangerous, being struck is very rare. You can stay safe by avoiding trees and open spaces during storms.

WINDSTORMS

Because of the way the world spins, wind doesn't flow in straight lines, but swirls into spirals. Sometimes, wind spirals grow into terrifying storms, such as hurricanes and tornadoes, which contain the fastest wind speeds on Earth.

A satellite picture of the hurricane Typhoon Odessa

Coriolis effect

Winds are caused by high-pressure air rushing toward low-pressure areas, called cyclones. But instead of moving straight into the cyclone, the air circles around it in a spiral. This is called the Coriolis effect, and it happens because the spinning of the Earth always pushes winds to one side.

Hurricanes

Hurricanes are huge, very powerful windstorms that can be hundreds of miles wide. They only form in very warm, wet conditions, usually over the sea in tropical areas near the Equator. No one knows exactly what makes a hurricane start.

The warm, wet air has a very low pressure, so cooler winds spiral towards it.

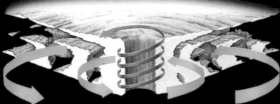

The damp air rises higher and condenses into thick clouds. They are blown into a spiral by the wind.

After hurricanes form, they sometimes hit land and cause massive damage. Winds of up to 240km/h (150mph) destroy buildings and rip trees out of the ground. But hurricanes die down soon after they hit land, as there is not enough moisture to keep them going.

Tornadoes

Tornadoes are much smaller than hurricanes, but can be even more dangerous. Tornadoes form during violent thunderstorms, when a hot, fast-moving upward air current meets a cold, downward air current. Because of the Coriolis effect, the hot and cold currents spiral around each other into a tight funnel of clouds between the thundercloud and the ground. The wind inside a tornado's funnel can be as fast as 480km/h (300mph), the fastest wind speeds measured on Earth.

Where the funnel touches the ground, it can be up to 500m (1,640ft) wide. It roars across the land, smashing everything in its path. People, animals and even cars can be dragged into the air by its powerful winds. But tornadoes are soon over. Although hurricanes can last 10 days, most tornadoes only last a few minutes. They grow weaker and fade away as the air inside grows colder, and the pressure evens out.

A tornado looks like a huge black or grey trunk, twisting from the thunderclouds down to the ground.

Tornado Alley

Some places have frequent thunderstorms and lots of tornadoes. Part of the U.S.A., between Texas and Illinois, has so many that it is known as Tornado Alley. The worst tornado ever recorded there hit Ellington, Missouri, on March 18, 1925. It lasted 3½ hours, destroyed four towns and killed 689 people.

Sea spouts

Sometimes a tornado forms over the sea. It sucks the water up into a towering spout, reaching into the clouds above. These tornadoes are called waterspouts. Sailors used to think they were long, snake-like sea monsters.

This engraving showing monstrous waterspouts is from a 19th-century book about the weather called L'Atmosphère

FLOODS AND DROUGHTS

Plants, animals and people need water to survive, and they rely on the weather to bring it to them. If there is too little rain, rivers dry up and crops fail. On the other hand, too much rain causes floods, which can damage crops and buildings and wash away precious soil.

Wet and dry

Some parts of the world always have more rain than others, and many places have wet and dry seasons. Rainy and dry periods like these are not usually a problem if they are regular, but too much or too little rain can be dangerous when unexpected weather changes take people by surprise.

This picture shows terrible flooding in Vietnam. People are forced to use boats to get around.

Too much rain

Normally, rainfall soaks into the ground or flows away in streams and rivers. Floods happen when there is suddenly too much water for the ground to hold, and streams, rivers and drains overflow. The extra water can come from rain, brought by heavy storms, from ice and snow on mountains melting and flowing into streams and rivers, or even from the sea spilling onto the land.

River Nile

Aswan High Dam

Lake Nasser

The River Nile floods naturally every summer, watering the land in the Nile Valley and making it fertile (good for growing crops). Lake Nasser is a reservoir formed by the Aswan High Dam.

Dirt and disease

Floods are very dangerous. As well as drowning people and animals and destroying homes and crops, floods can actually cause water shortages. They cover the land with dirty water, contaminating clean water supplies and helping diseases to spread.

Lack of rain can make soil harden, crack into lumps, and eventually crumble into dry dust.

This pump is an important source of clean water, but the dirty floodwater surrounding it could contaminate the water supply.

Not enough rain

A drought happens when there is less than the expected amount of rain. Droughts are often hard to predict, but they usually happen when winds change direction and no rainclouds are blown over the land. A bad drought may last several years and make the land completely infertile.

The effects of droughts can be made much worse if the land has not been used carefully.

From 1931 to 1938, a severe drought hit the Southern Great Plains of the U.S.A. The farmers had overworked the land, removing the grasses that held the soil in place. As the land dried out during the drought, the soil blew away, creating violent dust storms. The area became useless for farming and was named the Dust Bowl.

FREEZING AND FRYING

These Inuit people in Alaska, U.S.A., keep warm in traditional coats called parkas, which are made from animal skins.

The temperature on Earth can range from a bone-numbing -88°C (-127°F), measured at Vostok in Antarctica, to an unbearably hot 58°C (136°F), recorded at Al' Aziziyah, Libya. Extreme hot and cold weather can be deadly, and often has strange effects on people and places.

World of ice

Ice storms are caused by rain falling onto frozen surfaces. They happen when a mass of warm air passes through a cold area in winter, bringing rain that falls in the form of liquid raindrops, instead of as snow or hail. But when the drops of water hit freezing cold roads, cars, houses and trees, they immediately freeze into a coating of solid ice.

Ice storms are beautiful, but lethal. If enough rain falls, all outdoor surfaces can get covered in a layer of ice up to 6in (15cm) thick. It makes roads hazardous to drive on, builds up on rooftops until

This branch was caught in an ice storm that hit Kingston, Canada, in 1998.

they cave in, and coats tree branches, making them so heavy that they break. The ice also weighs down power lines until they snap. With the electricity and roads cut off, people can freeze to death in their own homes.

Blizzards

Blizzards are a combination of heavy snow and strong winds. They are especially dangerous because blizzard victims are blinded by the swirling snow, as well as being caught in the freezing cold. People who get stuck in a bad blizzard can sometimes get buried in the snow and freeze to death just a short distance away from warm houses, because they can't find their way to safety.

Heatwaves

A heatwave is a period of extra-hot weather. Heatwaves are caused by a combination of factors. Usually, a lack of wind and cloud allows the Sun to heat up the land and the atmosphere much more than normal. The hotter the air is, the more water it can hold in the form of tiny invisible droplets. This makes the air very humid, which makes it feel "sticky".

In some hot places, people have siestas ~ they sleep during the hottest part of the day to avoid the Sun.

This Egyptian boy's white clothes reflect the Sun's heat and help to keep him cool in hot weather.

Heatstroke

Heatstroke is caused by getting too hot ~ usually in the Sun. Normally, if you get too hot, your body sweats. The sweat evaporating from your skin helps you cool down. But heatstroke stops your body from sweating so that you get much too hot, and may go into a coma.

Heatstroke can happen quickly, especially inside a car, where the windows act like a greenhouse and stop heat from escaping. This is why animals and babies should never be left inside cars on hot, sunny days.

Sun and skin

Although the Sun provides warmth and energy, direct sunlight can be bad for you. It can cause wrinkles, sunburn and even skin cancer.

A poster warning Australians to wear T-shirts, sunscreen and sunhats

Hot and bothered

Hot, humid weather can even affect the way we behave. In New York, U.S.A., the murder rate rises as the temperature goes up. Most big riots start in cities on hot, humid nights. No one is sure why heat makes people get angry more easily.

This riot took place in the hot city of Los Angeles, in southern U.S.A., in 1992.

STRANGE WEATHER

U nusual, extreme weather, often called freak weather, can take people by surprise. Sometimes it can be so odd it doesn't seem like weather at all. Strange lights in the sky, showers of frogs, and even clouds that look like UFOs are all natural weather phenomena.

Weather beliefs

When strange weather strikes, people often think they're seeing something magical or supernatural. Weather may lie behind many traditional beliefs in fairies and ghosts, and also behind sightings of UFOs. One type of cloud, called a lenticular cloud, looks exactly like a flying saucer.

Lenticular clouds are shaped by waves of wind blowing around mountaintops. This one was seen at Mauna Kea, Hawaii, U.S.A.

Strange lights

The aurora borealis and aurora australis light up the sky around the poles with blue, red, green and white patterns. They are caused by streams of electrical particles which come from the Sun. When they interact with the gases in the Earth's atmosphere, they release energy which lights up the sky.

A solar flare is a storm on the Sun that sends electrical particles out into space, causing auroras on Earth.

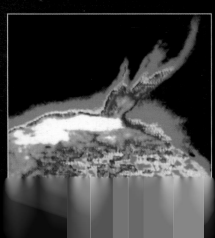

The aurora borealis appears in the northern skies, and is sometimes called the Northern Lights.

Raining frogs

"Rain" consisting of animals, fish or other objects has been reported many times through the centuries. The Roman historian Pliny reported a shower of frogs in AD77, and in the fourth century, fish fell on a town in Greece for three days. During a storm in England in 1939, so many frogs fell that witnesses were afraid to walk around in case they squashed them.

Showers like this, also known as "skyfalls", are probably caused by tornadoes* sucking up animals from ponds and rivers. Frogs are most often reported, but there have also been showers of snails, maggots, worms, pebbles and even sheep.

The common frog, a species seen falling from the sky

This magazine from May 1958 shows a skyfall of frogs which had recently been reported.

Big waves

Freak waves are one of the most dangerous types of unusual weather. Of course, not all big waves are freak waves. Hurricanes* can cause waves that swamp ships, and earthquakes can cause giant tsunami*. Some giant waves, though, appear from nowhere, even in calm weather. Scientists think waves like this may form when several smaller waves merge together.

These waves are especially dangerous because they often strike during otherwise good weather, when boats are not prepared for a storm and the crew may be out on the decks, so they can easily be swept away.

*Hurricanes, 84; tornadoes, 85; tsunamis, 44

WEATHER FORECASTING

Weather often seems random but, by careful observation, meteorologists (weather scientists) can learn how weather behaves and how to predict it. Radar and satellites* help them to track clouds and watch weather patterns from space.

This satellite image shows the temperature of the sea. Water evaporates from warm areas (shown in pink) and forms clouds. Maps like this are used to predict rain or droughts.

Measuring weather

Meteorologists measure different aspects of the weather, such as temperature, atmospheric pressure, and the amount of rainfall, at weather stations around the world. Weather balloons and weather planes carry instruments into the sky, where they can track the movements of clouds and high-altitude winds.

Weather technology

Weather satellites have been used since about 1960 to record the Earth's weather from space. From their positions in orbit above the Earth, satellites can take photographs and measure the temperature of the Earth's surface.

Geostationary satellites, like the weather satellite shown here, hover 36,000km (22,370 miles) above the Equator.

On the ground, radar equipment is used to detect cloud patterns. Radar waves are sent out, bounce off raindrops, and are collected by giant radar dishes. Computers collect the signals and create maps which show where rain clouds are heading.

Predicting weather

To forecast weather, readings from weather stations and satellites are stored in powerful computers. The data can then be examined to detect patterns and make predictions. For example, satellite images might show a hurricane forming over the ocean and heading for the coast. By calculating its size, speed, strength and direction, meteorologists can tell roughly when and where it will hit land.

At the moment, meteorologists can only predict weather a few days in advance. Weather can change so quickly that the forecasts are sometimes wrong.

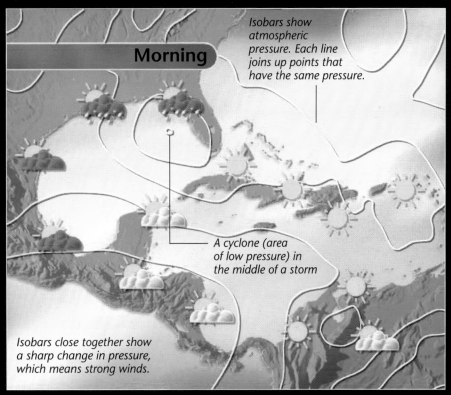

Morning

Isobars show atmospheric pressure. Each line joins up points that have the same pressure.

A cyclone (area of low pressure) in the middle of a storm

Isobars close together show a sharp change in pressure, which means strong winds.

Weather maps use lines called isobars to show differences in pressure, and symbols to indicate sunshine, rain and snow.

A satellite photograph of a hurricane over the Pacific Ocean

PLANTS AND ANIMALS

A red-eyed leaf frog

PLANT LIFE ON EARTH

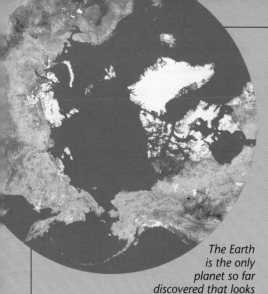

The Earth is the only
planet so far
discovered that looks
green from space.

The Earth is the only planet known to support living things, or organisms. There are millions of different kinds of living things on Earth. They fall into two main groups: animals and plants. To survive, nearly all of them need light and heat from the Sun, food, water and air.

The green planet

Most plants on Earth have green leaves and stems. This is because plants contain a green substance called chlorophyll, which helps them to make their food by a process called photosynthesis. From space, the Earth's land looks mainly green. This is because of the billions of plants covering most of its surface.

Plant food

Plants feed themselves by turning light from the Sun into food chemicals in their leaves. This is called photosynthesis, which means "building with light".

For photosynthesis to happen, plants also need water and nutrients* from the soil. They absorb these through their roots. They also take in carbon dioxide, a gas found in the air, through tiny holes in their leaves called stomata. They then use all these things to make glucose, a kind of sugar which they can feed on. Oxygen and water are produced too.

The Sun provides energy, in the form of light.

A plant's flowers contain parts that make seeds. These grow into new plants.

This part of the underside of a leaf has been magnified.

Leaves convert water and carbon dioxide into glucose and oxygen.

The stalk carries water and nutrients from roots to the leaves and flower.

Leaf stalk

Stomata let carbon dioxide in, and water and oxygen out.

Why we need plants

Plants are essential for life on Earth. Without them, the planet would look totally different, and there would be no people or animals. Animals ~ even meat-eaters ~ need plants, because plants form the basis of all food chains*.

Plants also give out oxygen and water, which animals and people need; and their roots hold the soil together. Without them, the soil would wash away into the sea. We use plants in many other ways, such as for wood and to make medicines, fabrics and perfumes.

The aloe, one of the thousands of plants from which we extract essences, is used in cosmetics and natural medicines.

Plant babies

Like all living things, plants reproduce (make new versions of themselves). They do this by making seeds. The seeds usually form inside the flower. They may then be carried a long way by the wind before falling to the ground and beginning to grow.

A sunflower contains hundreds of seeds like these. Like the seeds of many plants, they are an important source of food for people and animals.

Types of plants

Different types of living things are called species. There are millions of species of plants, from tiny flowers to enormous trees called giant sequoias, which are the biggest living things on Earth. Different species are suited, or adapted, to living in different parts of the world. In deserts, for example, where water is scarce, cactuses grow thick stems for storing water.

A giant sequoia tree. These are found mainly in California, U.S.A.

*Food chains, 100

ANIMAL LIFE ON EARTH

There are billions of types, or species, of animals living on the Earth. They include insects, fish, birds, reptiles, amphibians, and mammals such as humans. Unlike plants, animals have to move around to find food and water.

The bald eagle is a carnivore. It feeds mainly on fish, swooping down and snatching its prey from lakes and rivers.

How animals live

All animals have to eat in order to survive. Herbivores eat plants and carnivores eat animals. There are some animals, such as giant pandas, that eat both plants and animals. These are called omnivores. Most humans are also omnivores.

Honeyeaters are herbivores. They feed on nectar, a sweet juice found inside flowers.

Many animals have to watch out for predators, which are other animals that want to eat them. Their bodies have to be adapted to running fast or hiding. Some animals, such as zebras, are camouflaged, which means they are patterned so that they blend in with their background and are harder for predators to see. But some predators are also camouflaged, so they can creep up on their prey.

Tools for eating

Animals' bodies are adapted to suit the kind of food they eat. Herbivores usually have flat, broad teeth designed for munching plants, while most carnivores have sharp teeth and strong jaws for grabbing and tearing up their prey (the animals they eat).

You can see the long, sharp teeth in this badger's skull. They are good for grabbing and slicing through flesh.

In this roe deer's skull, you can see the long front teeth which are suited to biting off pieces of plants and flat molar teeth which are good for chewing plants.

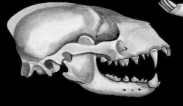

Natural selection

Why are animals and plants so well adapted to their way of life? One answer might be that they have gradually changed, or evolved, over a very long time to suit the places they live in and the food that is available to them.

In the 19th century, a scientist named Charles Darwin (1809-1882) put forward a theory, which he called "natural selection", to explain how these changes might happen.

According to Darwin, individual animals and plants sometimes have qualities that help them to survive. For example, in a green forest, a green bug would probably survive longer than a brown bug, because its appearance would help it to avoid being seen and eaten.

The individuals that survive the longest are likely to have more babies, and will pass on their useful qualities to them. Over a very long time, each species will very gradually develop all the most useful qualities for surviving in its own habitat.

Claws or talons

As a predator, the bald eagle has developed qualities such as good eyesight, flying skill and big strong claws, or talons. These help it to hunt and catch its prey.

Breathing

As well as eating food, animals need to breathe oxygen, a gas which is found in air and water. All animals take oxygen into their bodies, in a variety of different ways.

Gills

Fish have gills, which filter oxygen from the water as it flows through them.

Insects take in oxygen through tiny holes in their bodies, called spiracles.

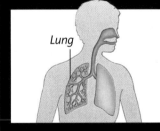

Lung

Humans and many other animals have lungs, which extract oxygen from the air.

Useful animals

Animals are very useful to humans, providing meat, milk, eggs, wool, silk, leather, and even medicines. Many animals are farmed carefully, but some species are in danger of dying out and becoming extinct, because humans have killed too many of them. You can find out more about these endangered species on page 103.

Guanacos are hunted for their long, thick wool.

ECOSYSTEMS

A place where a plant or animal lives is called its habitat. For example, seas, rivers, mountains, forests and deserts are all habitats. Together, a habitat and the group, or community, of plants and animals that live in it form a whole system, called an ecosystem.

Snowy owls and lemmings are part of the ecosystem in the Arctic. ★

Meat-eaters survive by eating other animals found in their habitat. These cheetahs are chasing a Thomson's gazelle.

Food webs

In an ecosystem, many different food chains intertwine to make up a complicated system known as a food web. Each animal in the web may eat many different species and be hunted by several others. The diagram below shows part of a food web in a mountain forest in a northern country, such as Canada. Each blue arrow points from a species that is eaten to a species that eats it. (This is a simplified diagram. In fact, there would be many more species than this in one ecosystem, and the whole food web would be too complicated to fit on the page.)

Food chains

The animals and plants in an ecosystem depend on each other for food. One species eats another, and is in turn eaten by another. This is called a food chain. Plants form the first link in a food chain, because they make their own food from sunlight, using a process called photosynthesis*. Plant-eating animals (herbivores) eat plants, and meat-eating animals (carnivores) eat herbivores and other carnivores

As in all ecosystems, plants form the basis of this food web. ★

Who eats who

A food web has several layers, known as trophic levels. There are different kinds of plants or animals on each level.

The Sun provides light and energy for plants.

Tertiary consumers
Animals that eat other meat-eating animals

Secondary consumers
Animals that eat plant-eating animals

Primary consumers
Animals that eat plants

Producers
Plants which use the Sun's energy to manufacture food

Decomposers
Organisms that feed on dead plants and animals and break them down in the soil*

The energy cycle

Plants and animals use food to make energy, which helps them grow, move, keep warm, make seeds and have babies. When plants or animals die, they are broken down by decomposers, such as fungi, and the energy goes back into the soil in the form of chemicals. These help plants to grow, and the cycle begins again.

Competition

Each type of plant or animal has a unique place in its ecosystem, known as a niche. Only one species can occupy each niche. If two different species try to exist in the same niche, they have to compete for the same food. The stronger species survives, and the other dies out or moves to a new habitat.

Different species in an ecosystem can survive side by side by eating slightly different types of food. For example, in African grasslands, elephants reach up to eat the higher branches of trees and bushes, small antelopes called gerenuks eat leaves lower down and warthogs nibble grasses on the ground. Each animal occupies a different niche, so they are not competing with each other.

Biomes

The Earth has several climate types, or biomes, such as rainforests and deserts. Each biome supports many ecosystems, but can also be seen as one big ecosystem. Together, all the biomes combine to form the biggest ecosystem of all, the Earth itself.

An elephant's long trunk allows it to reach to the tops of trees to collect food, while other animals eat the leaves lower down.

PEOPLE AND ECOSYSTEMS

Like every other plant and animal on Earth, you are part of an ecosystem. But there are now so many humans that we need more energy and make more waste than our ecosystem can deal with.

Using up energy

The first humans were suited to the ecosystems of the places they lived in. They ate the food that was available and used only as much energy as they needed to survive.

Now, though, we use up lots more energy than we really need to survive, because of all the things that modern humans do, such as running factories, getting around in cars and planes, and using electric lights and machines. We get most of our energy by burning fossil fuels*. This creates waste gases which can't be broken down quickly enough, so they build up around us as pollution.

Pollution

Pollution is any waste product that nature can't easily process and recycle. Things such as exhaust from cars, smoke from factories, and plastic packaging are all pollution.

Some pollution is just ugly, but some can be dangerous. For example, exhaust fumes that build up in the air can cause asthma, and chemicals that leak from farms into rivers can kill fish and upset the local food web*.

Smog is a kind of pollution caused when fossil fuels are burned and give off waste gases.*

Upsetting ecosystems

Each part of an ecosystem depends on all the other parts, making a natural balance. If one part is damaged or destroyed, it affects all the others.

If the plants in this food chain were destroyed, the animals further up the chain might starve.*

*Food chains, 100; food webs, 100; fossil fuels, 24

Using up space

Our farms, cities, roads and airports all need space. We use space that used to be the habitat of plants and animals. Without its habitat, an ecosystem can't work, and wild animals and plants die. If this happens too often, some species become extinct, which means they die out completely.

The dodo, which lived on the island of Mauritius, died out in about 1680 after it was hunted to extinction by Dutch settlers.

Many species have become extinct ~ for example, the dodo, a flightless bird. Extinction is sometimes caused by natural disasters such as volcanic eruptions, but usually it happens much more gradually. People now need so much space that plants and animals all over the world are dying out much faster than they used to.

Pollution, hunting, and introducing animals into new areas can cause extinctions. For example, several species of flightless birds were wiped out when humans brought dogs and cats to Australia and New Zealand.

Wind turbines like these convert the energy of the wind into electricity. This causes less pollution than burning fuel.

Conserving the Earth

Conservation means trying to reduce the damage done to the Earth and its species by pollution and other human activities. We can begin to conserve the Earth by using less energy, making less waste, and replacing as much as possible of the resources we use up. This is sometimes called sustainable living.

We cannot bring back plants and animals that are already extinct, but those that are in danger of dying out, known as endangered species, can be protected. Conservationists work to save natural habitats and protect rare wild animals from being hunted, so that they can build up their numbers and avoid extinction.

Snow leopards are an endangered species. They are now protected by laws and bred in zoos to try to save them.

POPULATION

Population is the number of people who live in a particular area. The population of the world has been rising for thousands of years, and is now going up faster than ever. In very crowded areas, it can sometimes be hard for people to get enough work, food or housing.

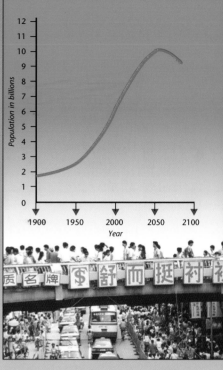

This graph shows how population is predicted to rise and then start falling.

Counting people

With thousands of people being born and dying every day, it can be hard to measure population. Many countries hold a census, or population count, every ten years. Each household fills in a questionnaire, saying how many people live there. Experts use the results to estimate the population of a country at any one time, and to calculate the total population of the world.

Rising numbers

The world's population began to rise quickly in the 17th century, when there were about 500 million people on Earth. There are now over six billion. Population is shooting up because the birth rate (the number of people being born in every 1,000) is higher than the death rate (the number of people dying in every 1,000). The death rate has dropped dramatically with advances in medicine and technology.

Predicting a fall

Population scientists, called demographers, predict that attempts to control population will soon have an effect. They suggest the world's population total will peak at around ten billion people in the 21st century and then begin to fall.

Over and under

The world's population is not spread out evenly. Some areas are overpopulated, with not enough food, water or work for everyone. Other areas, such as the French countryside, are underpopulated, as young people leave the towns and villages for the big cities.

Population density

Population density is the number of people living in a given amount of space. It is measured in people per sq km or sq mile. For example, Mongolia (a big country with a small population) has a low population density of less than two people per sq km (five people per sq mile).

Big populations

A third of the population of the whole world lives in just two countries – China and India. Although they have the largest populations, with over a billion people in each, they are not the most densely populated countries because they are so large.

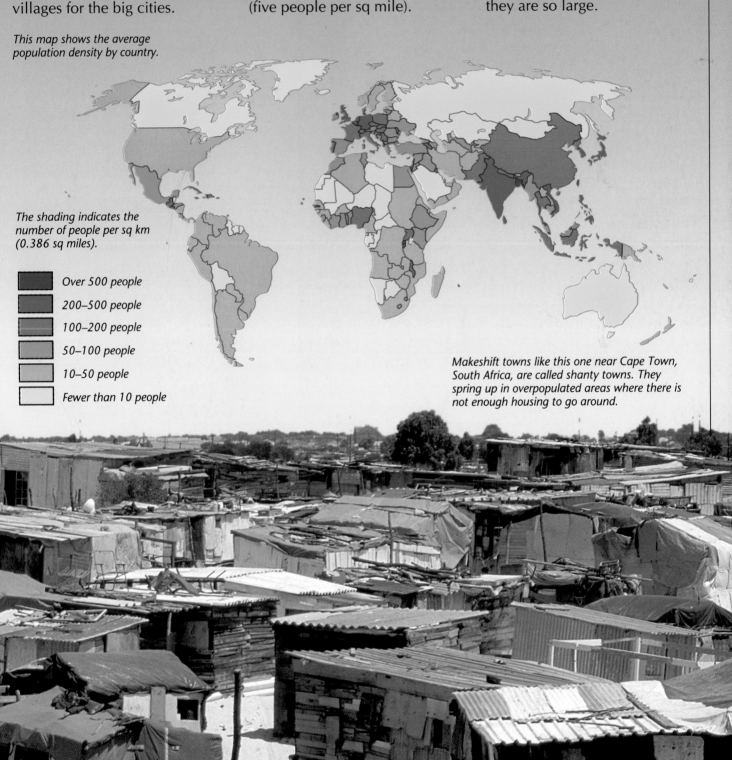

This map shows the average population density by country.

The shading indicates the number of people per sq km (0.386 sq miles).

- Over 500 people
- 200–500 people
- 100–200 people
- 50–100 people
- 10–50 people
- Fewer than 10 people

Makeshift towns like this one near Cape Town, South Africa, are called shanty towns. They spring up in overpopulated areas where there is not enough housing to go around.

FARMING

M ost of the things you eat, a lot of what you wear, and many of the things you use come from farms. Farming means growing plants or raising animals to meet human needs. It is the biggest industry in the world.

This pie chart shows how the world's land is used. Livestock farming uses more space than crop farming, but produces less food.

Types of farming

Growing plants is called crop farming or arable farming, and keeping animals is called livestock farming or pastoral farming. Many farmers do a mixture of both, and this is known as mixed farming.

Farmers choose what to farm according to the type of land they have, the soil and the climate. Farms can be tiny ~ just the size of a backyard ~ or huge, like Australian sheep farms that are so big farmers use planes to travel around them.

Yaks are adapted to surviving in high mountain areas. Farmers in the Himalayas keep them for milk and wool.

World industry

Around 45% of the world's workforce are farmers. Instead of just growing their own food, many farmers grow cash crops ~ crops grown specially to be sold and exported around the world. This is why, in some countries, you can buy different kinds of foods from all over the world in one supermarket.

Wet soil and a warm climate are ideal for growing rice. In hilly areas, farmers build steps of land, or terraces, to hold the water and soil in place. This picture shows rice terraces in China.

Growing crops

Combine harvesters are used to gather all kinds of crops. This one is gathering wheat. It is much quicker than harvesting crops by hand.

Crop farming uses up around 11% of the world's land. It is the best way of producing as much food as possible from the soil, so poor countries usually grow a greater proportion of crops than rich countries do. Planting, protecting and harvesting (collecting) crops is hard work, but many farmers use machinery to do these tasks.

Animal care

Like crops, livestock has to be looked after carefully. The animals need food and water, shelter, and protection from predators and diseases. Animal products also have to be "harvested", which means collecting the animals' milk, wool or eggs, or killing them for their meat.

Farm animals often have more than one use, producing wool or skins as well as meat. In many countries they also work, pulling carts or farm machinery.

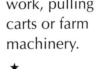

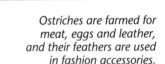

Ostriches are farmed for meat, eggs and leather, and their feathers are used in fashion accessories.

FARMING METHODS

Farmers want to get as much as they can from their land. There are various ways of improving the yield, or the amount of food or other things produced on a piece of land, but there can be problems as well.

Helicopters like this are used by intensive farmers to spray fertilizers or pesticides onto their crops.

Choosing the best

An important part of farming is selective breeding, which involves choosing the best plants and animals and developing them to make more useful varieties. For instance, wheat started off as a type of grass called einkorn, which grows naturally. Early farmers chose the einkorn with the biggest seeds for replanting, because these would provide more food. Gradually, einkorn developed into modern wheat, which has lots of large seeds on each stalk. Animals are developed in the same way, by selecting and breeding those with the most useful qualities.

★ *Modern farmed wheat*

A grass called einkorn, which was developed into modern wheat

Modern farm pigs, such as Landrace pigs (right), are descended from wild boar (below).

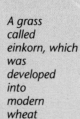

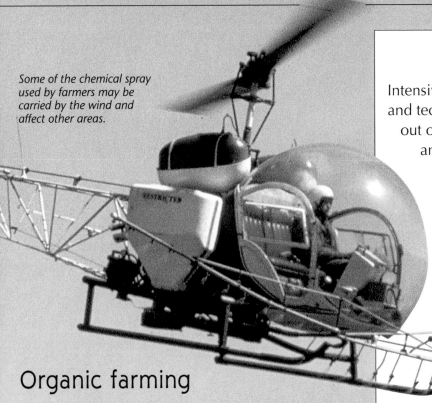

Some of the chemical spray used by farmers may be carried by the wind and affect other areas.

Intensive farming

Intensive farming means using chemicals and technology to get as much as possible out of the land. Intensively farmed animals, such as pigs or hens, are kept in small stalls or cages to save space. They are fed by automatic water and food dispensers and may be given drugs to make them grow faster. Intensive farming can increase yields, but the chemicals used can also cause pollution.

Chemical spray units attached to a helicopter

Organic farming

Organic farming means farming without using artificial chemicals or processes. Organic farmers use animal dung or compost instead of artificial fertilizer, and don't give animals drugs to make them grow faster. Organic food is expensive, because without drugs and artificial chemicals, diseases are harder to control and yields fall. However, there is a demand for organic products from people who are worried about their health, pollution and animal welfare.

Some people think intensive farming is cruel, because the animals are kept in unnatural conditions. "Free range" animals live in more natural conditions and are allowed to move around, or range freely.

Bug warfare

Insects and other bugs that eat farm crops can be a big problem. Intensive farmers (see right) often spray crops to kill insects, but organic farmers do not use chemical sprays. Instead, they sometimes try biological pest control. They change the ecosystem* in their fields by introducing another species to feed on the pest species.

These tiny aphids damage many crops. Instead of spraying, some farmers release other insects to eat the aphids.

Intensively farmed battery hens live in small cages and are usually fed by machines. The eggs they lay roll into a tray and are carried away on a conveyor belt.

*Ecosystems, 100

Pebbles on a beach in Oregon, U.S.A.

SHAPING THE LAND

SOIL

Soil covers most of the Earth's land surface. It is made up of particles of rocks and minerals, dead plant and animal matter, tiny living organisms, gases and water. Soil is vital to life on Earth, because it provides the food and conditions plants need to grow.

As they burrow through the soil, earthworms drag dead leaves and other organic matter down to the lower levels, and break them down into humus.

What's in the soil?

The particles of rocks and minerals that are found in soil have broken away from larger rocks. They range from big chunks of stone to tiny mineral particles which get dissolved by the water in the soil. Some minerals are taken in by plants and used as food. These are called nutrients.

Soil also contains organic matter ~ dead plants and animals. When they die they are gradually broken down into a substance called humus, by all the tiny creatures, bacteria and fungi in the soil. Humus is what makes soil rich and fertile (easy for plants to grow in).

Living things, such as bacteria and fungi, are a vital part of the soil. If they weren't there to break down dead plants and animals, the remains of things that have died would keep piling up on the Earth's surface.

Soil also contains spaces filled with water and gases. Water soaks into the ground from rain, and gases come from the air and from plants and animals. Plants absorb water and gases through their roots.

This earwig and her babies are among the thousands of insects and other small animals that live in soil.

Soil layers

If you looked at a slice of soil under the ground, you would see that it has several different layers, called horizons.

★

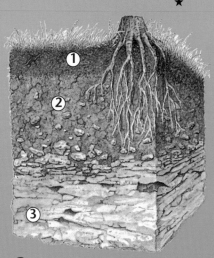

① *The topsoil contains a lot of humus and is full of tiny living creatures.*

② *Subsoil is made up of humus, rocks and minerals. Cracks and holes, or pores, in the subsoil help water to drain away, preventing the soil from getting too wet.*

③ *Bedrock is the lowest layer, or the rock that lies underneath the soil. Chunks of it sometimes break off into the soil.*

Types of soil

There are thousands and thousands of different types of soil. Some are more fertile than others, but different plants prefer different soils. So farmers can choose what to grow, depending on the type of soil they have on their land.

There are three main soil textures ~ sand, silt and clay. Sandy soil is rough and grainy. Silt has small particles, which are hard to see, while clay soil is made of fine particles, which bind together with water to form a thick, creamy mud. Clay is used to make pottery and china.

This picture shows parsnip roots reaching into the soil for water and minerals. Parsnips grow well in sandy and clay soils.

This hand contains sandy soil. Its grainy texture allows moisture to drain through it easily.

A handful of fertile soil contains up to 6 billion bacteria.

This hand contains loam soil. It is a very fertile soil containing a mixture of clay and sandy soils.

LOOKING AFTER SOIL

Why do we need to look after soil? The answer is that pollution, farming and cutting down trees can all damage soil and upset its natural balance. If we want to keep using the soil to grow food, we have to protect it, and replace all the chemicals that farming takes away.

This farmer in Minnesota, U.S.A., is loading up manure to spread over his land as a fertilizer.

The soil cycle

Where there is no farming, soil is part of a continuous cycle. Minerals are gradually dissolved into the soil. Dead plants and animals fall onto the ground, begin to rot, and are broken down into humus*. The minerals and the humus provide nutrients (food) for new plants, and the cycle starts again. This means that the nutrients that are taken out of the soil eventually get put back in.

But, when soil is used for farming, the crops are taken away to be sold, instead of rotting back into the ground. This causes the soil to become gradually less fertile* as it loses its nutrients.

Fertilizing

The best way to replace the nutrients in soil is to add a fertilizer. Fertilizers contain chemicals, such as nitrates, which plants need in order to grow. Manure (animal dung) is a natural fertilizer, but many farmers use specially made chemical fertilizers. Sometimes, if farmers use too much fertilizer, the chemicals can leak out of the soil into rivers, causing pollution.

Crop rotation

Crop rotation means changing the crop grown on a piece of land each year. It helps to keep the soil fertile, especially if the land is sometimes left to "lie fallow". This means the farmer doesn't harvest the crop, but lets it rot back into the soil. Plants such as legumes (peas and beans) or clover make good fallow crops because they put nitrates into the soil instead of taking them out.

Bright yellow oilseed rape is used to make cooking oil and as food for animals. Oilseed rape crops are often rotated with other crops on farms in Europe.

*Fertile, 112; humus, 112; terraces, 106

Soil erosion

In the natural environment, plants and trees hold soil together and stop it from being washed away by the rain or blown away by the wind. But farmers have to dig up the land to plant crops. This leaves the bare soil exposed to the wind and rain, so it is in danger of being blown or washed away.

This can also happen if trees are chopped down for firewood or to clear space for farming, especially on hillsides. Without the trees to protect it, the soil is soon washed away. This has resulted in whole forests disappearing. However, there are some ways to protect the soil.

With the trees cut down, the soil on this hillside could soon be washed away.

This cover crop protects the soil between rows of rubber trees. It also lets farmers grow two crops on the same land.

In some places, farmers can grow crops among the trees without cutting them down. If a crop leaves bare patches of soil, a crop called a cover crop can be planted in the gaps to stop it from eroding. In hilly areas, farmers build walls called terraces* to hold soil in place.

Lost forever

Ancient ruins show that there were once busy towns in places that are now desert, such as parts of Egypt and Saudi Arabia.

7,000-year-old pottery jars from an ancient civilization called Mesopotamia. The area where they were found is now desert.

The people who lived there may not have known how to look after soil and stop it from eroding. This may be why their civilizations died out.

WEATHERING

The holes in this limestone on Kangaroo Island, Australia, were caused by acid, in rainwater, eating away at it.

The rocks that make up the Earth's surface are constantly being worn away and broken down by the weather and by the actions of plants and animals. This process is called weathering.

How weathering happens

There are two main ways weathering can happen. Chemical weathering happens when chemicals, such as acid, in rainwater, gradually dissolve and eat away at rocks. Physical weathering makes rocks break apart in sheets, blocks or grains. It is usually caused by extremes of hot and cold.

Dissolving rock

Chemical weathering is usually caused by rainwater. The water absorbs gases from the air and the soil, making a weak acid. The acid eats away at certain types of rocks, creating cracks and holes which then let in more water and grow bigger.

Breaking apart

Heat makes most substances grow, or expand, very slightly. When rocks are warmed by the Sun, they expand, and when they cool down at night they shrink, or contract. The outer layer of the rock expands more, because it is directly exposed to the Sun's heat. Eventually it separates from the rock and peels off. This is called exfoliation.

Another type of weathering, freeze-thaw action, is caused when water seeps into cracks in rock and then freezes and expands.

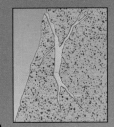 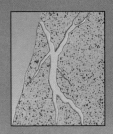 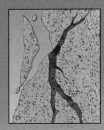

★

The process of freeze-thaw action begins when rain seeps into a small crack in a rock.

The water freezes, expands and widens the crack. When the ice thaws, more water can seep in.

As the temperature rises and falls, the crack gradually grows until the rock breaks apart.

Biological weathering

Weathering caused by plants or animals is called biological weathering. For example, lichens, which are organisms that grow on rocks, give out acidic chemicals which eat away at the rock surface. Animals burrowing and roots growing in the ground can also contribute to rocks breaking down.

As well as being dissolved by acidic rainwater, the Kangaroo Island rock on the left is being eaten away by lichens ~ the red areas on its surface.

Shaping the landscape

Because some rocks are harder and more resistant to weathering than others, they wear away at different rates. Harder rocks get left behind as outcrops, which stick up out of the surrounding land, or as long ridges. Over many years, weathering can produce amazing rock shapes, jutting mountain peaks and deep limestone caves*.

This cave is still being shaped by chemical weathering, as acidic water eats away at cracks in the rock.

*Limestone caves, 129

EROSION

E rosion happens when wind, water and gravity carry away particles of rocks and soil that have been worn down by weathering*. Gradually, eroded material is carried downhill and into rivers, and most of it ends up being washed into the sea.

You can sometimes tell old mountains from younger ones by how worn and flattened they are.

K2 in the Himalayas is 8,611m (28,250 ft) high. It is relatively young and still has pointed peaks.

Mount Baker in Washington, U.S.A., is 3,285m (10,778 ft) high. It has a flatter, worn shape, showing it was formed earlier in the Earth's history.

Wind and rain

Over hundreds of years, wind gradually blows away tiny particles from the surface of rocks. Many rocks contain different minerals, some harder than others. The wind wears them away at different rates, carving the rocks into wind sculptures.

Rain splashing onto rocks and soil washes away bigger particles and carries them into rivers. Farmers have to protect the soil* to prevent it all from eroding away in the rain.

These pinnacles in Arizona are striated, which means the wind has carved their surface into narrow grooves.

Moving mountains

On mountains, particles of rocks and soil are pulled downhill by gravity. Chunks of rock that break off near the top of a mountain fall down the slopes, knocking off other chunks as they go. Often a covering of loose stones, called scree, collects at the bottom of a slope.

Humans can add to this kind of erosion. Rock climbers sometimes dislodge scree and set off rockfalls, and walkers can slowly wear mountain paths away.

Wearing flat

As erosion carries particles of rocks and soil away from mountains and high ground towards the sea, the Earth's land masses become lower and smoother. However, new islands and mountains are sometimes formed by volcanoes* erupting and by the plates* that make up the Earth's crust grinding together. So as old land is worn away, new land rises up to replace it.

This photo shows the bare hillside left behind after a landslide in North Carolina, U.S.A.

Landslides

A landslide is a mass of earth and rocks suddenly slipping down a steep slope. One of the worst happened in 1903, when over 30 million m³ (40 million cubic yards) of rock fell down Turtle Mountain in Canada, and landed on the town of Frank, killing 70 people. This landslide, like most landslides, was caused by rainwater soaking into the soil and making it heavier. Landslides are particularly likely if water soaks into a layer of shale (a type of slippery rock made from compressed clay). The rocks, soil and trees on top may all slip down the mountainside.

Preventing erosion

A certain amount of erosion is normal, and we could never stop it completely. In some places, though, we can try to slow it down.

On mountains that are popular with walkers, stone or wooden paths help to protect the land from being worn away by feet. In hilly areas, trees help to keep the soil in place and prevent landslides, so people have learned not to cut down hillside trees.

A worker planting vegetation to prevent erosion near a roadside

119

A group of Atlantic salmon swimming

RIVERS AND OCEANS

RIVERS

The water in rivers comes from rainfall, from snow and ice melting from mountains and glaciers, and also from water inside the Earth, called groundwater. Rivers carry all this water downhill and into lakes and oceans.

Hippopotamuses live in and around slow, muddy rivers in Africa. This hippopotamus is providing a resting place for an egret.

A river's course

A river changes as it flows downhill along its path, or course. Many rivers begin in mountain areas, where rain and melting ice run into steep, clear streams. The water is rough, so the plants and animals that live in it have to be able to cling onto the rocks or swim against the stream to avoid being swept away.

As mountain streams reach the valleys, they begin to join together. Smaller streams and rivers that flow into a bigger, broader river are called tributaries. Away from the mountains, the water is warmer and flows more smoothly, so different plants and animals are found. As the land levels out, the river starts to meander, or twist from side to side, forming large loops and bends.

Finally, the river widens out into a broad estuary, or sometimes splits into a network of channels called a delta*, before flowing into the sea (or sometimes into a large lake). The part of a river where it meets the sea is called the river mouth.

Stonefly larvae live in mountain streams. They cling to stones with their claws so they don't get swept away by the rushing water.

Mountain streams, like this one in Connecticut, U.S.A., form series of mini waterfalls as they tumble down over the steep, rocky slopes.

Drainage

The area of land from which a river collects water is called its drainage basin. When water drains into streams and rivers, it forms different patterns, depending on the shape of the land and the type of rocks it is made of.

When there is only one type of rock, streams form a tree-like pattern like this. It is called a dendritic drainage pattern.

River records

The Manú River, a tributary of the Amazon, winding its way through the rainforests of Peru

The longest river in the world is the River Nile in Africa. It travels northward for over 6,600km (4,100 miles) from its source in Burundi to its delta in Egypt, where it flows into the Mediterranean Sea. But, the world's biggest river, or the one that holds the most water, is the Amazon in South America. It is about 6,440km (4,000 miles) long, and flows across South America from west to east. Every single second, it pours about 94 million litres (20 million gallons) of water into the Atlantic Ocean. At its mouth, the Amazon is 240km (150 miles) wide.

A Nile crocodile stalks its prey by swimming silently along in the river, with most of its body underwater.

RIVER EROSION

Rivers can carve through solid rock and move huge boulders hundreds of miles. Over many years, rivers have eroded deep gorges and huge waterfalls, and carried vast amounts of rock, sand, soil and mud to the sea.

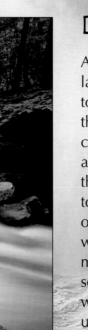

This satellite photo shows the Mahakam River, in Borneo. You can see how a network of channels and islands, or a delta, is formed where the river runs into the sea.

How rivers erode

As a river flows, the water sweeps along any loose soil, sand or rocks in its way. As they roll, slide and bounce along, the rocks and pebbles chip away at the riverbed, making it deeper and wider. They also grind against each other, which wears them down and breaks them into smaller pieces.

The river also forces water and air bubbles into cracks in the riverbed, breaking off more chunks of rock and soil. Another reason rivers erode is that river water is slightly acidic, because it comes from rain*. It gradually wears away some types of rocks by dissolving them.

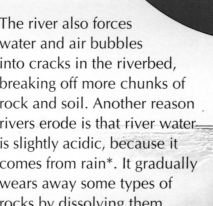

These rocks have been smoothed and rounded by the action of the water in the river.

Deposition

As a river flows over flatter land and slows down, it starts to drop, or deposit, some of the rocks and particles it is carrying. The biggest rocks are deposited first. Then, as the river gets slower, it starts to deposit sediment, made up of sand, soil and mud. This is why slow, wide rivers have muddy riverbeds. Near the sea, the sediment may form whole islands. The river splits up and forms a network of channels called a delta. The rest of the sediment flows into the sea and onto the seabed.

*Meander, 122; rainwater, 116

Changing course

Rivers flow faster around the outside of a bend, or meander*, than on the inside. The outside edge is gradually eroded, while the river deposits debris on the inside edge. This means that the meander grows longer and narrower over time. Eventually the two sides of the meander meet each other, and the river cuts through to form a new, straighter course. The entrance to the meander gradually fills up with sediment, leaving a lake called an oxbow lake, or billabong.

A river erodes the outside of a bend and deposits sediment on the inside, making a loop.

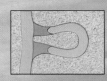
The loop grows longer and narrower until the river finally breaks through.

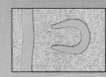
The river flows past the ends of the loop and they slowly become silted up.

Eventually the loop gets cut off completely and forms a lake called an oxbow lake.

This is the Horseshoe Falls, part of Niagara Falls, which is a huge waterfall on the border between Canada and the U.S.A. The waterfall moves upstream by around 3m (11ft) per year.

Waterfalls

Waterfalls begin when a river flows from an area of hard rock onto soft rock. The river wears away the soft rock more quickly and forms a ledge. Water falling over the ledge erodes a hollow at the bottom called a plunge pool. The action of the water and pebbles churning in the plunge pool can undercut the hard rock, creating an overhanging ledge. Chunks of the overhanging rock break off and very gradually, over hundreds of years, the waterfall moves backward, cutting a deep valley called a gorge.

This diagram shows how a waterfall is formed.

Waterfall cutting back

Falling water cuts away at the soft rock below.

Hard rock

Plunge pool

Softer rock

Spray undercuts here.

USING RIVERS

Rivers are central to the way human civilization has developed. They have been used for thousands of years for drinking and washing and as transport routes. Farming and industry depend on the water they provide and we can convert their flowing force into useful energy.

This engraving shows London, England, in 1631, with large ships plying their trade up and down the River Thames.

Amsterdam in the Netherlands is not on the sea, but is an important port, with over 80km (50 miles) of canals dividing it into over 80 islands.

River ports

A port is a city where ships can load and unload. When most international transport was by sea, many large ports, such as Montreal in Canada, Manaus in Brazil, and London in England, grew up near navigable rivers, that is rivers that can be used by ships. For example, most of the Amazon is navigable, because it is so wide and deep.

Canals

Canals are artificial waterways built to replace or extend rivers. Irrigation canals, for instance, divert water from rivers onto farmland. Navigational canals are built for boats or ships to travel on. For example, the Suez Canal joins the Mediterranean Sea to the Red Sea, so that ships can take a short-cut from Europe to the Indian Ocean.

Unlike natural rivers, canals do not change their course over time. They suffer less erosion* than natural rivers, because their beds and banks are usually built of brick or concrete, which wears down more slowly than natural rock and soil. Sometimes, especially in cities, natural riverbanks are rebuilt in the same way to prevent them from eroding.

*River erosion, 124

Clean energy

Electrical energy from waterpower is called hydroelectric power or HEP. An HEP plant usually consists of a dam built on a river to create a large reservoir or lake. High-pressure jets of water are released from the lake through narrow channels, and used to spin turbines which produce electricity.

Waterpower is increasingly important as an energy source. Unlike fossil fuels, it is renewable (it won't run out). It also causes very little pollution. But there can be problems when hydroelectric reservoirs take up precious land, or dams collapse.

Part of the Shasta hydroelectric dam in California, U.S.A. The spillway in the picture releases water to stop the dam from overflowing.

Dam disasters

The present-day ruins of the Malpasset Dam in France, which burst in 1959.

In the past, several large dams have caused disaster by breaking or overflowing. One example is the Malpasset Dam in Fréjus, France. It collapsed in 1959, causing a flood which killed over 500 people. The dam failed because it was built on a rock called schist, which cracks easily.

This small waterwheel generates electricity for a rural area of Washington State, U.S.A.

Waterpower

The energy in a river can be converted into electricity or other useful forms of energy. The earliest waterpower systems used a river or stream to turn a waterwheel. The turning force of the wheel was then used to drive machines, such as mills for grinding flour. Simple waterwheels like this are still used in many countries.

WATER IN THE GROUND

W ater doesn't just flow over the surface of the Earth; it flows under it too. As well as the rivers and lakes that we can see, there is a huge amount of water, called groundwater, stored underground in rocks and caves.

Bottling mineral water and spring water to sell as drinking water is a major industry in some areas.

Groundwater

Many types of rocks are porous, which means they can soak up and hold water like a sponge. Groundwater is rainwater that has soaked down through the soil and then been soaked up, or absorbed, into a layer of porous rock, such as sandstone, under the ground.

Groundwater seeps through the rock until it meets a layer of impermeable rock, which won't let water pass through it. The porous rock gets filled up with water. The top level of this water is known as the water table.

Aquifers are layers of porous rock that can hold water. Some stretch for thousands of miles under the ground. In some places they are an important source of fresh water.

Springs

A spring is a stream fresh water springir out of the ground. Springs form whe layer of water-fill porous rock mee the surface of th Earth, especial on a hillside. groundwater flows out of the rock and forms a s pool or stream.

Spring water is often clear sparkling because it has b filtered through layers of r Sometimes the water diss minerals from the rocks. S of these minerals are thou to be good for your health

Rain and snow seep through porous rock.

Mountain rivers

Rivers, lakes and springs may appear where an aquifer meets the surface.

A spring emerges where saturated rock meets the surface.

Water table

Saturated rock

Aquifer (porous rock)

Lake

Impermeable rock

Rivers under the ground

As well as soaking through rock, water can be found in underground rivers, waterfalls and even large lakes in caves and tunnels. These usually form in limestone, a type of rock that is easily dissolved by water. As water soaks into cracks in the limestone, it eats away at the rock by the process of chemical weathering* and eventually hollows out huge underground caverns and channels.

Stalactites and stalagmites

In some caves, long columns of stone, called stalactites, hang from the ceiling, and columns called stalagmites rise up from the floor. They are formed when water full of dissolved minerals drips from the cave roof. With each drop, a tiny deposit of rock is left behind. Over time, the deposit grows into a long pole. As the drips hit the cave floor, they deposit more minerals, which build up into stalagmites.

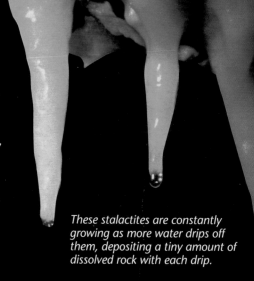

These stalactites are constantly growing as more water drips off them, depositing a tiny amount of dissolved rock with each drip.

Inside this cave in Mexico, long stalactites have grown down from the ceiling, while water has gathered to form a still underground pool.

RIVERS OF ICE

A glacier is a huge mass of ice that flows downhill, a little like a river. Glaciers flow much more slowly than rivers. But, because they are solid, they cut through the landscape more easily, gouging deep U-shaped valleys as they sweep rocks and soil along with them.

This is a glacier in Glacier Bay National Park, Alaska, U.S.A.

Ice force

Glaciers are very heavy and powerful. As a glacier flows along, the ice and the rocks caught in it scrape soil and rock from the sides and floor of the valley, carving a deep channel. When the ice melts, it deposits thick layers of debris, called moraine, on the valley floor. Glaciers also pick up boulders and deposit them further down the valley. These boulders are known as erratics.

How glaciers form

Glaciers are found in cold places, such as high mountains. At the top of a glacier, known as the accumulation zone, layers of snow collect and become packed down into hard, solid ice. As more snow falls on top, the mass of ice gets heavier and heavier, until it starts to move down the mountain.

As the ice gradually flows downhill, it gets warmer, because the air is warmer lower down*. At the lower end, called the ablation zone, the glacier melts and the icy-cold water, which is known as meltwater, flows into streams and rivers.

Fresh snow falls here.

Accumulation zone

As a glacier moves over bumps and around corners, it may develop cracks called crevasses.

Boulders carried along by the glacier scratch grooves in the rock below.

The glacier melts here.

Ablation zone

Meltwater

★

This diagram shows the different parts of a glacier and the way it moves downhill.

Glacial clues

If the climate gets warmer, glaciers sometimes melt, leaving behind a glacial valley. You can recognize a glacial valley by its deep, rounded U-shape and by debris, such as boulders and moraine hills, or drumlins, left on the valley floor. Sometimes, valleys called hanging valleys, that once joined the glacier, are left high above the main valley.

At the coast, some glacial valleys are filled in with seawater. They form narrow inlets called fjords.

This diagram shows some of the features that will help you to recognize a glacial valley. A glacial valley filled with seawater, like this, is called a fjord.

Smaller valleys that once joined the glacier are left high above the main valley. They are called hanging valleys.

★

A U-shaped glacial valley

Drumlins are low rounded hills, probably formed by deposited debris.

Boulders known as erratics are sometimes deposited by glaciers.

Ice sheets

Not all glaciers are found on mountains. They also form in very cold places near the poles, such as Greenland and Antarctica. Here, ice collects in huge sheets, called continental ice sheets. They flow outwards at the edges, as more snow falls, and more ice forms in the middle. Parts of the glacier can be pushed right into the sea and break off, forming icebergs.

Icebergs float away into the ocean, gradually melting as they reach warmer areas.

131

THE EDGE OF THE SEA

The coast, where the land meets the sea, is constantly being broken down and built up by the action of waves. The ebb and flow of the tide means that the environment at the seashore is always changing. Specially adapted animals and plants make their homes there.

Waves

Waves form far out at sea and are blown across the ocean by the wind. Although waves travel through water, they do not move the water itself forward. Instead, they make water particles move in circles under the surface. When a wave reaches shallow water, these circles are interrupted and the wave breaks.

Out at sea, wind blows the surface of the ocean into waves.

The waves make particles of water move in circular patterns under the surface.

On a shallow, flat beach, waves break before they reach the shore.

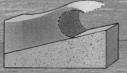

On a sloping coast, waves break at the shore and crash onto the beach.

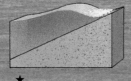

On a very steep slope, waves do not break, but surge against the shore.

Coastal erosion

This archway in Dorset, England, is called Durdle Door. It was created over many years by the destructive action of waves. It started as a headland with caves on either side. The waves gradually eroded the caves until, eventually, they broke through, creating an arch.

Waves that crash onto the shore are known as destructive waves, because they gradually wear away, or erode, the coast. When they break onto beaches, they drag sand, pebbles and other debris out to sea. When they crash onto rocky cliffs, any debris they are carrying is flung against the rock, wearing it down. Waves force water and air into cracks in cliffs, carving out caves.

Destructive waves erode the coastline at different rates. Soft rock wears down quite fast, and is worn away into curved bays. Hard rock is left behind, forming cliffs and jutting pieces of land called headlands. Sometimes two caves form on either side of a headland, and the sea breaks through, leaving an arch. The arch may collapse, leaving a tower of rock called a stack.

★

*Tides, 149

Building beaches

While destructive waves wear away parts of the coast, other waves, called constructive waves, wash up debris onto the shore, forming beaches. When a wave breaks gently onto a flat coast, it slows down and loses energy. This makes it drop any debris it may be carrying, such as pebbles and grains of sand previously broken off into the sea from cliffs and rocky shores. Over time, this deposited material builds up into a beach.

Stones and pebbles in the sea are polished and rounded by the action of the waves.

Tides

Tides* are caused by the gravity, or pulling force, of the Moon. The Moon pulls the sea slightly towards it. So, as the Earth spins, the part nearest the Moon has a high tide. There are roughly two high tides each day.

Animals and plants that live on the seashore have to be able to survive in the water at high tide, and in the air at low tide. They also have to find ways to avoid being smashed to pieces or swept away by crashing waves.

Crabs, like this rock crab, can breathe in both water and air. They have hard shells to protect them from the sea, and can burrow into the sand to hide from predators.

Coastlines

Over many years, the action of the sea changes the shapes of countries, as it builds up the land in some places and wears it away in others. Buildings near the sea sometimes fall in or get washed away as the land is gradually eroded.

For example, the coast of Holderness in Lincolnshire, England, has worn away very quickly. Over 50 coastal villages, which were listed in a national survey of towns and villages called the Domesday Book in 1086, have been washed away into the sea.

SEAS AND OCEANS

More than two thirds of the Earth's surface is covered with salt water. The Earth's five oceans and all its seas are connected, so sea water flows freely between them. The seas and oceans, and the creatures that live in them, still hold many mysteries for scientists to explore.

The ballan wrasse fish is found mainly near rocky shores in Europe.

Under the sea

Near the land, the seabed slopes gradually downhill, forming a wide shelf called the continental shelf. At the edge of the shelf, a cliff called the continental slope drops away to the deeper part of the ocean floor, which is called the abyssal plain.

A 3D map of part of the floor of the Atlantic Ocean

Just like the land, the abyssal plain has valleys, hills, mountains and even volcanoes. It also has ridges* where new rock is pushed out from inside the Earth, and trenches* where the Earth's crust is swallowed up again.

Exploring the sea

Sea scientists, called oceanographers, find out about how the Earth was formed and how life began, by studying the seabed and the creatures that live there. Oceanographers visit the seabed in mini-submarines called submersibles, or explore it from the surface using unmanned robots called Remote Operated Vehicles (ROVs). They also map the seabed using sonar. This sends out sounds which are reflected back as echoes, showing how deep the seabed is.

This diver is retrieving a rock from a remote-operated vehicle (ROV). The ROV has returned to shallow waters after collecting rock samples from the seabed.

*Food chains, 100; ridges, 18; trenches, 18

Life in the oceans

Seas and oceans contain a huge variety of plant and animal life, from the surface all the way down to the deepest trenches.

The loggerhead turtle lives in warm, shallow seas and comes ashore to lay its eggs.

The main food source in the sea is phytoplankton, a microscopic plant. Billions of phytoplankton drift near the surface of the sea, making food from sunlight, water, gases and minerals. They are the basis of the food chain* for millions of species.

Coral reefs

Coral reefs are amazing undersea structures made of the skeletons of tiny animals called coral polyps. When old polyps die, new ones grow on top of their bodies, and over many years a huge reef builds up.

Coral reefs develop in the warm, shallow seas of the tropics, and are home to the greatest variety of plant and animal life anywhere in the sea.

Part of a coral reef in the Red Sea, which lies between Egypt and Saudi Arabia

Ocean zones

The deeper down you go in the ocean, the darker and colder it is, and the fewer plants and animals are found.

Sunlit zone
Sea plants and many animals live here.

Down to 200m (650 ft)

Twilight zone
Many fish, such as swordfish, survive here.

Down to 1,000m (3,300 ft)

Sunless zone
Animals feed on dead food that falls from above.

Down to 4,000m (13,100 ft)

Abyssal zone
The water is cold and dark. Few creatures live here.

Down to 5,000m (16,400 ft)

USING SEAS AND OCEANS

For thousands of years, the sea has provided people with food. We also carry passengers and goods by sea and go on trips to the coast. But the oceans are often used as a place to dump waste, which causes pollution and may endanger wildlife.

Fishing

Most sea fish are still caught using nets, as they have been for centuries. There are three main types of nets. Purse seine nets are drawn closed, like a purse, around schools of herring or other fish that swim near the surface. Otter trawl nets are dragged along the seabed to catch fish that live there, such as plaice, while drift or gill nets have holes just large enough for a fish to get stuck in. They are left to drift near the surface or the seabed.

Above and top right: the many species of sea bass are the most common fish caught and eaten around the world. These were caught in Tokyo Bay, Japan.

Modern strong, lightweight materials mean that the nets themselves can be bigger than ever before. Fishing boats also use sonar* technology and even satellite* technology to find schools of fish.

Overfishing

Because of advances in fishing technology, fishing boats are now able to catch more fish than ever before, and the number of fish in the sea is falling rapidly. International laws have now been passed to restrict the areas where fishing boats can fish and the numbers and types of fish they can catch.

A Japanese fishing boat at work in Tokyo Bay, Japan, drawing a large net behind it.

CB3-50869

*Satellites, 11; sonar, 134

Container ships carry all kinds of goods in large metal boxes called containers. Cranes lift the containers off the ship quickly and transfer them to trucks or trains.

Shipping

Millions of different products, from oil and bananas to books and computers, are transported around the world on cargo ships. Ships travel more slowly than planes, but they can carry a lot more goods at once and are much cheaper to use.

World travel

A century ago, if you wanted to travel across the sea, you had to go by boat. Huge ocean liners carried people around the world, and travel could take months.

Today, most people go long distances by plane, but boats such as ferries, hovercrafts and hydrofoils are still used for shorter distances. The only ocean liners left are cruise ships, which take people on long, relaxing sea journeys.

Sea pollution

The seas and oceans are huge, and can absorb and break down a lot of the waste we pump into them. For example, a lot of sewage (waste from drains and toilets) goes into the sea and is broken down naturally into harmless chemicals.

However, some waste and litter doesn't break down fast enough, and ends up polluting the seas. Plastic, for example, dropped from ships or washed off beaches, can take up to 80 years to be broken down by the sea. Chemical and radioactive waste from factories, farms and nuclear power stations* can also end up in the sea and may poison plants, fish and other animals.

Oil tankers occasionally sink and spill the oil they are carrying. It can harm plants and animals, such as this seabird, by poisoning them or by coating them in oil so that they cannot breathe or move properly.

*Nuclear power, 25

*Stalactites and stalagmites in The Cave of the Winds,
Colorado Springs, U.S.A.*

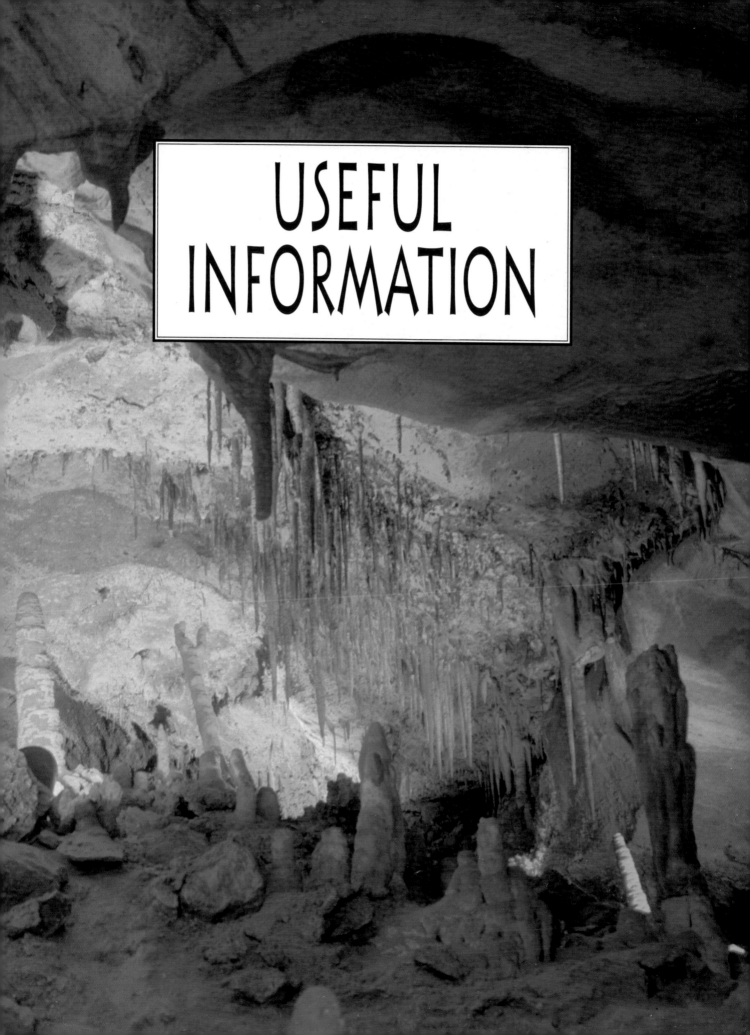

USEFUL INFORMATION

GLOSSARY

This glossary explains some of the words you may come across when reading about the Earth. Words in *italic type* have their own entry elsewhere in the glossary.

ablation zone The lower end of a *glacier*, where the ice melts and flows into streams and rivers, or into the sea.

abyssal plain A huge, flat expanse of seabed, about 4km (2.5 miles) deep, which forms most of the ocean floor.

accumulation zone The top of a *glacier*, where snow falls and is gradually compacted into ice, which then begins to flow slowly downhill.

acid rain Rain containing dissolved chemicals from polluted air. The chemicals make the water acidic, which means it can eat away at stone and damage plant life.

active An active volcano is one which might *erupt* at any time.

adaptation The way a plant or animal *species* develops over time to suit its *habitat*.

anti-cyclone An area of high *atmospheric pressure*, which pushes winds outwards. The opposite of a *cyclone*.

aquifer A layer of *porous* rock which can hold water and carry it along under the ground.

arable Arable land is suitable for growing crops (plants). Arable farming means crop farming.

asteroid A small rock which *orbits* the Sun. Asteroids sometimes hit the Earth or other *planets*.

atmosphere A layer of gases, about 400km (250 miles) thick, that surrounds the Earth.

atmospheric pressure The pressure caused by the *atmosphere* weighing down on the Earth. It can change according to how warm the air is and how high you are above sea level.

atom A tiny particle. All *elements* are made up of atoms.

aurora Flickering lights that sometimes appear in the sky near the *North Pole* (aurora borealis) or the *South Pole* (aurora australis). Auroras are caused by *magnetic* particles from the Sun.

autonomous underwater vehicle or **AUV** A small robotic submarine which can be sent to explore the seabed by itself and bring information back to the surface.

axis The imaginary line, running from the *North Pole* to the *South Pole*, around which the Earth spins.

bacteria (singular: **bacterium**) Tiny *organisms* that live in the soil, in the air, and in plants and animals.

bedrock The solid layer of rock that lies underneath the soil, covering the Earth's surface.

biome An area with a *climate* that supports a particular range of plants and animals. For example, deserts, mountains and seas are all biomes.

black smoker A *hydrothermal vent* which churns out black water containing many dissolved minerals. The minerals gradually build up around the vent, forming a chimney.

camouflage Patterns or features (such as a tiger's stripes) which help plants and animals to look like their background and avoid being seen.

canopy The thick upper layer of leaves and branches in a rainforest.

carnivore An animal or plant that feeds on animals.

chlorofluorocarbons or **CFCs** Chemicals that are thought to damage the layer of *ozone* in the Earth's *atmosphere*.

chlorophyll A green chemical in plants which enables them to convert sunlight into food.

climate The typical or average weather conditions in a particular place. For example, the Brazilian rainforests have a very wet climate.

community The group of plants and animals that live together in a particular *habitat*.

compass A device containing a *magnetic* needle that points to the *North Pole*. A compass is used to find your direction.

conservation Protecting and preserving *environments*, including the plants, animals and buildings that form a part of them, and trying to reduce damage caused by *pollution*.

continent One of the Earth's seven major land masses.

continental crust The parts of the Earth's *crust* which form land masses. Continental crust is made mostly of a rock called granite.

continental shelf A wide shelf of seabed which surrounds most land masses, making the sea much shallower near the land than it is in the middle of the oceans.

continental slope The steep slope at the edge of the *continental shelf*, leading down to the deeper seabed.

coral polyp A small tropical sea animal. Coral polyps live together in large groups, or colonies.

coral reef A structure made up of the skeletons of *coral polyps*, built up gradually as old polyps die and new ones grow on top.

core The central part of the inside of the Earth, which scientists think is made of the metals iron and nickel.

Coriolis effect The effect of the spinning of the Earth, which forces winds and *currents* into a spiral.

crevasse A crack in a *glacier*.

crop rotation Changing the crop grown on a particular piece of land each year, to help the soil recover.

crust The Earth's solid outer layer. It consists of *continental crust* which forms the land, and *oceanic crust* which forms the seabed.

currents Global systems of water and air which are constantly circulating around the Earth. For example, the Gulf Stream is a current that carries warm water across the Atlantic Ocean from the Caribbean to northern Europe.

cyclone An area of low *atmospheric pressure*. Cyclones suck winds towards them.

debris Any kind of loose rock, mud or other matter ~ such as the rocks carried along by a *glacier*, or the material carried and *deposited* by a flowing river.

deforestation Reducing or removing forests by cutting down or burning trees.

degree One 360th of a circle. Degrees are used with *latitude* and *longitude* to measure distance on the Earth's surface. One degree is one 360th of the distance around the Earth.

delta A fan-shaped system of streams, created when a river splits up into many smaller branches and *deposits debris* as it nears the sea.

deposition Dropping or leaving behind rocks or other *debris*. For example, when *glaciers* melt, they deposit rocks as *moraine*.

desertification The process of becoming a desert.

dormant A dormant volcano is not currently *active*, but could *erupt* again. The word dormant means "sleeping".

drumlin A small hill formed from *debris deposited* by *glaciers*.

dyke A barrier built at the coast to stop the sea from flooding the land at high *tide*.

ecosystem A living system that includes a group of plants and animals and the *habitat* they live in.

element A substance made of one type of *atom*. There are over a hundred elements on Earth, such as iron, oxygen and silicon.

El Niño A weather phenomenon that sometimes makes part of the Pacific Ocean get much warmer than normal, causing severe storms.

emergent A tree that rises, or emerges, above the main *canopy* in a rainforest.

environment Surroundings, including the landscape, living things and the *atmosphere*.

Equator An imaginary line around the middle of the Earth, exactly halfway between the *North Pole* and the *South Pole*.

erratic A large boulder which has been *deposited* by a *glacier* and is left standing away from its source.

eruption A volcanic explosion. When a volcano erupts, it shoots out *lava*, rocks, hot ash and gases.

estuary A wide channel which forms where a river joins the sea.

evolution The gradual development of plants and animals, over many generations, to fit in better with their *habitats*.

exfoliation When a rock exfoliates, its outer layers peel off like layers of an onion. This is caused by changes in temperature, which make rock shrink and expand.

extinct An extinct *species* is a type of plant or animal that has died out and stopped existing. An extinct volcano is one that has stopped being *active* or *dormant* and, it is thought, will never *erupt* again.

fallow Fallow land is farmland that is being left to rest and recover between crops.

famine A widespread shortage of food, which can lead to starvation and the spread of diseases.

fault A crack in the Earth's *crust*.

fault creep The gradual movement of two pieces of the Earth's *crust* scraping against each other along a *fault*.

fertile Fertile land is land that is good for growing plants. Fertile also means able to reproduce, or have babies.

fertilizer A substance, such as *manure*, which contains *nitrates* and other chemicals and is put on land to make it more *fertile*.

fold mountains A mountain range formed by the Earth's *crust* buckling up into folds when the *plates* of the crust push together.

food chain A sequence showing which plant and animal *species* eat which.

food web A network of *food chains* showing which *species* eat each other in an *ecosystem*.

fossil The shape or remains of a plant or animal that died long ago, hardened and preserved in rock.

fossil fuels Fuels such as coal, oil and gas, made from the compressed (squashed) bodies of plants and animals that died many years ago.

freeze-thaw action The action of water which seeps into cracks in rocks and then freezes, which makes it expand (grow). This expansion forces the cracks apart, so they gradually get bigger.

fungi (singular: **fungus**) Types of *organisms*, including mushrooms, that are similar to plants but have no leaves or flowers.

galaxy A huge group of stars and planets. There are millions of galaxies in the Universe.

geology The study of the Earth's rocks and *minerals* and the way they have developed.

geostationary A word that means "in one place". Geostationary *satellites* orbit the Earth at the same speed as the Earth spins, so they always stay above the same place on the Earth's surface.

geyser A hole in the ground where water and steam, heated up inside the Earth, shoot out in bursts.

glacial valley A deep U-shaped valley carved by a flowing *glacier*, and left behind after the glacier melts.

glacier A mass of ice that gathers on top of a mountain or land mass, and flows very slowly downhill.

global warming The gradual warming-up of the Earth, possibly due to the *greenhouse effect*.

gorge A deep, narrow valley, shaped by a river gradually cutting through the land it flows across.

gravity The pulling force which holds the *atmosphere* and objects onto the Earth and stops them from floating out into space.

greenhouse effect The effect of certain gases in the *atmosphere* which trap heat from the Sun, causing the Earth to heat up.

greenhouse gases Gases, such as carbon dioxide, which contribute to the *greenhouse effect*.

groundwater Water which has soaked into the ground and is stored inside *porous* rock.

habitat The place where an animal or plant *species* lives is called its habitat.

hanging valley A smaller valley found high up the side of a *glacial valley*. Hanging valleys once contained mini-glaciers that flowed into a large glacier. When glaciers melt, hanging valleys are left behind, high up the mountainside.

heat expansion The way many substances, such as wood and rock, expand (grow) as they get warmer.

hemisphere Half of the Earth. For example, the northern hemisphere is the half that is north of the *Equator*.

herbivore An animal that eats plants.

horizons In soil science, horizons are the layers or levels found in soil. "Horizon" also means the line where you can see the land meeting the sky when you look into the distance.

hot spot A weak area of the Earth's *crust* where *magma* can break through and form a volcano.

hot spring See **thermal spring**.

humidity The amount of water contained in the air.

humus The part of soil that makes it *fertile*. Humus is made from rotted plant and animal matter.

hydroelectric power or **HEP** Power created from the energy from flowing water.

hydrothermal vent A *hot spring* on the seabed. See **black smoker**.

Ice age A period when the Earth was much colder than average. There have been several Ice ages since the Earth began.

iceberg A huge chunk of a *glacier* that has broken off into the sea. Icebergs can float far away from their glaciers and cause shipwrecks.

ice sheet A huge sheet of ice covering a large area, such as the ice that covers the *North Pole*. An ice sheet is a type of *glacier*, but flows outwards instead of downhill.

igneous Igneous rock is formed when *magma* escapes from inside the Earth, cools and hardens.

impermeable Impermeable rock is rock that does not allow water to soak through it.

infrared A type of energy which *radiates* from hot things. It is invisible to the human eye, but can be detected by infrared cameras.

intensive Intensive farming means using chemicals and technology to increase *yield*.

interglacial A period of time within an *Ice age* when the climate gets slightly warmer for a while.

isobars Lines which link points with the same *atmospheric pressure*. The isobars on a weather map show the different patterns of atmospheric pressure.

landslide A sudden slippage of rocks and soil down a hillside, often caused by heavy rain or earthquakes.

latitude A measurement of how many *degrees* a place is north or south of the *Equator*. Lines of latitude are imaginary lines around the Earth, parallel to the *Equator*.

lava Hot molten rock which bursts or flows out of volcanoes. Lava also sometimes seeps out of holes in the ground, called vents.

leap year A year every four years which has 366 days instead of 365. The extra day is always added in February, to make February 29th.

lichen A kind of living *organism* which grows on rocks, and is made up of an alga (a type of plant) and a *fungus* living together.

longitude A measurement of how many *degrees* a place is east or west of the *Prime Meridian Line*. Lines of longitude are imaginary lines that run around the Earth from north to south.

magma Hot, melted rock inside the Earth.

magnet An object that has magnetic force, an invisible force that attracts iron and steel. The two ends of a magnet are known as its poles.

magnetic poles The Earth behaves like a giant *magnet*, and the ends of this magnet are called the magnetic poles. They move gradually over time, and are not in exactly the same place as the geographic *North Pole* and *South Pole*.

malaria A dangerous disease, which affects millions of people, spread by insects called mosquitoes.

mantle The thick layer of rock under the Earth's *crust*. Some of it is solid and some is *magma* (molten rock).

manure Animal dung which can be used as a *fertilizer*.

meander A bend or long loop in a river. Meanders form when rivers flow across gently sloping land.

Mediterranean A type of climate that has warm winters and hot summers, and is good for growing many types of crops. It is named after the region around the Mediterranean Sea, but is also found in other parts of the world.

megacity A name for a city that has more than a million people.

metamorphic Metamorphic rocks have been changed by heat or pressure. For example, when a rock called shale is squashed, it hardens into a type of metamorphic rock called slate.

meteorology The study of the weather and how to predict it.

migration Moving from one place to another. Many animals migrate each season to find food.

mineral A non-living substance found in the Earth, such as salt, iron, diamond or quartz. Most rocks are made up of a mixture of minerals.

mirage An image of something that is somewhere else, caused by light bending in the *atmosphere*.

molecule Two or more *atoms* bonded together. Many substances are made up of molecules.

monsoon A season of strong winds and heavy rain which affects some areas of Asia.

moon A natural *satellite orbiting* around a *planet*. The Earth has one moon which orbits it once a month.

moraine Boulders, clay and other *debris* left behind by a *glacier*.

natural selection The theory that those animals and plants that are best suited to their *environment* are the most likely to survive.

navigable A navigable river is one that ships can travel along.

niche A particular plant or animal *species'* place in an *ecosystem*.

nitrates Chemicals found in soil that help plants to grow.

Northern Lights See **aurora borealis**.

North Pole The most northern point on the Earth, and one end of the *axis* the Earth spins around.

nuclear power Energy produced by splitting *atoms* of a *radioactive element* called uranium.

oasis A *fertile* area in a desert, supplied by water from an *aquifer*.

oceanic crust The parts of the Earth's *crust* which form the seabed. Oceanic crust is made mostly of a rock called basalt.

oceanic ridge A raised ridge on the seabed, caused by the *plates* of the Earth's *crust* pulling apart and *magma* pushing up in between.

oceanic trench A deep trench in the seabed that forms where one *plate* pushes underneath another.

oceanography The study of seas and oceans.

omnivore An animal that eats both meat and plants. Omnivore means "everything-eater".

orbit The path of one object as it travels around, or orbits, another. For example, the Earth orbits the Sun once a year.

ore Rock which contains metal that can be extracted. For example, iron is often extracted from an iron ore called haematite.

organic Organic farming means farming without artificial chemicals and methods. Organic food is food that has been produced in this way and contains no artificial chemicals.

organism A living thing, such as a plant, animal or *bacterium*.

outcrop A rocky piece of land that stands out from the surrounding area.

oxbow lake A curved lake left behind when a river *meander* gets cut off from the rest of the river.

ozone A type of oxygen in which each molecule contains three oxygen atoms instead of two.

ozone layer A layer of *ozone* in the Earth's atmosphere, from 20 to 50km (12 to 30 miles) above the Earth's surface, which protects the Earth from the Sun's rays. The ozone layer may be being damaged by *chlorofluorocarbons* or *CFCs*.

Pangaea The name scientists give to a huge continent that they think once existed on Earth. It gradually broke up to form the *continents* we have today.

pastoral Pastoral farming means raising and breeding animals.

permafrost A layer of ice that never melts. It is found underneath the soil in *Arctic* areas.

photosynthesis A chemical process in plants, which converts sunlight into food.

planet A large ball of rock which *orbits* a *star*. For example, Earth and Mars are planets which orbit the Sun.

plates The separate pieces of *crust* which fit together like a jigsaw puzzle to cover the Earth.

plate tectonics The theory that the *plates* of the Earth's *crust* gradually move around and rub against each other.

poles The *North Pole* and the *South Pole*, the coldest parts of the Earth which are farthest away from the *Equator*.

pollution Waste or dirt, such as exhaust from cars, which builds up faster than it can be broken down.

population The number of people living in a particular place.

porous Able to soak up water. Porous rock can soak up water like a sponge and store it underground.

port A town or city where ships can load and unload.

precipitation Rain, snow, hail or any other water falling from the sky.

Prime Meridian Line An imaginary line that runs from north to south through Greenwich, England, at zero *degrees* of *longitude*.

projection The way the curved surface of the Earth is distorted (stretched) so that it can be shown on a flat map.

radar A system that detects objects such as clouds by sending out radio waves and collecting the signals that bounce back. Radar stands for **RA**dio **D**etecting **A**nd **R**anging.

radiation Energy, such as light, heat or *radioactive* particles, that radiates (flows outwards) from an energy source. For example, the Sun radiates light and heat.

radioactive Radioactive substances, such as uranium, give off particles which can be harmful.

remote-operated vehicle or **ROV** A remote-controlled robot used for exploring the seabed.

remote sensing Recording information from a long distance away; for example, measuring sea temperatures from a *satellite*.

rift valley A valley formed on land where two *plates* of the Earth's *crust* pull away from each other.

Ring of Fire A group of volcanoes and *faults* that forms a huge ring around the Pacific Ocean.

satellite An object that *orbits* a *planet*. Many satellites are built to do particular jobs, such as monitoring the weather.

sedimentary Sedimentary rock is rock made up of particles of sand, mud and other *debris* that have settled on the seabed and been squashed down to form hard rock.

seismology The study of earthquakes and other, smaller movements of the Earth.

selective breeding Developing plants and animals by choosing those with good qualities for farming.

sewage Waste and dirty water from sinks and bathrooms.

shanty town A makeshift town that grows up on the outskirts of overpopulated cities, when people build their own homes out of junk.

slash-and-burn A method of destroying trees quickly to make room for farmland.

smog A mixture of smoke and fog. Also a general word for *pollution*.

solar system The Sun and the *planets* and *satellites*, including the Earth, that *orbit* it.

solar year The amount of time it takes the Earth to *orbit* the Sun once. A solar year is about 365¼ days.

sonar A method of bouncing sounds off objects and measuring the results in order to make maps. Sonar is used to map the seabed.

South Pole The most southern point on the Earth, and one end of the *axis* the Earth spins around.

species (plural: **species**) A type of plant, animal or other living thing.

stalactites Columns of stone that hang down inside caves, made by water dripping from the cave roof and *depositing* dissolved minerals.

stalagmites Towers of stone which rise from the ground in caves, formed by water dripping onto the cave floor and *depositing* dissolved minerals.

star A huge ball of burning gas in space. The Sun, in the middle of our *solar system*, is a star.

stomata (singular: **stoma**) Tiny holes in leaves that allow gases and water in and out. See **transpiration**.

strata (singular: **stratum**) Layers of rock.

subduction zone An area of the seabed where one *plate* of the Earth's crust plunges underneath another, forming a deep trench.

submersible A small submarine used by scientists to explore the seabed.

subsoil A layer of rough soil underneath the *topsoil*. The rocks and cracks in subsoil help water to drain through it.

temperate A mild, damp *climate*, between extremes of hot and cold.

terraces Large steps dug into hillsides to hold soil and water in place for farming.

thermal spring A place where hot water, heated by underground rocks, comes to the surface of the Earth. Also known as a hot spring.

tidal wave Very large waves are sometimes called tidal waves. However, *tsunamis* are not tidal waves, as they are caused by underwater volcanoes or earthquakes and have nothing to do with tides.

tides The daily movement of the sea up and down the shore, caused by the gravity of the *moon*.

topsoil The rich, uppermost layer of soil. It contains *humus* and various *organisms* which make soil *fertile*.

transpiration A process that takes place in plants. Water that the plant has sucked in through its roots travels up to the plant's leaves, and transpires, or evaporates, out through the *stomata*.

treeline The height up a mountain after which there are no more trees (because it is too cold and windy for them to survive).

tributary A river that flows into a bigger river, instead of into the sea.

tropics The warm, wet areas on either side of the *Equator*.

tsunami A giant wave caused by an earthquake or volcano on the seabed making the water vibrate.

tundra A type of land in which the soil is always partly frozen. It is found in the *Arctic*.

turbine A machine that converts turning power (such as the spinning of a waterwheel) into electricity.

ultraviolet or **UV** A type of invisible light *radiation* from the Sun which can cause skin damage.

understorey The level of a rainforest where small trees and plants grow, between the *canopy* and the forest floor.

vulcanology The study of volcanoes.

water table The top level of the *groundwater* that is stored in underground rock.

yield The amount of food or other produce that is grown on a particular piece of land.

MAPS AND LINES

The Earth is a huge, round ball of rock moving through space. It has no "top" or "bottom" and no lines marked on it. Lines such as the Equator, the Arctic Circle and the International Date Line, which are explained here, are all imaginary. They are used to help us measure distances and find places on maps.

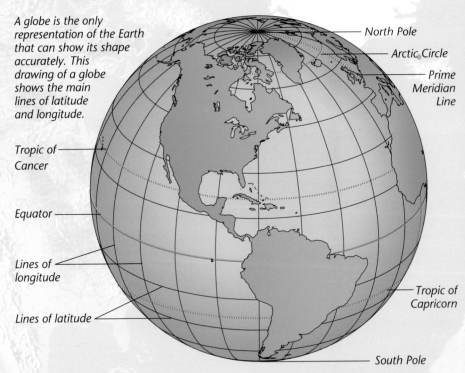

A globe is the only representation of the Earth that can show its shape accurately. This drawing of a globe shows the main lines of latitude and longitude.

North Pole
Arctic Circle
Prime Meridian Line
Tropic of Cancer
Equator
Lines of longitude
Lines of latitude
Tropic of Capricorn
South Pole

What do the lines mean?

• **Lines of latitude**, or **parallels**, run around the globe, dividing it into flat slices. Lines of latitude get shorter the closer they are to the poles, but they never meet each other.

• The **Equator** is the biggest and most important line of latitude. It runs around the globe halfway between the North Pole and the South Pole. The other lines of latitude are measured north and south from it.

• **Lines of longitude**, also known as **meridians**, run from the North Pole to the South Pole, dividing the globe into segments, like the segments of an orange. They all meet at the North Pole and at the South Pole.

• The **Prime Meridian Line** is the most important line of longitude, because all the other lines are measured from it. But it is not longer than any of the others; the lines are all the same size. It was decided in 1884 that the Prime Meridian would run through Greenwich, near London in England.

• **Degrees** (°) are used to measure distance on the globe. One degree is one 360th of the way around the globe. Lines of latitude are measured in degrees north and south of the Equator, while lines of longitude are measured in degrees east and west of the Prime Meridian Line. For example, somewhere that is 50°S and 100°E has a latitude 50 degrees south of the Equator, and a longitude 100 degrees east of the Prime Meridian Line.

• **Minutes** (') and **seconds** (") are smaller distances, used for making more precise measurements. There are 60 minutes in one degree, and 60 seconds in one minute.

• The **Arctic Circle** is a line of latitude at 66°30' north. The area north of it includes the North Pole and is known as the **Arctic**.

• The **Antarctic Circle** is a line of latitude at 66°30' south. It contains the South Pole and the area south of it is known as the **Antarctic**.

• The **tropics** are two lines of latitude near the Equator. The **Tropic of Cancer** is at 23°27' north and the **Tropic of Capricorn** is at 23°27' south. The hot, stormy area that lies between these two lines is also sometimes known as the **tropics**.

• The **International Date Line** is near the 180th meridian (the line at 180° longitude, directly opposite the Prime Meridian Line). It runs mostly through the Pacific Ocean, and is not straight but bends to avoid the land. It is part of the system that is used to define international time zones (see opposite). The date changes from one side of the line to the other.

Map projections

A flat map cannot show the world as it really is. So, to represent the round Earth on a flat surface, it has to be distorted (stretched) or divided into pieces. Some methods of doing this, called projections, are shown here.

• A **cylindrical projection** is similar to what you would get if you wrapped a piece of paper around a globe to form a cylinder, then shone a light inside the globe. The shapes of the countries would be projected onto the paper. Near the Equator they would be accurate, but near the poles they would look distorted.

A cylindrical map projection

• In the **Robinson projection**, the longitude lines curve in at the poles, so countries in the far north and south don't look too big. The curved lines can be confusing, but the map represents the Earth's proportions quite well.

The Robinson map projection

• The **Peters projection** stretches the countries near to the Equator, so that all the countries are the right size in relation to each other. But this makes them look too long, so they aren't the right shape.

The Peters map projection

• The **Homosline projection** splits the globe up into sections. It makes each country almost the right shape and size, but it's not very useful for working out distances and routes, especially if you live near one of the edges!

The Homosline map projection

• The **Mercator projection** is probably the most well-known projection. It was invented by Gerardus Mercator in 1538. It is like a cylindrical projection, but is stretched out at the poles. The countries are the right shape, but those nearest the poles look too big.

The Mercator map projection

Time zones

Because the sun rises and sets at different times across the world, the Earth is divided into 24 time zones. In each zone, people set their clocks to their own standard time. There is a new zone every 15 degrees of longitude, but this is only a rough guide, as whole countries or states usually keep to the same local time instead of sticking to the zones exactly. In some countries, they use a different Summer Time. This map shows how the time zones work. The zones are measured in hours ahead of or behind Greenwich Mean Time, or GMT, which is the time at the Prime Meridian Line.

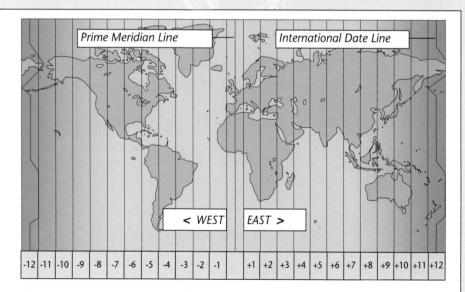

This diagram shows the 24 time zones. The areas ahead of GMT meet the areas behind GMT at the International Date Line (on the opposite side of the world from the Prime Meridian Line). If you travel east across the International Date Line, you go back 24 hours. If you travel west across it, you go forward 24 hours.

THE EARTH'S CYCLES

The Earth is constantly going through repeated processes, or cycles, such as the orbit of the Earth around the Sun, the way it spins and tilts as it moves through space, the orbit of the Moon around the Earth, and the sequence of the tides.

Days and years

Days and years are created by the movement of the Earth in relation to the Sun. Here are some facts and figures about the Earth's orbit.

• One **day** is the amount of time it takes the Earth to spin around on its axis. We divide each day into 24 hours of 60 minutes each.

• The exact amount of time it takes the Earth to make one complete orbit around the Sun is 365.26 days. This is known as a **solar year**.

• Instead of having 365.26 days, a normal **year** on Earth has exactly 365 days (because this is easier for us). Every four years another day is added to make up the difference. A year with an extra day in it is called a **leap year**. The extra day is added to February, so in leap years February has 29 days instead of 28.

• Making every fourth year a leap year does not even things out exactly, so some leap years are missed. Usually, every fourth year is a leap year, such as 1988, 1992 and 1996. But century years, such as 1700, 1800 and 1900, are not leap years. However, millenium years, such as the year 2000, *are* leap years.

Calendars

A **calendar** is a system of measuring years, months, weeks and days. People don't all agree when the world began, so years cannot be measured from then. Several different calendars, mostly based on religious beliefs, are used today.

Years ago	Christian Calendar	Muslim Calendar	Chinese Calendar	Hebrew Calendar
5,800				
5,600				*This is when Hebrews believe the world began.*
5,400				
5,200				
5,000				
4,800				
4,600				
4,400			*Emperor Huang Di is said to have invented the Chinese calendar 4,600 years ago.*	
4,200				
4,000				
3,800				
3,600				
3,400				
3,200				
3,000				
2,800				
2,600				
2,400				
2,200				
2,000				
1,800	*The Christian calendar begins with the birth of Christ, the founder of Christianity.*			
1,600				
1,400				
1,200		*This is when the Muslim prophet Mohammed fled from Mecca to Medina.*		
1,000				
800				
600				
400				
200				
0				

This chart shows how many years ago the different calendars began. When the Christian calendar is on the year 2000, the Muslim calendar is on the year 1378, and so on.

The Moon

A **moon** is a ball of rock orbiting (moving around) a planet. The Earth only has one moon, but some planets have more. Jupiter, for example, has at least 16 moons.

Our Moon orbits the Earth once every 27 days, 7 hours and 43 minutes. The Moon "shines" because it is reflecting light from the Sun. Whether we see a full moon, a thin crescent moon, or something in between, depends on what position the Moon is in and how much sunlight it can reflect onto the Earth. These different shapes are called the phases of the Moon.

This diagram shows the phases of the Moon as it orbits the Earth.

New
moon

Half
moon

Full
moon

*Light rays
from the Sun*

Half moon

1. New moon
2. Waxing crescent
3. Half moon
4. Waxing gibbous
5. Full moon
6. Waning gibbous
7. Half moon
8. Waning crescent

Phases of the Moon

• A **new moon** does not shine at all. The Moon's cycle begins when the Moon is between the Earth and the Sun, so none of the light it reflects can reach the Earth.

• A **half moon** appears when the Moon has moved around and is alongside the Earth. We see half of it reflecting the Sun.

• A **full moon** is what you see when the Moon is on the opposite side of the Earth from the Sun. All the sunlight the Moon reflects can be seen from the Earth, so the Moon looks like a complete circle.

More Moon facts

• When the Moon is moving away from the Sun and growing fuller, it is **waxing**. When it moves around towards the Sun again and seems to be getting smaller, it is **waning**.

• A **crescent moon** is between a new moon and a half moon, and looks like a crescent or C-shape.

• A **gibbous moon** is between a half moon and a full moon, and is a fat oval shape.

• A **lunar month** is the amount of time it takes the Moon to complete its cycle: 29 days, 12 hours and 44 minutes. This is longer than the orbit time, because while the Moon is making its orbit around the Earth, the Earth is moving around the Sun and so changing its own position.

• Like the Earth, the Moon spins around on its axis. It does this every 27 days, 7 hours and 43 minutes. This is exactly the same amount of time as the time it takes to travel around the Earth, which means we always see the same side of the Moon from Earth. However, we can see the other side of the Moon in pictures taken by spacecraft.

• The Moon is 3,476km (2,160 miles) across, about a quarter of the width of the Earth. Its circumference is 10,927km (6,790 miles) and its distance away from the Earth varies between 356,399 and 384,403 km (221,456 and 238,857 miles). It orbits the Earth at about 3,700 km/hr (2,300 miles per hour).

• A **month** on Earth is a period of time based on the Moon's cycle. But to make 12 months fit into a year, an average month is about 30 days long, slightly longer than a lunar month.

• A **blue moon** happens when there are two full moons within one Earth month. The second full moon of the two is called the blue moon.

Tides

The water in the Earth's seas and oceans rises and falls twice a day. These movements are called tides, and they are caused by the gravity of the Moon.

As the Earth spins, different parts of its surface move past the Moon. The part nearest the Moon has a high tide, when the water rises as the Moon pulls it.

At the same time, a high tide also happens on the opposite side of the Earth, because of a reaction called centrifugal force, created by the way the Earth and the Moon move around each other.

While this is happening, there is a low tide on the parts of the Earth's surface that are not facing or opposite the Moon. Each part of the world has two high tides and two low tides every day.

SCIENCES AND SCIENTISTS

Many scientists are involved in studying all the different aspects of the Earth. The sciences that relate to the Earth are often called the Earth sciences or geosciences. *Geo* is Greek for "Earth", and it appears in the names of many of these sciences.

The table below shows some of the Earth sciences and the scientists who study them, and describes which area each science deals with. Some of the sciences overlap; for example, geologists and paleontologists may both study fossils.

Science	Name of scientist	What is it?
Geography	Geographer	The study of the Earth's features and processes, climates, resources, maps, and the way people relate to the Earth.
Geology	Geologist	The study of the rocks the Earth is made of and how they formed.
Paleontology	Paleontologist	The study of fossils and the organisms that formed them.
Mineralogy	Mineralogist	The study of minerals.
Geophysics	Geophysicist	The study of the forces that affect the Earth, such as its magnetic field, its movement through space, and gravity.
Geochemistry	Geochemist	The study of the Earth's chemicals and how they occur naturally, both on the Earth's surface and inside the Earth.
Geomorphology	Geomorphologist	The study of landforms, or the shapes and features on the Earth's surface, and the processes which cause them.
Vulcanology	Vulcanologist	The study of volcanoes.
Seismology	Seismologist	The study of earthquakes and earth tremors.
Oceanography	Oceanographer	The study of seas and oceans and the seabed.
Sedimentology	Sedimentologist	The study of sedimentary deposits ~ layers of rock, minerals, mud or other substances which have settled on land or on the seabed.
Meteorology	Meteorologist	The study of the weather and weather forecasting.
Climatology	Climatologist	The study of climates past and present.
Ecology	Ecologist	The study of the relationship between living things (including humans) and their surroundings on Earth.
Pedology	Pedologist	The study of soil. This is also often known as soil science.
Cartography	Cartographer	The science of designing and making maps, and collecting the information needed to make them.

Earth scientists

These are some of the famous scientists who have contributed to our understanding of how the Earth and its processes work.

Agricola, Georgius (1494-1555)
German scientist who studied rocks and minerals scientifically, at a time when most theories about what they were made of were based on superstition. His book *De Re Metallica* (1556) was a guide for miners and geologists.

al-Idrisi (c.1100- c.1165)
Arabic geographer and author who explored the Mediterranean region, created an early map of the world, and wrote a book, *The Book of Roger*, describing his travels.

Aristotle (384BC-322BC)
Greek scientist and philosopher who wrote on many subjects. He realized that the Earth was a sphere, although it took a long time for everyone to accept this. (Until about 1500AD, many people still thought the Earth was flat.)

Darwin, Charles (1809-1882)
English scientist who developed the theory of natural selection, which argues that plant and animal species change, or evolve, over long periods of time. This theory was controversial, partly because it suggested that the Earth was much older than many people believed.

Davis, William Morris (1850-1934)
American geologist and meteorologist who founded the science of geomorphology. He developed a theory of how the process of erosion forms a cycle and was famous for his detailed diagrams showing how features of the Earth's crust are formed.

Democritus (c.460BC-c.370BC)
Greek philosopher who was the first to claim that all matter was made up of tiny particles, or atoms. He also studied earthquakes, volcanoes, the water cycle and erosion.

Eratosthenes (c.276BC-c.196BC)
Greek scientist and geographer who made the first measurement of the distance around the Earth, using the stars as a guide.

Flammarion, Camille (1842-1925)
French astronomer who wrote and illustrated a popular book about the weather, *L'Atmosphère* (The Atmosphere, 1872) which was translated into many languages. Flammarion's picture of waterspouts is reproduced on page 85 of this book.

Gardner, Julia Anna (1882-1960)
American geologist and paleontologist. Her studies of fossils were important because they increased understanding of rock layers, or strata.

Gould, Stephen Jay (born 1941)
American geologist and paleontologist who built on the theories of Charles Darwin. He has written many popular books such as *Wonderful Life* (1989).

Henry the Navigator (1394-1460)
A prince of Portugal who planned and paid for many journeys of exploration to Africa. He opened a school which taught explorers how to navigate (find their way) and record their discoveries.

Humboldt, Alexander von (1769-1859)
German explorer who contributed to the sciences of geography, geology, meteorology and oceanography. He explored South America and wrote a 5-volume book, *Kosmos* (The Cosmos), in 1844, describing the geography and geology of the world.

Hutton, James (1726-1797)
Scottish scientist who studied rocks and minerals, and is sometimes called "the father of geology". He said that the Earth's crust changed gradually through erosion, volcanic eruptions and other processes.

Lyell, Sir Charles (1797-1875)
Scottish geologist who developed the theories of James Hutton. He was also a friend of Charles Darwin and his ideas helped Darwin with his theory of natural selection.

Ptolemy (c.100AD-c.170AD)
Egyptian geographer and astronomer. He devised an early system of latitude and longitude and used it to create many maps.

Schmitt, Harrison Hagan (born 1935)
American geologist and astronaut who was on the Apollo 17 mission to the Moon in 1972. He is famous for his 22-hour journey in a moon buggy to collect geological samples ~ the longest trip ever made on the Moon.

Torricelli, Evangelista (1608-1647)
Italian mathematician and physicist who studied atmospheric pressure. In 1643, he invented the barometer (an instrument that measures atmospheric pressure).

Varenius, Bernhardus (1622-1650)
German geographer. He wrote a major book, *Geographia Generalis* (General Geography) in 1650, and also studied the islands of Japan.

Wegener, Alfred (1880-1930)
German meteorologist who claimed that all the Earth's continents had once been joined together in one big continent, which he named Pangaea. Wegener's theories were not accepted at the time, but were used in the 1960s when they helped scientists develop the theory of plate tectonics, about how the Earth's continents have moved.

WORLD RECORDS

Here are some of the Earth's longest rivers, highest mountains and other amazing world records. But the world is always changing; mountains wear down, rivers change shape, and new buildings are constructed. Ways of measuring things can also change. That's why you may find slightly different figures in different books.

Highest mountains	
Everest, Nepal/China	8,850m (29,035ft)
K2, Pakistan/China	8,611m (28,251ft)
Kanchenjunga, India/Nepal	8,597m (28,208ft)
Lhotse I, Nepal/China	8,511m (27,923ft)
Makalu I, Nepal/China	8,481m (27,824ft)
Lhotse II, Nepal/China	8,400m (27,560ft)
Dhaulagiri, Nepal	8,172m (26,810ft)
Manaslu I, Nepal	8,156m (26,760ft)
Cho Oyu, Nepal/China	8,153m (26,750ft)
Nanga Parbat, Pakistan	8,126m (26,660ft)

Longest rivers	
Nile, Africa	6,671km (4,145 miles)
Amazon, South America	6,440km (4,000 miles)
Chang Jiang (Yangtze), China	6,380km (3,964 miles)
Mississippi/Missouri, U.S.A.	6,019km (3,741 miles)
Yenisey/Angara, Russia	5,540km (3,442 miles)
Huang He (Yellow), China	5,464km (3,395 miles)
Ob/Irtysh/Black Irtysh, Asia	5,411km (3,362 miles)
Amur/Shilka/Onon, Asia	4,416km (2,744 miles)
Lena, Russia	4,400km (2,734 miles)
Congo, Africa	4,374km (2,718 miles)

Biggest natural lakes	
Caspian Sea, Asia	370,999 km² (143,243 mi²)
Lake Superior, U.S.A./Canada	82,414 km² (31,820 mi²)
Lake Victoria, Africa	69,215 km² (26,724 mi²)
Lake Huron, U.S.A./Canada	59,596 km² (23,010 mi²)
Lake Michigan, U.S.A.	58,016 km² (22,400 mi²)
Aral Sea, Asia	41,000 km² (15,830 mi²)
Lake Tanganyika, Africa	32,764 km² (12,650 mi²)
Lake Baikal, Russia	31,500 km² (12,162 mi²)
Great Bear Lake, Canada	31,328 km² (12,096 mi²)
Lake Nyasa, Africa	29,928 km² (11,555 mi²)

Deepest ocean	

The Mariana Trench, part of the Pacific Ocean, is the deepest part of the sea at 10,911m (35,797ft) deep.

Deepest lake	

Lake Baikal in Russia is the deepest lake in the world. At its deepest point it is 1,637m (5,370ft) deep.

Biggest islands	
Greenland	2,175,600 km² (840,000 mi²)
New Guinea	800,000 km² (309,000 mi²)
Borneo	751,100 km² (290,000 mi²)
Madagascar	587,040 km² (226,656 mi²)
Baffin Island, Canada	507,451 km² (195,928 mi²)
Sumatra, Indonesia	437,607 km² (184,706 mi²)
Great Britain	234,410 km² (90,506 mi²)
Honshu, Japan	227,920 km² (88,000 mi²)
Victoria Island, Canada	217,290 km² (83,896 mi²)
Ellesmere Island, Canada	196,236 km² (75,767 mi²)

Tallest inhabited buildings	
Petronas Towers, Malaysia	452m (1,483ft)
Sears Tower, U.S.A.	443m (1,454ft)
Jin Mao Building, China	420m (1,378ft)
CITIC Plaza, China	391m (1,283ft)
Shun Hing Square, China	384m (1,260ft)
Plaza Rakyat, Malaysia	382m (1,254ft)
Empire State Building, U.S.A.	381m (1,250ft)
Central Plaza, China	373m (1,227ft)
Bank of China, China	368m (1,209ft)
Emirates Tower, U.A.E.	350m (1,148ft)

Biggest cities and urban areas	
Tokyo, Japan	26.4 million
Mexico City, Mexico	18.1 million
Bombay, India	18.1 million
Sao Paulo, Brazil	17.8 million
New York, U.S.A.	16.6 million
Lagos, Nigeria	13.4 million
Los Angeles, U.S.A.	13.1 million
Calcutta, India	12.9 million
Shanghai, China	12.9 million
Buenos Aires, Argentina	12.6 million

Famous waterfalls	Height
Angel Falls, Venezuela	979m (3,212ft)
Sutherland Falls, New Zealand	580m (1,904ft)
Mardalfossen, Norway	517m (1,696ft)
Jog Falls, India	253m (830ft)
Victoria Falls, Zimbabwe/Zambia	108m (355ft)
Iguacu Falls, Brazil/Argentina	82m (269ft)
Niagara Falls, Canada/U.S.A.	57m (187ft)

Natural disasters

Natural disasters can be measured in different ways. For example, some earthquakes score highly on the Richter scale, while others cause more destruction. The earthquakes, volcanic eruptions, floods, hurricanes and tornadoes listed here are among the most famous and destructive disasters in history.

Earthquakes	Richter scale	Disastrous effects
Shansi, China, 1556	unknown	830,000 people died
Calcutta, India, 1737	unknown	300,000 people died
San Francisco, U.S.A., 1906	7.9	3,000 people died in resulting fire
Messina, Italy, 1908	7.5	Over 70,000 people died
Concepcion, Chile, 1960	8.7	2,000 died; possibly biggest quake
Alaska, U.S.A., 1964	8.6	125 people died in this huge quake
Tangshan, China, 1976	7.9	Over 655,000 people died
Mexico City, Mexico, 1985	8.1	20,000 died, with $5bn damage
Manjil-Rudbar, Iran, 1990	7.7	50,000 people died
Kobe, Japan, 1995	6.8	6,400 died, over $147bn damage

Volcanic eruptions	Disastrous effects
Mount Vesuvius, Italy, AD79	Pompeii flattened; up to 20,000 died
Tambora, Indonesia, 1815	92,000 people starved to death
Krakatau, Indonesia, 1883	36,500 drowned in resulting tsunami
Mount Pelee, Martinique, 1902	Nearly 30,000 people buried in ash flows
Kelut, Indonesia, 1919	Over 5,000 people drowned in mud
Agung, Indonesia, 1963	1,200 people suffocated in hot ash
Mount St. Helens, U.S.A., 1980	Only 61 died but a large area was destroyed
Ruiz, Colombia, 1985	25,000 people died in giant mud flows
Mt. Pinatubo, Philippines, 1991	800 killed by collapsing roofs and disease
Island of Montserrat, 1995	Volcano left most of the island uninhabitable

Floods	Disastrous effects
Holland, 1228	100,000 drowned by a sea flood
Kaifeng, China, 1642	300,000 died after rebels destroyed a dyke
Johnstown, U.S.A., 1889	2,200 killed in a flood caused by rain
Frejus, France, 1959	More than 500 died after dam burst
Italy, 1963	Vaoint Dam overflowed; 2–3,000 killed
East Pakistan, 1970	Giant wave caused by cyclone killed 250,000
Bangladesh, 1988	1,300 died, 30m homeless in monsoon flood
Southern U.S.A., 1993	$12bn of damage after Mississippi flooded
China, 1998	Chang Jiang overflow left 14m homeless
Papua New Guinea, 1998	Tsunamis killed 2,000 people

Storms	Disastrous effects
Caribbean "Great Hurricane",1780	Biggest ever hurricane killed over 20,000
Hong Kong typhoon, China, 1906	10,000 people died in this giant hurricane
Killer tornado, U.S.A., 1925	Up to 700 people died in Ellington, Missouri
Tropical Storm Agnes, U.S.A.,1972	$3.5bn damage, 129 dead
Hurricane Fifi, Honduras, 1974	8,000 people died and 100,000 left homeless
Hurricane Georges, U.S.A., 1998	Caribbean and U.S.A. hit; $5bn of damage
Hurricane Mitch, C. America, 1998	Over 9,000 killed across Central America

Amazing Earth facts

The Earth is 12,103km (7,520 miles) across. Its circumference (the distance around the Equator) is 38,022km (23,627 miles) and it is 149,503,000 km (92,897,000 miles) away from the Sun.

To make one complete orbit around the Sun, the Earth has to travel 938,900,000km (583,400,000 miles). To do this in just a year, it has to travel very fast. Because of the atmosphere surrounding the Earth, you can't feel it moving. But in fact you are zooming through space faster than any rocket.

• **Orbit speed** The Earth travels around the Sun at a speed of about 106,000kph (65,868mph).

• **Spinning speed** The Earth also spins around an axis, but the speed you are spinning at depends on where you live. Places on the Equator move at 1,600kph (995mph). New York moves at around 1,100kph (684mph). Near the poles, the spinning is not very fast at all. (You can see how this works by looking at a spinning globe.)

• **Solar System speed** The whole Solar System, including the Sun, the Earth and its moon, and the other planets and their moons, is moving at 72,400kph (45,000 mph) through the galaxy.

• **Galaxy speed** Our galaxy, the Milky Way, whizzes through the universe at a speed of 2,172,150kph (1,350,000mph).

MEASUREMENTS

Measuring things – distance, area, weight, volume, time and temperature – is one of the most important parts of science. There are two main systems of measurement: metric and imperial. This page shows how each measuring system works, and also how to convert from one into the other.

Imperial

This system of measurement is very old, dating from the 12th century or even earlier. It can be hard to use because it is not based on the decimal (base 10) system which we use for numbers. Some of the units have symbols or abbreviations. For example, the symbol for an inch is ".

Length and distance

12 inches (") = 1 foot (')
3 feet = 1 yard (yd)
1,760 yards = 1 mile
3 miles = 1 league

Area

144 square inches = 1 square foot
9 square feet = 1 square yard
4,840 square yards = 1 acre
640 acres = 1 square mile

Weight

16 drams (dr) = 1 ounce (oz)
16 ounces = 1 pound (lb)
14 pounds = 1 stone
2,240 pounds (160 stone) = 1 ton
2,000 pounds = 1 short ton

Volume and capacity

1,728 cubic inches = 1 cubic foot (ft³)
27 cubic feet = 1 cubic yard (yd³)
5 fluid ounces (fl oz) = 1 gill (gi)

20 fluid ounces = 1 pint (pt) (U.K.)
16 fluid ounces = 1 pint (U.S.)
2 pints = 1 quart (qt)
8 pints (4 quarts) = 1 gallon (gal)

Temperature

The imperial unit of temperature is one degree (°) Fahrenheit (F). The freezing point of water is 32° F and the boiling point of water is 212° F.

Metric

The metric or decimal system is based on the metre or meter, a unit of measurement which was first used in France in the 1790s. Metric units are multiples of each other by 10, 100 or 1,000. Countries around the world are gradually switching from imperial to metric. Many of the metric units have both U.S. spellings (-er) and European spellings (-re).

Length and distance

10 millimeters/millimetres (mm) =
        1 centimeter/centimetre (cm)
100cm = 1 meter/metre (m)
1,000m = 1 kilometer/kilometre (km)

Area

100 square mm (mm²) =
        1 square cm (cm²)
10,000 square cm =
        1 square m (m²)
10,000 square m = 1 hectare
1,000,000 square m = 1 square
        kilometer/kilometre (km²)

Weight

1,000 grams (g) = 1 kilogram (kg)
1,000 kilograms = 1 tonne (t)

Volume and capacity

1 cubic cm (cc or cm³) = 1
        milliliter/millilitre (ml)
1,000ml = 1 liter/litre (l)
1,000l = 1 cubic m (m³)

Temperature

The metric temperature unit is one degree (°) Celsius (C). Water freezes at 0°C and boils at 100° C.

Conversion tables

You can convert between metric and imperial with this table. Use a calculator to do the multiplications.

To convert	into	multiply by
cm	inches	0.394
m	yards	1.094
km	miles	0.621
grams	ounces	0.35
kilograms	pounds	2.205
tonnes	tons	0.984
cm²	square inches	0.155
m²	square yards	1.196
km²	square miles	0.386
hectares	acres	2.471
liters/litres	pints	1.76
inches	cm	2.54
yards	m	0.914
miles	km	1.609
ounces	grams	28.35
pounds	kilograms	0.454
tons	tonnes	1.016
square inches	cm²	6.452
square yards	m²	0.836
square miles	km²	2.59
acres	hectares	0.405
pints	liters/litres	0.5683

INTERNET LINKS

Throughout this book, we have recommended websites to visit where you can find out more about the Earth. For links to these sites, go to the Usborne Quicklinks Website at **www.usborne-quicklinks.com** and enter the keywords "planet earth". There you will find links to click on to take you to all the sites.

Internet safety

When using the Internet, please make sure you follow these guidelines:
• Ask your parent's or guardian's permission before you connect to the Internet.
• If you write a message in a website guest book or on a website message board, do not include any personal information such as your full name, address or telephone number, and ask an adult before you give your email address.
• If a website asks you to log in or register by typing your name or email address, ask permission of an adult first.
• If you receive an email from someone you don't know, tell an adult and do not reply to the email.
• Never arrange to meet anyone you have talked to on the Internet.

Site availability

The links in Usborne Quicklinks are regularly reviewed and updated, but occasionally you may get a message saying that a site is unavailable. This might be temporary, so try again later, or even the next day. If any sites close down, we will, if possible, replace them with suitable alternatives, so you will always find up-to-date links in Usborne Quicklinks.

Downloadable pictures

Some pictures from this book can be downloaded from the Usborne Quicklinks Website and printed out for you own personal use. Look for pictures with a ★ beside them. To print out the downloadable pictures, follow the instructions at the Usborne Quicklinks Website.

What you need

Most of the websites described in this book can be accessed with a standard home computer and a web browser (the software that enables you to display information from the Internet).

Some websites need additional free programs, called plug-ins, to play sounds, or to show videos, animations or 3-D images. There is usually a button on the site that you can click on to download the plug-in. Alternatively, go to **www.usborne-quicklinks.com** and click on "Net Help". There you can find links to download plug-ins. Here is a list of plug-ins you might need:
• RealOne™Player – lets you play videos and hear sound files
• QuickTime – enables you to view video clips
• Flash™ – lets you play animations
• Shockwave® – lets you play animations and interactive programs

Note for parents and guardians

The websites described in this book are regularly reviewed and the links in Usborne Quicklinks are updated. However, the content of a website may change at any time and Usborne Publishing is not responsible for the content of any website other than its own.

We recommend that children are supervised while on the Internet, that they do not use Internet chat rooms, and that you use Internet filtering software to block unsuitable material. Please ensure that your children read and follow the safety guidelines printed on the left. We also strongly recommend that you buy anti-virus software to protect your computer and update the software regularly. For more on Internet safety and computer viruses, see the "Net Help" area on the Usborne Quicklinks Website.

ACKNOWLEDGEMENTS

Every effort has been made to trace the copyright holders of the material in this book. If any rights have been omitted, the publishers offer to rectify this in any subsequent edition, following notification. The publishers are grateful to the following organizations and individuals for their contributions and permission to reproduce material (t=top, m=middle, b=bottom, l=left, r=right):

Cover Desert image © Jamie Harron; Papilio/CORBIS; all other images Digital Vision; **endpapers** CORBIS/Wolfgang Kaehler; **p1** CORBIS/Yann Arthus-Bertrand; **p2** CORBIS/Joseph Sohm, ChromoSohm Inc; **p4** CORBIS/Ralph A. Clevenger; **p6** © Digital Vision; **p8** (l) © Digital Vision; (tr) Gary Bines; (br) Jeremy Gower; **p9** (tr) NASA; (br) Gary Bines; **p10** (tl and br) © Map Creation Ltd; (bl) © Digital Vision; **p11** (tr) European Space Agency/Science Photo Library (br) © Digital Vision; **p12** (tr) © Digital Vision; (ml) CORBIS/Dave G. Houser; (mr) CORBIS/Galen Rowell; (b) Jeremy Gower; **p13** (mr and bl) © Digital Vision; (br) CORBIS/Bill Ross; **p14** (bl) Jeremy Gower; (tr and b) © Digital Vision; **p15** (tl) Chris Lyon; (tr) Gary Bines; (b) Simon Fraser/Science Photo Library; **p16** (main) © Digital Vision; (insert) Gary Bines; **p17** (tl) Jeremy Gower; (mr) Andy Burton; (bl) Chris Lyon; (br) Howard Allman; **p18** (tr) Jeremy Gower; (mr) Guy Smith; (br) Jeremy Gower; **p19** (tr) Guy Smith; (mr) CORBIS/Yann Arthus-Bertrand; (br) CORBIS/Galen Rowell; **p20** (main) G.S.F Picture Library © Dr. B. Booth; (ml, m, tr and mr) Mike Freeman; **p21** Mike Freeman; **p22** (bl) CORBIS/Kevin Fleming; (tr) Jeremy Gower; **p23** (l) Mike Freeman and Roberto de Gugliemo/Science Photo Library; (tr) Rosenfeld Images Ltd/Science Photo Library; (br) CORBIS/Dorothy Burrows, Eye Ubiquitous; **p24** (main image and bl) © Digital Vision; **p25** (tr) © Digital Vision; (br) Laura Fearn; **p26** CORBIS/Douglas Peebles; **p28** G.S.F. Picture Library © Dr. B. Booth; (bl and mr) Jeremy Gower; (br) Chris Shields; **p29** (br) Chris Shields; **p30** (bl, tr, br) Jeremy Gower; (tl) © Digital Vision (r) Julian Cotton Photo Library; **p32** (main) CORBIS/Michael T. Sedam; (tr) Jeremy Gower; **p33** (tl) CORBIS/Ralph White; (br) D. Drain/Still Pictures; **p34** (main) CORBIS/Amos Nachoum; (b) Jeremy Gower; **p35** (tr) G.S.F. Picture Library © Solarfilm A; (b) CORBIS/Douglas Peebles; **p36** (main) G.S.F. Picture Library © Univ. California; (bl) CORBIS/Philip James Corwin; **p37** (br) Jeremy Gower; **p38** (main) © Vinay Parelkar/Dinodia, Oxford Scientific Films (tr) CORBIS/Grant Smith; **p39** (tl) Photo courtesy of Kinemetrics Inc; (r) Peter Bull; **p40** (main) CORBIS/Kevin Schafer; (ml, bl and br) Jeremy Gower; **p41** Jeremy Gower; **p42** (t) Jeremy Gower; (b) CORBIS/Roger Ressmeyer; **p43** (bl) Jane Burton; (r) CORBIS/Richard Cummins; **p44** (tr) © Costas E. Synolakis; (bl) Jeremy Gower; **p45** (tr) Jeremy Gower; (b) FOTO-UNEP/Still Pictures; **p46** CORBIS/Scott T. Smith; **p48** (main) CORBIS/George Hall; (tl) © Digital Vision; (l) CORBIS/Jonathan Blair; (ml) NASA; (bl) © Digital Vision; **p49** (tr) NASA/Science Photo Library; **p50** (r) NASA/Science Photo Library; **p51** (t) Los Alamos National Laboratory/Science Photo Library; (background and bl) Shuttle Views the Earth: Oceans from Space, compiled by Pat Jones and Gordon Wells, courtesy of LPI; **p52** (tr) Dr. Jeremy Burgess/Science Photo Library; (mr) Peter Bull; (bl) CORBIS/Karl Switak, ABPL; **p53** (tl) Nick Cobbing/Still Pictures; (mr) CORBIS/Chinch Gryniewicz, Ecoscene; (bl) Peter Bull; **p54** (main) CORBIS/Vince Streano; (tr) CORBIS/Ron Boardman, Frank Lane Picture Agency (bl) © Digital Vision; **p55** (t) CORBIS/Wolfgang Kaehler; **p56** (tr) CORBIS/Dewitt Jones; (m) PLI/Science Photo Library; **p57** (bl) CORBIS/Paul A. Souders; (br) © Digital Vision; **p58** (main) CORBIS/Reinhard Eisele; (bl) Nicola Butler; **p59** (tr) © Digital Vision; (ml, mr and bl) Ian Jackson; **p60** (main) CORBIS/Buddy Mays; (tr) Nicola Butler; **p61** (t) CORBIS/Buddy Mays; (mr) Ian Jackson; (br) CORBIS/Anthony Bannister, ABPL; **p62** (main) CORBIS/Kit Kittle; (bl) Jeremy Gower; **p63** (t) Yann Layma/Tony Stone; (tr) David Scharf/Science Photo Library; **p64** (main) CORBIS/Christine Osborne; (tr) Nicola Butler; (m) CORBIS/Jeremy Horner; **p65** (mr) Ian Jackson; **p66** (tr) Nicola Butler; (bl) CORBIS/Gail Mooney; **p67** (tr and b) Carlos Guarita/Still Pictures; (ml) Richard Passmore/Tony Stone; **p68** (tl) Nicola Butler; (r) CORBIS/Stuart Westmoreland; **p69** (tl) CORBIS/Ron Watts; (tr) CORBIS/Stuart Westmoreland; (br) CORBIS/George MacCarthy; **p70** (tl, tr, bl and br) Ian Jackson; **p71** (t) CORBIS/Dan Guravich; (b) CORBIS/Paul A. Souders; **p72** (main) CORBIS/Galen Rowell; (tr) CORBIS/David Muench; **p73** (tr) CORBIS/William A. Bake; (br) CORBIS/Catherine Karnow; **p74** (main) © Digital Vision; (tr) Arc Science Simulations/Science Photo Library; **p75** (tr) Kevin Schafer/Still Pictures; (bl) © Digital Vision; **p76** CORBIS/Steve Kaufman; **p78** (background) CORBIS/Craig Aurness; (l) CORBIS/Michael Yamashita; (tr) Ian Jackson; **p79** (t) © Digital Vision; (ml) Ian Jackson; (br) CORBIS/Wolfgang Kaehler; **p80** (tr) Scott Camazine/Science Photo Library; (bl) Peter Dennis; **p81** (background, tl and tr) Shuttle Views the Earth: Clouds from Space, compiled by Pat Jones, courtesy of LPI; (ml) CORBIS/Wolfgang Kaehler; (bl) © Digital Vision; (br) Ian Jackson; **p82** (main) Glen Allison/Tony Stone Images; (bl) Shuttle Views the Earth: Clouds from Space, compiled by Pat Jones, courtesy of LPI; **p83** (tr) Werner Burger/Fortean Picture Library; **p84** (main) John Lund/Tony Stone Images; (tr) Shuttle Views the Earth: Clouds from Space, compiled by Pat Jones, courtesy of LPI; (b) Guy Smith; **p86** (main) CORBIS/Michael S. Yamashita; (tr) Shuttle Views the Earth: Geology from Space, compiled by Peter Francis and Pat Jones, courtesy of LPI; **p87** (tr and ml) © Digital Vision; **p88** (tr) Michael Sewell/Still Pictures; (bl) Robert H. Pearson, Canada; **p89** (tr) Seymour Snowman Sun Protection Campaign, NSW Cancer Council and NSW Health Department, Sydney, Australia, 1997/8; (bl) Will and Deni McIntyre/Tony Stone Images; (br) CORBIS/Peter Turnley; **p90** (main) Pekka Parviainen/Science Photo Library; (tr) Magrath/Folsom/Science Photo Library; (bl) © Digital Vision; **p91** Llewellyn Publications/Fortean Picture Library; (m) CORBIS/Alamay and E. Vicens; **p92** (main and tr) © Digital Vision; (bl) European Space Agency; **p93** (tr) Courtesy of International Weather Productions; **p94** CORBIS/Michael and Patricia Fogden; **p96** (tl, tr, bl) © Digital Vision; (br) CORBIS/Ron Boardman, Frank Lane Picture Agency; **p97** (tl) © Digital Vision; (r) CORBIS/Galen Rowell; (bl) Howard Allman; **p98** (main) CORBIS/Stuart Westmoreland; (ml) Ian Jackson; (bl and br) Chris Shields; **p99** (tr, mr and b) Ian Jackson; (br) Jeremy Gower; **p100** (tr) Ian Jackson; (ml) CORBIS/Tom Brakefield; (br) David Wright; **p101** (tl and r) © Digital Vision; **p102** (main and bl) © Digital Vision; **p103** (tr) © Digital Vision (ml) Michael Viard/Still Pictures; (br) Ian Jackson; **p104** (main) CORBIS/Hans Georg Roth; (tr) Still Pictures/Ron Giling; **p105** (m) Craig Asquith; **p106** CORBIS/Keren Su; (tr) Fiona Patchett and Laura Fearn; (ml) Ian Jackson; **p107** (tl) CORBIS/W. Wayne Lockwood, M.D.; (mr) Ian Jackson; **p108** (tr and bl) Ian Jackson; (br) Rachel Lockwood; **p109** (tl) CORBIS/Richard Hamilton Smith; (tr) Ian Jackson; (br) © Digital Vision; **p110** CORBIS/Ric Ergenbright; **p112** (tr) CORBIS/Robert Pickett; (bl) CORBIS/Ken Wilson, Papilio; **p113** (tl) Andrew Beckett; (tr) CORBIS/Michael Boys; (b) CORBIS/Bob Rowan, Progressive Image; **p114** (tr) CORBIS/Richard Hamilton Smith; (b) CORBIS/Eric Crichton; **p115** (tl) CORBIS/Dean Conger; (tr) Ancient Art and Architecture; (b) Alan Watson/Still Pictures; **p116** (main) CORBIS/John Farmer, Cordaiy Photo Library Ltd; **p117** (tr) Jeremy Gower; (br) CORBIS/Robert Holmes; **p118** (main) CORBIS/Layne Kennedy; (tr) Jeremy Gower; **p119** (tl) CORBIS/Richard A. Cooke; (br) CORBIS/Wolfgang Kaehler; **p120** CORBIS/Lawson Wood; **p122** (tr and bl) © Digital Vision; (br) Ian Jackson; **p123** (tl) Shuttle Views the Earth: Geology from Space, compiled by Peter Francis and Pat Jones, courtesy of LPI; (tr) Frans Lanting/Tony Stone Images; (b) © Digital Vision; **p124** (main) CORBIS/John and Dallas Heaton; (tr) CORBIS/Digital Image ©1996 CORBIS; original image courtesy of NASA; (bl) CORBIS/David Muench; **p125** (tl and br) Jeremy Gower; **p126** (tr) Mansell Collection/Visscher; (m) CORBIS/Charles and Josette Lenars; **p127** (tl) CORBIS/Michael T. Sedam; (tr) CORBIS/Charles and Josette Lenars; (b) CORBIS/Philip James Corwin; **p128** (t) Evian Natural Mineral Water; (tr) Photography courtesy of The Strathmore Mineral Water Co; (bl) Jeremy Gower; **p129** (tr) CORBIS/Richard Hamilton Smith; (b) CORBIS/Macduff Everton; **p130** (main) CORBIS/Neil Rabinowitz; (bl) Chris Lyon; **p131** (t) Jeremy Gower; (mr) Ralph A. Clevenger; **p132** (background) © Digital Vision; (ml) Laura Fearn; (bl) Chris Lyon; (mr) Shaun Egan/Tony Stone Images; **p133** (tr) CORBIS/Anthony Bannister, ABPL; (b) © Digital Vision; **p134** (tl) CORBIS/Lawson Wood; (m) Dr. Ken McDonald/Science Photo Library; (b) CORBIS/Amos Nachoum; **p135** (tl and b) © Digital Vision; (tr) Peter Dennis; **p136** (main, tr and ml) CORBIS/Michael S. Yamashita; **p137** (tl) CORBIS/Charles O'Rear; (br) © Digital Vision; **p138** CORBIS/David Muench; **p140, p142, p144** © Digital Vision; **p146** (tr) Map Creation Ltd; (bl) Nicola Butler; **p147** Nicola Butler; **p149** Susannah Owen/Nicola Butler; **p150** © Digital Vision; **p152 and p154** © Digital Vision.
With thanks also to Susannah Owen for additional design work.